Moreton Morrell

UNDERSTANDING THE CONSUMER

Also by David A. Statt

PSYCHOLOGY: MAKING SENSE
THE CONCISE DICTIONARY OF PSYCHOLOGY
THE CONCISE DICTIONARY OF MANAGEMENT
PSYCHOLOGY AND THE WORLD OF WORK

UNDERSTANDING THE CONSUMER

A PSYCHOLOGICAL APPROACH

David A. Statt

MACMILLAN
Business

First published 1997 by
MACMILLAN PRESS LTD
Houndmills, Basingstoke, Hampshire RG21 6XS
and London
Companies and representatives
throughout the world

ISBN 0–333–66062–5 hardcover
ISBN 0–333–66063–3 paperback

A catalogue record for this book is available
from the British Library.

This book is printed on paper suitable for recycling and
made from fully managed and sustained forest sources.

10 9   8   7   6   5   4
06 05 04 03 02 01

Printed & bound by Antony Rowe Ltd, Eastbourne

To Elliot and Stan
and all the Brookwood Boys
in celebration
of what we believed in

Contents

List of Figures and Tables

Figures

Tables

Preface

While this book is intended for use as a text on consumer behaviour, with all the appropriate content and coverage, it should also be accessible to the non-specialist reader interested in the topic.

It is written by a psychologist using a wide range of ideas and research findings from the psychological and social scientific literature and integrating these with marketing examples throughout. In trying to understand consumer behaviour I have therefore been conscious of the complementary experience of the individual consumer and the individual marketer.

In preparing this book I have engaged with the two disciplines of psychology and marketing very seriously but not, I trust, too solemnly, and that is no doubt reflected in the writing. What I hope is also reflected is how much I enjoyed writing it.

I would like to thank my editor, Jane Powell, for being both professional and pleasant to deal with during the writing of this book. My greatest debt of gratitude, as ever, is to my wife Judith, who performed her usual magic and transformed vast mountains of my illegible scrawl into an elegant typescript with the roughest edges smoothed off. Responsibility for the end product is mine alone.

David A. Statt

Acknowledgement

The publishers and author are grateful to Routledge Publishers Ltd for permission to reproduce Figures 6.3 and 8.1.

PART I
The Consumer in Context

■ Introduction

In the first Part of the book we place the consumer within his or her recognized social context, that is, in relation to the producer and to the market place in which buying and selling takes place.

In doing so we follow Peter Drucker's view that a business has only two important functions: marketing and innovation. In Chapter 2 we deal with the way producers market their products to consumers and in Chapter 3 the way they develop and market new products and innovations. But before that, in Chapter 1, we set the scene for this psychological approach to understanding the consumer by discussing the importance that *being* a consumer has on our lives.

People as Consumers

■ Introduction

Whatever else we may be in our lives – child, parent, student, worker, lover, jogger or stamp collector – we are all consumers, all of our days. We buy and use goods and services constantly; to eat, to wear, to read, to watch, to play, to travel in; to keep us healthy, to make us wealthy and, if not wise, at least better educated. The act of consumption is therefore an integral and intimate part of our daily existence. And that is true whether we have a lot of money to spend on it or very little.

The prevalence of consumption in our lives is such that we are often unaware of its importance in shaping our lives, and exploring the implications this has for us will be one of the important themes of this book. In every large country of the world billions of purchases of goods and services are made every year. In the United States, for example, this activity now accounts for most of the economy – some $4 trillion, or about two thirds of the annual gross national product. In this chapter we will raise basic questions about how and why people behave as consumers, as well as ways in which this behaviour might be studied.

■ Studying People as Consumers

Research on people as consumers only dates from the mid 1960s. The main impetus for this research was practical: marketing managers wanted to know how the social and behavioural sciences could help them find the specific causes of consumer actions and, in particular, their buying decisions. Why did people choose Brand X as opposed to Brands Y or Z? And, most importantly, how would the consumer react to a new and improved Brand X? This focus on what the consumer would do under certain specified conditions was known as the positivist approach to research.[1]

The positivist approach is the traditional form in which scientific research has been conducted. As such it makes several assumptions about what is being studied, the most important of which are as follows:

- All behaviour has objectively identifiable causes and effects, all of which can be isolated, studied and measured.
- When faced with a problem or a decision, people process all the relevant information available to deal with it.

- After processing this information people make a rational decision about the best choice to take or decision to make.

As all the other social and behavioural sciences have found, one of the limitations of this practical approach is that it leaves an awful lot of human behaviour totally unaccounted for.

Precisely because consumption is such a universal and frequent activity there is a temptation to see virtually *all* human activity in consumer terms, and to view all consumer activity with a positivist lens. Thus the relationship between a doctor and a patient may be discussed in terms of the provision (by the doctor) and the consumption (by the patient) of health care, even when the health care is free at the point of delivery and there is no direct buying and selling, as in the British National Health Service. Similarly the relationship between teacher and student may be characterised as the provision and consumption of education.

This is known as the *reductionist* view of the doctor–patient and teacher–student relationships because it reduces the content of these relationships to the buying and selling of services, just like plumbing or piano tuning. What is missing from this view is the psychological content of the relationships that are involved. It does not explain, for example, why so many doctors and teachers do so much more than they are paid to do. It does not tell us how a doctor's care and concern, and a patient's appreciation of it, may do more healing than the impersonal use of expensive medical equipment.

To the extent that people have some relationship with each other, therefore, the act of consuming is an infinitely more complex one than that of simply buying and selling. Indeed the people involved at either end of the process may not even see it as the provision and consumption of a service at all but as an important social or professional role in their lives. The nature and quality of the relationships that occur is often regarded as an essential part of the job for the professionals involved and something unquantifiable, hence the frequent outcry at attempts to introduce performance related pay for doctors, nurses, teachers or police officers.

But the element of relationship in the act of consumption is much more widespread even than this. Think of the sitcom 'Cheers', for instance, where a complex web of human interaction revolves around the buying and selling of booze. These kinds of relationship are also found in every local pub in the United Kingdom and every local café in France or Italy. They are important to us in understanding the consumer because they affect the buying decisions and consumption patterns of everyone involved. Despite the prevalence of consumer activity, in other words, it has to be understood within the context of human interaction, and that is the perspective of the more recent *interpretivist* school of research. In contrast to the positivists the interpretivists base their approach on the following key assumptions:[2]

- Cause and effect cannot be isolated because there is no single objective reality everyone can agree on.

- Reality is an individual's subjective experience of it, so each consumer's experience is unique.
- People are not simply, or always, rational information processors or decision makers, because this view takes no account of an individual's emotional life (what has been called 'fantasies, feelings and fun').[3]

The interpretivist school would therefore regard the act of buying as only a small part (however important) of a consumer's activities. And this buying behaviour has to be interpreted in the light of a person's entire consumer experience, and indeed his or her entire life experience. Many commentators in this field now regard the positivist and interpretivist approaches as complementary to each other. They see the need for prediction and control in *trying* to isolate cause and effect in buying behaviour, while emphasizing the importance of *understanding* the life of the consumer in all its messy complexity. And that is the view we shall adopt here.

■ **Buyers, Customers and Consumers**

In understanding how and why people behave in their role as consumers most of our attention will be focused on the act of *buying*. However it is immediately obvious that people do not buy goods and services always or only (or even sometimes at all) for their own use. The simplest example of this is a mother shopping in the supermarket for her family. Clearly she will be influenced, at least to some extent, by what her husband and children like to eat, and she may well buy things for them that she herself will not consume.

But she is also subject to the same influences at the point of sale as someone buying solely for themselves, in terms of price, quality, packaging and so on, and these will affect her actual buying decisions. While it is therefore very important for providers to know who will actually use their product they also need to know who will buy it (and who they are buying it for) in order to market it most effectively.

Another distinction worth making at this stage is that between *customers* and consumers. 'Consumer' is the more general term. It refers to people buying groceries rather than shopping specifically at Safeway; buying a family saloon car rather than a Ford. The term 'customer' usually implies a relationship over time between the buyer and a *particular* brand or retail outlet.

As encouraging repeat purchases and brand loyalty is crucial to the marketer, this is obviously one more relationship that provides a key to our understanding of the consumer. And this relationship may be deliberately invoked by providers of goods and services. It is probably not by chance that the newly privatized British railway companies, for example, now talk about 'customers' rather than 'passengers'.

■ Consumer Behaviour

The much-used term 'consumer behaviour' includes all the examples we have been looking at. That is, it involves the buyers of and customers for products as well as the people who actually use them. It deals with the buying decision itself and far beyond. Consumer behaviour extends all the way from 'how do we know what we want?' – not as obvious a question as it may sound – to 'what do we do with something we no longer want?' In between these two phases consumer behaviour deals with issues such as:

- How do we get information about products?
- How do we assess alternative products?
- Why do different people choose or use different products?
- How do we decide on value for money?
- How much risk do we take with what products?
- Who influences our buying decisions and our use of the product?
- How are brand loyalties formed, and changed?

... and many more.

To summarise then, a typical definition of consumer behaviour would therefore be: 'The mental, emotional and physical activities that people engage in when selecting, purchasing, using, and disposing of products and services so as to satisfy needs and desires'.[4] We will spend the rest of this book unpacking that definition.

■ The Consumer Environment and the Consuming Society

We have already noted how prevalent the act of consumption is. This is not, of course, accidental. Indeed the whole of our economy is based on it. Continued, and in fact *ever-increasing*, consumption is generally considered essential to our prosperity. Every year, for example, the figures for the sales of new cars are greeted with satisfaction and approval if the trend is upward, widespread gloom if it's downward. A fall in sales is taken to be unequivocally bad because of falling profits – and decreased share values – for the companies that make cars and car components, and the threat of job losses for their workers that is always linked to such a trend.

Car sales are considered to be a barometer of economic performance and therefore especially important, but they mirror public attitudes about virtually every other product. And that is why we are bombarded by many hundreds of advertisements every day of our lives – on radio and television,[5] in newspapers and magazines, on buildings and billboards, in buses and trains; with bright colours, flashing lights, loud music and, everywhere, smiling faces. All encouraging us to buy more.

The most important feature of the consumer environment, therefore, is the universal and all-encompassing view that buying is not just a necessary activity but an attractive and highly approved way of behaving; a good in itself. Until recent years this way of viewing consumer behaviour has been virtually unquestioned. If it produces an ever-higher standard of living for more and more people, what can possibly be wrong with it?

We will deal with this issue in some detail in Part V of this book, on Consumerism, but for the moment we should simply mention some basic questions now being asked about this scenario of ever-increasing consumption, questions that are beginning to have an effect on the consumer environment. Perhaps the most immediate of these questions is the one dealing with the earth's resources. For example fossil fuels such as oil and coal are a finite resource, unlike, say, wave power or solar energy. When they are used up there won't be any more. They won't be used up tomorrow of course, but they will be one day in the foreseeable future. When that happens what will we run our cars on, or our electricity generating stations?

Allied to this practical question are the economic, political and moral ones lying behind the fact that the vast majority of the earth's resources are consumed – either directly like energy or indirectly like food and manufactured goods – by a handful of the world's richest countries. Is this the most morally just/politically stable/economically viable way to organise the world?

These kinds of question have prompted a different kind of accounting that figures out the hidden or real costs of goods and services other than the purchase price to the consumer. What is the unit price of cigarettes, for instance, when the cost of the resulting ill-health (to both smokers and passive smokers) in terms of medical care and lost work days is added in? How much should a new car cost to take account of the environmental damage it will do?

■ The Consumer and the Market Place

There has been trade between producers and consumers ever since people discovered that the folks in the next valley made some very interesting firewater but lacked their own suregrip axe handles. It has always been an integral part of the relations between different groups of people, from the Stone Age clan to the modern nation state. This *trading nexus* is a necessary condition for the growth of small groups into complex societies with their systems of law, government, finance, education, administration and so on.

At the heart of the trading nexus is the act of *exchange* between producer and consumer for their mutual benefit. Originally this took the form of bartering goods, a form of exchange that still exists today, of course, particularly at the international level where a country might exchange oil for aeroplanes, for instance. Historically, as trading centres were established and grew into ports and cities, metals such as gold and silver came into use as a medium of exchange that was acceptable to both consumers and producers. This medium of exchange developed into coinage of various denominations – originally made out of metals such as silver or bronze, but as larger amounts were traded paper money was introduced. Plastic cards came into use in the middle of the twentieth century as a safer and more convenient medium of exchange, and at the end of the century they have taken the place of many cash transactions.

■ Markets and Marketing

All the activity of the trading nexus described above is usually referred to as the operation of the *market place.* However the modern market place is often a vastly more complex place than the simpler historical examples we have been considering. Individual producers and consumers do sometimes still trade directly with each other, as when we buy handmade goods from stallholders in open-air markets, or when a florist buys his or her stock directly from a greenhouse.

But the most typical buying behaviour in our society is done through retail (or even wholesale) outlets that do not themselves manufacture the products they sell. The products must therefore be *marketed* to potential consumers by the combined efforts of the producer and the retailer, and the people they hire to do their advertising and market research.

Before the development of the factory system and the industrial revolution in the eighteenth century, producers and consumers were in much closer contact than they are now. Consumers could make their needs and preferences known directly and producers could, whenever possible, adjust their products accordingly. Indeed in the case of goods such as clothing or furniture, which were crafted by hand of course, many more customers could have items made to order than in today's luxury markets. There was little need for producers to carry large stocks or worry too much about distribution.

It is interesting to note that many of today's business gurus urge producers to return to such conditions. Staying close to the customer, customizing goods whenever possible and using just-in-time methods to minimize inventory are now widely accepted aspects of conventional wisdom. But for much of the last couple of centuries the customer has not always been king, unless of course the customer *was* a king or someone equally wealthy.

The mass production methods that arose after the industrial revolution, culminating in Henry Ford's assembly line in 1913, were enormously successful in producing vast quantities of identical products. And this mass production required mass markets. So mass production led to mass consumption, which stimulated further mass production. The relationship between producer and consumer at that time is captured in Henry Ford's famous saying 'you can have any colour of Model T you like as long as it's black'.

This dominance of the producer over the consumer in the market place was first noted in 1779, at the beginning of the industrial revolution, by 'the father of political economy' and expounder of the market system, Adam Smith:

Consumption is the sole end and purpose of all production; and the interest of the producer ought to be attended to, only so far as it may be necessary for promoting that of the consumer. . . . But in the mercantile system the interest of the consumer is almost certainly sacrificed to that of the producer; and it seems to consider production, and not consumption, as the ultimate end and object of all industry and commerce.[6]

This view of the market place is a very far-sighted critique of what came to be known as the *production orientation*. When demand for a product exceeds supply, consumers are forced to buy what there is rather than what they really want. Under these conditions producers know they can sell whatever they produce, without having to bother too much about consumer needs, desires or preferences. They can therefore concentrate all their resources on simply turning out as many items as they can as quickly as possible.

The production orientation is usually held to be the defining characteristic of planned, centralized economies such as the former Soviet Union. While the production orientation worked well for traditional heavy industry in the Soviet Union – when it collapsed it was producing far more steel per annum than the United States – it was catastrophic for consumer goods. Soviet products were certainly cheap (affording them was never the problem) but they were generally scarce, poorly made, unattractive, of low quality and largely unrelated to consumer needs. The usual reason given for this type of situation is the lack of a consumer market place.

But this disregard for the consumer also occurred in capitalist countries – where there *was* a consumer market place – right up until the mid 1950s. Again it was a case of supply and demand. It was only in the 1950s that the global economy, emerging from the depression of the 1930s and the war of the 1940s, was able to meet the basic demand for consumer goods, and producers then found themselves in the novel position of having to compete for buyers. This was especially true in the United States, where there was much more productive capacity for staple products than even its huge domestic market required.

In the 1950s the production orientation in capitalist countries was therefore challenged by a different perspective on the market place that came to be known as the *marketing concept*. This perspective required a producer to identify first what the needs, wants and preferences of consumers were and then to satisfy them better than the competition could. In other words producers shifted their focus from selling whatever they could make to making whatever they could sell.

It was Peter Drucker, the granddaddy of all the business gurus, who first gave voice to the new need to become consumer-driven, and he did so with stark simplicity: 'There is only one valid definition of business purpose: *to create a customer*'.[7] Based on this philosophy Drucker identified the most important things that businesses could do, and again these could not have been described more succinctly: 'Because its purpose is to create a customer, the business enterprise has two – and only these two – basic functions: *marketing* and *innovation.* Marketing and innovation produce results; all the rest are costs'.[8]

It is these two functions – marketing and innovation, which are now endorsed as vital by virtually all business gurus and commentators – that will occupy us for the rest of Part I. Figure 1.1 illustrates this in a plan for the rest of the book.

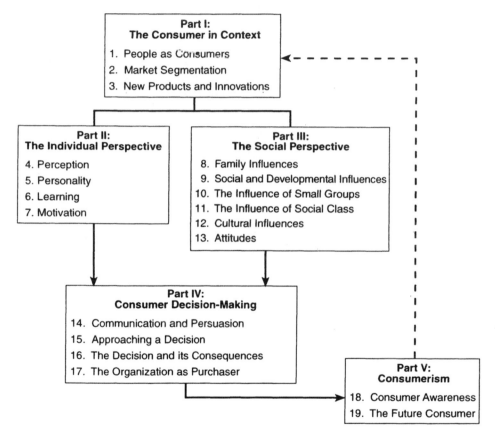

Figure 1.1   Plan for understanding the consumer

After placing the consumer in a general context we adopt two complementary perspectives – *individual* and *social* – to study consumer behaviour. Part II examines the core psychological processes shared by each individual, such as perception, the development of personality, learning, memory and thinking, and motivation. This perspective is that of the individual consumer facing the world.

We then consider the same consumer's behaviour from the viewpoint of society facing the individual as it were. Here we consider the influences on the individual of the family and society in general, as well as both the small and large groups whose membership links the individual to his or her society. We then consider the importance of the cultural and subcultural influences that cut across the other forms of social influence. Finally in Part II we analyse the formation and changing of attitudes about being a consumer in general, as well as about specific products.

The sum of both these individual and social perspectives provides us with a rounded view of the consumer and allows us to tackle the core issue of consumer behaviour, that of decision making. Part IV is therefore concerned with the forms of communication and persuasion that surround this decision, how the consumer goes about making a decision and then deals with its consequences. We end Part IV by looking at the way organizations do the same thing.

In Part V we draw on all four previous parts to deal with issues of consumerism. We analyse how consumers come to see themselves as a separate interest group and how this affects the producer and the marketer. As well as making use of previous research, we shall also refer back to Part I, where we were concerned with placing the consumer in context. Our analysis of consumerism in Part V shows us how that context has been changing in recent years and how it is likely to develop in the future.

■ Further Reading

Kassarjian, H. and T. Robertson (Eds.), (1991), *Handbook of Consumer Behavior,* 4th edn. (Englewood Cliffs, NJ: Prentice-Hall, 1991). An authoritative account of the most important concepts used in consumer behaviour, with a detailed review of relevant research.

Katona, G. *The Powerful Consumer* (New York: McGraw-Hill, 1960). A pioneering work on consumer behaviour by one of the first social scientists to combine, in a systematic way, economic and psychological thinking on this topic.

It is also worth browsing through the latest issues of the following periodicals: *Advances in Consumer Research, Harvard Business Review, Journal of Consumer Research.*

■ Questions for Discussion

1. What is the difference between the 'positivist' and the 'interpretivist' approach to understanding the consumer? What are the strengths and weaknesses of each?
2. Distinguish between a buyer, a customer and a consumer.
3. Why is ever-increasing consumption so important to the consumer economy? What are the social implications?
4. How does the marketplace function for producers and consumers? What is the difference between the 'production orientation' and the 'marketing concept'?
5. Why is the marketing concept considered so important? What would marketers do if it didn't exist?

CHAPTER 2

▌Market Segmentation

■ Introduction: The Origin of Segmented Markets

In the first chapter we quoted the original business guru, Peter Drucker, to the effect that marketing and innovation are the only things that really matter to a business organization. In this chapter we consider the first of these two functions. In particular we are concerned with the way that marketers target prospective consumers of their products by segmenting the market according to a number of different criteria.

We noted in the last chapter that the *marketing concept*, with its emphasis on consumer wants, needs and preferences, appeared in the mid 1950s. As part of this focus on the consumer rather than the producer end of the market place the term 'market segmentation' was also introduced at that time.[1]

Mass production came to dominate the developed economies from the time of the industrial revolution, but manufacturers bothered little about marketing their products, as demand exceeded supply. What little marketing was done was mass marketing; that is, consumers were treated largely as one big, undifferentiated, market. What different groups of consumers wanted in a product – still less what individuals wanted – was more or less treated as irrelevant.

In this context the famous quotation from Henry Ford mentioned in the last chapter is worth looking at again: 'You can have any colour of Model T you like as long as it's black'. This really doesn't make commercial sense. What would it have cost Ford to have a few red, white or blue paint sprays instead of black at the end of the assembly line? If there was an extra cost it would have been tiny. So why not make customers happy by giving them the colour of their choice?

I think Ford's statement only makes sense if we consider it psychologically, and looked at in this light it is about power and control. Ford was really saying: 'I have it in my power to give you a car in any colour your heart desires but I'm going to withhold the fulfilment of that desire. Instead, you will have the colour I want you to have and no other'. And every one of his 15 000 000 *black* Model Ts that he saw reinforced this feeling.

Put like this it sounds like the behaviour of a rather harsh and punitive parent, and that, I would argue, is a pretty good summary of the prevailing relationship between producers and consumers, of which Henry Ford in the 1920s represented the high-water mark. It was a manipulative one that betrayed a paternalistic contempt for the consumer. As we will see throughout this book, that relationship did not disappear entirely with the advent of the marketing concept.

What the marketing concept did was to provide a focus for a changing producer orientation from one of unthinking control and dominance of the producer – consumer relationship to one of greater sophistication. Market segmentation is generally regarded as the essence of the marketing concept, but though the term itself was only introduced in the mid 1950s the more thoughtful producers had in fact been practising the concept for many years – indeed since Henry Ford's time.

In the early 1920s, when the Ford Motor Company dominated the car market, five small and ailing American car manufacturers (Chevrolet, Pontiac, Oldsmobile, Buick and Cadillac) formed a new company, the General Motors Corporation. Within the new conglomerate each of these five companies retained its own identity as a distinctive brand, and each brand was marketed with a different segment of the market in mind.

Chevrolet was the cheapest brand, aimed at young, first-time buyers. Cadillac of course was the top-of-the-range car for the consumer who had 'made it'. The other three brands were intended as intermediate stages on life's automotive journey, and were marketed accordingly. This basic form of market segmentation was highly successful in turning a large number of consumers into life-long GM customers. Within a few years GM had overtaken Ford, and thereafter dominated the American car market for nearly sixty years.[2]

We now take it for granted that every major car manufacturer will provide a range of models at different prices. But Henry Ford didn't. And one of the most intriguing aspects of GM's success is that it did it by using exactly the same components for all its models and even (with the exception of the Cadillac) the same assembly line.[3]

The General Motors example also shows the importance of *positioning* a product in the market, a technique that is closely allied to market segmentation. The position of a product in the market reflects the way consumers perceive it in relation to its competitors. The particular attributes of the product and the way it is promoted are the ingredients of the strategy the marketer will use to position a product for its target segment of the market. This implies, of course, that the marketer has first segmented the market and identified the preferred target. Attempting to position a product without doing so would be pointless.

Market segmentation has reached the point where the American consumer can now choose from over 300 kinds of vehicle – and where the average supermarket contains over 21000 products.[4] This explosion of market segmentation, and indeed of marketing, has been greatly encouraged over the past forty years by the parallel development of the computer. Computers are able to store very large amounts of data and analyse them very quickly – ideal if you have a total market of hundreds of millions of people and the target consumer for your product is a green-eyed, left-handed, highly educated, football-loving, vegetarian female who is over six feet tall, under the age of twenty-five and living in rented accommodation in the country-side.

We have now reached the stage where computer databases are enabling marketers to generate lists of individuals in their target market segment and send them personalised communications based on who they are, where they live, what they do and so on. This process has been called 'a segment of one'[5] and it represents the ultimate in market segmentation, or to put it another way, a return to the relationship between producer and consumer that prevailed before the advent of mass production and mass marketing.

It is widely agreed that a number of market conditions have to be met if a segmentation strategy is to work. These may be described as:

- *Identity*: how identifiable, and distinguishable from other consumers, is a prospective segment and how easy is it to obtain the necessary information on such people?
- *Access*: how easy is it to reach people in this segment with marketing communications?
- size: does the number of people in the segment, and their purchasing power, justify the cost of marketing to them?

For the rest of this chapter we will consider some of the most important forms of market segmentation: geographic, demographic, psychological, usage and benefit.

■ Geographic Segmentation

This involves segmenting the market by location on the assumption that people living in one location will have similar needs, wants and preferences, and that these will differ significantly from people living in other locations. There are some obvious limits to this assumption. People all over the world drink Coca Cola, for instance, and buy Japanese electronic goods. Indeed some marketing specialists have suggested that global communication systems, for example satellite television, have now made geographical boundaries obsolete.

However, while the important effects of global communication must certainly be considered – and we will do so in various ways in other chapters – the issue is a complex one. Coca Cola for instance, which is renowned for its global marketing strategy, has also developed a strategy for more localised markets.[6] Another internationally known brand, Campbell's soups, has divided the American market into 22 regions and attempted to devise a separate strategy for each. Moreover this has even extended to differentiating the product itself, for instance the Californian version of Campbell's nacho cheese sauce is much spicier than its mid-western version.[7] This process is now known as *micromarketing*.

One aspect in which geographic segmentation makes obvious sense is when there are large climatic variations to be considered. There is a greater demand for convertible cars and swimming pools in Florida than in Illinois for instance. This is an obvious factor to consider when marketing overseas. The United States is one of the few domestic markets that is physically large enough for climate to be a significant marketing factor, but other aspects of geography may be of interest in much smaller countries. In the United Kingdom, for example, the water supplied to most of Scotland is much softer (with fewer impurities, and soap is easier to lather), than it is in London because of their geological differences. This has implications for the marketing of soaps and shampoos as well as water softeners.

When you think about it from the viewpoint of the consumer, *most* buying behaviour is actually local. Apart from the mail order business – which has certainly seen a resurgence in recent years – and a few famous or speciality retail outlets, people tend to buy goods and services where they live and work. And this is true even of globally marketed and distributed products.

Localised consumer behaviour is often expressed through the presence of a significantly large cultural or subcultural group that is different from the mainstream. The spicier version of Campbell's nacho cheese sauce that is available in California and the south-west is obviously related to the region's high concentration of Hispanic people. Sometimes a local cultural product may be successfully marketed much more widely, for example the New York Jewish bagel or the Balti Indian cuisine of Birmingham, or most black American music for that matter.

There are also geographically based differences between consumers for reasons that are more complex or obscure. It is not immediately obvious why the Scots eat a lot more confectionery than the English, or why people in the eastern United States drink a lot more whisky than those in the south. But knowing that they do, can be important to a marketing strategy.

Advertising to a geographic segment can also be a highly cost effective way of reaching a target market. Advertising in local newspapers, radio and television is much cheaper and more closely focused than in their national counterparts. Even more so, of course, is in-store or point-of-sale advertising within a single retail outlet.

Marketing promotions aimed at this ultimate geographic segment are known as *store-specific marketing* and are often associated with key supermarkets in well-defined neighbourhoods. For example Kraft tried this approach recently in the United States, where it used information from checkout scanners to find out local preferences and then heavily promoted these items in special displays. Sales increased by 150 per cent in one year.[8]

■ Demographic Segmentation

Demographic segmentation deals with the many ways of statistically categorizing all the people in a national population. For example a national population can be divided into subgroups by age, sex, income, education, occupation, social class, family size, race and religion. In a sense these are also different ways of looking at the same individual consumer, because of course we all belong to each of these groups. Different aspects of our identity will be relevant to different products at different times. Baby foods can only be marketed to parents of young children, for example, and a middle-class, middle-aged, middle-income, middle-manager is more likely to be in the market for an exercise bike than a motor bike.

Many of the categories mentioned above will be examined in more detail in later chapters. In the context of demographic segmentation we will simply introduce the more important of these groupings. First though we should consider some general demographic trends and their implications for marketing. While it is important for the marketer to know the number of people in any given population group it is just as important to be aware of the ways in which this number has shifted over time and how it is likely to change in the future.

Several broad demographic trends can be discerned in most of the industrialised world:

- The population is *ageing*. Life expectancy for both men and women has increased during the course of the twentieth century, so people are living longer and older people are making up a larger proportion of the total population.
- The members of the post-war *baby boom* are now middle-aged. There was a huge increase in the birth rate between 1946 (just after the end of the Second World War) and the early 1960s. People born at that time are now in the 35–55 age range, and this is now the largest and most influential age group.
- The proportion of *young people* in the population, especially those aged 15–20 is declining.
- Average *household sizes* have declined, with a large increase in one-person households.
- Women are having *fewer children* and giving birth later in life.

Marketers are now tending to focus much of their effort on the middle-aged consumer. But there is a large and growing secondary market of older people, some of whom have a considerably larger disposable income than that of previous generations. Sheltered housing, nursing homes and health care products are some of the more obvious marketing possibilities here, but with increasing levels of fitness and education among older people, travel and leisure pursuits are also providing increased opportunities.

Bearing these trends in mind, we will now look at some of the more important specifics of demographic segmentation:

■ **Age**

Age is perhaps the most frequently used demographic variable in market segmentation. One reason for this is that the life cycle has been divided up by society into what seem to be easily recognisable groups that are clearly differentiated from each other – infants, children, teenagers, young adults and so on. To these biologically based groups may be added groups such as the 35–50-year-old baby boomers (the result of the greatly increased birth rate following the Second World War) and their 18–29 year-old children, sometimes known as generation X, as well as yuppies (young upwardly mobile professionals), dinkies (dual income no kids) and so forth. This allows marketers to target a particular age group nationally or even globally (think of 'the Pepsi generation' for instance).

Another reason for the extensive use of age segmentation is that knowing someone's age can often tell you a lot about them. A 17 year-old is unlikely to be a home-owning, newspaper-reading parent for instance; a 37 year-old is a much more likely bet. Disposable income generally increases with age, at least until retirement, and we saw earlier in the chapter how General Motors used this basic trend successfully for most of the twentieth century to market different models to different age groups.

However from the consumer's point of view the issue of age is not quite so straightforward and there is a psychological dimension to this variable that marketers would do well to bear in mind. It is that people do not always look like, feel like, or act like they are supposed to at their chronological age. The period of 'old age', for example, is generally assumed to begin when people start to receive official retirement benefits, often around 65 years of age. Yet many people aged 70 or more still consider themselves 'middle aged' and behave – and consume – as though they are. In other words their *perceived age* is out of sync with their chronological age.[9] But it is this age that marketers have to deal with, at the risk of insulting their target market if they don't. The converse is apparently true of many younger people. Up to the age of about 30 many people consider themselves, or wish to be considered, older than they are.

■ **Sex**

Dividing the market into male and female segments is another frequently used strategy. But even here the old marketing certainties are breaking down. It used to be a safe bet for marketers to target do-it-yourself products exclusively at men and supermarket shopping at women. But with the larger increase in single-occupant households and one-parent families (most of them female) many more women are now repairing and decorating their own homes and many more men are shopping in supermarkets.

In addition more women than men buy for other consumers. Women are still the main buyers of baby products, for instance, and frequently buy underwear for their menfolk, a role that men are apparently still very reluctant to undertake for women – apart from special occasions such as Christmas or Valentine's Day, when their manhood is less likely to feel threatened.

■ **Socio-Economic Status**

A person's Socio-Economic Status (SES) is determined by *education, income* and *occupation*. Though there are many exceptions, of course, these three factors are often in alignment. More highly educated people tend to do managerial and professional jobs that bring a relatively high income, and vice versa. For obvious reasons most marketers are more interested in people with high rather than low SES. Nonetheless there are many essential purchases that even people of the lowest SES have to make – food being the most obvious example – and these are usually in high-volume markets.

Income is often considered the most important SES variable because it is so easy to quantify and because it dictates entry to certain markets. But income by itself can be quite misleading. A college professor and a used car salesman may have the same income but one is more likely to go to the opera and the other to a football game – at least in North America and the United Kingdom. Marketing both events to both people is therefore probably a waste of resources. In Italy, on the other hand, where the popularity of both opera and football transcends occupation and education, income probably will be the deciding factor, but not in attendance *per se*, rather in terms of *frequency* of attendance and price of ticket.

■   **Geodemographic Segmentation**

The final market segment we will consider in this section is actually a hybrid that combines demographic segmentation and the geographic segmentation examined above. As the word 'geodemographic' implies, this segment is based on the idea that people who live in the same neighbourhood will tend to have the same socio-economic status, and each of the three SES factors – income, education and occupation – will also be similar. People in a given neighbour-hood thus tend to have similar needs, wants and preferences and a similar amount of money to spend on them. It is a way of identifying ready-made clusters of households with similar lifestyles and patterns of consumption – ideal for marketers with clearly identified and detailed targets.

Geodemographic segmentation became popular in the 1970s after the invention of the silicon chip dramatically increased the power and decreased the cost of computing. Highly sophisticated systems for mapping all the consumer neighbourhoods in an entire country were devised, using census data and market research on patterns of consumption, such as PRIZM in the United States and ACORN in the United Kingdom. PRIZM stands for 'Potential Rating Index by Zip Market'. It is a means of using the 36 000 or so postal districts in the United States (each with its own zip code) to divide the population into 40 categories using factors such as the ones described above plus race, religion, family, mobility and so on.

The Claritas Corporation, which developed PRIZM, established an SES ranking (or 'zip quality') of these neighbourhood clusters throughout the coun-try that ranged from 'blue blood estates' at ZQ1, where the most affluent Americans live, to 'public assistance', comprising the most indigent people in the inner cities at ZQ40.[10] Along the way there are clusters such as 'blue-chip blues' at ZQ10 (the most prosperous blue-collar communities) and 'Grain Belt' at ZQ33 (the most sparsely populated rural communities).

ACORN (A Classification of Residential Neighbourhoods) performs the same function in the United Kingdom.[11] In its most recent version 38 types of neighbourhood have been listed with a similar housing categorization to PRIZM. ACORN has been expanded to include types of lifestyle such as 'younger very affluent suburban couples and families' and 'older suburban singles', which take account of both household composition and age structure. Systems such as ACORN and PRIZM are now routinely used for direct marketing via leaflets, mailing lists and local newspaper inserts, as well as planning the most appropriate sites for new stores and stocking existing stores.

■ Psychological Segmentation

Useful though demographics and demographic market segmentation have been to advertisers and providers of goods and services, they have only given us a broad-brush approach to understanding the consumer; an aggregate approach to consumers rather than a detailed one. They are concerned with breadth rather than depth of understanding.

What is missing from this picture of the consumer is an analysis of the way the consumption of particular products relates to the rest of the consumer's life. Sampling the richness of this picture of the consumer as an individual human being is the goal of *psychological* segmentation. This form of market segmentation is at the heart of the approach to consumer behaviour taken by this book. We will briefly consider it here, but it is examined in detail in Part II and at other points throughout this book.

This form of market segmentation is sometimes described as *psychographics* or *lifestyle* segmentation. However the approach is based on fundamental psychological factors such as motivation, perception, personality patterns, learning, and the formation and changing of attitudes. The intention of this approach is to gain some insight into what makes consumers tick and to arrive at individual profiles that capture the essence of a target consumer.

The attempt to come up with a practical form of consumer profile has concentrated on three areas of behaviour: activities, interests and opinions.[12]

- *Activities:* how do people spend their time? (For example work, entertainment, shopping.)
- *Interests:* What are people most interested in? (For example family, job, recreation, food.)
- *Opinions:* how do people view themselves and their world? (For example politics, business, education, the future.)

This type of profile is now widely used in marketing. A typical piece of research would use a battery of several hundred statements and respondents would be asked how they rated each one on a scale from 'strongly agree' to 'strongly disagree'. Typical statements might include the following:

- I am an impulse buyer.
- I'm a demanding person.
- When it comes to the way I dress I'm not particularly fashion conscious.
- My family is the most important thing to me.
- I would be willing to pay more for a product with all natural ingredients.
- We are more likely to try new products than most of our friends and neighbours.
- We are a particularly good looking family.

Using this approach, one study of some 3300 people categorised the American population into ten types of lifestyle, five for male and five for females.[13] The female psychographic profiles in particular have been widely quoted. They were marketed to marketers with a set of catchy titles, as follows:

- *Thelma*: 'the old-fashioned traditionalist' (25 per cent of the population)– devoted to husband, children and home ... socially and politically conservative ... keen churchgoer ... no higher education ... watches vast amount of television.
- *Candice*: 'the chic suburbanite' (20 per cent of the population)– highly educated and sophisticated ... pillar of the community ... aware of social and political issues ... reads newspapers and magazines ... watches little television.
- *Mildred*: 'the militant mother' (20 per cent of the population)– married and had children when relatively young ... husband in insecure, badly paid job ... she is unhappy and frustrated with her lot ... likes rock and soul music ... watches vast amount of television.
- *Cathy*: 'the contented housewife' (18 per cent of the population) – a younger version of Thelma, but without the religion ... avoids news programmes on television and looks for 'wholesome family entertainment' instead.
- *Eleanor*: 'the elegant socialite' (17 per cent of the population) – a big city version of the suburban Candice, though career rather than community oriented.

Simplistic and general though these profiles may be, they have been used with apparent success in various marketing campaigns, for example to sell women's underwear – sorry, ladies' intimate apparel. A company making a traditional old-fashioned line for the Thelmas and Cathies of America came up with two profitable new lines, one for Candice and Eleanor and the other for Mildred.[14]

A similar system in the United Kingdom identified eight groups, each with 10–15 per cent of the population.[15] They are labelled as follows:

- 'The young sophisticates'
- 'Middle-aged sophisticates'
- 'Cabbages'
- 'Coronation Street housewives'
- 'Traditional working class'
- 'The self-confident'

- 'The penny pinchers'
- 'The homely'

The most elaborate form of psychological segmentation is an American system known as VALS (values and life styles).[16] The basic research for VALS was carried out in the late 1970s and was updated a decade later as VALS-2. It is seen as a form of classification that can pigeonhole every adult American consumer into one of eight (originally nine) categories with the usual imaginative names ('survivor', 'sustainer', 'belonger', 'believer', 'struggler', and so on).

Like all lifestyle/psychographic systems, VALS is open to the criticism that millions of people do not fall neatly into a few categories for everything they buy and stay in those categories throughout their lives. Indeed this criticism is to some extent accepted by the Stanford Research Institute of California, which developed the system. Nevertheless many large American companies and advertising agencies rely on it heavily in their marketing strategies. But as we shall see later in this book, it is extremely difficult to link someone's attitudes, opinions and interests to their actual behaviour. There is a lot of psychology in between.

■ Segmentation by Usage

This form of segmentation is based on information about volume and frequency of purchase for a given product. It is a popular way of segmenting markets because there is a lot of readily available information about patterns of usage for most goods and services. In fact, with so many transactions now electronically recorded, a great deal more data is available than is actually used. Perhaps the most familiar usage data is provided by the electronic point of sale (EPOS) systems used by supermarket checkouts. Not only are all the purchased items listed, together with their prices, but so is the date and exact time of purchase and the method of payment used.

The market is usually divided into users and non-users, with users subdivided into light, medium and heavy. Only a small proportion of consumers are heavy users of a product but they usually account for most of its sales. This is sometimes called the 80–20 rule (where 80 per cent of sales are accounted for by 20 per cent of buyers), but of course the actual percentages may vary around these figures.

These figures refer to *frequency* of usage but in some cases infrequent buyers buy the product in bulk: when they are buying for institutions or food co-operatives for example. Some companies have understood this aspect of marketing their products and offer discounts and other incentives for bulk buying.[17] There is also some evidence that it is easier to increase sales by persuading existing buyers to increase their usage. Although it may be possible to find new users for a product it is more difficult to accomplish.[18]

Another aspect of frequency of purchase that should be considered is *time*.

Are we talking about current or future usage? For example the attitude of major banks towards students as customers depends on whether they are concentrating on their current pattern of usage (frequent use but small amounts) or their potential future usage after graduation (possibly less frequent but much larger amounts, and therefore bank profits).

Banks that choose the longer-term strategy are in fact trying to build up a customer relationship that will encourage *brand loyalty*. Although this is a primary aim of all marketers it is a more complex relationship than it might seem at first glance. Brand loyalty cuts across all groups and all market segments. Any consumer may exhibit brand-loyal or even store-loyal behaviour, and it is very difficult to discern any pattern in this behaviour.

Moreover consumers who are loyal to a certain brand may only buy a little of it; you may have been loyal to Bayer aspirin or Band Aids since childhood but only use them two or three times a year. And brand loyalty seems to be product-specific; that is, it does not extend to other products with the same brand name. The family that automatically reaches for Heinz Baked Beans may choose Crosse and Blackwell when it comes to Spaghetti Hoops.[19]

One final aspect of usage segmentation worth considering is that of time as represented by a particular occasion or situation. Linking a product to a particular occasion is a staple technique of the greetings card business for instance, which majors in Christmas cards of course, but in addition practically invented Mother's Day and Father's Day. There is probably no definable moment of life from birth to death – from birthdays, barmitzvahs and graduations to weddings – that can not be marked with a greetings card (large or small, plain or fancy, serious or funny). Other businesses have been quick to spot these selling opportunities – florists and confectioners being the most obvious examples.

Time also affects usage in at least one other important way: the consumer's *situation*. Take travelling for instance. Retired people can travel at more or less any time they choose and so they can plan ahead and travel at off-peak times. They can therefore take advantage of cheaper rates at hotels and on trains and planes, as well as discounts for booking far in advance. The business traveller, on the other hand, to whom time is invariably more valuable than money, often has to travel at short notice and at peak periods, and pays a great deal more for the same services.

■ Segmentation by Benefit

This form of market segmentation is based on a knowledge of the benefits that consumers seek from a particular product. The task of the marketer is to include the appropriate characteristics – or the impression of them – in the design of particular goods or services. In a sense this kind of segmentation is at the heart of the entire marketing concept – find out what people want and provide it for them.

This strategy involves a great deal of market research on consumer motivation. But as we will see in Chapter 7 on motivation, people cannot always tell you what they *really* want and still less why they want it. That is, the real reason (or at least the deepest reason) for their buying and consuming behaviour may be hidden even from themselves. In this respect consumer motivation is like any other form of motivation: a highly complex and sometimes deeply emotional part of our psychology that is very difficult to understand – and therefore to influence directly.

What people tell market researchers is therefore often superficial: what they think the questioner wants to hear, or what they think will show them up in a good light, or even what they may have gleaned from advertisements for the product. This last kind of response is a particular headache for researchers because it makes the whole process circular. So it is quite dangerous for a marketing strategy always to take consumers' statements about their needs and motivations entirely at face value. Like all psychological data they need to be interpreted by people who understand the processes involved.

One way to cope with this difficulty is instead to ask consumers what *problems* they have with a particular product, under which situations, how frequently and so on. This approach was tried with some success for canned dog food.[20] The problems were apparently threefold: the smell, the cost and the lack of different sized cans for different sized dogs. When each of these problems was dealt with (cost by the use of cheaper ingredients) sales improved.

Benefit segmentation requires a sharp differentiation to be made between the benefits of a particular product and those of its competitors. Ultimately this involves customising a product as far as possible to meet the buyer's specifications. This has always been the selling point of services such as quality tailoring, for instance, but is now being applied to manufactured products too.

Perhaps the most striking example of this is provided by the Japanese company Matsushita, which sells customised bicycles tailored precisely to each consumer's dimensions.[21] In the retail outlet the customer sits on a frame to be measured, the measurements are faxed to the company's computer, which then produces an exact blueprint for robots to cut the materials to size and weld them together. The bicycle is then assembled, decorated by hand and road tested. The entire process takes three hours, though customers are usually made to wait a couple of weeks so that they appreciate it more.

A final aspect of benefit segmentation worth noting is that increased sales of a product to existing users, or even the creation of new markets, can be accomplished by making minimal changes to the product that have the effect of introducing a new benefit (a form of repositioning). A particularly striking example of this has been the trend in recent decades towards 'healthy eating'. Obvious examples here are decaffeinated coffee, skimmed milk, low-sugar baked beans and even vegetarian sausages, which contain the cereals and spices of ordinary sausages but without the (usually minimal) meat content.

■ Further Reading

Crimp, M., *The Market Research Process* (Englewood Cliffs, NJ: Prentice-Hall, 1981). A solid introduction to market research.

Engel, J. F., H. F. Fiorillo and M. A. Cayley, *Market Segmentation: Concepts and Applications* (New York: Holt, 1972). A good and accessible source of the basic ideas and usage of market segmentation.

Garreau, J., *The Nine Nations of North America* (New York: Avon, 1981). An influential anthropological approach to the North American market that deals in cultural boundaries rather than the political ones of country, state and region.

Holman, R. and M. R. Solomon, *Advances in Consumer Research*, vol. 18 (Provo, Utah: Association for Consumer Research, 1991). The most prestigious series of research reviews in the field. Updated every year or two. The 1991 edition contains a number of particularly important articles on market segmentation.

Levitt, T., *The Marketing Imagination* (New York: Free Press, 1983). A much quoted account of the ideas behind marketing and how marketers operate.

Piirto, R., *Beyond Mind Games: The Marketing Power of Psychographics* (Ithaca, NY: American Demographic Books, 1991). The leading authority on the practical applications of psychographics. Includes the history and development of VALS.

It is also worth browsing through the latest issues of the following periodicals: *Journal of Marketing, Journal of Marketing Research, Advertising Age, Admap, American Demographics.*

■ Questions for Discussion

1. What is the origin of the 'marketing concept'? What is its importance to (a) marketers (b) consumers?
2. What are the benefits and costs to the marketer of market segmentation? How does it relate to positioning?
3. What kinds of producer might best market their products on the·basis of the following kinds of segmentation (a) demographics, (b) usage, (c) benefit, (d) psychological?
4. What would be an appropriate segmentation strategy for the following products: (a) a course on consumer behaviour, (b) a jazz radio station, (c) chocolate flavoured coffee beans, (d) a cheap lager?
5. How are the following segmented and positioned, (a) Calvin Klein jeans, (b) British Airways, (c) McDonald's hamburgers, (d) Honda cars?
6. You can also try the process of market segmentation for yourself via the Internet. The address is http:#future.sri.com/vals/.

CHAPTER 3

New Products and Innovations

There is no such thing as a commodity. All goods and services can be differentiated and usually are (Theodore Levitt).[1]

Introduction

In Chapter 2 we examined the practical implications for consumers of the marketing concept. In this chapter we will look at the other key functions of the business enterprise that help form the consumer context: innovation and the development of new products.

As the twenty-first century approaches, one of the most striking things about being a consumer is the number of new products there are to consume. Every trip to the supermarket may well reveal something new. The exact number of new products coming on to the market is practically impossible to calculate, but it is huge. Recent estimates put the *annual* number of new products appearing on supermarket shelves at between 1000 and 5000, and these represent a very small proportion of all the new product ideas that are actually tested. Estimates of the failure rate of these marketed products is also imprecise but just as huge, ranging from 80–90 per cent at a cost of many billions of dollars.

As nearly all large companies are in the business of introducing new goods and services the worldwide scale of this activity is quite colossal. And so is the scale of the waste involved: the waste of time, materials and human brainpower. This is an important issue that needs to be dealt with separately and we will tackle it in Part V on consumerism. In this chapter we will study the way in which new products and innovations are marketed to the consumer and how the consumer responds to them.

Developing New Products

One aspect of this process is clear already: there are many more failures than successes, and even the biggest and most successful companies have failures. Sony had the Betamax video cassette recorder, Polaroid had the Polavision instant movie camera and Ford had perhaps the best-known flop of all time, the notorious Edsel. These companies were large enough and had enough profitable lines to absorb the losses, but many smaller companies in a similar position have gone under.

There are various pressures on all companies constantly to increase the number of new products in their field. One of these is the declining birth rate in the industrialised world since the baby boom ended in the mid 1970s. There are simply fewer new consumers in the potential market place, and therefore new products have to be sold mainly to existing customers.

Another source of pressure in all areas of goods and services is the constant technological innovation that companies have to be aware of and adapt to. As we saw in the previous chapter this has been particularly true of the microchip and the electronic computer/information technology it has spawned. Related to this is a perceived shortening of the lead time in which to profit from technological and product innovations. Du Pont's invention of nylon in the 1930s put the company decades ahead of its competitors and Polaroid's introduction of instant photography in the 1960s gave it several years of exclusivity. Six months is now considered a long time.

For some industries, for example pop music, computer software and women's fashions, innovation is a matter of life or death, but even when no products are involved there is still great pressure on most organisations, even in the public sector, to introduce innovations in the way they operate. This may involve changing the organizational structure, the training of management, the development of staff or even changing the personality of the chief executive in order to focus on different ways of doing things.

There is nothing new about this view of innovation. Peter Drucker has been writing about it for most of the past half century. For example:

> every managerial unit of business should have responsibility for innovation and definite innovation goals. It should be responsible for contributing to innovation in the company's product or service. In addition it should strive consciously to advance the art in the particular area in which it is engaged: selling or accounting, quality control or personnel management.[2]

More recently another business guru, Rosabeth Moss Kanter, concluded from a survey of 105 innovations in leading American companies that competitive advantage derives from the encouragement of 'idea power'.[3]

What has changed in recent years is the awareness of senior management that innovation is not just a luxury or a nice theory, or even a specialised function of the research and development division, but a universal necessity. And this awareness has not been brought about by the existence of a new breed of enlightened senior managers but the hard realities of intense, ever-increasing global competition and an economic and political climate, especially in the United Kingdom and North America, of quick profits and low public spending.

■ The Total Product Concept

As we will see throughout this book, the producer's view of a particular product may not always be indentical to that of the consumer. There may be a psychological gap between the two. This is particualrly evident with the introduction of new products, where marketers often unduly emphasize the newness of the product – its innovative aspects – and neglect boring old things such as ease of

installation or the availablility of spare parts, which might well be more important to the potential consumer.

It is therefore vital for marketers to bear in mind that the simple question
'what is the product we are marketing?' usually has a complex answer. Theodore
Levitt's 'total product concept' is a useful way of thinking about this question.[4]
Levitt sees a product as a combination of various attributes that increase in complexity through four levels, as follows:

- *Generic product:* the substantive content (the car, the shoes, the hamburger
  the life insurance) that forms the core of the product that reaches the market.
- *Expected product:* the generic attributes *plus* the buyer's minimum expectations
  of it (price, packaging, delivery and so on).
- *Augmented product:* the generic and expected attributes *Plus* those attributes
  the marketer has included to differentiate the product from its competitors
  (bonuses or free gifts such as tapes with a VCR, training in new software with
  a computer system, an extra rumple treatment to make a baggy suit even
  baggier).
- *Potential product:* generic, expected and augmented attributes *plus* ... and the
  plus is where the new products and innovations come in. So the potential
  product is what is possible but not yet attained.

Figure 4.1 illustrates this idea graphically:

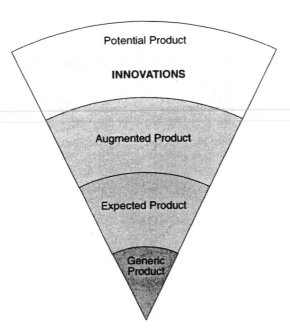

Figure 3.1   Levitt's total product concept

■ **Successful Innovation**

Most of the writers who have commented on what makes for successful innovation agree that the most potent secret lies in changing some aspect, however small, of the way society is organized, which results from satisfying a need that consumers were perhaps unaware that they had. We can see this most clearly in the spectacularly successful innovations that have arisen since the Second World War, for instance fast food outlets, photocopiers, word processors, portable telephones, personal stereos and, probably most important of all, supermarkets. Each of these innovations has changed the way people relate to each other, in important and less important ways.

The supermarket, for example, changed the way people shopped, ate and travelled. A single outlet, situated out of town, that could supply all a consumer's food and household requirements meant the demise of many local specialist shops, as well as an increase in car ownership and usage in order to get there and stock up. And because for many people shopping became a major once-a-week activity rather than a minor daily routine, people had to buy food that would last the week, hence the rise of frozen foods and of freezers to keep them in, and then of microwave ovens to defrost them with.

The word processor has encouraged the writing of many more books and articles than would have been possible with typewriters. It has also influenced marketing, for example by enabling firms to send out mass mailings to prospective customers and to 'personalise' these by using the recipients' names.

These are all spectacular innovations that very quickly cornered a large market or created a new market. But what of less spectacular innovations; what makes them successful? Another celebrated business guru, Tom Peters, has pointed out that there is no substitute for getting as close to the customer as possible – indeed forming a partnership with the customer.[5]

This in itself, of course, represents a change in the way society is organised, the idea that producers and consumers might be part of the same enterprise and not on opposite sides with opposing interests. For the producer it implies that executives, no matter how senior, have to be in direct touch with the customer at the point where their goods or services are actually supplied. It suggests that, whatever professional consumer research they may commission, it is still crucial that they themselves actually talk – live, face-to-face, in person – to their customers.

The most successful innovators seem to do something like this. The Campbell's Soup Company, for instance, requires its senior managers to do their own food shopping. The board of directors regularly meets at the back of a supermarket after a session discussing Campbell's products at the front – something the chief executive spends his own Saturday mornings doing. At one point the company was successfully introducing 42 new products a year to the supermarket, a staggering hit rate.[6]

Innovation at this level is a form of continuous improvement; something we have learned from the Japanese, who call it *kaizen*. One end point of this process is the total customising that we saw in the previous chapter with the

Matsushita bicycle, which was literally built to each customer's individual specification. A leading British business executive has recently testified to the commercial advantages of this approach to innovation: 'Big leaps forward are much more satisfying than small incremental changes. Yet, making money from a great invention is notoriously slow and difficult. It is the small innovations, targeted directly to someone's needs, that produce the quick and generous pay-back.'[7]

■ The Product Life Cycle

It is frequently claimed that all products have a limited profitability lifetime. The very market success that makes something profitable guarantees that it will become a target for competition, and of course the greater the profitability the greater the competition. Some products become obsolete because of advances in technology (radio valves), though others may survive in drastically reduced markets (horseshoes), and still others may find a new niche market (nylon stockings).

However it does seem that some products appear to have an indefinite lifespan. Mars Bars have been around for half a century or so and Pears Soap for over a century. It might be questioned, though, to what extent these are still the same products; Mars Bars are now also being marketed as ice cream and Pears Soap has gone downmarket since the nineteenth century. In a sense it might be fair to say that, even if a recognisable product is around for a long time, periodically it has to reinvent itself as times, tastes and technology change.

The life cycle of a product is often depicted graphically as an evenly distributed 'normal curve', as in Figure 3.2, with five different stages along the way.

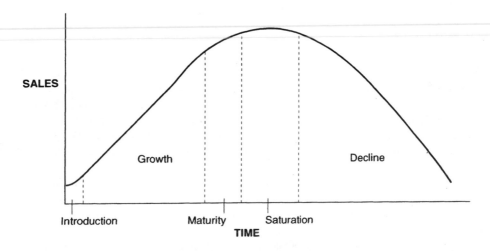

Figure 3.2 Product life cycle

A 'normal curve' in statistics is simply a way of describing how a particular collection of data looks when plotted on a graph. For example the various heights of adult males would plot as a normal curve on a graph, the range going from about five feet to about seven feet and the average being about six feet. Similar normal curves could be drawn for weight, age and any other naturally occurring characteristics.

There is nothing 'normal', however, about the curve of a product life cycle in terms of sales. The five stages of the life cycle are common to all products, but the *shape* of the curves differ depending on the product, the market and a whole host of environmental factors. It is simply a convenient model for thinking about the process and bears about as much relation to a particular product as a fashion model does to a particular woman.

Producers usually have a range of products in the market at any given time, covering the five stages of the life cycle. The amount spent on marketing, advertising and promoting a product depends on where it is in the product life cycle. Activity is naturally highest during the introductory and growth phases, but is reduced as the product is accepted by the market during the maturity phase and hits its sales peak in the satiation phase. At some point during the decline phase the producer needs to make a decision about the cost effectiveness of maintaining the product on the market or removing it from sale.

These phases seem perfectly straightforward and one would expect companies to introduce new products as others decline. That would be the rational thing to do. However organisations, and particularly large organizations, have a certain amount of irrationality and inertia built into them – because they are staffed by people and not robots – and the most appropriate marketing decision may not be chosen, or it may be chosen (or implemented) later than it should.[8]

■ The Effects of Personal Influence

■ Product Champions

The effects of personal influence on innovation are important for two groups; producers and consumers. From the producer's viewpoint it has been suggested that the more innovative a new product or idea is the more it needs devoted support from key members of the organisation, sometimes called 'product champions'.[9] These people are considered necessary because of the inbuilt resistance to change that is standard, as noted in the preceding paragraph, in all organisations.

The central dilemma for organisations is that successful innovators are likely to be unusual people and they are usually difficult to work with. Tom Peters describes their personal characteristics as follows:

(1) energy, (2) passion, (3) idealism, (4) pragmatism, (5) cunning, (6) towering impatience, (7) an unrealistic unwillingness to allow any barrier to set him

back, and (8) love–hate relationships among his subordinates . . . the impassioned champion is anathema to everything that traditional, civil, organized corporate endeavor stands for. But we must hire him, even though he will alienate some good people, irritate almost everyone, and in the end fail more often than not.[10]

The product champion may sometimes be the head of the company, as in the case of the mercurial Soichiro Honda in the early days of the company that bears his name.[11] As the founder of the company he had more latitude to break the rules than most mavericks of course. And breaking rules seems to be an essential part of innovation. Indeed sometimes the most successful innovations can be traced back to people who disobeyed orders from senior management to abandon a project and continued to work on it in secret, at the risk of losing their jobs, because they believed in it so much. This was the case, for instance, with the production of the disk memory unit that was a key component of IBM's early success.[12]

■ Opinion Leaders

As consumers opinion leaders are not always themselves innovators although they will be more open than most to new ideas. Their influence derives more from their judgment about *when* it is appropriate to try a new product and *which* new products to accept.

Most people apparently need more than the information provided in mass media advertising to come to a buying decision. For reasons we will go into in some detail in Chapter 14, most of us feel a need for the personal opinion of individuals we can trust. These individuals obviously exert a considerable influence on the market by what is often known as 'word-of-mouth' communication. Indeed favourable word-of-mouth advice can have far more influence on buying behaviour than the most sophisticated and extensive advertising campaign.[13] This is something that has long been accepted in the marketing of items of popular culture such as books, films and music.

It is difficult to estimate how many opinion leaders there are of course, but figures for the United States vary – depending partly on the market – from 10–25 per cent of the population. The most commonly used products, such as cars and electronics, probably have the highest concentration of opinion leaders. Inasmuch as we have any idea of what an opinion leader is like, research studies suggest they are pretty much what you would expect (we will look at this in more detail in Chapters 10 and 14).

Opinion leaders, while belonging to the same social groups as the people they influence, tend to be more outgoing, enthusiastic and knowledgeable about the products in question. They read the relevant specialist magazines, for example, and are familiar with performance details and technical specifications. In terms of personal characteristics they tend to have higher self-esteem and self-confidence than the average consumer.[14] Although there is some overlap between different product areas, it is unlikely that any one person can be an opinion leader for all products.[15] The range of available goods and services is simply too vast.

It is important to note the obvious fact that people can only be opinion leaders if other people are willing to be their followers – as in any other kind of leadership. This implies that there is a continuing relationship between opinion leaders and followers and that the relationship provides the leaders with something that is important to them. The status of being an expert or a pioneer within a group is an attractive one and opinion leaders enjoy the respect and attention this brings them.

Advertisers sometimes aim their pitch directly at the self-perceived opinion leader rather than the general consumer, as in the personal profiles series for Dewar's Scotch Whisky (pronounced 'do-ers' in the United States). But more often in the mass media a *simulated* opinion leader–follower relationship is used, in the form of a popular celebrity who comes into our home and gives us a 'personal' word-of-mouth message.

A variation on this theme was the successful campaign of the American sports shirt manufacturer La Coste. In its early days the company gave its products away to tennis stars and other sporting and media celebrities and encouraged them to wear the shirts, with their distinctive alligator logo, in all sorts of social situations where they could be observed and emulated by the relevant opinion leaders.

■ The Diffusion of New Products and Innovations

The accepted definition of diffusion is 'the process by which an innovation ... is communicated through certain channels over time among the members of a social system'.[16] It is therefore a macro or group process compared with the micro or individual process of adopting new products and innovations, which we will look at below.

The process of diffusion has been studied in a much wider context than just consumer goods and services, though consumer behaviour has been at the heart of this research. One indication of the social importance of this field is the fact that over 3000 studies of it have been carried out by researchers from a dozen different disciplines of the social and behavioural sciences.

Three main types of innovation have been identified: *continuous, dynamically continuous* and *discontinuous*.[17] Before we consider each of these types, it would be as well to remind ourselves that the great majority of new products and ideas are not diffused at all; they simply disappear. Others may be diffused, but not very far. This has been the fate of several bright hopes of the information technology industry that have performed far below expectation. American predictions in the 1980s, for instance, were that by 1990 some three million people would subscribe to home banking. The actual number was 100 000.[18]

- *Continuous* innovation involves the modification of an existing product and requires only a relatively minor change in consumer behaviour. Examples are new models of cars, new flavours of yoghurt or low fat cheese. The great majority of consumer innovations fall into this category.
- *Dynamically continuous* innovation requires a little more change in consumer behaviour. It can involve the modification of an existing product or the creation of a new one, such as compact disc players, telephone answering machines or wholefoods.
- *Discontinuous* innovation involves a new product whose use requires some new form of behaviour by the consumer; that is, behaviour that is 'discontinuous' from existing behaviour. This is the rarest form of innovation – usually the result of great technological discoveries – but the one with the greatest social and psychological impact. Examples include the telephone, car, radio, television, personal computer and microwave oven.

The importance of being able to predict the very small number of successful innovations in any category is obvious. There is, of course, no standard recipe but it is widely agreed that there are five product characteristics that determine consumer response.[19] These are:

- Relative advantage
- Compatibility
- Complexity
- Testability
- Observability

Relative advantage is the first and perhaps the most important factor to be considered. To what extent does the innovation represent an improvement on existing products? An improvement, that is, in the perception of the *consumer*. Debit cards seemed like a good idea to the banks and retail companies that introduced them, but so far consumers do not seem to share their opinion. On the other hand the fax machine has been a great success because of its clear relative advantage over mail and courier services, allowing consumers to transmit documents in a matter of seconds, as opposed to hours or days, for a fraction of the cost.

Compatibility deals with the issue of how well the innovation fits in with the potential consumer's existing values, attitudes, interests and behaviour. Introducing new bacon products to the Middle East is unlikely to be a winner, for instance. On the other hand a non-alcohol lager might be worth considering.

Complexity refers to the perceived difficulty of using a product. The easier it looks to use the more likely it is that people will try it. That is probably why self-assembly products always come in boxes with pictures of confident, smiling punters effortlessly assembling whatever it is (the reality of course is quite different). And that is what puts a brake on the sale of home computers as opposed to microwave ovens for instance.

Testability: is it possible to try out, or sample, the product on a limited basis? This is a simple matter if the product is a detergent or a breakfast cereal, or even a magazine. It is obviously more difficult with consumer durables, though cars can be test-driven, computer systems leased and television sets displayed. What do you do about washing machines or refrigerators though?

Observability: this factor is sometimes called *communicability* because it is concerned with how easily the benefits of the innovation can be conveyed to potential consumers. In this respect tangible products have an advantage over services, and publicly visible products (telephones, cars, clothing, the Sony Walkman) have an advantage over privately used products, for example those concerned with health and hygiene.

■ The Adoption of New Products and Innovations

The processes of diffusion and adoption may be usefully linked by considering the dimension of time, as outlined in Figure 3.3. The top half of this diagram depicts the life cycle of three generations of a family, the grandfather (GI) born in 1920, the father (GII) born in 1950 and the grandson (GIII) born in 1980. The bottom half of the diagram shows the diffusion and adoption of some of the twentieth century's most successful product innovations.

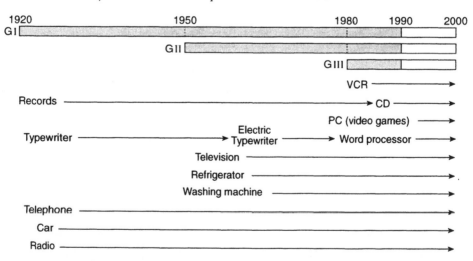

Figure 3.3   The time dimension

I think the following important points are suggested by this simple illustration:

● different generations grow up with different innovations. So whilst the grandfather would have learned to type on a manual machine, the son might well have learned on an electric machine and the grandson on a word processor (a form of dynamic discontinuity). What would be natural to the grandson would require some effort by the father and might be totally beyond the grandfather.

- Some innovations, for example the telephone, the car and the radio, have become so widely diffused that they are now taken for granted by all three generations that grew up with them.
- Some innovations are so user friendly that even a generation that did not grow up with them will adopt them very rapidly. This is the case with the refrigerator and the television set.
- Some innovations may achieve an appreciable penetration of the market because of their perceived usefulness, while only being user friendly to a fraction of buyers (usually the youngest). That is why most families have a video cassette recorder although few people over the age of fifteen can actually work it properly.
- No innovation, even when highly successful, will ever be adopted by everyone in the market at the same time. People have different timetables at different stages of their lives (as well as different values, needs, incomes and so on).

Time is also important when considering global markets. Different countries have different timetables of diffusion and adoption of innovations. New innovations have invariably begun or been adopted first in the United States then spread to other rich countries and finally the rest of the world but there is some evidence that the time lag is diminishing. It took 12 years for black and white television sets in Japan and Western Europe to achieve the same penetration as they did in the American market, compact disc players did it in three years.[20]

Even more important are the different individual timetables noted above. These have been the subject of some research attention. It has been suggested that these individual timetables, when plotted for society as a whole, will form a normal curve, as in Figure 3.4.[21]

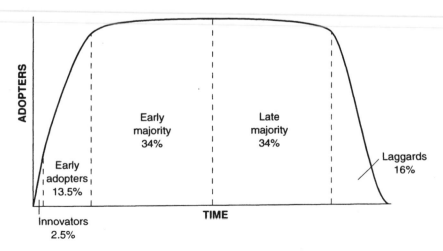

Figure 3.4 The normal distribution of adoption

- *Innovators,* as you would expect, are thought to be adventurous consumers who are willing to take social and financial risks (for example the person who bought the first telephone).
- *Early adopters* tend to be opinion leaders, discussed earlier, who are more linked in to their community and have a relatively high status within it.
- *Early majority* members are more cautious about the innovation.
- *Late majority* members are frankly sceptical about it.
- *Laggards* are downright suspicious about it and wonder, loudly, what was wrong with steam-driven typewriters anyway?

Both these categories and the numbers attached to them are only suggestions. In real life the process is a continuous one, with one attitude towards the innovation shading into another.   Moreover, to the extent that there are recognisably distinct stages, they may not follow this neat linear pattern. Some of the 'laggards' for instance may in fact have rejected the product at the same time as the 'innovators' accepted it and only tried it when the price decreased dramatically over time, as prices usually do. Conversely some of the first eager innovators may have grown tired of the product after six months.

It is also important to note that the normal distribution model assumes 100 per cent adoption of an innovation throughout the population. This has never been true of anything, not even the telephone, the television set and the car in the United States (though they have all come pretty close). Still less is it true of microwave ovens and video cassette recorders, let alone home computers and services such as home banking and cable television. In other words some commercially successful innovations are actually rejected by most of the population.

These huge exceptions to the normal curve may actually represent sizeable markets for alternative goods and services. To take one small example, although there are far more cars than households in the United States many residents of Manhattan (the sane ones) don't own a car. They are therefore in the market for a decent public transport system, a painfully obvious fact that is being discovered by marketers in the industry generally as America's passionate love affair with the car grows ever cooler.

The most important point made by the normal curve model, I would suggest, is that the adoption of innovations is a process that continues *over time* and is never immediate. The process invariably takes longer than producers would wish or anticipate, and quitting the field too soon probably accounts for a sizeable proportion of innovations that are not successfully adopted.

■ Further Reading

Goldberg, M. E., G. Gorn and R. W. Pollay (eds), *Advances in Consumer Research*, vol. 17 (Provo, Utah: Association for Consumer Research, 1990)

Holman, R. H. and M. R. Solomon (eds), *Advances in Consumer Research*, vol. 18 (Provo, Utah: Association for Consumer Research, 1991). This is the most prestigious series of research reviews in the field and is updated every year or two. The 1990 and 1991 editions contain a number of particularly important articles on product innovation and diffusion.

Mahajan, V. and R. A. Peterson, *Innovation Diffusion: Models and Applications* (Beverly Hills: Sage, 1985). A detailed and technical account of new product marketing and market forecasting.

O'Shaughnessy, J. *Why People Buy* (New York: Oxford University Press, 1987), puts the case for the importance to marketing of a psychological interpretation of buying behaviour.

Porter, M. E. *Competitive Advantage* (New York: Free Press, 1985). Competitive advantage is understanding which new products will appeal most to the customer.

Robertson, T. S., *Innovative Behavior and Communication* (New York: Holt, Rinehart & Winston, 1971). An accessible work by a leading researcher that emphasizes psychological aspects of product innovation and adoption.

Rogers, E. M. and F. Shoemaker, *Communication of Innovations* (New York: Free Press, 1971). This deals with the cultural factors that influence the speed of new product diffusion as well as the personal characteristics of adopters.

It is also worth browsing through the latest issues of the following periodicals: *Journal of Consumer Research, Journal of Marketing Research, Journal of Advertising Research, Journal of Consumer Marketing, Journal of International Marketing.*

■ Questions for Discussion

1. What is the 'total product concept'? What are its implications for the marketing of a new product?
2. What factors make for a successful new product? How does this relate to the idea of a 'product life cycle'?
3. How does personal influence operate? What are its implications for the marketer?
4. What is the difference between (a) continuous, (b) dynamically continuous and (c) discontinuous diffusion? Give an original example of each (that is an example not contained in the chapter).
5. In what way are the diffusion and adoption of new products and innovations linked over time?

PART II
The Individual Perspective

■ Introduction

In Part II we will focus on individual consumer behaviour and in doing so we will examine the core psychological processes we all share.

Chapter 4 examines how far we can trust what our senses tell us about a product. Chapter 5 examines how our individual personality influences what we buy. Chapter 6 examines how we learn what to buy, and finally Chapter 7 deals with the key question of why we buy the things we buy.

CHAPTER 4

Perception

■ Introduction

Can we trust what our senses tell us about a product?

You know that old joke about the optimist and the pessimist sitting side-by-side in a bar and contemplating their drinks?

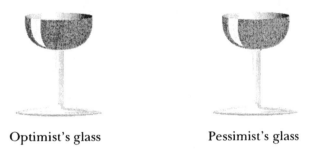

Optimist's glass   Pessimist's glass

Objectively there is exactly the same amount in each glass – about half. But whereas the optimist's glass is half *full*, the pessimist's is half *empty*.

This simple illustration neatly captures the central truth about the way we see the world as consumers; there is no such thing as objective reality. We each perceive the world differently, and we have to construct our own reality out of it. The way we do so and the equipment we use to do it with are the subjects of this chapter.

It seems glaringly obvious to say that the first point of contact we have with our physical environment is through our senses, but it needs saying nonetheless because we need to understand the *information processing* our brain does with the sensory messages it receives before we can appreciate the psychological interaction we have with our environment, and the vast amount of consumer information it bombards us with. First we will examine how we use the senses that equip us to find our way around the world.

■ Using our Senses

Information about the environment is conveyed to the brain from the eyes, ears and other sense organs. Traditionally people have referred to the five senses of

41

vision, hearing, touch, taste and smell. We now know that this is an oversimplified description of the human senses. The sense of touch, for instance, is really four different senses – pressure, pain, cold and warmth. There are four senses of taste – salt, sweet, sour and bitter. Even the sense of vision has to be divided into two – colour vision and black-and-white vision. In addition to these familiar senses, psychologists now add two less familiar ones – bodily movement and balance.

Our senses are more wide-ranging, complex, delicate and sensitive than we normally realise and in everyday life we use only a fraction of their power. Thus on a clear dark night we are capable of seeing a candle flame over 30 miles away, and in a quiet room the tick of a watch can be heard at a distance of 20 feet. But each of our senses, however acute, can nonetheless be bettered by some member of the animal kingdom. A hawk, for example, has sharper vision than ours, a dog can hear sounds inaudible to us and many animals have a much better sense of smell. So a vast amount of sensory information about the world is not picked up by our sense organs and is therefore unavailable for processing by the brain. But it is the *range* and *coordination* of the human senses together with their sensitivity that provides us with a unique quantity and quality of information about the environment.

■   **Vision**

We rely most on our sense of vision to navigate our way through our daily life, so much so in fact that we tend to take our eyes for granted until they fail us. This they begin to do with age, for instance by our mid forties virtually all of us need at least reading glasses. Packaging designers are aware of this process, but they are also aware of the fact that we don't always use our glasses, and they incorporate this knowledge into their work by making packages as easy as possible to recognise, identify and read (except for the list of ingredients of course).[1]

■   **Hearing**

Next to seeing, hearing provides us with the information about our environment that we rely on most. Our experience and our ability to make sense of the world is largely shaped by these two senses. In both seeing and hearing, our sense organs react to waves of energy from the environment: our eyes to light waves and our ears to sound waves. Just as light waves activate the optic nerve at the back of the eye, sound waves are focused by the outer ear on the eardrum, where they stimulate nerve endings that send messages to the auditory nerve and from there to the brain.

In terms of hearing and consumer behaviour, for the past thirty years psychologists have been interested in the effects that in-store background music may have. The first factor to be studied was the sheer volume of sound. It was found that people spent less time shopping when the music was loud than did their luckier counterparts who shopped to quiet music, but they spent just as much money![2]

A later study examined the effect on consumer behaviour of quiet music played at different tempos. It found that when slow music (60 beats per minute) was played customers walked more slowly and sales by value increased by 38 per cent compared with the playing of fast music (108 beats per minute).[3] Perhaps the converse of this is also true: if the business relies on a steady throughput of customers should it play loud, fast music? Is this why junk food outlets tend to have megadecibel rock music? Perhaps not though, because most junk food consumers tend to be young, and therefore are more likely to be rock fans. Indeed a more recent study has found that consumers will spend more if the background music is their kind of sound.[4]

■ The Hidden Power of Smell

The senses of smell and taste, which we normally think of as being quite different, are actually very closely tied to each other. In fact if we didn't have a sense of smell the food we eat would have very little taste. You've probably experienced this yourself when you had a head cold and your nose was blocked. If not, try holding your nose while you taste a piece of raw potato and a piece of raw apple. You probably won't be able to tell the difference.

The receptors for the sense of smell are high up in the nasal cavity – too high, in fact, to be in the direct line of the airflow through the nose and down into the lungs. Unless the odour is very strong, therefore, we have to sniff in order to force the air up the nose to the receptors, which are then activated and pass their message along to the brain. This is what wine tasters and connoisseurs are doing when they put their nose into glasses of wine and inhale deeply. And they often describe flavour using images of smell ('I'm getting a ripe sensation of old socks and camel dung with this one ...').

The receptors for the taste sensations are found mainly in the taste buds on the tongue. The tip of the tongue is most sensitive to sweet and salt, the sides of the tongue are most sensitive to sour, and the back of the tongue is most sensitive to bitter. Food producers are well aware of the fact that what we refer to as taste depends heavily on our sense of smell, but with prepared foods there's not a lot they can do about it. Perhaps this may help to account for their efforts to stimulate the basic sweet and salty sensations by using vast amounts of sugar and salt in the manufacture of these products. More subtle food products in restaurants owe a great deal to the scent of fresh herbs and spices, such as cumin in Indian restaurants and garlic in Italian ones.

Perhaps because we rely so heavily on vision and hearing for sensory information we tend to overlook the importance of smell, but it is of course the basis of a vast global industry, both in the production of perfumes to be used on the skin and in adding scents to household products such as washing up liquid and lavatory cleaner.

Like everything else in our society, perfumes tend to be gender-based – women's products being heavily floral and men's products tending more towards wood, tobacco, leather and other traditionally masculine associations. Indeed

Donna Karan has recently produced one that exudes suede and motor oil. Women seem to be somewhat more susceptible to scents than men, buying perfume mainly for themselves and buying most of their menfolk's perfumes too.

One piece of research in this field, done many years ago, throws some interesting light on this susceptibility. Some 250 women in a small American town were each asked to judge the quality of four pairs of stockings and to select the best pair. Half the women chose one particular pair, but it had nothing to do with quality because the stockings were identical.

What was different about them was that three different scents had been added to three of the pairs, though only six of the subjects noticed anything (hence the effect on the others may have been subliminal – an issue we will take up later in the chapter). The most popular pair had been treated with a floral scent, while the unscented pair attracted only 8 per cent of the subjects. Yet the women justified their choice in terms of quality values such as fineness of knit and texture.[5]

■ Multi-Sensual Marketing

We are used to associating particular consumer environments with specific senses, for instance a supermarket with vision or a perfume counter with smell, but clever marketing makes use of as wide a range of sensory stimuli as possible. Thus a successful upmarket bookstore may have acres of well-laid-out shelves, piped classical music, soft carpeting and a coffee shop that emits an appetizing aroma. Indeed a recent advertisement for Toyota's Lexus luxury car plays on this theme by talking about the smell of the leather upholstery, the car's sleek looks, 'the feel of gentle lumbar support', and so on through all the senses.

■ Common Properties of the Senses

■ Thresholds of Awareness

Before we can become aware of any stimulation from the environment, a stimulus has to be strong enough for our sensory receptors to pick it up. Below a certain level of intensity we simply won't experience the stimulus. A point of light in a dark room, for example, has to be bright enough to cross our threshold of vision before we can see it. This threshold is known as the *absolute threshold* because it marks the difference between sensing and not sensing. Different people have different absolute thresholds, however, and a person's ability to sense a certain stimulus may also vary according to her or his psychological and physiological condition at the time; for example drunk, sober, excited or depressed.

An understanding of how the absolute threshold operates has long been used in the design of products and packaging. Manufacturers want their new products, or redesigned existing products, to be immediately distinguishable in the consumer's environment, especially, of course, distinguishable from competing products. A lot of research may therefore be done to determine where the consumer's absolute threshold might be in this environment in terms of shape, size, colour and so on.

There is another sensory threshold and this operates when we try to discriminate between two stimuli. Suppose that two slices of your favourite cake are left on the shelf and you're trying to decide which is bigger. In order for you to decide, the difference between them has to be sufficiently large for you to notice. The minimum amount of difference that you can detect is called the 'Just Noticeable Difference', or JND. Once you have detected a JND between one stimulus and another, you have crossed the *difference threshold* between them.

Difference thresholds are also quite variable, depending on the two stimuli in question, and not only in sensory experience. We can see this in our everyday life. A one dollar increase in the price of a night at the Waldorf-Astoria would probably not be a JND; the same increase in the price of a hamburger probably would be. The manipulation of the consumer's difference threshold is also a commonly used technique of marketing. For example:

- A new product that claims to *last longer* than its competitors, for example a battery or a washing powder, should ideally last just long enough for the consumer to notice the difference, otherwise the extended product life will eat into profits.
- Those favourite chocolate bars that you remember so fondly from your child,- hood now seem much smaller. You may have attributed this to your increased size and age. In fact it's probably the case that the bar really *is* much smaller, although if you had remained a steady customer over the years you would not have noticed the change. In order to keep the price of a product fairly stable manufacturers will often decrease its size, in increments carefully calibrated to be less than the consumer's JND.[6] Of course prices do increase over time, but here again each price rise will be less than a JND if at all possible. The other relevant variable, *quality*, is also subject to the same manipulation, though the JND here may be more sensitive than either price or quantity, except at the cheapest end of the market, where the lowest grade teabags or instant coffee may be degraded even further when the price of their raw materials rises.
- Knowing where to pitch a sales *discount* for maximum effect is another marketing use of the JND that cuts across all retail sectors. An oft-quoted figure in the trade for an effective JND is 15–20 per cent of the existing price.

In the first and last of these examples it is important that the consumer notices the differences being made to the products. In the middle example it is crucial that the consumer does *not* notice.

■ Sensory Adaptation

As you read this book you are probably not aware of any pressure on your skin.

Yet if you wear a watch or clothes with elastic in them, when you take these things off you may find that your skin has been marked by their pressure. If you have ever visited a fish market you may have wondered how the people working there could stand the smell. Had you asked them, they might have replied 'What smell?' and assured you that people get used to it in time.

In both these cases the sense organs involved have done the same thing – they have adapted. Just as people in fish markets get used to the smell, you can get used to the feel of what you wear, and stop feeling the pressure on your skin. The sensory adaptation involved helps us live through everyday situations without the mind-boggling necessity of stopping to examine the meaning of every stimulus from the environment picked up by our sense organs. In fact if the stimulus is constant and familiar the sense organs become insensitive to it and stop sending information about it to the brain. If the stimulus changes, the sense organs swing back into action. You are probably most familiar with the visual form of adaptation – between conditions of light and dark.

There is a limit to sensory adaptation of course – if your watch strap is so tight that it causes you discomfort, you won't adapt to it, you'll change your environment by loosening the strap. If your usual brand of toothpaste now contains an added ingredient that makes you nauseous you'll change your toothpaste. But below the level of pain or nausea, our senses can adapt very efficiently to a wide range of environments.

We also 'adapt' to advertising, both generally and specifically. That is why advertisers go to such lengths to be noticed amongst all the other ads. And that is also why advertising campaigns are changed so frequently, so that we continue to notice them.

■ Perception: Processing Sensory Information

The sense organs provide our brain with a steady flow of information about our environment and the brain's task is then to take this raw material and use it to help us make sense of that environment through the process of *perception*. And the brain does its job so smoothly and well that we're not even aware of what it does.

Occasionally we come across incidents in our daily lives where the 'sense' we have made of our environment is seen to be illusory. Walking home late at night we turn a corner and jump as we see a mugger lurking in the shadows. A split second later we realize the 'mugger' is actually a bush. Why did we make the mistake and what did we actually see? Well, what we saw was a bush but what we *perceived* was a mugger.

Presumably if we lived in an environment where there were no muggers, and only sabre-toothed tigers lurked in shadows, we might well have seen a sabre-toothed tiger as we turned the corner. The raw material provided by our sensory apparatus is thus a very important component of perception, but it is not the only one. What we see, hear and feel is quite unlearned but if we had to rely only on these sensations to make our way about the world we would be as help-less as an infant. We have to learn how to interpret and order these sensations in such a way that the environment becomes secure and predictable.

Not only does our past experience of dealing with the world enter into our perceptions but so does our current emotional state and our needs, wishes, fears and desires. Some people are more likely than others to mistake bushes for muggers (or sabre-toothed tigers). There are times when and places where we would all make the same mistake.

■ Focusing and Attention

Our consumer environment is, of course, only part of our total psychological environment. Yet it has been calculated that most of us are bombarded with many hundreds of advertisements every day. The total amount of sensory information we receive every day is therefore enormous. Given the vast amount of stimuli picked up by our sense organs, why is our perceptual process not continually swamped? The answer seems to be that, as very few of the stimuli that impinge on us at any given time are of any *immediate* importance, we filter out the ones that are important simply by paying attention to them and ignoring the rest.

We focus on whatever stimuli are most important in the environment at any given time. We ignore a constant hum from an air conditioner, for instance, but immediately focus on the machine if it suddenly stops, providing us with a new and possibly important stimulus. If the steady hum returns, the sound of the air conditioner becomes unimportant once more and it recedes to the edge of our awareness. We refer to this process of focusing our perceptions, bringing them in from the edge, as *attention*, and attention (as we'll see in Chapter 6) is crucial to learning something and committing it to memory.

By attending to certain sensory stimuli and not to others we give them access to our sensory memory, the first stage of the memory process, and from there they can then move to the short-term and then the long-term memory. Underlying this series of psychological processes are corresponding physiological processes. Thus when one channel of communication between a sense organ and the brain is occupied and has our full attention, the other physiological pathways to the brain are apparently blocked so that we don't become confused and overwhelmed by the other sensory messages.

We follow the same process of focusing when we go shopping. As long as we know what we want to buy, as in the weekly trip to the supermarket, we use this process very efficiently, though it helps to make a list – and not leave it on the kitchen table. But we've all had experience of this process breaking down, when we decide to go and browse through the winter sales for example. If we're not focused on a particular purchase we very quickly become aware of the constant hammering intensity of stimuli we are not normally subjected to or influenced by, and perhaps may even become quite disoriented by the experience.

■   **Selective Perception and Distortion**

We have seen that in order to make sense of our sensations our perceptions have to be selective. But how do we go about making the selection? In order to perceive something we have to give it our attention. But we know from experience that our attention is continually shifting. What determines which stimuli will capture our attention?

Psychologists refer to external and internal factors in trying to understand attention-getting and selective perception.

☐   *External Factors*

In our example of the air conditioner we noted that the sound of the machine stays at the edge of our awareness until it stops, whereupon it captures our attention. It is the stimulus provided by change in the environment that is most important. The change can take many forms. *Contrast* (between sound and silence, for example) is one of them. A man seven feet tall stands out much more on the street than he would on a basketball court. A white television news-caster wearing a see-through dashiki would attract more attention than one in a dark pin-striped suit. A large amount of white space rather than text in a print advertisement would have a similar effect.

Movement in the environment is another important kind of change. People are quite automatically very responsive to visual movement. Even very young babies will try to follow movements with their eyes, and adults will have their attention caught by moving neon signs rather than by stationary ones.

Sheer *repetition* of a stimulus is also an effective way of getting our attention, a particularly important phenomenon in advertising. In what psychologists call the 'mere exposure' effect it has been found that not only does repetition gain our attention, it actually encourages us to have a slightly more positive attitude towards the stimulus in question.[7] It follows from this that the more familiar we are with a product's brand name then, other things being equal, the more highly will we regard it. And more to the point, there is a good chance we'll actually buy it. Though it's not an immutable law, it does appear that the most extensively advertised products are often the ones that sell best if the choice to be made is not of earthshaking importance. People faced with shelves full of different washing-up liquids may well just grab the first brand they recognise as they all do the same job anyway.

This seems to hold true in other sectors of the economy as well, as the following American example suggests:

> Several years ago, the Northwest Mutual Life Insurance Company conducted a nationwide poll to find out how well the public recognised its name. It came out thirty-fourth among insurance companies. Two weeks later the company repeated the poll. This time it came out third in name familiarity. What caused this amazing leap from obscurity to fame? Two weeks and $1 million worth of advertising on television.[8]

Size can also be an important external factor. This is why newspapers and magazines grade the importance of their headlines by the size of the type they use: the more important the message, the bigger the type.

Finally the *intensity* of a stimulus is also used to catch our attention. Bright colours and loud sounds are routinely used at public events for instance – whether commercial, cultural or political – to gather crowds and focus attention. And many television commercials begin with a flood of colour or a loud sound – which is why others start off in quiet monochrome.

☐ *Internal factors*

The external factors outlined above refer to stimuli from the environment. However the person perceiving these stimuli does not do so as a neutral observer; different people react to the same sensations in different ways. A woman may put on a sweater because the room is too cold, while her husband throws open the windows. She may sleep through the ringing alarm that wakes him up for work but is instantly awake at the baby's first whimper. When they read the same magazine she will pick out the features on women's clothing and he the men's.

This man and woman, bring different interests and motives to each situation they share. Their emotional and physical states change, and if they don't happen to feel the same way at the same time they may well have different reactions. But the most important internal factor in perception is what people *expect* to see or hear in each situation. The woman has a perceptual set to hear her baby cry. She expects it to happen. The man has a *perceptual set* to hear the alarm go off at the same time each morning – so much so that he wakes up a few seconds before it goes off.

■ **Perceptual Distortion**

Sometimes this set may be so habitual or so important to a person that he or she may perceive things that aren't there – like the bush we mistook for a mugger earlier in this chapter. Psychologists have discovered some striking examples of such *perceptual distortion*.

In one study a group of white people who were known to be highly prejudiced against blacks were shown a picture and afterwards were asked to describe it from memory. The picture depicted a subway carriage with several people in it. The central characters in the scene were a black man and a white man. One of these men was well-dressed and standing quietly in the middle of the carriage. The other was poorly dressed, rough-looking and standing in front of the first man threatening him with an open razor. The first man was black, his attacker was white. But the prejudiced white subjects in this study did not have a set to see what the picture showed and so they reported a rough-looking black man threatening a well-dressed white. They had distorted their perception to fit what they *expected* to see.[9]

This may seem like a dramatic and unusual example, but it illustrates something that psychologists have long known about – that we are quite capable of perceiving anything we have a *need* to perceive, from little green aliens to the infallible workings of our favourite patent medicine. At its most basic our

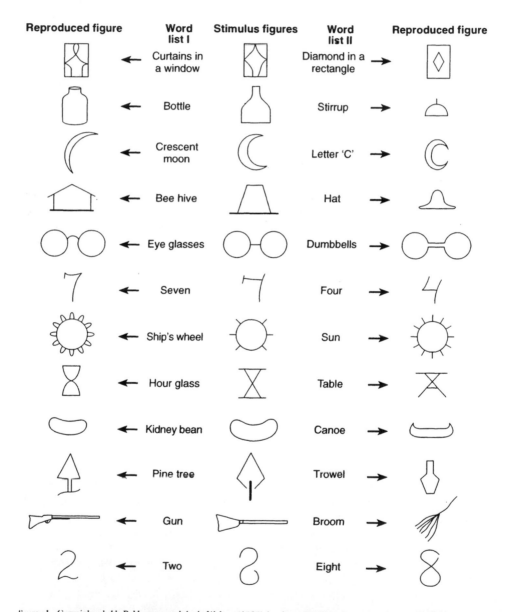

Source: L. Carmichael, H. P. Hogan and A. A. Walter (1932) in *Journal of Experimental Psychology*, 15, 73-86.

Figure 4.1   Distortions of schemas

perception of an object can be altered by a simple suggestion that may have important consequences, as Figure 4.1 demonstrates.

The subjects in this experiment were all shown the drawings of stimulus objects in the centre column. Then half of them were given the description of the object in Word List I and half in Word List II. When the subjects were later asked to reproduce the drawings from memory they were clearly influenced by the different descriptions they had been given. Their eyes had all received the same sensory stimulation but their perceptual set had been biased towards the description offered.

A classic study in marketing looked at the suggestive effects of branding on (male) consumers' perceived liking for beer. In the first part of the study each subject was given a six-pack of unlabelled beer to drink. Each of these packs contained three different brands, one of which was the subject's particular favourite. A week later, in the second part of the study, they were given another six-pack of the same three beers but this time bearing their usual brand labels.

The subjects were asked to rate the beers after each test, and the differences between the two tests were striking. In the 'blind' test the consumers were barely able to differentiate between the three brands. In the 'labelled' test not only did they rate all the beers more highly, but they rated their own favourite highest of the three.[10] Simply labelling the beers had restored the consumers' perceptual set, as without this set they had been unable to identify their favourite beer. Of course the deliberate upsetting of a perceptual expectation has long been a favourite technique of advertisers to gain attention. Memorable examples in the print media include a tough-looking biker lovingly cradling a tiny baby (financial services) and a 'pregnant' man (health education).

■ Organising Perceptual Cues

■ Illusions

Internal factors can thus lead us to perceive things differently from the way they really are. But so can some external factors. The important difference is that while each person brings a unique group of internal factors to a perceptual situation, the external factors are the same for everyone. There are some perceptual situations, for example, where we will all react the same way, perceive the same thing, and be completely wrong.

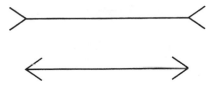

Figure 4.2 Length of line illusion

For example in Figure 4.2 the top line is seemingly longer than the bottom line. But if you measure them you'll find they are exactly the same length.

Perceptual illusions such as this are very exceptional however, and in our daily lives our perceptions are normally accurate and perfectly reliable. But the existence of such illusions has been helpful to psychologists interested in the normal process of perception. Out of a vast number of careful studies has emerged an understanding that the way in which we perceive is highly organized and well ordered. We do not live in a world of changing sound and light waves but in a world of objects, people, music and events. With our perceptions we make sense of our sensations according to some well-established principles that are partly learned and partly due to the structure of the brain and the nervous system. These principles allow us to navigate our way through the world, even though they are not perfect.

☐   *Figure and Ground*

Perhaps the most basic of these perceptual principles is the way we perceive things against a background; the way we need a background before we can pick out an object in the environment. If we cannot separate figure and ground we are unable to see the object; it is hidden or camouflaged. Many animals make use of this principle to evade their predators, for example the chameleon changes colour to blend in with its background.

You too are making use of this principle in reading this book. You are perceiving black print against a white background. When you close the book and put it on the desk it doesn't disappear. You can see it clearly outlined against the background of the desk. We can separate figure and ground in this fashion because of our ability to perceive contour. Contours mark off one thing from another, an object from its background and even a musical theme from its surrounding chords. Figure and ground illusion are both necessary for our perceptions, and as Figure 4.3 shows, they can be interchangeable at times.

Figure 4.3   Length of line illusion

When you perceive the white figure, the human profiles, the black part is the ground. When you perceive the black vase, the white part becomes the ground. Note that you can't see both figures at the same time and that no matter how hard you try to focus on one of these figures your attention will shift after a time to focus on the other.

The figure–ground principle has several applications to advertising. I once did some advertising market research for the drink Campari and found that people generally enjoyed the ads for the product and recalled them clearly. The only problem was they couldn't remember whether they were for Martini or Cinzano. In this case the brand name formed the (forgetable) background and the characters in the ad the (memorable) figure.

Similarly the music for an ad is sometimes remembered but not the accompanying message (or even brand name). And some ads are so clever that figure and ground merge, so that people simply can't tell what is being advertised, or even by whom.

☐ *Grouping*

Another simple but important way in which we structure our perceptions is by grouping things into patterns. In Figure 4.4 we see six single lines on top but three pairs of lines on the bottom.

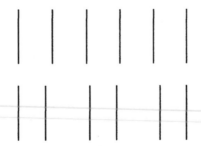

Figure 4.4 Grouping

The wearing of uniforms is a common form of grouping the similar and identifying the dissimilar as applied to people. This is perhaps most obvious in the case of the police or airline staff, where we see and react to the uniform rather than the person inside it. But it is also true of the dark conservative suits that group together on Wall Street or in the City of London.

☐ *Closure*

Despite the fact that they are incomplete the three drawings in Figure 4.5 are recognisable as a triangle, a square and a circle. If certain things are familiar to

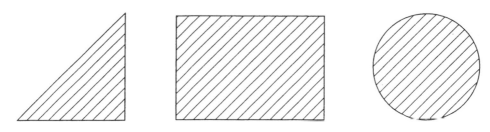

Figure 4.5   Closure

us our perceptual process will close the gaps in the picture, thereby providing the necessary contour lines for us to perceive it as a distinct object. We do much the same thing with our language when we read a telegram or a newspaper headline.

Because of this need to complete an incomplete picture, things that we cannot complete tend to bother us, and therefore stick in the memory.   In psychology this effect is known as the *Zeigarnik effect*, after the woman who discovered that people working on a variety of tasks best remembered the ones where they had been interrupted and prevented from completing.   Advertisers sometimes make use of this effect by stopping a jingle or catchphrase in the middle, as in ' Sshh ... you know who' or 'You can take Salem out of the country but ...'

■ *Gestalt* Psychology

The principles of perception we have been discussing come mainly from the work of a school of German psychologists who took the view that what we perceive is more than just the sum of the sensory stimuli that impinge on us from the environment.   We perceive something, they argued, as a *gestalt*, a German word meaning 'form' or 'configuration'.   Each gestalt has a lot more meaning to the perceiver than just its sensory properties of size, colour or weight.   A book, a painting or even a chocolate bar may have a meaning for us (and be able to affect our behaviour) that is far beyond a cataloguing of its physical properties, no matter how detailed.

Therefore, in perceiving, not only is the whole greater than the sum of its parts, but the parts themselves are not important or even perceived.   We search constantly for patterns, for order, for wholes that make sense of the parts.

■ Perceptual Constancy: Colour, Size and Shape

There are several other factors we might consider here in discussing the way our perceptions are organized.   One of these is the fact that while the sensations we receive from the environment are ever-changing, our perceptions of things remain constant.   You know for instance that as the eye operates like a camera, images of the objects you look at will appear on your retina as they would on a photograph.   So if you set your coffee cup down in front of you and take a picture of it, the picture will show what you see – an elliptical object. But you know your coffee cup is not an ellipse. It's round. How do you know that?

When you're surrounded by people on the street it's quite easy to judge how tall each person is to within a few inches. If you were on a country road and you saw a man coming towards you from a great distance the image of him on your retina would make him about as tall as an insect. How would you know he's not?

Apparently what we see is not always what we perceive, not just in visual illusions but in our everyday perception. We have to learn the meaning of what we see. Among the things we learn are that black snow at night is really white, that an opening door does not disappear into a vertical line and that buildings seen from the air are really bigger than matchboxes.

■ Depth and Distance

Just as perceptual constancy is so completely a part of our lives that we take it for granted until it is pointed out to us, the fact that we see a three-dimensional world seems totally unremarkable until we realize that the retina, like the lens of a camera, is a two-dimensional surface. How do we use the two-dimensional information of right–left and up–down that our eyes see to perceive a world of objects, of depth and distance?

, It appears that in judging the distance of objects we are very sensitive to various cues from the surrounding environment in a fashion similar to the figure–ground phenomenon noted above. These cues include the play of light and shadow, perspective and the positioning of other things in the environment. The fact that we have two eyes that give us slightly different images of what we're looking at also plays a part in judging distance.

■ Movement: Movies and the Phi Phenomenon

The final area of perception we should examine in trying to make sense of what we see is that of movement. Some of the movements we perceive, such as a bird flying past the window, can be explained simply as visual stimuli moving across our visual field and stimulating different parts of the eye. However much of the movements we perceive are quite illusory and cannot be explained in this fashion.

The most common illusion of movement is perceived when watching a film. A film consists of a series of still photographs, each one slightly different from the preceding one, flashed onto a screen at the rate of about twenty frames per second. At this speed we don't perceive a series of stills, we perceive movement on the screen.

This illusion was studied extensively by the Gestalt psychologists at the beginning of this century when movies were first introduced. They were able to isolate the simplest form of the illusion and examine the conditions under which it appeared.

They discovered that if they flashed two lights on and off in quick succession, given the right time interval between the flashes, people perceived the light as moving between two points. They called this illusion of movement the *Phi phenomenon* and in addition to being active in our perception of films, it underlies the effectiveness of the moving neon advertising displays that attract our attention in big cities or when driving down a highway at night.

■ Subliminal Perception

In the late 1950s the owner of a private research company in the United States, James Vicary, claimed to have found a way to encourage consumer spending without those involved being aware of it. Vicary reported that he had flashed brief ads for popcorn and Coca Cola onto a movie screen at a speed so fast that viewers had been unaware of seeing them, that is, the stimulus had been below the absolute threshold (or 'limen') discussed above. Over a period of six weeks these subliminal ads, in the form of the slogans 'drink coke' and 'eat popcorn', had apparently increased the sales of popcorn by about 18 per cent and Coca Cola by about 58 per cent.

As you can imagine there was tremendous and universal interest in Vicary's findings. The United States Congress even went so far as to hold hearings on the subject and discussed the possibility of banning all subliminal advertising as it could be seen as a form of 'brainwashing'. Academic researchers immediately tried to replicate Vicary's findings under controlled scientific conditions but were unable to do so.

Vicary himself was challenged to replicate his own test, but when he did the previous dramatic findings were not repeated. Hardly surprising really as Vicary was a fraud who later confessed to having fabricated his original findings in order to get some publicity for his own failing company.[11]

So can we safely conclude that there is nothing to subliminal perception? Well, not quite. There is some reliable evidence that we are capable of subliminal perception. In other words we can perceive stimuli that we can't consciously see or hear. Indeed we may even be influenced by these stimuli without being aware of it.[12] You'll recall the finding that sheer amount of exposure to a stimulus can increase our general feeling of liking for it. The same seems to be true at the subliminal level, though in a weaker and less reliable way.

For instance people may show a particular fondness for certain geometrical shapes that they are not aware of having seen. They may even feel more thirsty after subliminal exposure to the word 'coke'. But the message 'drink coke' will *not* make them any more likely to do so.

Other reports have suggested that subliminal messages can have a more specific application. Thus a New Orleans supermarket claimed to have greatly reduced pilfering by secreting in the piped Muzak the subliminal phrases 'I am honest. I won't steal. Stealing is dishonest'. In the absence of controlled replication of these claims they must, of course, remain suspect. But nevertheless the possibilities of subliminal advertising continue to fascinate a lot of people in marketing, advertising and psychology.

At this time I think we can safely conclude that while there may well be some influence on us through subliminal perception, the effects are probably not very great or very specific. Indeed all the evidence from well over a century's research in perception (and in advertising) seems to suggest strongly that the more aware we are of the stimulus in question the greater its effect is likely to be.[13]

■ Product Images, Self-Images and Consumer Behaviour

In later chapters we will examine in some detail the concept of 'self-image', its origin and content. For the purposes of this section it is sufficient to note that we each have an image of ourself and this image includes a view of ourself as a consumer. Are we part of 'the Pepsi generation' or 'the Geritol set'? Would we feel comfortable shopping at Harrods in London or Bloomingdales in New York, or is Woolworths more to our taste?

The view we have of ourself includes an image of the products and services we consider *appropriate* to buy. Middle-class, and particularly college-educated, people may find it difficult to accept that consumers can exclude themselves from a particular market for any reason other than lack of money. But self-imposed psychological restrictions are a real and potent force.

In my family, for instance, nobody in my parents' generation was college-educated, but I was forever being assured that education was a good thing because 'if you're educated you can talk to anybody'. And that included waiters in fancy restaurants and assistants in fancy stores such as Harrods and Bloomingdales. Even when they could afford more my parents' generation was much more comfortable psychologically at the Woolworths end of the market. This personal experience has been borne out more generally by relevant research into consumers' choice of shops and stores. Leading stores and retail chains do seem to have a distinct image or 'personality' for people and they will only shop in places that correspond to their own self-image.[14]

It is therefore important to be clear about the strong element of self-selection by consumers in to and out of different markets. And of course many retailers, manufacturers and service providers do have a clear idea of where their primary market is located in the consumers' psychological map, and position themselves accordingly. Attempts to reposition a product, brand or company, particularly up or down-market, must therefore pay careful attention to the existing map before setting off in a new direction.

The way a product is *perceived* by consumers is a much more important influence on their behaviour than any objective characteristic it may have – as witnessed by the beer study we looked at above, when people could not distinguish the taste of their favourite beer until the presence of the brand label made it look (was perceivable as) familiar. Companies try to influence consumer perceptions by, for instance, encouraging associations between themselves and a desirable and appropriate image (a process we will explore in Chapter 6). The

Travelers Insurance Company in the United States, and The Abbey National and Legal and General in the United Kingdom all use the image of an umbrella.

Of course our self-image is not a fixed and unalterable thing, it changes as we change and as we move through the life cycle. Young people and old people represent consumer markets that overlap in some areas but are vastly different in others. People's needs may change quite quickly as they go from being single, to being part of a couple, to becoming parents. As their self-image changes they continue the process of selecting themselves in to or out of a new series of markets.

We are also aware of the image that other people may have of us, and this is often based on what we do for a living. Thus the Chrysler Corporation has created, and frequently updated, a brand-image 'map' of the way people perceive different cars. It has been found that certain associations are made between different occupations and the cars that are considered appropriate for people in those occupations.[15] For example:

- Young executive: BMW
- Senior executive: Mercedes/Cadillac
- Nurse: Toyota
- College professor: Volvo
- Teacher: VW Rabbit
- Doctor: Mercedes

I came up with similar findings in a piece of market research I did for the Ford Motor Company in the United Kingdom in the early 1980s.

■ Perceiving Risk

As consumers we make a steady stream of buying decisions about goods and services, and the outcome of many of these decisions may be quite uncertain. If (and only if) we are consciously aware of this uncertainty are we *perceiving a risk*, to some degree at least, about the consequences of our decisions. Six forms of risk have been identified:

- *Performance*: will it do what it's supposed to? For example, will new Reek after-shave really make me irresistible to women?
- *Financial*: will it be worth the money? For example, will this expensive course on marketing really increase my future income?
- *Physical*: will it be safe? For example, will this powerful new food processor include my fingers in the process?
- *Time*: will it be time-consuming to return? For example, will I really have to start shopping all over again if she doesn't like the colour of this suit?
- *Social*: and even if she likes the suit, will the office? For example, will my reputation for quiet but powerful elegance suffer yet another blow?

- *Psychological*: is it me? For example, will this nose stud really say what I want it to say about me?

There are also several types of situation that will influence our feeling of uncertainty about the outcome of a purchase and hence our perception of the risk involved.[16] For example:

- Uncertainty about *purchase goals* (is the car primarily for commuting or occasional trips?)
- Uncertainty about best *alternative choice* (blue or red hair rinse to achieve a more youthful look).
- Uncertainty about the satisfactory consequences of *making/not making* a given purchase.

We do not all perceive risk in the same way, of course. As we saw in the case of sensory stimulation, everyone has a different threshold. So where some consumers will perceive some risk in a buying decision, others won't; some people will perceive high risk, others low risk.

It has also been found that some people are more likely to *accept* risk than others.[17] Indeed a personality type, Type T (for 'thrillseeker') has been identified in the United States: this type actively looks for risk when making consumer decisions.[18] Type T's have been estimated at 25 per cent of the American population. Car ads emphasizing speed and exotic adventure are obviously aimed at this group.

Our perception of risk also varies with the kind of product we are considering. Buying a headache cure is usually perceived as more risky than buying spaghetti, for example. And perception of risk also seems to vary with the buying situation. Shopping by mail or telephone or from door-to-door salesmen is usually seen as riskier than buying in a store. However with the recent increase in specialist catalogue shopping this assessment of risk may be changing.

■ Coping with Risk

Uncertainty in any area of our psychological life leads us to feel anxious. So the more uncertain the consequences of a buying decision the more anxiety will we feel, and the more will we try to relieve that anxiety. That is, we will seek to reduce the perceived risks listed above that may be attached to that decision. There are several ways in which we might do this, including information gathering, relying on brand loyalty, the image of a major new brand, the image of the store we shop in, or some official seal of approval.

Research has found that, generally speaking, relying on *brand loyalty* is the most popular strategy for reducing perceived risk. The least popular strategy is buying a product because of its price and trusting that the most expensive model will have the lowest amount of risk attached to it.[19] There are obvious implications here for marketing strategy, particularly for new products entering the market place. While companies will try to reduce perceived risk by means related to the product, for example offering specific guarantees, it is interesting to note that it is the psychological relationship between buyer and product (which is implicit in brand loyalty) that seems to be most important to the consumer.

■ Further Reading

Key, W. B., *Subliminal Seduction* (New York: New American Library, 1973). A book for the general reader, which suggests that subliminal erotic cues are hidden in alcohol advertisements and are aimed at unconscious sexual impulses.

Schiffman, H. R., *Sensation and Perception: An Integrated Approach* (New York: Wiley, 1976). A sound and accessible account of the Gestalt school and the principles of perception.

Zeithaml, V. A., A. Parasuraman and L. L. Berry, *Delivering Quality Service: Balancing Customer Perceptions and Expectations* (New York: The Free Press, 1990). An account by leading researchers in the field of the way in which customers perceive quality of service.

It is also worth browsing through the latest issues of the following periodicals: *Psychology and Marketing*, vol. 5 (Winter 1988). *Advances in Consumer Research, Journal of Consumer Research, Journal of Marketing, Advertising Age.*

■ Questions for Discussion

1. What are the human senses we rely on most? Why? Give examples of marketing appeals aimed at one of the senses. Give a current example of a marketing campaign that is aimed at as many of the senses as possible.
2. What is the 'difference threshold?' How do marketers make use of JNDs?
3. How does the process of sensory adaptation affect our response to advertising? How can marketers use this to draw our attention to their products?
4. What is the importance of 'figure and ground' to perception? How do marketers make use of the process in print and television advertisements?
5. What perceptual effect does subliminal advertising attempt to manipulate? Does it work? Should it be allowed?
6. What kinds of risk do consumers perceive in buying situations? How do they deal with them? Is there anything the marketer can do to minimize the perception of risk for a given product?

CHAPTER 5

Personality

■ Introduction

How does our personality affect what we buy?

Personality factors are so pervasive in the study of consumer behaviour that we have encountered them several times already in this book:

- In Chapter 2 (Market segmentation) we met a colourful cast of characters: Mildred the militant mother and Candice the chic suburbanite, along with the survivor, the sustainer, the struggler, the penny pincher and lots more of their alliterative chums. This psychological segmentation of the market was an attempt to achieve some depth of understanding about what made people buy the things they did. Marketers use this approach widely to draw up consumer profiles, or *psychographics*, of the typical lifestyles favoured by their target consumers.
- In Chapter 3 (New products and innovations) we discussed how the essential characteristics of people identified as product champions, opinion leaders and innovators are of particular concern to both researchers and marketers.
- In Chapter 4 (Perception) we noted how we each perceive the world differently and that we construct our own individual reality out of the raw sensations of our brain processes. We also noted that people have different ways of reacting to the perception of risk when making consumer decisions, with some people, labelled Type T (for 'thrillseeker') actively seeking out such risk.

What we shall do in this chapter is take a more systematic look at the concept of personality in general and its relevance to understanding the consumer in particular. In doing so we will consider how psychologists use the term, and take a very brief look at the most important formal theories of personality. This should help us to put the practical applications we are so familiar with into their proper intellectual context, and thus increase our understanding of what we can and cannot do with them.

■ What is Meant by Personality?

The term 'personality' is commonly used in both psychology and everyday speech, and like most terms with dual usage it does not mean quite the same thing in each context. Psychologists interested in this subject want to know what makes someone a unique person. What are the characteristic ways in which she behaves? What is the overall pattern of how she relates to other people and how they react to her?

In everyday speech we talk about someone as being 'tough and aggressive' or having 'an attractive personality', showing that we are trying to discern characteristic patterns in their behaviour. These patterns are categories of behaviour, as defined by our society, that we have learned to recognise from our previous experience with people. Where the difference lies is that unlike the psychologist, other people do not normally try to assess the *uniqueness* of an individual at the same time as they place him or her in categories that emphasize his or her 'sameness'.

It is interesting to note that one of the attributes of a great novelist or play-wright is the ability to create characters of some psychological complexity and subtlety. But we don't always have the time in our daily lives to be as reflective as novelists or playwrights. In fact our way of life usually encourages us *not* to be considered and reflective when relating to others.

We know little or nothing about many of the people we come across in the day-to-day business of life, and very often we have nothing to go on but appearance – someone's colour, sex, size, clothing, gestures and so on. When you get on a bus, for instance, how unique does the driver seem to you as opposed to his sameness to all the other bus drivers you've seen? If you stopped to appreciate the uniqueness of this individual the people standing behind you in the rain might not appreciate *your* uniqueness. But a balance between the two can also be observed: I once heard that a bus driver resigned after his wife got on his bus one day and walked right past without recognising him.

Both the psychologist and the layman use the term 'personality' to make sense of an individual's behaviour; after all behaviour is all we have to go on. We can never know for sure why people have acted in a certain way; all we can do is observe their behaviour and infer what inner processes motivated them to do it. And this is just as true of psychologists as it is of anyone else. It is important to realise therefore that both psychologists and lay people carry out this procedure by referring to a set of ideas – a theory if you like – about what personality is, how it came into being and how it operates. The difference is that psychologists make their theory of personality explicit while that of lay people usually remains implicit and not consciously thought about.

■ Formal Theories of Personality

There are many formal theories of personality. There always have been. They go back to Aristotle, Plato and beyond. The history of psychology is dominated by attempts to understand and explain the human personality. From the time of the earliest thinkers to the present day it is this aspect of psychology that has excited the greatest interest. Indeed it is a subject of intrinsic fascination to most people.

For our purposes we need only consider the four theories that have excited most interest among consumer researchers and marketers: Freudian psychoanalysis, neo-Freudian psychoanalysis, self theory and trait theory.[1] But before we look at these theories we need a definition.

My favourite dictionary of psychology defines the term personality thus:

> The sum total of all the factors that make an individual human being both individual and human; the thinking, feeling and behaving that all human beings have in common, and the particular characteristic pattern of these elements that makes every human being unique. Theorists in this field often stress the integrated and dynamic nature of an individual's personality and the important role of unconscious processes that may be hidden from the individual but are at least partly perceptible to other people.[2]

The key words in this definition are 'characteristic pattern' and 'unconscious processes'. Whenever I use the term 'personality' in this book, that is the definition of it I have in mind.

All formal theories of personality attempt to do something extremely difficult: they attempt to explain why people are the way they are and why they do what they do. They are general theories of human behaviour, in other words, that are centrally concerned with motivation and are integrated around the concept of a complete person. The working of motivation is itself so complex that it is usually abstracted for closer study as a separate process, and we will do that in Chapter 7.

It is important to note that no formal theory of personality comes even close to fulfilling its ambitions. Human lives are much too complex and multivariate (or, if you prefer, rich and interesting) to be subsumed under, or explained with, or predicted by any one existing theory. The best we can hope for, therefore, are useful guidelines or helpful clues leading towards a partial understanding.

■ Freudian Psychoanalysis

The psychoanalytic approach is most intimately related to the work of Sigmund Freud, of course, and we will use Freud's theory to represent this approach. Personality theories have their roots either in the psychological laboratory or, more often, in the consulting room. Freud's theory, like most theories of personality, emerged from his clinical experiences as a psychotherapist.

Freud thought of the human personality as comprising three parts: the id, the ego, and the superego:

- *Id*: the id is composed of powerful drives, raw impulses of sex and aggression that demand to be satisfied immediately. We are not usually aware of the id; it is unconscious.
- *Ego*: we are aware of the ego. It is the rational, conscious, thinking part of

our personality. Our self-image would be contained within Freud's description of the ego. The ego gets its working energy from the id, but when the id impulses are too strong and threaten to take over the ego, it represses them and defends itself from knowing about them.

- *Superego*: the superego, like the id, is usually unconscious so we are unaware of its workings. It is the part of our personality that deals with right and wrong, with morality, with the correct and proper way to behave, feel and think. The superego can be just as powerful as the id in its demand on the ego that we behave the way we should – or take the consequences of feeling guilty.

This way of conceiving of personality has often been depicted as an iceberg, and Freud himself was very fond of using hydraulic metaphors to illustrate his theory (Figure 5.1)

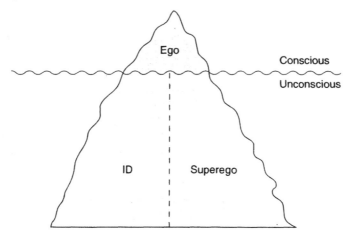

Figure 5.1 The Freudian iceberg

These three aspects of the personality are constantly interacting with each other as we move through life. Frequently they are in conflict. This conflict appears in the ego as the conscious feeling of anxiety, whose source we are unaware of because both the id and the superego, with their conflicting demands, remain unconscious. The id growls 'Do it,' the superego cries 'No, no,' and the poor old ego is caught in between, doing its best to separate them and keep the peace.

To the extent that the ego succeeds, the personality is well adjusted, balanced, content and happy, allowing the individual, as Freud emphasized, to love sexually and to work productively. To the extent that the id and the superego influence someone's personality, he or she suffers conflict, feels anxious and therefore behaves in a disturbed, *neurotic* fashion.

Freud believed that the first few years of a person's life are absolutely crucial in shaping the adult personality. Conflicts that inevitably arise in early child-hood between id, ego and superego are at the root of neurotic behaviour in adulthood. These conflicts are repressed into the unconscious and the job of the psychoanalyst is to help patients become conscious of these problems and to strengthen their egos so that they may bring them squarely within the image they have of themselves and face them unflinchingly.

Repression is not simply a passive business of not wanting to know certain things. On the contrary it is an active process that takes up a huge amount of psychic energy to hold things down in the unconscious. For this reason Freud referred to the 'dynamic' unconscious, and the psychological processes involved in it are often referred to as *psychodynamics.*

The psychoanalytic or psychodynamic view of the human condition – that the most important causes of human behaviour are unconscious, and therefore closed to external observation – was a powerful one that attracted an important following around the world, first in a clinical or psychiatric setting and later in virtually every area of life. We will trace the influence of the unconscious on various other aspects of psychology and consumer behaviour, including motivation, family influences and even learning.

■ Freud's Developmental Stages

Freud's theory of personality is a developmental one. He believed that from birth to psychological maturity the individual would normally pass through a series of developmental stages in a particular order and at a particular time. Successful negotiation of all these stages resulted in a healthy personality; unsuccessful negotiation inevitably led to psychological problems in later life. He related these psychological stages to biological stages of development and called them the *oral, anal* and *phallic* stages. Unresolved conflicts at any stage led to a *fixation* with the particular features of that stage, which found later expression in certain corresponding adult personality characteristics.

□ The Oral Stage

The mouth is the most important source of gratification and physical stimulation for the first couple of years of life. It is the medium through which infants first learn about the world. A lack of sufficient gratification at this stage can produce a hostile sarcastic kind of personality much given to making 'biting' remarks about other people. On the other hand too much gratification can also lead to fixation of a different kind leading to someone being too dependent on others, or being gullible and liable to 'swallow' anything.

□ The Anal Stage

At around the age of two the child realises that some control can be exerted over the muscles of the anus and therefore over the elimination or retention of faeces.

This control produces its own gratification, a source of gratification that meets external authority for the first time in the form of parental toilet training. A child may be fixated at this stage by toilet training that is too strict or too lax. Strictness leads to an anal personality that is obsessively clean, controlled and ordered – and this concept is supported by some contemporary research.[3] Laxity leads to disorder and messiness.

☐   *The Phallic Sage*

At about four years of age the child should be entering the phallic stage of development, where gratification is associated with sensuous pleasure from the genitals, including masturbation and fantasy. This is the stage at which the famous *Oedipus complex* appears. In ancient Greek mythology Oedipus was a king who inadvertently killed his father and later unknowingly married his mother.

Freud used the story as a metaphor for the attraction the child has to the parent of the opposite sex, accompanied by an unconscious wish to remove the parent of the same sex. Anxiety about retribution from the rival parent leads the child to identify with that parent instead, and thus obtain at least vicarious satisfaction. The guilt the child experiences for having these feelings forms the basis of the primitive superego.

Though the Oedipus complex is repressed after the age of five, it remains a crucial part of the personality for life and plays a large part in determining someone's attitudes, not only towards the opposite sex but also towards people in positions of authority. Freud considered his discovery of the Oedipus complex (which came to him while watching a performance of 'Oedipus Rex' in Paris) to be one of his most important contributions to psychology. It is also one of his most contentious of course, though there is some research evidence to support it.[4]

■ Freudian Applications to Consumer Behaviour and Marketing

The essence of Freudian psychology is its emphasis on the unconscious nature of much of the causes of our behaviour. What this means for marketing is that the consumer is often unaware of the needs a product is satisfying beyond the most immediate and obvious ones.

Many people wear jeans, for example, but why do some people just have to have (expensive) stone-washed Levis? If any old jeans satisfy the need to be clothed, then these particular jeans must have some subjective significance for the buyer. And the reason given for buying the jeans (for example 'they're the best', or 'everyone in my group wears them') may not be the deepest or most important reason and may have more to do with acting out the fantasies (aimed at the pleasure principle of the id) suggested by the product advertising.

This approach to understanding consumer behaviour was popularised by Ernest Dichter, a keen Freudian who studied psychoanalysis in Vienna in the 1930s before emigrating to the United States, where he founded the Institute for Motivational Research. It was Dichter who first proposed the famous interpretation that men regarded the owning of a convertible car as the psychic equivalent of having a mistress.[5]

We will look specifically at the effects of sex in advertising in Chapter 14 and we will consider the work of Dichter in more detail in Chapter 7. For the present we should simply note that while a great deal of modern advertising encourages wish fulfillment and fantasising about basic biological drives such as sex – but also aggression and affiliation with others – there is nothing new about this. Copywriters were doing the same thing a hundred years ago, before anyone had even heard of Freud.

In other words, crude and uncertain and difficult to verify though these interpretations might often be, they are clearly tapping into matters of some importance to the consumer. One of the most frequently used techniques that marketers have adopted to try to ride this powerful current is aligning products with consumer lifestyles (with the key element of wish fulfilment) rather than extolling the attributes of the products themselves. You see this with advertising for trainers, jeans, cars, cigars, pension schemes and many, many more products, especially those containing alcohol (beer, wine, spirits, liqueurs, perfume and aftershave).

Advertising and market research companies derive their ideas for product campaigns from panels of consumers, and they have a number of written and visual techniques to help them tap into the kind of unconscious processes we have been considering. All these techniques are variants of standard personality tests based on Freudian theory. We will take a brief look at three of the most important tests: the MMPI, the TAT and the Rorschach.

The aim of a personality test is to get behind the public face that individuals present to the world and obtain a picture of what they are 'really' like; that is, an account of their inner life, of which they themselves may not be fully aware. The personality test therefore acts like a probe into the unconscious.

□   *The MMPI*

The most commonly encountered personality test (often called a paper-and-pencil test) is in the form of a questionnaire that can be administered to a large group of people and has a standardised (often computerised) method of dealing with the responses. There are dozens of these tests, of which the best-known is the Minnesota Multiphasic Personality Inventory (MMPI).[6] The MMPI has 550 statements, to which the subject has to answer 'true', 'false' or 'cannot say'. The statements deal with a vast range of thoughts, feelings and behaviour, as the following examples show:

● My way of doing things is apt to be misunderstood by others.
● I am bothered by acid stomach several times a week.
● I have never indulged in unusual sexual practices.
● I like to read newspaper articles on crime.
● I never worry about my looks.

- Someone has been trying to poison me.
- I often feel as if things are not real.
- If I were an artist I would like to draw flowers.

This may seem like an odd mixture of innocuous and dramatic statements to use when trying to understand someone's personality, and any one of them by itself would certainly reveal nothing. But responses to a great many statements like these have been shown to reveal *patterns* of behaviour and attitudes that can give psychologists some clues – and they are no more than that – about deep-lying aspects of personality such as anxiety or depression, or feelings about masculinity/femininity, or even a tendency towards schizophrenia.

Taken over the whole range of the MMPI's 550 statements – complete with cross-checks on consistency of response – it is considered likely that people will reveal more of their inner life than if they are asked directly about, say, their masculinity/femininity. The direct approach is thought more likely to elicit the kind of reply the individual considers to be socially acceptable.

☐   *The TAT*

The kind of personality tests that require the subject to *project* whatever is in his or her mind onto some vaguely defined picture are considered more powerful than the paper-and-pencil test. These are called projective tests, of which the Thematic Apperception Test (TAT) is perhaps most widely used.[7] The TAT consists of 20 black and white pictures (drawings and photographs) most of which contain one or two people. The emotions portrayed by, and the relationships between, the people in these pictures are made deliberately ambiguous, allowing the subject scope to identify with the situation being depicted. The subject is asked to make up a story about what is happening in each picture, what led up to it and what will happen in the future. The picture thus acts like a screen upon which parts of the person's inner life may be projected. These stories are then analysed to see what recognisable themes may be perceived (hence the name of the test), and this is used to gain some clues about the person's unconscious mind.

☐   *The Rorschach Ink Blot Test*

Named after its inventor, the Swiss psychiatrist Hermann Rorschach, this projective test is perhaps the most famous of all psychological tests.[8] Ten pictures of actual ink blots are used, five of them in colour. The subjects are asked what they see in the ink blot; what it reminds them of. There are no right or wrong answers, of course, and the theory is that each person will see people or things that are important to them alone. Psychologists experienced in the use of the Rorschach claim that the subjects' responses to the shape and colour and detail of the ink blot can reveal a great deal of their unconscious life, as projected onto the picture.[9]

It is important to note that each of these personality tests was developed for use with disturbed people in a clinical setting. Companies that use some adaptation of them to get information from people assumed to be normal are therefore in some danger of abusing the tests (and also perhaps the people they are used on), with serious implications for the validity of their findings. As the better part of psychological skill lies in the *interpretation* of test or interview findings, this activity really should be left in the hands of trained and experienced psychologists.

■ Neo-Freudian Psychoanalysis

Some of Freud's successors, especially in the United States, have tended to de-emphasize the importance of the id in favour of more ego-related *social* factors. That is, they feel that Freud gave too much weight to the effects on people's behaviour of biological drives such as sex and largely ignored the interaction that takes place between individuals and the people who form the world they live in. These neo-Freudian psychoanalysts believe that interpersonal relationships, and particularly those between parents and children, are crucial to the development of an individual's personality.

One neo-Freudian theorist, Karen Horney, produced a model of human behaviour that has been used in research by consumer psychologists. Horney suggested that there are three major orientations by which people can be classified in their relationships with others:

- The *compliant* orientation includes people who tend to move *towards* others. They are particularly dependent on other people for love, affection and approval.
- The *aggressive* orientation includes people who tend to move *against* others. They have a particular need for power and the ability to manipulate other people.
- The *detached* orientation includes people who tend to move *away* from others. They stress the need for independence and self-reliance and avoid developing emotional bonds with other people that might involve them in obligations.

A CAD (Compliant Aggressive Detached) personality scale has been derived to measure the orientations of individuals as consumers. This scale was used in the 1960s with American undergraduates on business studies courses, where differences between the three orientations were found for a wide variety of products.[10]

For example, of the three types 'compliant' people expressed a greater preference for recognised brand names such as Bayer aspirin or Right Guard deodorant, and they also used more mouthwash and toilet soaps. 'Aggressive' types were significantly more in favour of razors, as opposed to electric shavers , and were more likely to use after-shave and cologne. (Old Spice was their favoured deodorant.) 'Detached' subjects had the least interest of the three groups in branded goods and were more likely than the other groups to drink tea (an odd beverage in 1960s America).

More recent research on the CAD orientations found that, in general, the detached subjects were far less interested in being consumers than either the compliant or aggressive types.[11] Generally speaking this line of research has not been as fruitful as it looked like being in the 1960s. However in practical terms there are plenty of advertising examples that are aimed at each of the CAD orientations. Assessing the effectiveness of these appeals is of course a much more difficult proposition.

■ Self Theory

Self theory grew out of the school of thought known as *humanistic psychology*, a diverse and eclectic approach to the study of human beings. The sources of humanistic psychology include Zen Buddhism and psychedelic drugs, for instance, along with the more mainstream study of group dynamics (which we will examine in Chapter 10) and the self-actualization ideas of Abraham Maslow (which we will consider in Chapter 7). But perhaps the most representative source is the person-centred work of Carl Rogers.

Carl Rogers is often taken to be the primary personality theorist in humanistic psychology, which takes an optimistic view of the existence of creativity and the potential for growth within every human being. The fact that this potential so often remains unfulfilled, Rogers and others would argue, is due to the oppressive effects of family, school and all the other social institutions that shape the lives of individuals.

The key to overcoming these influences, and so unlocking the human potential hidden underneath, is for everyone to take responsibility for their own lives. If people can take this first, crucial step they can then start to explore and then enrich their 'inner life' – their unique experiences and their deepest feelings – and eventually free themselves from what Rogers called 'the conformity of institutions and the dogma of authority'.[12]

Like Freud, Carl Rogers' theory of personality grew out of his clinical experience as a therapist. However Freud was a physician while Rogers was trained as a psychologist and their differing professional backgrounds are reflected in their differing approaches to understanding personality. Freud's underlying view of human nature was that people are driven largely by irrational forces that only a well-ordered society can hold in check. Rogers on the other hand believed that people are basically rational and are motivated to fulfil themselves and become the best human beings that they can be.

Rogers stresses the importance of the *conscious self-image* in this theory; he is not very interested in the workings of the unconscious. To the extent that people are maladjusted in their behaviour, their self-image is out of touch with reality, like academics who consider themselves to be stimulating teachers despite the fact that students tend to fall asleep in their classes.

■ The Origin of the Concept of Self

The concept of self , which would fall within the Freudian term 'ego', is widely used by personality theorists as the basic building block of personality. As such it is important that we understand how our sense of self originates.

We are not born with a sense of self, of who and what we are; it develops throughout our childhood and youth and continues to change, however slowly, for as long as we live. As newborn infants develop into people, their conception of themselves is the most important one they will ever form. It is pivotal to how they perceive the world and everyone in it.

The self concept is formed during the process of interacting with other people. From the moment of birth people respond to infants' behaviour and the infants react in turn. From the very beginning of life they receive feedback from other people about themselves; how they are regarded by them, the effects of their behaviour on them.[13] The basis of the self-image is physical – a body image – and it will remain so throughout life.

At first infants have difficulty knowing where they end and the environment begins. Gradually they begin to be aware of their own bodies and, at about the age of ten to twelve months, start to distinguish 'me' from 'not me'. During the first few years of life infants are closely concerned with exploring their own bodies, seeing what's there and finding out what it can do. As various groups of muscles mature they take delight in using them, gaining more and more mastery over themselves, and exploring the environment.

By about the third year of life children begin to be aware of themselves. They think of themselves as separate objects but still have only the crudest idea of themselves as people. They have trouble, for example, distinguishing processes internal to themselves from those of their environment. Dreams may be located 'in the room' or 'beside the bed'.

Children also have great difficulty, as they acquire language, in using personal pronouns. Children start to use the word 'I' to refer to themselves when they are two or three years old, but they won't use it consistently. They hear people talking about objects called 'table', 'dog', and 'ball', and they very quickly learn to use these terms correctly. But they hear people refer to them both as 'you' and as 'George/Georgina', and so they may also refer to themselves in both these ways. At the same time they are learning that people announce their wants and intentions with the word 'I', so they try out that one too.

All this early exploratory activity normally takes place, of course, within the social context provided by the family and in particular by the mother, with whom much of the activity takes place. The feelings other people have about the children and the way these feelings are expressed can exert the most crucial influence on their development. If children feel secure and loved and encouraged in their earliest explorations of themselves and their world, they are off to a good start in their development as people. If not, both their intellectual and their emotional development may suffer.

With the broadening of children's horizons that comes with the development of language, there also appears a more detailed self-image. As at every other stage of life, their self-image is a product of the interaction between the children and the people around them.   But whereas later in life it is possible to reinterpret the judgements of these others or to seek out different judgements, young children have no alternative but to believe that they are what their parents tell them they are.   If the message from their parents is that they are unlovable then that is the judgement they will make of themselves, so the parents should not be surprised if they then start to behave in an unlovable fashion.

By the end of adolescence the outlines of our concept of self have been set and the crucial question of our self-image, whether or not we like ourselves and have high or low self-esteem, has been answered.   In one sense though our concept of self is never completely formed or finally finished, and our self-esteem can be raised or lowered to some extent by social factors.   Thus it has long been known that if people are deliberately treated by their group as popular and attractive they will come to *feel* popular and attractive and behave in the way that popular and attractive people behave – to the point where the in group begins to believe that these people really are popular and attractive.[14]

■ Marketing and the Concept of Self

The concept of self has long been of great interest to marketers because of its subjective element.   People's self-image is composed of their view of themselves, all that they are and all that they have, physically, mentally, emotionally, socially and in terms of material possessions.   The nature of that view may well be different from the more objective view of the consumer researchers, with their interviews, questionnaires and pre-existing categories.   The way I make sense of your behaviour in building up a picture of you, in other words, may not be the same as the way *you* do it – and your way will include the particular goods and services you choose to buy.

A number of studies have attempted to explore the relationship between self-image and specific products, especially cars.   Following the lead of Ernest Dichter, noted above, researchers in the 1960s found some suggestion of a certain congruence between buyers' self image and the image of their cars. Owners of Volkswagen beetles, for instance, thought of themselves and all the other owners of these cars as being a particular kind of person and quite different from the owners of other (similarly priced) cars.[15]

Consumer researchers have recently adopted a more complex approach to self-image however, and now tend to split the concept into four:[16]

- *Actual self-image*: the traditional concept of how people actually see themselves.
- *Ideal self-image*: how people *would like* to see themselves.
- *Social self-image*: how people think *others* see them.
- *Ideal social self-image*: how people *would like* others to see them.

The assumption here is that consumers will be influenced by different self-images in different situations.   Thus the actual self may purchase cars or cleaning fluids while the ideal (or ideal social) self buys the clothes and the perfume. And many advertisements appeal to different aspects of the self of course, which is why American Express 'says more about you than money ever can' and a Patek Philippe watch 'doesn't just tell you the time. It tells you something about yourself'.

Behaviour based on self-image is largely at the level of conscious awareness, whereas a great deal of the real causes of our behaviour, as we saw earlier in the chapter, may well be unconscious. Nevertheless self-image may still be important to marketers in terms of *specific* buying choices, and I would suggest that this is particularly true when an individual is trying to change an *actual* physical self-image into an *ideal* one.

And this is an integral part of everyday consumer behaviour. Why else would people spend so much money on cosmetics, scents, hair products, contact lenses, plastic surgery and so on? There used to be a flourishing market in hair straighteners for black people, for example, until the self image of black people began to change in the 1960s.

■ Trait Theory

There is one final kind of formal personality theory we need to consider. Unlike the three we have already looked at, it is not based on a particular approach to understanding the human condition. It is, on the contrary, empirically based; that is, it sets out to identify and measure all the relatively stable characteristics of someone's personality at any given time, using the methods of experimental psychology and statistics. Each of these characteristics is known as a trait, either physical (such as height and weight) or psychological (such as imagination, assertiveness or even intelligence). While traits are therefore shared by everyone, people may differ from each other on each trait.

We are concerned here with the use of the trait concept in the attempt to build up a general theory of personality. The leading theorist in this field is Raymond Cattell. The fundamental technique used by trait theorists such as Cattell is a sophisticated one known as factor analysis, which we shall only describe very briefly. For a full technical explanation you should look to the relevant authorities on the subject.[17]

Factor analysis is a statistical procedure for identifying a small number of underlying dimensions: patterns of factors contained within a much larger set of data. It is a way of both reducing and summarising the original data set. Given that the English language contains an estimated 4500 adjectives that describe behavioural traits, for instance, the first task of a trait theorist must be to reduce these to a manageable number. However, as many terms are virtually synonymous (for example reserved, detached, cool, reticent, taciturn, aloof, restrained, laconic, remote and distant) the task is not quite as difficult as it might seem. Cattell eventually came up with sixteen different factors, each forming a continuum, as follows[18]:

- Outgoing .... Reserved
- More intelligent .... Less intelligent
- Emotionally stable .... Affected by feelings
- Assertive .... Humble
- Happy go lucky .... Sober
- Conscientious .... Expedient
- Venturesome .... Shy
- Tender-minded .... Tough-minded
- Suspicious .... Trusting
- Imaginative .... Practical
- Shrewd .... Forthright
- Apprehensive .... Placid
- Experimenting .... Conservative
- Self-sufficient .... Group-dependent
- Controlled .... Casual
- Tense .... Relaxed

Identification of these sixteen factors allowed Cattell to score people on each one and so obtain a 'personality profile' for any given individual. This personality test is now widely used as the 16PF in job selection and vocational guidance. Later exponents of factor analysis have carried Cattell's narrowing down process even further and have come up with only five factors,[19] as shown below, although this classification has not yet been as widely accepted as Cattell's.

- *Extroversion* – for example: Talkative .... Silent
- *Agreeableness* – for example: Good natured .... Irritable
- *Conscientiousness* – for example: Fussy .... Careless
- *Emotional stability* – for example: Calm .... Anxious
- *Culture* – for example: Intellectual .... Unreflective

Cattell suggested that there were three important sources of data about any given individual personality, life data, self-report questionnaire data and objective data from personality tests. Life data consists of ratings on various factors by people who know the person being studied and objective data comes from the kind of personality tests that we encountered earlier in this chapter. It is interesting to note therefore, that despite his rigorously empirical and statistical approach Cattell was happy to accept the influence of unconscious forces, and indeed the psychoanalytic concepts of ego and superego.

There have been many attempts to relate particular personality traits, factors or types to particular products using the kind of instrument outlined above. But attempts to find practical applications for this kind of personality theory have been no more successful than those for any other theory.

A recent survey of over 300 such studies covering various theories found only a few that seemed to have strong links between specific aspects of personality and particular products. The results of the rest were 'questionable or perhaps meaningless'.[20] There are a number of probable reasons for this:

- The techniques used were often adapted from instruments devised for a very different, clinical, purpose.
- Both personality and consumer choice, as we have already seen in this book, involve very complex psychological processes and reducing these to a correlation between one product, or even brand, and one tiny aspect of personality is virtually a caricature.
- Even if an attempt is made to deal with the entire personality of a consumer, that would still be only a part of the causal jigsaw puzzle that lies behind the specifics of buying behaviour. There are many other situational factors in both the consumer's life and the purchasing context that might have more influence on the final choice. Money and availability are only two of the most obvious such factors.

■ Brand personality

A more modest and attainable use of personality factors in marketing, and in the understanding of consumer behaviour, lies in the development of a *brand personality*. This is a way of characterizing the image of a brand by giving it personal associations, as though it were an individual. Would the brand be described as 'masculine' or 'feminine', for instance, as 'old-fashioned', 'aggressive', 'elegant' or any one of the large number of personality attributes mentioned in this chapter?[21]

More elaborate than this fairly widespread marketing technique are attempts to provide brands with a whole, rounded and consistent personality of their own – usually with proper names such as Dr Pepper or Mr Coffee in the States and Mr Bradford and Mr Bingley in the United Kingdom. The aim is to make the brand immediately recognisable, and if possible respected and liked, the way an individual might be. We saw in Chapter 4 how repeated exposure to a subject can induce some positive feelings for it.

An important part of brand personality is colour. Some colours have been associated throughout history with certain characteristics. In Western countries white has always been associated with purity and cleanliness for instance, and in virtually every society gold has meant wealth and often royalty. The red end of the colour spectrum is often associated with passion and excitement and is considered a 'warm' colour, whereas blue is more associated with authority and is considered a 'cool' colour. Black, which traditionally has had negative associations in Western society, is now also considered sophisticated, mysterious and powerful.[22] Could this be why every piece of electronic equipment in the galaxy is now matt black?

■ Further Reading

Blackwell, R. D., J. F. Engel and W. W. Talarzyk, *Contemporary Cases in Consumer Behavior* (Chicago: Dryden, 1990). A compilation by leading researchers in consumer behaviour that includes some interesting work on personality factors.

Burgess, S. M., *Personal Values, Consumer Behaviour and Brand Image Perceptions* (Johannesburg: University of the Witwatersrand, 1990). The evolution of values according to psychological theory.

Freud S., *The Standard Edition of the Complete Psychological Works of Sigmund Freud,* J. Strachey (ed.) (London: Hogarth, 1953–74). The authoritative translation of Freud's work.

Ward, S. and T. S. Robertson (eds), *Consumer Behavior: Theoretical Sources* (Englewood Cliffs, NJ: Prentice-Hall, 1973). Contains some detailed discussions on personality factors and psychological theory as related to marketing.

Wells, W. D. (ed.), *Life Style and Psychographics* (Chicago: American Marketing Association, 1974). A useful compilation by a leading researcher in the field.

It is also worth browsing through the latest issues of the following periodicals: *Advances in Consumer Research, Journal of Consumer Research, Journal of Marketing Research, Journal of Consumer Psychology.*

■ Questions for Discussion

1. If every personality is a unique individual, why is the concept of 'personality' used so much in consumer research on marketing?
2. How might the id, ego and superego of Freudian theory affect particular purchase decisions? Give examples of advertising that appeals to each of these aspects of personality.
3. Why is it important for a marketer to know that one's sense of self tends to be consistent over time?
4. Choose a product to market on the basis of consumer self-image. How effective would each of the four types of self-image be?
5. What is the attraction for marketers of the trait theory of personality? What are its practical limitations?
6. How does 'brand personality' relate to the basic concept of human personality?

CHAPTER 6

■ Learning

■ Introduction

How do we learn what to buy?

When a human infant comes into the world to start life, he or she is not very well equipped for the journey. Unlike many animal infants, a human baby is completely helpless for a relatively long period of time, and for several years is physically dependent on adults for sheer survival. Contrast this with several species of birds that start to get about and forage for themselves shortly after they are born, for example chickens. However, while the baby bird will grow up to do not a lot more than getting about and foraging, our human baby may grow up to be Billie Holliday or Sigmund Freud.

A great deal of animal behaviour is preprogrammed, or instinctive, but the higher up the animal kingdom you go the less important instinct becomes, until you arrive at human beings who probably have no instincts at all. What we have instead is the capacity to learn. The effects of learning on behaviour are easiest to see in young children, for whom the world is new and waiting to be discovered. As they become increasingly aware of their environment their society socializes them, instructs them in how to behave (a process we will examine in Chapters 8 and 9).

In the process of being socialized children must learn the approved ways of walking, talking, eating, excreting and thinking, to list just a few of the more obvious kinds of behaviour. They must also learn how to make sense of life in the fashion approved by their particular society; whom to like and whom to dislike, how to deal with advertising and how to make buying decisions. *All* consumer behaviour is therefore learned behaviour. Because the process of learning is so important to understanding the consumer, we need to examine it in a little detail, along with the associated process of memory.

■ What is Learning?

We will start with a definition of learning. Most psychologists would now agree with something like the following: 'learning is the relatively permanent process by which changes in behaviour, knowledge, feelings or attitudes occur as the result of prior experience'.

You will notice immediately that this is a very broad definition. It is in fact an attempt to surround the process. As we will see, learning is too complex a process to allow anything more focused. The key words in the above definition are *relatively permanent, behaviour, knowledge* and *prior experience.*

By *relatively permanent* we mean an outcome that is not due to the effects of temporary situations such as taking drugs or alcohol, or being very tired, any of which can dramatically affect the way we behave for a limited period of time. When we say that learning is the result of *prior experience* we exclude the changes that accompany the physiological process of growing up and maturing. And we also exclude, of course, any changes that may occur as the result of brain damage or other injury.

The other two key terms in our definition of learning, *behaviour* and *knowledge*, refer to the two major 'schools' or approaches to the study of learning, *behaviourist* and *cognitive*. Because of the practical difficulties involved in studying the learning process in people, much of the basic work of these two schools was done on animals, though the same processes can often be seen in human learning.

■ The Behaviourist Approach

The behaviourist approach to learning stems from one of the two most influential general theories of psychology, behaviourism. The other major theory, which we have already encountered in this book, is of course psychoanalysis. The two theories could not be more different in their view of psychology. Behaviourism was founded early in the twentieth century by J. B. Watson who described it thus:[1] 'Psychology as the behaviourist views it is a purely objective branch of natural science. Its theoretical goal is the prediction and control of behaviour'.

Unlike Freud, Watson did not believe in the existence of the unconscious mind. But then he didn't believe in the existence of the conscious mind either, or any other kind of mind. There was nothing else to be studied but someone's observable physical behaviour, he argued. Watson, in other words, was firmly of the opinion that in psychology what you see is what you get, and what you can't see and don't get doesn't exist. The experimenter provided the stimulus, noted the subject's response to it and didn't worry about what happened in between.

■ Pavlov and Classical Conditioning

The question of what occurred between stimulus and response was, however, something that greatly concerned Ivan Pavlov. Pavlov was not a psychologist, he was a very distinguished physiologist who won the Nobel Prize in 1904 for his work on digestion. But in the course of his research on the digestive system of dogs he came to demonstrate the working of a process that was clearly psychological.

Pavlov had known for a long time that when dogs are fed, their digestive glands start to function and they salivate. What he began to observe in the course of his research was that the dogs in his lab began to salivate *before* they were fed, in fact as soon as they recognised the man who was coming to feed them. This aroused Pavlov's curiosity, and he designed an ingenious series of experiments to find out what was going on.[2]

A dog salivating when it is given food is a perfectly automatic inborn response. This does not depend on any other conditions being present, so that both the stimulus of presenting the food to the dog and the dog's response of salivating are unconditioned – unconditioned stimulus (US), unconditioned response (UR).

A dog salivating when it is merely shown food or simply sees someone bringing it food is not producing an inborn response because there is a condition attached to it. The condition is that the dog is able to associate what it now sees with what it has previously tasted; that it is able to recognise this as food. When the dog recognises food, its brain flashes a message to its digestive system and it starts to salivate. Thus the stimulus of seeing the food (or even food provider) and the response of salivating are both conditioned – conditioned stimulus (CS), conditioned response (CR).

What Pavlov wanted to find out was what kinds of conditioned stimuli could produce the conditioned response of salivating. After starting out by simply showing the animal food and getting it to salivate, he substituted a whole host of conditional stimuli such as bells, buzzers, metronomes and lights, and found that with any of them he could produce the conditioned response and get the dog to salivate. The experimental procedure he used is known as *classical conditioning*:

1. Food (US) leads to salivation (UR).
2. The sound of a bell (CS) by itself leads to nothing.
3. The sound of a bell (CS) followed by the presentation of food (US) leads to salivation (UR).
4. When this process has been repeated enough times for the dog to associate the bell (CS) with the food (US), he will salivate (UR) at the sound of the bell alone.
5. At this point the animal's salivation has become conditional on hearing the bell rather than unconditional on being given food. Thus the bell (CS) now results in salivation (CR) just as effectively as the food (US) had resulted in salivation (UR). The animal, in other words, has been conditioned to salivate at the sound of a bell.

The classical conditioning process is presented schematically in Figure 6.1.

J. B. Watson was very taken with Pavlov's work and incorporated it into his theory of behaviourism. Here was a clear and objective way of understanding why a given stimulus produced a given response without recourse to talk of mental processes or the mind. Moreover it should be possible to use the conditioning method to change someone's behaviour in a desired direction, an exciting prospect indeed for a man who would shortly leave the academic world for a successful career in advertising with the J. Walter Thompson Company.[3]

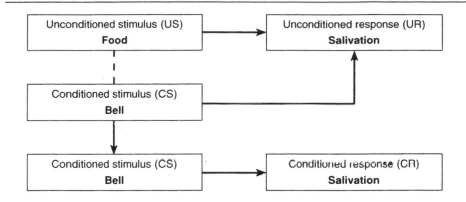

Figure 6.1   The classical conditioning process

■ Consumer Applications

Behaviourists point out that quite a lot of human behaviour can also be explained by simple conditioning. If you usually have your dinner at about the time that someone else in the house watches a soap opera, for instance, it will take no more than the opening bars of the signature tune to get you salivating just like Pavlov's dogs! And if you hear the same tune in a different time and place your mouth will still water even though it's not dinnertime.

In fact the basic link in classical conditioning between the conditioned stimulus and the unconditioned stimulus is at the heart of a great deal of consumer advertising. The goal here is to associate a product (US) with a particular image (CS) that is thought to be attractive to the potential customer. Think of all the products – from booze to life insurance – that are associated with sun-filled leisure, far from the everyday world, usually on a golden beach empty of all but a handful of beautiful people. You can see why J. B. Watson did well in advertising. Figure 6.2 shows how this application of classical conditioning is done. How effective it is is another matter.

A laboratory study has shown how people can be conditioned by the music in an advertisement to choose one colour of pen rather than another. The subjects in the experiment tended to like one of two pieces of music and dislike the other. The advertisement in which the background music was playing featured the use of either a beige or a light blue pen (both previously evaluated as 'neutral'). Nothing was said to the subjects about the colour of the pens; the story was that an advertising agency was looking for a suitable piece of music.

At the end of the study the students were invited to take one of the pens away with them. The study found that when the liked piece of music was played the colour of pen used in the advertisement was greatly preferred to the other one. With the disliked background music the colour of pen *not* displayed in the advertisement was preferred.[4] However it is important to remind ourselves that

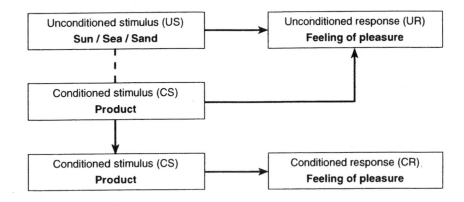

Figure 6.2 Application of classical conditioning

people do not normally watch advertisements under laboratory conditions and many other factors may influence how they react in their usual circumstances.

We have sketched above the merest outlines of what has become a very complex and rather technical procedure, but before leaving the topic of classical conditioning we need to consider a little further two major aspects of it: stimulus generalization and stimulus discrimination.

Stimulus generalization was discovered by Pavlov as he systematically varied the different factors in his conditioning technique. He discovered that his dogs would salivate not only at the sound of the usual bell or buzzer that was used, but also at other bells and buzzers that had a similar sound. The animals were generalizing from the particular stimulus they had been conditioned with to a wider range of stimuli that sounded like it.

We do something similar when we look favourably on some of the other 56 varieties of Heinz because we liked their baked beans so much as children. Indeed that factor probably had a lot to do with the huge extension of the company's product lines. It is obviously a lot cheaper to extend an existing successful range than to produce a completely new product, and about 80 per cent of the new arrivals on the American market each year are either brand or product extensions.[5]

The effect of stimulus generalization also explains why there are so many flourishing 'me too' products on the market that eat into the brand leader's sales. Conversely it is also the psychological process behind the successful licensing of branded company names and trademarks, from Walt Disney to Manchester United. Company names are often jealously guarded. Thus McDonald's have sued McTravel and McSleep because they were getting too close. One wonders what people called McDonald make of it all.

Stimulus discrimination is the opposite effect. Pavlov demonstrated that a dog can be conditioned *not* to generalize to any other stimulus. He showed that the animal could be trained to distinguish between its original conditioned stimulus and any other conditioned stimulus. He simply rewarded the animal with food if it salivated to one particular sound and did not reward it for responding to any other sound.

Stimulus discrimination also has the opposite effect in marketing. While imitators want potential customers to *generalize* the product stimulus, market leaders – or anyone who wants to establish the uniqueness of their product – want them to *discriminate*. Hence the problems faced by Campari and Cinzano drinks, or Goodrich and Goodyear tyres, or even the Bank of Scotland and The Royal Bank of Scotland.

Indeed the ownership of a registered trademark may be lost and become public property if the courts believe it has become generic (generalized) rather than remaining company specific (discriminated). That has been the fate of many products over the years, including aspirin, cornflakes, linoleum and the thermos flask.

■ Skinner and Operant Conditioning

We have seen that classical (or Pavlovian) conditioning is a very basic form of learning that depends on a stimulus (S) being given to an animal, which results in a particular response (R). The animal's behaviour in this pattern of stimulus–response is said to be elicited from it. The animal does not initiate the conditioning process by its own behaviour. However, much of an animal's behaviour is not elicited by outside stimuli but is part of the animal's own spontaneous actions. Without waiting for a push from the outside an animal will often begin to explore its surroundings, to 'operate' on its environment. An animal engaging in such activity is said to exhibit *operant behaviour* and this brings us to the work of another famous psychologist, B. F. Skinner.

Skinner carried Pavlov's work on conditioning a step further and showed that it was possible to shape an animal's behaviour in some very ingenious ways by using conditioning techniques.[6] This process is known as operant conditioning, or sometimes *instrumental conditioning*. He designed an environmentally controlled cage for a laboratory-bred white rat. With this cage (now known as a 'Skinner box', Figure 6.3) he could control the amount of light, heat and sound that the animal was exposed to. But the crucial feature of the Skinner box was a small bar set low down on one wall. When this bar was pressed a food pellet automatically dropped down into a tray below it.

As the rat explored the Skinner box it accidentally pressed the bar, winning itself some food. It ate the food but didn't make the connection. In the course of moving about it pressed the bar again and this time the idea clicked. The rat now made the connection and associated the bar pressing with the appearance of food. It then proceeded to press the bar as often as it could. As with classical conditioning, as long as the rat's operant behaviour of bar pressing was rein-forced by the appearance of food – in other words positive reinforcement – it continued the behaviour. When Skinner withdrew the food and the rat was no longer rewarded for this particular operant behaviour, it stopped doing it.

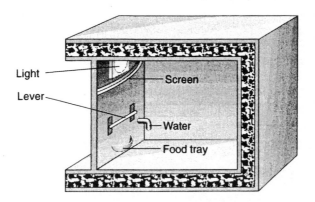

Figure 6.3 Skinner box

Skinner also neatly demonstrated that the avoidance of pain is at least as important in reinforcing operant behaviour as the gaining of a reward. Through the floor of the box he produced a mild electric shock that could be turned off by pressing the same bar that had produced food in the previous experiment. The rat went through the same random movements before pressing the bar accidentally and turning off the current. As before it quickly learned to press the bar as soon as the current came on, thereby avoiding further shocks. Skinner called this *aversive conditioning* and it results from a schedule of *negative*

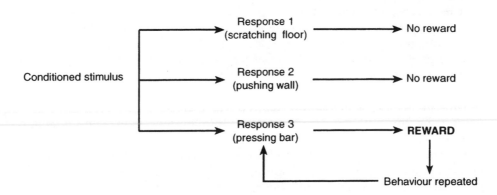

Figure 6.4 Operant conditioning

reinforcement. This is not the same as *punishment,* by the way. Punishment, such as receiving a shock when pressing a bar, is intended to *discourage* the behaviour in question.

When discussing Pavlov's work we saw that animals can learn to generalise from one conditioned stimulus to others and conversely to discriminate between one particular stimulus and any other stimuli. Skinner has shown that these principles also apply to operant conditioning. In fact by building up the animal's learning step-by-step he has shown that animals can learn some very complex tasks.

Animal trainers in zoos and circuses are actually applying operant conditioning by reinforcing the animal with food when it exhibits the desired behaviour. It is by this means that they can get horses to dance and dolphins to perform acrobatics. Skinner himself actually taught pigeons to play ping pong and demonstrated it to his students, a feat he later regretted as he became fed up with talking about it!

■ Consumer Applications of Operant Conditioning

Behaviourists argue that examples of operant conditioning in consumer behaviour are many and various. For example if your supermarket has a new brand of yoghurt on offer and you decide to try it, future purchase of the product will depend on whether your response is 'reinforced' or 'rewarded' by your liking it. If it is you will add it to your shopping list, if it isn't your original buying behaviour will probably be 'extinguished'. The same applies to any other product you like, producing what we recognize as *brand loyalty*.

Clearly it is important for marketers to ensure if possible that their products are rewarding to their consumers each time they use them. They want at all costs to ensure that no incidence of 'punishment' follows the buying decision. It only took the discovery of one dead fly in one bottle of the mineral water I used to buy to put me off the brand for life.

It has been found that simply telephoning to say 'thank you' to a customer after a purchase is seen as rewarding and can lead to increased sales, especially if the caller does not tout for business at the same time.[7] You can't get a cheaper form of positive reinforcement than saying 'thank you', but even, though this is widely employed, in many cases it is made ineffective or even irritating by its patent insincerity. 'Thank you for calling X ...' is my favourite. If your sister is arriving on Sardine Seater Airlines and you call their office to find out when the flight is due they will end the conversation with a bright 'thank you for calling Sardine Seater'. Who else could you have called?

In planning promotional campaigns marketers employ operant conditioning in many of their techniques. For existing customers, money-back and points-for-purchase programmes are often used by supermarkets, airlines and hotel chains to reinforce usage. To attract new customers techniques such as low introductory offers, free gifts, free product samples or trial periods are used for a vast array of products from cars to newspapers. The aim is to reward the consumer for engaging in an activity desired by the marketer. The hope is that the consumer's experience of the product will be pleasant enough for continued usage of it to become a habit even when the original reward is no longer there.

There is a difference of opinion among psychologists as to how applicable operant conditioning is to consumer buying decisions, but probably most would agree with a former president of the Association for Consumer Research that, at least for products with little personal importance or significance to the consumer (choice of detergent, oranges, or taxicabs for example), the simple explanations of behaviourism are quite adequate.[8] People find they like a product and (other things, such as price, being equal) will buy it again the next time the need arises.

However most psychologists would probably argue that for major and complex buying decisions that are of some significance to the consumer the behaviourist explanation is not enough. Indeed for these types of decisions it might be argued that behaviourism provides a *description* of the behaviour involved rather than an *explanation* of how and why the consumer came to make the eventual decision.

■ The Cognitive Approach

When dealing with complex and important decisions most psychologists would turn to the definition of learning provided at the beginning of this chapter (learning is the relatively permanent process by which changes in behaviour, knowledge, feelings or attitudes occur as the result of prior experience), and place the accent on *knowledge* (and feelings and attitudes) rather than behaviour. The difficulty with this approach is that you can't actually see someone's knowledge (or attitudes or feelings), all you can see is what they *do*, and you have to *infer* from that behaviour what they think or feel.

Until people show what they think about a product by picking it off the shelf, or telling a market researcher (that is, verbal behaviour), their consumer preferences or attitudes don't really exist. But when they do engage in consumer choice we are then faced with the problem of interpreting what their behaviour means, and in any field of psychology – as we have already seen and will see again – interpretation is the most difficult and contentious of psychological skills. This is the problem that psychologists who take a cognitive approach to learning have to deal with.

■ Insightful Learning

As with the classical and operant conditioning techniques of the behaviourist approach to learning, the cognitive approach was founded on work with animals. In our discussion of conditioning we looked at a very simple and basic form of learning behaviour. Even in an operant conditioning situation, where the animal takes some initiative, the learning involved is accomplished by trying out the behaviour many times until it is satisfactory to the trainer. Circus tricks performed by animals require a great deal of patient, step-by-step training, and a lot of trials have to be undertaken and a lot of errors corrected before the animals learn the trick. *Trial and error* learning is thus a slow and laborious process. People, as well as animals, learn by this means but a lot of human learning is due to insight, where the understanding of a situation or the solution to a problem seems to occur quite suddenly and without any careful step-by-step process of learning.

The phenomenon where everything seems to click all at once (an 'aha!' reaction), also occurs among other intelligent animals. Early in the twentieth century Wolfgang Kohler described some striking examples of insight in the behaviour of the apes he studied.[9] In a typical experiment, a banana was placed outside a chimpanzee's cage but well beyond its reach, even with the aid of the short stick provided by Kohler. Just outside the cage was another stick, and this was long enough to reach the banana from the cage. The animal reached for the fruit, first with its hand and then with the short stick lying inside the cage. It was unable to reach the banana of course and gibbered about in frustration. After a time it calmed down, backed off and surveyed the situation once more, taking in all the elements of the problem. Suddenly the answer came to it. It used the short stick to pull in the longer stick then successfully hauled in the banana with the new tool at its disposal.

By such a process of *insightful learning* Kohler's apes solved much more complex problems than this. They made and used tools and they combined various elements in their environment (for example ropes and sticks) to reach distant objects. But there is a limit of course to animal insight, and even the brightest chimps cannot learn beyond the level of a three- or four-year-old child.

The greatest advantage of an insightful solution is that, unlike trial and error learning, it can be applied to new situations. No specific skill or set of movements is learned, but an understanding of the *relationship* between the means and the end is gained.

The cognitive school of learning emphasizes the importance of knowledge, understanding and insight; of higher mental processes such as the 'aha!' reaction of Kohler's apes as opposed to the conditioned responses of Pavlov's dogs. Psychologists of this school feel that the sheer formation of habits, no matter how complex, cannot entirely account for the ability of people and animals to cope successfully with problems *they have never experienced before.* Some other process, they argue, takes place inside the learner's head that, for example, allows him or her to use the habits already learned and then go a step further into unknown territory.

Moreover learning through trial and error is simply too dangerous in the acquisition of some skills: flying a 'plane and performing brain surgery spring immediately to mind. Some cognitive processes (evaluative, mental activity) do seem to be at work here. In a sense we all like to think of ourselves in terms of cognitive learning when we consider our own consumer behaviour. We are, after all, the kind of consumers who ask a wide range of people for their opinions and read the information provided in Consumer Reports before we ever dream of buying a new electronic widget demystifier, aren't we?

The cognitive approach to learning is therefore concerned with our need to make sense of the world we live in, with the search for meaning. As noted in Chapter 4, this need induces us to search constantly for patterns, for order, for wholes that make sense of the parts. You will recall from that chapter that this approach to dealing with the vast amount of stimuli we are subjected to constantly is central to the theory of Gestalt Psychology, and Wolfgang Kohler –

whose work on chimpanzees we have just looked at – was indeed a founder of that school.

Just as the way that we process environmental stimuli is crucial to our perception, the way that we process information is crucial to our learning. And there is a link between the psychology of perception and the psychology of learning: the concept of *memory*.

■ Information Processing and the Concept of Memory

Whatever we learn would be of no use if we had no way of storing it, ready to be retrieved when needed. This procedure is often referred to as *information processing*. Whenever we learn something the brain engages in various activities that probably result in some kind of physical traces. We then store this information and experience in our *memory*. Exactly how this happens and what these physical traces are like, psychologists can only speculate about. It is quite conceivable, however, that some trace of past learning will always remain. The problem is to retrieve it. Whatever can be retrieved is *remembered*; whatever cannot be retrieved is *forgotten*.

There are several ways in which you can try to retrieve previous learning from your memory. If you are asked the name of a product advertised on television last night you are being urged to *recall* what you learned. Similarly, if you are asked by a market researcher to name all the brands of toothpaste you can, you have to recall previous learning in order to answer the question.

If you were shown some advertisements and asked if you remember seeing them before, then only *recognition* of previous learning would be called for. You would normally be able to recognise more of the advertisements than you could recall. However it has been found that recognition is a less reliable method than recall as people sometimes claim to 'recognise' advertisements that have never been shown before and which they couldn't possibly have seen.[10]

There is a practical marketing issue involved in this discussion of memory and the retrieval of what has been learned. Should the marketer attempt to trigger recognition or recall of the brand name? The answer appears to depend on the environment in which the buying decision is to be made.[11] If the product in question is a drink, for example, and the consumer is in a bar there will be enough stimuli around for him or her to recognize the brand immediately. However if he or she is in the office and wants to order a bottle of the stuff by telephone as a gift for a client, he or she will need to *recall* the brand name.

It is also important for the marketer to decide whether to aim for recognition or recall in planning an advertising campaign. Recognition should be a much cheaper option.

These two processes of recall and recognition are two different kinds of response to the same stimulus; to the same jogging of the memory. In discussing how much learning has been retrieved or remembered by these means and how much forgotten, it must be understood, as mentioned earlier in this chapter, that we have no direct access to learning processes. When we look at test results and see that Joe remembered more than Moe but less than Flo, we are talking about performance. And various factors other than what is learned and what is remembered can affect performance.

The actual process of committing something to memory seems to involve three distinct stages, as outlined in Figure 6.5. When the sense organs react to environmental stimuli by sending information to the brain, a fleeting trace of the stimulus remains after the message is sent. For example if you just glance at a telephone number you will have a very brief memory of it as it registers in your brain. This sensory memory lasts for less than a second and if you want to use the information from your senses it has to be transferred onto the next stage of memory. Advertising images are also processed in this way. The advertiser's problem is not getting a product image into the memory system, but keeping it there.

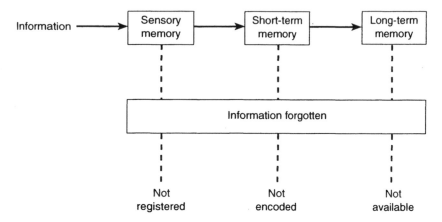

Figure 6.5   The memory system

The second stage of memory lasts slightly longer (up to 30 seconds), long enough to work through the task in hand and decide whether or not the incoming information is worth keeping.[12] As most information is not worth keeping it is not encoded, it is tossed out, or in other words forgotten. If you call half a dozen local stores to find out whether they have a certain make of computer you will not remember their telephone numbers for very long. Nor would you want to remember this kind of information; it would be a waste of time and effort, and confusing to boot. But some of the information we have to consider in this *short-term memory* stage is important enough to be recorded permanently (names, dates, formulae, and so on), and it must then be transferred to the third and final stage in the process.

This third stage is called *long-term memory,* and in order to get there the information has to be processed while being held in the short-term memory. New information is constantly passing from sensory memory to short-term memory, and as it does so it pushes out information already there. Information that is earmarked for long-term retention is therefore repeated or rehearsed (for example, by saying it aloud or writing it down) so that it sticks.

It is then *encoded* by the brain in such a way that what we consider essential about it is retained and the rest is discarded. Consumers are encouraged to encode a package of product information in the form of brand symbols, such as McDonald's golden arches or the Apple Company logo. There may be some differences in the way men and women encode information. When a television advertisement is based upon a social relationship, for instance, women are more likely to remember it than men.[13] The information is then ready to be placed alongside similar information in long-term memory storage, where it may well remain forever.

Contrary to widely held belief, memories that are filed away in long-term storage do not fade with time, although they may change somewhat. Our memories of school, for instance, or the 'fashionable' clothes we used to buy, may become distorted as we add things that didn't occur or subtract things that did in an attempt to make better sense of what actually happened and the way we experienced it at the time. Information in long-term memory storage is therefore not static but in a constant state of reorganization as our understanding is updated.

If our memories are permanently stored and do not fade away, why then do we forget things that have happened and information we have learned? The answer depends on *why* we cannot remember. It may be that the stimulus we are given is not sufficient for us to retrieve the memory, or it may be that we *don't want* to retrieve the memory.

As we saw in our discussion of recall and recognition, the form in which the stimulus is presented can determine how much is remembered and how much is forgotten at any given time. Another sign that the stimulus given may not be sufficient to retrieve the desired information from the memory is the sensation, familiar to everyone at some time, that the answer is on 'the tip of the tongue' but can't quite be produced.

It seems that verbal information that is stored away in the long-term memory is filed under several different systems – the way it sounds, the way it looks and what it means.[14] Thus if the word you want is the navigational instrument sextant, but you can't get it past the tip of your tongue, you may actually produce the word sextet, which looks and sounds similar, or the word compass, which has a similar meaning. For similar reasons you might confuse Campari, Cinzano and Martini.

Failure to retrieve information because we don't want to is a different matter altogether. It involves the unconscious repression of certain memories because experiencing them again would cause pain – reliving an unhappy period of childhood for example. This kind of 'motivated forgetting' may seem a long way from consumer behaviour, but sometimes people can't remember certain products or brand names because they are associated, by a process of conditioning, with something awful that happened to them. We sometimes have a *need* to forget certain information.

Such instances are striking because they are fairly unusual. We are more likely to be motivated to remember information in our long-term memory bank, whether it's material for an exam or the name of a restaurant we once stumbled across and where we had an unusually good meal. Given this basic motivation to remember, there are all sorts of techniques to help us process information efficiently and retrieve it effectively; to learn, memorize and reproduce.

■ Making Learning Meaningful

The desire to make human learning as efficient as possible has promoted an enormous amount of research for many years. A lot of this research has been devoted to the study of different methods of learning.[15] We will just concern ourselves here with a few of the concepts and techniques that are most relevant to consumers and product advertising. These techniques between them apply to almost all advertising, though only one or two of them might be applicable to any given advertisement.

□ *Repetition*

The most obvious and immediate technique for learning something is simply to repeat (or 'rehearse') the information. As we saw in the discussion of memory above, this is how information is passed from short-term to long-term memory storage. Radio and television commercials make extensive use of this technique – you will recall that 30 seconds is usually enough time for information to enter long-term memory – by repeating the brand name and/or the selling point throughout the advertisement.

By and large the technique works, but only up to a point.[16] In the course of an advertising campaign more consumers will learn more of the message with repetition. However the repeated message produces diminishing returns, with each repetition adding less to the consumer's learning than the previous one did. The more motivated the consumer is to learn about the product, the fewer the number of repetitions required to learn the message.

Somebody who is currently in the market for a particular product will be especially attentive to the relevant advertisements and may learn their message from a single exposure. This applies mainly to relatively expensive and infrequent purchases such as cars or life insurance. Soap powder or dog food will probably require a few more repetitions to make an impact. However this effect is complicated by the amount of competition there is. Repetition can be very effective when there is little competitive advertising, but when a lot of competing advertisements are all using repetition they may simply cancel each other out.[17]

□ *Visuals*

The Chinese saying that 'one picture is worth a thousand words' does seem to have some validity in advertising. This apparently is the case in print advertising as well as point-of-sale material and even brand names. You will recall that in our discussion of how material is encoded into long-term memory it was suggested that a visual representation of the material was one way of coding it.

This may be why visual representation is such a popular marketing device. Anything that includes the word 'royal' in its brand name, for instance, will often portray a crown or a crowned head. King Edward cigars are packaged with a portrait of the gentleman himself. This widespread usage is supported by research findings that brand names are more easily learned if they come with visual representation.[18]

☐ *Self-referencing*

It has been found by psychologists that when people are asked to relate information to their own lives, their memory of the material is increased.[19] As with visual imagery this is probably because of increased access to the way the material is encoded and stored in the long-term memory. The representation of the self is a complex and highly organized affair, as we saw in Chapter 5. Because of its psychological importance to the individual it has great power – if triggered by the stimulus material – to retrieve information from long-term memory storage. This trigger can apparently be pulled simply by using the word 'you' and referring to previous consumer experiences.[20]

☐ *Mnemonics*

In ancient Greece, public speaking was practically a spectator sport and orators were highly skilled at making long and elaborate speeches without notes. They were able to do this in the same way that modern entertainers perform amazing feats of memory for a living: they developed their own system of coding information into 'chunks' that could easily be retrieved from their long-term memory bank.

Thus the Greek orators would break up their speech into paragraphs and associate each paragraph with a statue in their favourite temple. As they were making their speech they would take an imaginary walk through the temple, and each succeeding statue they came to would be the stimulus to trigger the retrieval of the paragraph associated with it. Such devices are called *mnemonics*, from the Greek word for remembering.

We sometimes use mnemonics ourselves. Many of us learned the number of days in each month by reciting the jingle, 'Thirty days hath September...'. Spelling was made a little easier by putting 'i before e except after c'. Even in the absence of mnemonics we like to group and cluster things together as though we are making keys that will unlock doors where more information is stored away. As long as we can remember where we put the keys, we're in business.

For instance if I rush into a telephone booth at Heathrow Airport to call someone urgently at the Edinburgh University Management School whose number I don't have with me, I may have to retrieve eleven digits from memory to get the information I need: 01316508069. Now, if that's how the number was presented to me I would have a hard time remembering it. The normal memory span is able to cope with about seven digits.[21] However all the memorizing I have to do is in three chunks: 0131-650-8069. I know you have to dial 0131 for Edinburgh, and I know the University prefix is 650. So all I really have to learn is the individual number: 8069.

■ Meaningfulness

The thread running through these methods of learning is the search for meaning, for understanding, for ways of making sense of the information we encounter. That is the essence of the cognitive approach to learning. We search for patterns, codes, keys and rules that will make our learning easier, and we *must* do this because there is so much to learn.

We learn new things by linking them with things we already know. We interpret unfamiliar new information in terms of what is familiar to us. We strive constantly for logic and order and have difficulty learning if we don't find it. In a word we *organize* our memories, and the organized packages that we form are sometimes called *schemas*. Tapping into these schemas is the goal of every marketer.

■ Modelling

There is one last form of learning that we should consider. It has been claimed by both the behaviourist and the cognitive camps and indeed aspects of it are common to both. It is usually referred to as *modelling* or *observational learning*, and sometimes as *vicarious learning*. In this kind of learning people observe the behaviour of others and use them as models for their own behaviour.

It has been argued that this is how children learn social behaviour from parents, older siblings and valued peers. That is, they learn about the behaviour vicariously – without actually experiencing it themselves. That is why antidrug campaigners are so keen to present models who just say 'no', and it is a crucial aspect of any public health campaign on issues such as drug abuse, drunken driving, unsafe sexual behaviour and so on.[22]

In commercial advertising models are, and always have been, widely used in a positive sense to demonstrate new products and the rewards that come with using them. Hence the traditional 'housewife' advertisements that present ecstatic women with shining, manageable hair as a result of using Grungeoff floor cleaner or feeding their cute children on Doggomeat. Indeed this use of modelling has become so hackneyed that there is now a whole genre of advertisements based on mocking them – the Barr's Irn Bru soft drink for instance – while still using a desirable model to sell the product. One Irn Bru advertisement depicts an attractive middle-aged woman with an unattractive teenager. The woman is saying, 'Barr's Irn Bru keeps me young and beautiful, unlike my daughter'.

■ Further Reading

Anderson J. R., *Cognitive Psychology And Its Implications* (New York: W. H. Freeman, 1985). A thorough account of cognitive processes, including information processing, and their links with everyday behaviour.

Bandura, A., *Principles of Behavior Modification* (New York: Holt, Rinehart & Winston, 1969). A leading social psychologist's account of how and why human behaviour can be shaped.

Mackintosh, N. J., *Conditioning and Associative Learning* (New York: Oxford University Press, 1983). An exposition of the links between the conditioning process and cognitive learning theory.

Robertson, T. and H. H. Kassarjian (eds), *Handbook of Consumer Behavior* (Englewood Cliffs, NJ: Prentice-Hall, 1991). The authoritative source of concepts and theories of consumer behaviour. The 1991 edition contains some useful articles on the application of conditioning and other learning theories.

It is also worth browsing through the latest issues of the following periodicals: *Advances in Consumer Research, Journal of Consumer Research, Journal of Marketing, Journal of Marketing Research, Journal of Advertising Research.*

■ Questions for Discussion

1. Why is learning so important to the understanding of consumer behaviour? What are the two major forms of learning theory?
2. Which of the three major types of learning we have discussed (classical conditioning, operant conditioning or cognitive learning) could best explain the following purchases: (a) chewing gum, (b) low-tar cigarettes, (c) designer jeans?
3. How are stimulus generalization and stimulus discrimination used by marketers?
4. How would an advertising strategy relate to (a) sensory memory, (b) short-term memory, (c) long-term memory?
5. When might an advertiser aim a message at the process of recall rather than at recognition, and vice versa?
6. What is the importance of (a) repetition and (b) visuals in an advertiser's attempt to make a message meaningful to an audience?

CHAPTER 7
Motivation

Introduction

Why do people buy what they buy?

We have encountered the concept of motivation more than once in this book:

- In Chapter 6 (Learning) we discussed the role of motivation in learning, remembering and forgetting. We saw that people might be motivated, unconsciously, to forget a certain brand name if it was associated in their mind with an unpleasant experience. We also saw that it is more usual for people to be motivated to remember information and that this is important for successful learning.
- In Chapter 5 (Personality) we discussed the work of Ernest Dichter, the founder of 'motivational research', a system of interpreting consumer behaviour in terms of Freudian psychoanalysis. This system, which places great importance on a consumer's unconscious reasons for buying a product, will be explored in greater detail in this chapter.
- In Chapter 2 (Market Segmentation) we noted the importance of individual motivation in the way an individual consumer structures his or her lifestyle, and how market researchers have developed psychological techniques to tap into this process.
- We will also encounter the concept of motivation later in this book, perhaps most notably in Chapter 13 (Attitudes). It is in fact difficult to overstate its importance for a psychological approach to understanding the consumer.

What is Meant by Motivation?

Motivation asks the key question 'Why?' about human behaviour. A small word, perhaps, but an enormous question. 'Why did he put his foot through the television screen?' 'Why did she run off with her brother-in-law?' 'Why do they prefer McDonald's hamburgers to Grease Boy Burgers?' 'Why do more people buy Coca Cola than any other soft drink?' 'Why are you reading this book?'

Very few answers to 'Why?' questions are simple, straightforward or singular. Even the last question in the preceding paragraph could have more than one answer. You might say 'I'm reading this book because I need to know what's in it to pass the exam' (highly likely). But you might also say 'I picked it up in the bookstore/library and found it so fascinating and well written that I just couldn't put it down' (wildly improbable, though a theoretical possibility). Or your reply might combine more than one factor: 'I needed a book on consumer behaviour and this is the shortest one I could find'. No one observing your behaviour could know for sure why you are reading this book.

You will recall that when we discussed personality issues in Chapter 5, I pointed out the following. Both the psychologist and the layman use the term 'personality' to make sense of an individual's behaviour; after all behaviour is all we have to go on. We can never know for sure why people have acted in a certain way; all we can do is observe their behaviour and infer what inner processes motivated them to do it. And this is just as true of psychologists as it is of anyone else.

In this chapter we will concentrate on trying to understand that inferential process – which we usually refer to under the broad description of 'motivation' – to help us make better sense of consumer behaviour.

■ Defining Motivation

The Penguin *Dictionary of Psychology* describes motivation as an 'extremely important but definitionally elusive term'.[1] Having attempted to define he term myself I can assure you that this is no cop-out. What I finally decided on was the following: 'a general term for any part of the hypothetical psychological process which involves the experiencing of needs and drives, and the behaviour that leads to the goal which satisfies them'.[2] You can see what they mean by 'definitionally elusive', can't you?

The key words in this definition are 'needs', 'drives', 'goal' and 'satisfies', and we will return to them as we surround the topic and close in on it. We can say here though that any behaviour whose object is to reach a particular goal is motivated behaviour. That's an awful lot of behaviour and it includes, of course, consumer behaviour, or why people buy what they buy.

A diagram may help clarify the place of motivation in buying behaviour. Figure 7.1 shows that a given instance of buying behaviour is the result of three factors multiplied by each other, the *ability* to buy something, the *opportunity* to buy it and the *motivation* (the wish, need, desire) to do so.

Figure 7.1 Motivation and buying behaviour

Let's say I ask someone to get me half a pound of caviar. Will she do it or not?

- *Ability.* Does she know what caviar is? Is she physically able to go and buy it?

If I'm asking an 85-year old housebound peasant woman, the answer to both questions is probably 'no'.

- *Opportunity.* Let's say my 85-year-old shopper is in robust health and grew up on the shores of the Caspian Sea, where the finest caviar comes from. The next issue to be dealt with is that of opportunity. Is there anywhere round here that sells the stuff? It just so happens that the local delicatessen is trying to move upmarket and has a special introductory offer on caviar this week.

- *Motivation.* So now my healthy 85-year-old shopper who knows all about caviar has a place to buy it. Will she get me the caviar or not? This brings us finally to the question of motivation. Why *should* she buy me the caviar? What wish, need or desire of hers would be fulfilled by doing so? Well if the woman had never seen me before the answer is probably 'none'. But what if I offered her a thousand dollars and told her to keep the change? Or what if she was my mother, who liked nothing better than to see her children enjoying their food? Either of these situations might provide her with a sufficient incentive to influence her buying behaviour, one of them (the relationship) *internal* and the other (the money) *external*, as Figure 7.2 demonstrates. The need (or wish or desire) to buy the caviar is triggered by the incentive of either love or money and either will lead to the required behaviour.

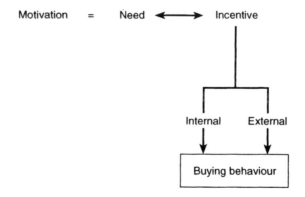

Figure 7.2   Components of motivation

However it is important for marketers to realise that, as Figure 7.1 points out, motivation is only one of the essential elements that contribute to buying behaviour. No amount of love or money could motivate the old lady to get me my caviar if she is housebound or there is no caviar to be had.

Similarly a lot of people may be highly motivated to attend your sale of men's clothing, but if you only open on weekdays until 5.00 pm you're not giving them much opportunity to act on their motivation. Or if you represent a supermarket that has heavily advertised a new product line, it's a good idea to ensure that all your outlets stock it – a simple but too often absent synchronization. Nor does it make much sense to advertise expensive products to people who don't have the money (ability) to pay for them, or cheap products in an out-of-town location to people who don't have a car in which to get them there.

■ The Fulfilment of Needs

There are several major theories of motivation, although the best known and most widely accepted among psychologists are ones that deal with the fulfilment of needs. Needs are often divided into *primary* biological or physiological needs ssuch as food, drink and shelter, and *secondary* psychological needs such as love or power. Primary needs must be satisfied before secondary needs, simply because of the overriding importance of survival. The brilliant young artist starving in a garret may be a romantic notion, but if he is truly starving he won't produce much art.

The need to eat can only be postponed for a limited amount of time, no matter how dedicated the artist, before the *physiological* drive that the feeling of hunger produces motivates food-seeking behaviour. Unless the hunger is sufficiently satisfied for the drive (and the tension that accompanies it) to be reduced it will take over the individual's life. Very few people reading this book will have experienced the hunger drive to that extent. We are able to reduce the tension long before it gets to the level of starvation. Nonetheless we need food and drink to survive in a way that we don't need power or achievement.

■ Maslow's Hierarchy of Needs

This common observation has given rise to various attempts at classifying human needs, the best known of which is that of Abraham Maslow.[3] Maslow was one of the founders of humanistic psychology, which he saw as a more positive and optimistic way of understanding the human condition than either behaviourism or psychoanalysis, whose basic approaches we have considered in previous chapters. He was most interested in the human potential for growth. He talked about five levels of need that form a loose hierarchy, as illustrated in Figure 7.3.

People strive to fulfil their needs, firstly at the most basic physiological level necessary for survival. When these needs are fulfilled they are no longer motivated by them, but other needs will always take their place that *are* motivating. These will be psychological needs for social acceptance and personal achievement. As people continue striving to have their needs fulfilled they arrive finally at the level of self-actualization. At this level they seek to express personality characteristics such as independence and autonomy, to strengthen and deepen personal relationships, and to maintain a sense of humour and a balanced view of life.

Maslow did not coin the term 'self-actualization' (that was done by a Gestalt theorist called Kurt Goldstein), but he did a great deal to popularise it. What Maslow meant by the term, in brief, was the need to actualize, or realize, all of

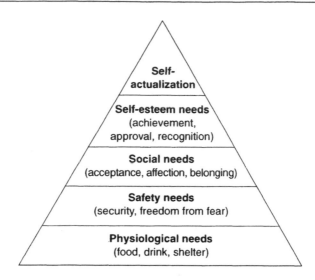

Figure 7.3 Maslow's hierarchy of needs

one's unique potential; to be all that one can be. In a sense this need can never be fulfilled, so that even people who have reached this level – and Maslow thought them to be a small minority of the population – will still have no shortage of motivation. The more self-actualized people become, the more they want to become. This is a motivation with its own inner dynamic.

Maslow did not intend these five levels to form a totally rigid hierarchy. Although lower-level needs are usually more easily satisfied, or satisfiable, than higher-level ones, more than one level of need can be experienced at the same time by the same person. Moreover people could have different priorities of needs, depending on how hungry they are for instance, and there are always people who are willing to make sacrifices for others and give up the chance to fulfil their own needs.[4]

■ Consumer Applications of Maslow's Hierarchy of Needs

Maslow suggested that people are influenced by higher-order needs even when all of their lower-order needs have not been entirely satisfied. It is as though, on average, our physiological needs are satisfied say 80 per cent of the time, and so on through the hierarchy, to having our need for self-actualization satisfied say 10 per cent of the time.[5]

What this implies for marketers is that virtually everyone is in the market, at some level, for the whole range of need satisfaction and that people may quite consciously trade off needs in some areas to spend more on other needs. Thus people might decide to spend as little as possible on housing (physiological) in order to release resources to spend on education (self-esteem or self-actualization).

Marketers have generally found Maslow's hierarchy, despite its lack of specifics, to be conceptually stimulating in their understanding of consumer motivation (at least in Western societies) and useful in practical terms as a framework for both marketing and advertising strategies. Specific products are often targeted at specific levels of need, for example:

- *Physiological*: housing, food, drink, clothing.
- *Safety*: insurance, burglar alarms, fire alarms, cars with air bags.
- *Self esteem*: luxury or high-status brands, goods or services (from reading the *Observer* or *New York Times* to owning the *Observer* or *New York Times*.
- *Social*: greetings cards, gifts, group holidays, team sports equipment.
- *Self-actualization*: educational services, skills, experiences (from learning Sanskrit to wilderness camping)

The element of consumer choice in satisfying all these needs, even the physiological ones, is of particular importance to marketing. I can satisfy my thirst with tap water so why should I choose a soft drink? And why Coke rather than Pepsi? It is also important to note that many products can be used to satisfy several different levels of need, for example a sweater, a car, a book or even a telephone.

It has more recently been suggested that Maslow's framework is a useful way of identifying 'emotional triggers' in consumers so that marketers can go beyond specific product benefits and appeal to the psychological needs they may be trying to satisfy.[6] You may recall that in Chapter 2 we discussed this issue under the heading 'psychological segmentation'. In that section we considered the *psychographic* or *life-style* approach that had resulted in consumer profiles concentrating on three areas of behaviour: activities, interests and opinions. This strategy is widely used in the positioning of products and the content of their advertising.

Both before and after Maslow's work, psychologists interested in specifying human needs have come up with long lists of them. As this is more a way of describing the issues than analyzing them I shall not burden you with such lists. What I would like to do instead is to consider how different needs relate to each other within individuals and to look a little more closely at a few needs that have been identified as being particularly important.

■ The Motivational Mix

■ Multiple Motives

If you see someone in a shopping mall and you ask 'Why are you here?', the immediate and obvious answer you will get is 'to buy things'. But if you followed this up with the question 'Why else are you here?' you might be met with a blank stare. Yet research has discovered that there are many other reasons why people visit shopping malls, some of which they may be aware of and others of which they may be quite unconscious.[7] Some of the reasons on this list may include the following:

- shopping gets you out of the house and breaks up the routine.
- shopping is a form of entertainment (and window shopping is free entertainment).
- shopping allows you to meet friends.
- shopping can make you feel important and needed as the household provider.
- shopping can also give you a sense of being important, and even powerful, when you are waited on by deferential and attentive assistants.
- shopping gives you the opportunity to exercise your hunting and bargaining skills, and success gives you a feeling of achievement.

■ Approach and Avoidance

Another important example has been identified where more than one motive may be operating in a given situation. This one was suggested in the 1930s by a psychologist of the Gestalt school called Kurt Lewin. Lewin is also known as 'the father of group dynamics' and we will deal with his work in that connection in Chapter 10.

Lewin suggested that motivational pressures can be either positive or negative in direction; that is, we may feel pressure to move (psychologically) towards a goal object – approach – or away from it – avoidance.[8] Conflict can arise in three situations where the motive strengths are about equal:

- *Approach–approach conflict:* this is a common form of conflict in which the consumer has to decide between two alternatives, both of which are equally desirable. For example whether to go on holiday to an exciting city or a quiet lakeside resort; whether to have chocolate fudge cake or lemon meringue pie for dessert.
- *Avoidance–avoidance conflict:* this is the opposite of the previous situation and much more unpleasant. The consumer has to decide between two alternatives, both of which are equally undesirable. Happily this form of conflict is also more rare than its opposite. By the nature of the conflict, though, people are tempted to put off making a decision because whichever alternative they choose will be unpleasant. The maintenance versus replacement of household items is a frequently quoted example. Thus your ancient vacuum cleaner is now held together by faith and sticky tape; getting it repaired will be expensive but buying a new one will cost twice as much. What do you do?
- *Approach-avoidance conflict:* in this fairly common situation the conflict is between positive and negative aspects, usually of a single product. The simplest such situation is when the price of a desirable item is only just affordable. Thus the positive aspect of owning the house or car of your

dreams is offset by the negative aspect of having to shell out a vast amount of money to get it.

You will recall that we dealt with the issue of perceived risk in Chapter 4, where we noted that consumers have devised various ways of dealing with the risks of making a bad purchase decision in terms of finance, performance, social esteem and so on. We noted there that relying on brand loyalty was the most popular strategy for reducing perceived risk. There is clearly room here for marketers to help prospective customers part with their money by emphasizing the 'approach' aspect of the sale. In addition they can always reduce the 'avoidance' by reducing the price, and this is the goal of having sales, discounts, interest free credit, part exchanges and so forth.

■ The Force of Inertia

In focusing on the motivational force of both approach to and avoidance of a goal we may lose sight of the fact that this force has to be strong enough to move people *at all*, let alone in a particular direction. Unless we are actively seeking certain products we will follow our established buying habits which, like any other habits, will have been learned over a period of time and become part of our life.

As we saw in Chapter 6, changing habits that have been well learned, and appear to serve us well, requires a great deal of effort. It will therefore take a lot of persuasion for us to overcome the force of inertia. So powerful is this force that even clear appeals to our self-interest, and indeed personal safety, may not be enough to overcome it.

Defective Ford Pinto cars and Firestone tyres in the United States were recalled by the companies concerned and repairs and replacements were offered free of charge. After two years of heavy publicity by the companies, over one third of the defective cars and over half of the tyres were still on the road, despite the fact that the defects were potentially lethal.[9]

■ Involvement

The concept of 'involvement' was first suggested by Herbert Krugman in the 1960s and has since been of considerable interest to specialists in consumer motivation.[10] It is essentially concerned with the *relationship* that a consumer has with a product. As such it refers to the personal importance that a given product in a given situation has for a particular individual. What does it do for the needs and values that are the behavioural expression of his or her self-image? The greater the involvement of the individual with the product and its perceived benefits, the more motivated he or she is to buy it. It is therefore crucially important to realise that in the following discussion of involvement it is the way the individual consumer *makes sense* of the product, the situation and so on that is the key.

There has been a great deal of research on involvement and this is usually discussed under the headings 'antecedents', 'properties' and 'outcomes of involvement'.

These are the factors that precede involvement and determine its extent. They are usually divided into person, product and situation.

- *Person.* This set of factors is concerned most directly with the consumer's self-image, and the needs, drives, values, interests, wishes and fantasies that can be translated into buying behaviour. People who have a close and intimate relationship with their cars, for instance, are likely to take part in car rallies, watch motor racing and buy appropriate magazines, thus demonstrating high involvement. People with low involvement on the other hand will simply regard cars as a means of transport.[11]
- *Product.* People react to the same product in different ways. It is therefore consumers' *perception* of the product, combined with the personal factors just described, that affects their level of involvement. Level of involvement increases, for instance, the greater the differential the consumer perceives between products.[12] That is, the less generic and the more specific a product is, the more scope there is for the consumer to establish a relationship with it. Involvement also increases with the amount of risk the consumer perceives to be involved in the purchase.[13] We dealt with the various kinds of risk consumers might encounter earlier in this chapter and more extensively in Chapter 4. As in any relationship the risks, and of course the rewards, are going to be much greater than those found in a more casual connection.
- *Situation.* A consumer's level of involvement can also be influenced by the situation in which a product is being purchased, for example purchasing a gift as opposed to buying something for one's own use.[14] A gift usually implies a relationship with another person, and so what might be a mundane purchase (such as chocolates or flowers) becomes imbued with some significance, and hence involvement, if you have somebody else in mind when you buy it. Moreover the level of involvement and the quality of the product chosen can change in that kind of situation. Thus people tend to buy different wine for dinner guests than they do for themselves.[15]

These properties refer to the feelings that the consumer experiences and the behaviour exhibited when his or her sense of involvement is aroused. Consumers who are highly involved will spend a great deal of time and effort on making purchase decisions. They will seek out as much information as possible on different brands, models and so on, and will pay particular attention to relevant advertising.[16]

They will also tend to process this information both thoroughly and critically and they will be swayed more by the content of the argument than the style in which a particular message is conveyed. That is, they are actively engaged, as opposed to people with low involvement who are more passive recipients of information. This is an issue that we will return to from a different angle in Chapter 14. Different media appear to have different properties of involvement in advertising.[17] Television, as a passive medium, usually requires a low level of involvement and does not encourage the processing of information. Print advertisements, on the other hand, demand closer attention and more effort in processing content, and therefore a higher level of involvement.

☐ *Outcomes of Involvement*

The outcomes of involvement will depend, of course, on the interaction between the preceding two sets of factors. The passive processing of information mentioned in the last paragraph leads to passive consumers who allow television and other advertising to wash over them, largely without registering the ads in their consciousness. Brand names will therefore have a hard time entering the awareness of consumers with low involvement, even after repeated exposures.[18] Relationships will not be formed with specific brands and differentiation between brands will scarcely exist.

On the other hand mere exposure to a sufficiently heavily advertised brand, as we saw in Chapter 4, may be enough to get a consumer with low involvement to buy the product if he or she has not formed a relationship with any of the competing brands. The problem for the marketer is that for many purchase situations many consumers have little motivation to learn about and evaluate alternative products and brands – but that doesn't stop them from buying things.

Various attempts have been made to devise scales of involvement for different products. One important research project, carried out in France, considered fourteen products spanning the range of consumer goods from toiletries to television sets. The research looked at several dimensions of each product, for example the purchase risk involved and the psychological significance of the product. They found that dresses rated highest for involvement and detergents lowest.[19]

We will return to the issue of consumer involvement in the context of advertising and persuasion attempts by marketers in Chapter 14 (Communication and Persuasion).

■ Specific Needs

We will end this part of the chapter by looking at three specific needs that have been abstracted for study from the motivational mix. Each of these needs is considered to be of particular importance in our society: the need for *achievement*, *affiliation* and *power*. All of these have great implications for consumer behaviour and are relevant to vast areas of marketing.

☐ *The Need for Achievement*

The need for achievement is probably the best known of these three specific needs. It was one of twenty needs motivating behaviour suggested by Henry Murray[20], who developed the Thematic Apperception Test (TAT) (discussed in Chapter 5) as a way of gauging the strength of these needs. David McClelland then used the TAT to concentrate on the need for achievement (which he labelled n Ach), and tried to find both historical and cross-cultural evidence for its collective importance to societies.[21]

People high on n Ach, McClelland maintained, have a preference for particular situations, where:

- the degree of risk involved is neither high nor low but moderate;
- feedback on their performance is provided;
- individual responsibility is acknowledged.

Moderately risky tasks would provide a reasonable probability of success for people high on n Ach whereas low-risk situations would be unchallenging and unlikely to engage their interest. However tasks that look too daunting would also be avoided for *fear of failure.* Thus it is not making the attempt that counts, but the outcome. Failure would apparently be too damaging to self-esteem, regardless of the worth and importance of the goal.

A sense of personal accomplishment is crucial to people with high n Ach and this would place them in the self-esteem or self-actualization categories in Maslow's hierarchy (see Figure 7.3). One of McClelland's major findings was that people in the sales and marketing departments of companies have more of this need than people in engineering, finance or production. So you might expect marketers to have an inbuilt advantage when aiming at this market! We would expect this market to be particularly receptive to innovative goods and services, unusual (though not wild) holidays and financial products that contain a moderate degree of risk.

☐ *The Need for Affiliation*

The need for affiliation would be placed lower than the need for achievement in Maslow's hierarchy – in the category of social needs (see Figure 7.3). This need is characterized by the particular importance to the individual of love and acceptance, and the feeling of belonging to key groups such as family, peers, sports teams and so on. Most teenagers are obvious targets for an appeal to this need because of the life situation they are in, struggling to establish an identity of their own and heavily influenced by the judgements, values and interests of their peer groups. The Coke and Pepsi advertisements are classic appeals to this need.

However the enormous area of romantic love is relevant to the need for affiliation, including 'sex appeal', which we will look at in more detail in Chapter 14. Magazines aimed at young men and women are perhaps the most systematic carriers of advertisements that tailor their appeal to this need (almost regardless of product). But our entire society is saturated with messages that address some aspect of the need for affiliation, from the necessity of ensuring you have loving pets and children by giving them Whiskas or baked beans, to the importance of selecting a retirement home in the right location.

☐ *The Need for Power*

The need for power would be placed at an even more basic level of Maslow's hierarchy than either of the other two needs – at the level of safety. That is, people who have much of this need seek a feeling of security by trying to control as many elements of their lives and their environment as possible, including other people. Successful managers in companies, for instance, tend to have a relatively large need for power and little need for affiliation.[22] Powerful cars, computers and other machines would be particularly relevant in appealing to this need.

■ Unconscious Motivation

We have seen at various points in previous chapters how much of our psychological life we are unaware of: the way we perceive the world, the way we learn, the way we make sense of our own personality and that of other people. But no aspect of our life contains more that may be hidden from us than our motivation. There are times when we literally do not know why we did something (buying that ugly terracotta sculpture comes quickly to mind). We usually try to think up plausible reasons (I thought it would go nicely with the ugly terracotta sculpture we've already got), but they will simply be ways of justifying our behaviour.

We owe most of our understanding of the unconscious and how it works to Sigmund Freud, of course, whose work was summarized briefly in Chapter 5. You might find it helpful to reread that section and refresh your memory before we consider how psychologists have tried to apply this work to the study of consumer motivation.

■ Motivational Research

The most direct application of Freudian theory came in the 1950s with the work of Ernest Dichter, a Viennese psychoanalyst who settled in the United States and founded the Institute for Motivational Research.[23] The term 'motivational research' is restricted to the workings of unconscious consumer motivation.

Up to that point twentieth-century advertising research and marketing strategy had been largely dominated by the behaviourist orientation of stimulus–response that we have come across several times already in this book. In

Chapter 6 particularly, we noted the importance of the first theorist of behaviourism, J. B. Watson, and how he later imported his ideas and techniques into the world of advertising through a highly successful career with the J. Walter Thompson company.

That was in the 1920s, and by the 1950s the fads and fashions that occur in consumer psychology as in everything else were ready to swing away from behaviourism towards psychoanalysis. Soon no self-respecting advertising or market research agency was complete without its in-house analyst, whose job it was to get at the deep and hidden motivation of consumer respondents.

Ernest Dichter was the major spokesman for this approach and quite a few of his interpretations about the meaning of common products have passed into the folklore of consumer behaviour. We have already encountered the idea that a convertible car for a man could have the same unconscious function as having a mistress. Here are a few other juicy interpretations:[24]

- When a woman bakes a cake and pulls it out of the oven she is (unconsciously and symbolically) going through the process of giving birth.
- Men who prefer to hold their trousers up with braces (suspenders in the US) are dealing with their anxiety about castration.
- Ice cream taps into unconscious feelings of love and affection for many people because it symbolizes an abundant and nurturing mother.

This approach to consumer motivation generated a great deal of interest among advertisers and marketers and informed a lot of the agency work of the 1950s and early 1960s. However, as noted in our discussion of personality tests and projective techniques in Chapter 5, these ideas and methods of interpretation, and the individual in-depth interviews used when generating them, were originally devised for quite a different purpose.

Freud and his colleagues developed and used these tools to help them understand and treat emotionally disturbed people. Moreover they emerged over a period of years in a context of trust between patient and analyst and in a situation where the patient wanted help and the analyst knew a great deal about his or her life and background. None of these things are true of motivational research. Finally there was the sheer practical difficulty that agencies had in turning these interesting interpretations into advertising copy or marketing strategy, especially when the interpretations they were offered were often the views of a single researcher.

Not surprisingly, then, motivational research went into something of a decline from the late 1960s onwards, though it was always a fertile source of stimulation for some agencies. But the pendulum of fashion never stops and by the late 1980s it had swung back in Dichter's direction.[25] Leading agencies such as Ogilvy and Mather and D'Arcy Masius Benton and Bowles are once more doing motivational research for major companies such as Chrysler, Colgate-Palmolive, American Express and Visa.

This more recent use of motivational research is probably a little more sophisticated than it was in the 1950s. Ideas that emerge in the course of *qualitative* work with small groups, or in-depth interviews with individuals, are often passed on to *quantitative* market researchers for incorporation into large-scale surveys. And by using this approach it is sometimes possible to identify accurately the real reasons behind some consumer behaviour.

One striking example of this concerns the sales of a cockroach killer in the United States. This product, called Combat, was contained in a small plastic tray that enabled cockroaches to be killed in a cleaner and more efficient way than the traditional spray cans. Yet it was not selling well to an obvious target market: women living in poor areas of the South, who retained their preference for sprays. McCann-Erickson, the agency commissioned for this project, devised a projective technique where a sample group of these women were asked to draw the cockroaches and say what they felt about them.

The researchers were intrigued to discover that all the insects were drawn as males. And the stories that accompanied the drawings were clearly about the men in these women's lives. Thus 'killing the roaches with a bug spray and watching them squirm and die allowed the women to express their hostility toward men', and it also afforded them a feeling of power and control over their immediate environment.[26] How could a bit of plastic compete with something as therapeutic as that?

■ Creating Needs

This study also helps provide an answer to that ancient question about marketing: 'can needs be created?' Here an important consumer need was being met that the manufacturer of the product, its marketers and advertisers were *totally unaware of.* The consumers decided for themselves that the psychological satisfaction obtained from using the cockroach spray was more important to them than the need for a cleaner and more efficient product.

The fear that people express of having needs created for them is reminiscent of the concern about subliminal research discussed in Chapter 4. You may recall that my conclusion about that argument was that while there may well be some influence on us through subliminal perception, the effects are probably not very great or very specific. That is also my conclusion on the creation-of-needs argument. There is no evidence whatsoever that anyone can *create* a need in a consumer.

What marketing and advertising *can* do is try to stimulate an existing need, or channel it in a certain direction towards one product or brand rather than another; but the results are still pretty unpredictable. As we saw in the cockroach spray example, and in many of the other areas of consumer behaviour we have dealt with, the consumer is never a totally passive recipient of manipulation by clever people. Companies may not always believe this however. Ernest Dichter was held responsible for just such manipulation in the 1950s.[27] After his work was attacked he received a lot of telephone calls from business people, who said 'What you're doing is terrible: How much does it cost?'[28]

■ Semiotics

Current work in the area of motivational research makes use of a recently developed field of study called *semiotics* (or sometimes semiology). Semiotics is concerned with the meanings that signs and symbols have for people, both consciously and unconsciously. Though we are not usually aware of it we live in a world full of signs and symbols and we use them all the time.

Think of the meaning associated with a country's flag, for instance. What do trainers or portable telephones symbolize to you? Rituals associated with eating are among the most basic areas of everyday life where symbolism plays an important part. Think of a formal dinner party, for example, where people wear special clothes, bring a gift (often a bottle of wine) for the host or hostess, use special implements (fish knives, grapefruit spoons), have several courses in a particular order and so on. All this elaborate behaviour is built upon the simple and universal need to reduce hunger tension. Such ritual symbolism varies from one culture to another of course, as Western business people discover in Japan or Saudi Arabia.

All these symbols and situations are regularly used in advertising to convey a great deal more content – especially emotional content – than is put into words. Drambuie liqueur, for instance, is not shown in the setting of Sunday lunch with the family but as the accompaniment to a fancy dinner party in a tropical location.

Recent research has focused on small-scale and concrete symbols, particularly animal symbols such as penguins (the cool but friendly inhabitants of Diet Coke advertisements, among others) and teddy bears, which have been the subject of at least one celebrated study. In the 1980s Lever Brothers marketed a highly successful fabric softener with the aid of a teddy bear called Snuggle. The company employed a psychologist to analyze Snuggle's appeal to the consumer and she told them: The bear is an ancient symbol of aggression; but when you create a teddy bear, you provide a softer, nurturant side to that aggression. As a symbol of tamed aggression, the teddy bear is the perfect image for a fabric softener that tames the rough texture of clothing.[29]

Because symbolism is by its very nature non-verbal it makes psychological interpretation – which is never easy – particularly difficult. We can, after all, only make an educated guess about what a symbol means to an individual consumer. Moreover, even when the psychologist is fairly sure about the subjective meaning of the symbol for someone, the marketer and the advertiser may not be able to do much with the information. We will end this chapter with an example from Ernest Dichter's own work in the 1960s.[30]

Dichter was asked by the California Sunsweet Growers Association to investigate the declining sale of prunes. Why did fewer people like them? What Dichter found was that a lot of people in America *did* like prunes, or at least the taste of them. But what many people found off-putting was the prune as a *symbol,* and what the prune symbolized to them was the following:

- *Old age and waning vitality:* prunes were an old person's food – they even looked old and shrivelled!
- *Health problems:* the prune was a laxative for people (often old) with digestive or other problems and was also used by faddists obsessed with their health.
- *Parental discipline:* prunes were something your parents made you eat because they were good for you, not something you would choose for yourself.
- *Low prestige:* prunes lacked class. They might be good for you but you wouldn't offer them to others. They were not something you'd want the neighbours to catch you eating.

The difficulty for the marketers was that the consumers seemed to have a pretty clear idea of the product's characteristics and the kind of people who used it and when. This very clarity made the prune a potent symbol to consumers and crystallized their unfavourable feelings about it. After more than 30 years of trying, prune marketers have still not been able to overcome the symbolism of the product.

■ Further Reading

Hirschman, E. C. (ed.), *Interpretive Consumer Research* (Provo, Utah: Association for Consumer Research, 1989). An authoritative review of the important 'interpretive' approach to consumer behaviour emphasizing subjective aspects of consumption and the consumer's motivation.

Olson, J. and K. Sentis (eds), *Advertising and Consumer Psychology* (New York: Praeger, 1986). A good selection of articles dealing with key topics raised in this and other chapters.

Piirto, R., *Beyond Mind Games: The Marketing Power of Psychographics* (Ithaca, NY: American Demographics Books, 1991). The leading authority on the practical applications of psychographics.

Robertson, T. and H. Kassarjian (eds), *Handbook of Consumer Behavior* (Englewood Cliffs, NJ: Prentice-Hall, 1991). The authoritative account of the most important concepts used in research on consumer behaviour. The 1991 edition has some particularly useful articles on motivation.

It is also worth browsing through the latest issues of the following periodicals: *Advances in Consumer Research, Journal of Consumer Research, Journal of Marketing, Journal of Marketing Research*.

■ Questions for Discussion

1. Why is motivation so important to the understanding of consumer behaviour? What are its marketing implications? What factors can override motivation when a purchase is being made?

2. What makes up Maslow's 'hierarchy of needs'? Name three products that might appeal to more than one level at the same time.
3. Why is the subjective perception of the consumer so important to the concept of 'involvement'? Develop a high-involvement scenario and a low-involvement scenario and suggest appropriate marketing strategies for them.
4. What problems does unconscious motivation pose for marketers? How does motivational research try to deal with them? How successful has it been?
5. Are people right to worry that consumer needs can be created by marketers? Why/why not?
6. What is 'semiotics' and how does it relate to motivation?

PART III
The Social Perspective

■ Introduction

In Part III we will focus on all the societal influences that impinge upon the individual consumer we studied in Part II.

We will examine the effects of our family upbringing in Chapter 8 and the effects of school in Chapter 9. In Chapter 10 we will analyse the workings of the small groups to which we all belong and which link us to the wider society. Chapters 11 and 12 are concerned with the effects of membership of wider groups: those of social class and culture. Finally, in Chapter 13 we will look at how the attitudes we acquire from all these social groups towards products are formed and how they change.

CHAPTER 8

Family Influences

The family is a nursery, a school, a hospital, a leisure centre, a place of refuge and a place of rest. It encompasses the whole of society. It fashions our beliefs. It is the preparation for the rest of our life (Margaret Thatcher).[1]

If a family is a factory for turning out children then it is lacking in the most elementary safety precautions. There are no guard rails round that dangerous engine the father. There are no safeguards against being scalded by the burning affection of the mother. No mask is proof against the suffocating atmosphere. One should not be surprised that so many lose their balance and are mangled in the machinery of love (Alan Bennett).[2]

■ Introduction

How does our upbringing affect us as consumers?

Above are two contrasting views of the family. Margaret Thatcher's view is largely a social one, in keeping with her belief that 'there is no such thing as society, only individuals and their families'. The view of Alan Bennett, the playwright, is a psychological one in that he is concerned with *relationships* between family members. Both of these eloquently expressed viewpoints contain essential truths about the family, and both are, of course, only partial views (in both senses of the word).

Alan Bennett is concerned with the emotional power that is generated in families and how dangerous that can be – a staple source of material for playwrights through the ages. It was the subject 'of Sophocles' play 'Oedipus Rex', which so inspired Freud, and of the greatest plays by another playwright Freud greatly admired, Shakespeare. Think of what 'Hamlet' and 'King Lear' are about for instance. But of course what playwrights are less interested in (because it lacks drama) is the kind of family where the relationships are mutually supportive and loving.

Similarly, while it is possible for a family to perform all the functions that Margaret Thatcher claims for it, there are many that do not. While the family can be a place of refuge and a place of rest it is also the place where you are, statistically, most likely to be assaulted, raped or murdered, especially if you are female. As well as a nursery, a school, a hospital and a leisure centre, the family can also be a prison and a torture chamber.

However virtually all psychologists would agree with the last two sentences of

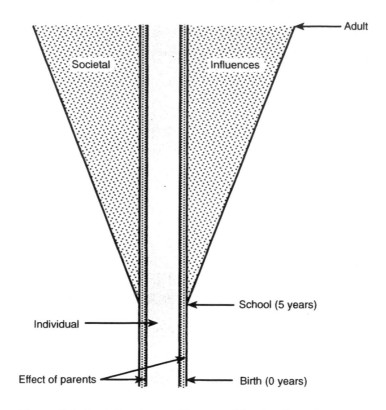

Figure 8.1 Socialization as illustrated by the Statt Cone

the Thatcher quotation: our beliefs are fashioned in the family when we are growing up and our experience of it affects us for the rest of our lives. Figure 8.1 illustrates how we carry our early influences into adult life.

As we saw in Chapter 5, childhood experiences are crucial to the formation of adult personalities. What happens in families seems to be of intrinsic interest to everyone, whether or not they've ever seen 'Hamlet' or 'Oedipus Rex'. The huge and abiding popularity of soap operas testifies to that. And we shouldn't forget that soap operas were given that name in the 1950s because they were seen as ideal vehicles for advertising soap powder (washing powder).

There have been some significant changes in families and family life since the 1950s, and these are partially mirrored by changes in the soap operas themselves. We will discuss these changes, and their marketing implications, later in the chapter. In all that follows, however, it is extremely important to understand that we are dealing with a psychological environment of the greatest complexity. When we try to isolate particular behaviours such as buying and consuming specific products, and ask what effects family relationships have on them, we are attempting something very difficult indeed. Often we will oversimplify our interpretation. Sometimes we won't have the vaguest idea.

■ What is a Family?

The answer to this question is not quite as obvious as it seems.   Until fairly recently though a visiting Martian could have answered it easily by looking at our advertising: a family is an attractive, smiling mother and father plus two cute children (one male, one female), plus a friendly dog, all living in a large house – the McTypicals. If this type of family was ever 'typical' in any sense outside a television studio it is no longer. In the United States today it would represent no more than a quarter of all families. Yet the stereotype dies hard and it can still influence our view of what a family is *supposed* to be – and therefore what it is supposed to consume.

■ Definitions

The most common definition of a family in Western society is that it is 'a group of two or more people living together who may be related by blood, marriage, or adoption'. So two sisters are just as much a family as the McTypicals.

Families may also be *nuclear*, consisting of a husband and wife plus one or more children (that is, the McTypicals), or *extended* (the McTypicals plus). An extended family may extend over time (to include grandparents) or (psychological) space (to include relatives such as cousins and in-laws whose links are a little more distant from the nuclear core). The family one is born into is known as the *family of origin* (or orientation). The family one helps create by reproduction is the *family of procreation*.

Because the family is also a social group – indeed the prototypical social group in any society – two other defining terms should be mentioned, *primary group* and *reference group*. Every family is a primary group because of the face-to-face interaction that takes place between its members on a regular and continuing basis. Families can also be reference groups, up to a point, as long as members refer to family values and ways of behaving as a guide to their own decisions and action (see Figure 8.1).

Whatever constituents a family has, the family as a group is of great importance to the marketer. That is, apart from the effects that our family of origin has on our individual consumer behaviour, the family as a buying organization exercises enormous economic influence. That is why marketers have a vested interest in understanding and supporting the concept of the family. For example the Christmas festive season, the prime time for family buying and consumption, accounts for over half of all sales and profits in the United States.[3]

■ Changes in the Family

The extended family is now quite rare in Western countries, and where it still exists it is usually to be found in ethnic subcultures. In many Eastern and Middle Eastern countries, however, it is still a very important part of society and the marketing strategies that are used to target Western families would be quite inappropriate there. The decline of the extended family in the West was due mainly to large-scale economic changes that led to geographical mobility as people (especially young people) left their home communities in search of work and a higher material standard of living.

There have also been changes within the nuclear family in the past 20–30 years due to economic factors. The McTypicals had a father who worked full-time and a mother who was a full-time housewife. There have been changes in the position of each parent. Full-time employment for men is much more pre-carious than it was a generation ago, with many men losing their jobs or being forced into early retirement.

Many more women have come into the workforce during that time, and in most Western countries there are now roughly as many women as men in paid employment. It is now very rare, therefore, for the man to be the sole bread-winner in a family and most women now have their own source of income, even if it is usually less than their man's.

The rate of divorce has also increased greatly over this period of time, with almost half of all Western marriages now ending in divorce. This has meant a great increase in the number of single parent (usually female) families. Marriage is still a popular institution however – the vast majority of the population will try it at some point in their lives – and many divorced people remarry, often to become stepparents.

■ Households

The term 'household' is often used in the same context as 'family' in discussions of consumer behaviour. They don't mean quite the same thing however. A household refers to all those, whether related to each other or not, who occupy the same unit of housing, be it a room or a castle. That is, a household is based on *where* people live rather than with whom. This makes it a more inclusive term than family, covering nearly all the population. The only people not in a house-hold are those who live in institutions, for instance soldiers in military barracks, monks in monasteries and patients in mental institutions.

There is, of course, a considerable overlap between families and households. In Western countries families will typically form over two thirds of all house-holds. But there is one very important group of non-family households: people who live alone. They now comprise about a quarter of all households and rep-resent a key segment of the population for many marketers.

The term 'household' is preferred by official statisticians, in census bureaux for example, though the focus of interest for some marketers is still the family (for example children's cereals). Often though, the terms are used inter-changeably, just as people move in to and out of family households throughout their lives as they leave home, live in a college dormitory, share a house with friends, get married and form a family household again, get divorced and live alone, remarry, and so on. Figure 8.2 illustrates this movement in the life of a given individual.

Family Household	Non-family Household	Non-Household
0–18 years (family of origin) 28–38 years (family of procreation) 43–78 years (stepparent)	22–28 years (sharing house) 38–43 years (divorced)	18–28 years (college) 78–85 years (nursing home)

Figure 8.2   Movement of an individual through households

■ Socialization

■ Childhood

Socialization is the process whereby an individual becomes a social being. Although it is a lifelong process it is considered particularly important in childhood when society is represented by, and through, a child's parents, as well as the rest of his or her family (see Figure 8.1). Socialization is therefore the way in which an individual child becomes an adult person and a functioning member of his or her society.

The term 'socialization' is sometimes used as though it describes something that is done to people without their consent or participation. We talk of people 'being socialized' into society but never of people 'socializing themselves' into society. In fact however socialization is very much a two-way process. People influence their social world and are influenced by it from birth onwards. We separate the two forms of influence artificially to enable us to study each more closely, but in real life they are closely interwoven.

Psychologists have observed for example that some newborn infants are more active than others. This simple difference means that people will react to them differently, and have different expectations of their future behaviour. The infant will in turn react to their reactions and the process of socialization – and the construction of personality – will have begun. In a very real sense children can socialize their parents just as parents socialize their children. Each can influence and even manipulate the other's behaviour.[4]

■ The Effect of Institutions

As we shall see in the next few chapters, we all live our lives among groups of other people. Some of these groups are more important to us than others in our socialization. A few groups are important to everybody and are officially recognised as such by our society. What happens in these groups is crucial to the working and the future of our society, so it watches over them carefully, passes laws and creates regulations dealing with them, and thus turns them into *institutions*.

The institutions that have the most powerful influence on our socialization are the family, the school and the nation-state. Figure 8.1 illustrates the individual's progress towards being recognised as a fully adult member of his or her society, via these three institutions.

□ *Family*

Most children in our society, until they go to school, live their lives mainly within their family. Freud was not the first to argue that children's family experiences are crucial in determining their adult personalities, but he was certainly the most influential. Probably the great majority of modern psychologists would agree with him on this point, especially with regard to the influence of parents.

That is why in Figure 8.1 I have represented parental influence as two parallel lines that accompany the individual from birth onwards. In the first few years of life the behaviour of their parents is of paramount importance to children. They are all-powerful (no matter how benign). They always know the answers. They know what to do in every situation. And their way of dealing with the world becomes the children's way of dealing with the world.

As children grow up and increase their contacts outside the home they begin to put their parents and family within a wider social framework. They acquire a perspective on their family as they come into contact with other families and other models of behaviour. As they broaden their social horizons their parents become less and less of an immediate, daily, physical presence, and their influence is diluted by other social influences.

But in a psychological sense children's parents remain with them in some form for the rest of their lives, for they will have internalised what they have learned from them. And one of the things they will have learned is an image or model of what being a consumer means. So it should come as no surprise to us that in emotionally important areas such as food consumption, for instance, people may retain for the rest of their lives the eating habits and preferences they learned at the family dinner table – or in front of the family television set.

□ *School*

The next important institution that children meet links them to the education system. Our society requires its members to achieve certain academic skills – at least the ability to read, write and count – and we tend to regard this as being the function of school. This is obviously an essential part of the socialization process and nobody can be a fully accepted member of our society unless he or she has acquired these skills. But to a psychologist the school has a much more important task: it prepares children for their adult role in society.

In their family setting children are probably used to having someone around to whom they can turn for information or explanation about the world as it filters through to them, for example in the form of comic books or television. But in school they actually become part of the world and must deal with it alone. Play gradually gives way to work, and even play must be performed in a certain way at a certain time with other people.

This is children's first non-academic lesson in socialization: how to behave in an extremely complex mass society where everyone has to fit in, while being expected to maintain and develop their individuality at the same time, at least in Western societies. The teenage years in particular are where this dilemma achieves its most crucial form. You can see the expression of this in the way teenagers dress, expressing their desire to fit in by wearing jeans and T-shirts, and their individuality by the type of jeans and the particular rock group or football team emblazoned on the T-shirt.

Schools therefore reflect the values of the society around them and instruct their members in those values. As we are dealing here with the psychological processes of learning, these processes will operate regardless of the social desirability of the outcome. What some children may learn is that drugs are wonderful and people in authority are hypocrites, or that ever-increasing consumption is gross and immoral.

As children go through school the other children who accompany them from grade to grade (their peer group) will assume an ever-increasing importance to them, and eventually the opinions of their peers will influence them more than those of their parents.

☐ *Nation-state*

At a certain point in his or her life, society recognises that the individual has become a fully adult human being – socially. Psychologically, as we saw in Chapter 5, individuals of adult age may be at various stages of maturity in their development as persons. The official age of adulthood varies with time and place, as with the particular social behaviour we choose to look at, but certainly by the age of 21 people in our society are regarded as adults. They can now fulfil all aspects of citizenship, they may have entered the world of work, and they will certainly come into contact with the third key socializing institution, the nation-state.

The most important single fact about the way people on this planet are divided up socially is that virtually everyone is the citizen of a national government. The few people who are not have no social existence; they cannot travel (having no passport) nor do they have the right to live and work in any country. National governments are the only *legitimate* sources of social power in a given country (controlling the police and the army), with the ability to raise taxes and pass laws.

Individuals in their role as citizens come into contact with these social influences as taxpayers, voters, drivers, soldiers, buyers of alcohol and signers of all kinds of legal documents. These are all signs that the socialization process has achieved its purpose and produced adult social beings who are able to behave in the ways expected of them.

Different nation-states may produce different kinds of adult social beings. People are taxed, vote, drive, drink alcohol and fight under similar but different systems of values. These values in turn are reflected in different education systems and family patterns. In a federal system the state or province may be the appropriate authority for some of these roles.

There is some evidence that even nations with such similar institutions as the United States and Canada can produce people who regard the world, and their own place in it, in very different ways.[5] To a psychologist such differences are neither good nor bad, merely interesting. But whatever the effects that socializing institutions have on people, whatever kind of people they are meant to produce, they form the boundaries within which the psychological development of the person takes place, and they select from the vast range of psychological possibilities those aspects of behaviour that they consider most valuable.

The institutions of family, school and nation-state are all linked together, of course, and normally share the same social values and reinforce the same kinds of behaviour. Typically the basic ways of relating to the world that are laid down in the family are expanded upon and applied in school and elsewhere to actual forms of behaviour, behaviour which the individual then engages in as an adult. Increasingly, over the past two generations especially, the mass media of communication have become the nerves and sinews that link these institutions to each other and to the individual – something we will explore further in the next few chapters.

■ **Consumer Socialization**

In the last section we saw how important parents are in the general socialization of their children. That obviously includes their socialization as consumers. Parents don't do this by providing specific training as they might in road safety, for instance. They do it by going shopping with their children, known as *coshopping*, and they do it by acting as role models for their children.

Coshopping – usually mother plus child – has probably increased in recent years, partly because of the demographic changes caused by the falling birth rate in most rich countries. This has meant a greatly increased incidence of one-child families, where the child is more used to communicating with adults than children from larger families. Also, with more women working than ever before it has become a useful way of mother and child spending time together.

On these shopping trips children learn about such basic consumer skills as budgeting, pricing and choosing between different products and brands, as well as more complex skills such as getting value for money, how to choose an appropriate store and even how to decipher and evaluate advertising.[6] As we saw in the last section, socialization is a two-way process between adults and their children and children can exert considerable influence during coshopping trips, a factor of obvious interest to marketers.[7]

Parents also indirectly teach their children a lot about consumer behaviour simply by being *role models* for them. Sometimes this may involve a pivotal choice, such as when a young man about to start shaving decides to follow his father's example and use an electric shaver rather than a safety razor. A lifetime's use of shaving products may be decided right there. That kind of decision may be one of the last that a parent can influence, as teenagers usually look more to their peers than to their parents for role models.

By this age children may well become role models for their parents at times, particularly if the product in question did not exist during the parents' childhood socialization, for example VCRs, CDs and home computers. Teenage children may also be more aware of new trends in consumer behaviour and can influence their parents by virtue of their greater knowledge and awareness of the issues. Something like this seems to have happened with the environmental movement. In one recent American study one third of the parents sampled said they had changed their buying and consumer behaviour because of their children's influence.[8] In other words this is really a process of *adult socialization*.

However intergenerational influence doesn't stop there, because adult children can have an important influence on the buying and consuming decisions of their aged parents – who in retirement will find themselves in the final phase of consumer socialization as they adjust to a new lifestyle.[9] Consumer socialization is thus a very fluid and dynamic process and therefore difficult for marketers to get a direct handle on. There is a lot more to it than the cosy picture of brand loyalty being passed down through the generations.

And the process is even further complicated by the fact that not only do children and parents influence each other, but children – and certainly teenagers – are a major buying force in their own right. An interesting question in consumer socialization is what young consumers do with their pocket money and earnings, a topic to which we will return a number of times.

■ Family Buying Decisions

We have already seen several times in this book how difficult it is to find the specific causes of an individual's buying decisions. When dealing with the buying decision of a family (even a two-person family) the problem is vastly more complex. There is usually more than one person involved in the decision, or in influencing the person who makes it, and one decision may well be linked to another because of the relationships involved ('we bought him that expensive

Garbagini Whinger for his birthday so we have to give his sister more than a plastic Junior Bimbo set'). Finally, unlike the small groups we will consider in Chapter 10, it is very difficult to study the family group directly.

■ Family Roles

Marketers have traditionally regarded the woman of the family as having the dominant buying role or control of the 'purse strings', certainly as regards food, clothing and household purchases. It is indeed true that women still do most of the actual buying but they usually have other family members in mind when they do so.[10] It is this gap between buying behaviour and what it represents that we will concentrate on in this section.

Social scientists who study group behaviour have often divided the roles involved into two kinds: *instrumental* and *expressive*. The instrumental role is a functional one; that is, it is about getting the group's tasks done successfully, usually by providing material support and the authority of 'leadership'. It's what you would traditionally expect of Mr McTypical, whereas Mrs McTypical is expected to perform the expressive role, which is concerned with the emotional support of the group and the encouragement of its aesthetic expression.[11]

We will come across these two sets of roles again when we discuss small groups in Chapter 10. These roles and the dichotomy between husband and wife have been changing for about a generation, though our images of family buying behaviour still lag behind somewhat. Nor should we forget that the McTypicals are still a pretty large clan.[12]

There are many specific roles to be played in the course of a family purchasing decision, and they have been given a variety of names. The following are perhaps the most frequently used: initiator, influencer, decision maker, buyer, user and gatekeeper.

- *Initiator:* the person who first identifies a need or raises the idea to buy something.
- *Influencer:* a kind of family opinion leader who provides information and persuades the family about what to buy and why.
- *Decider:* a family member with the authority to make the buying decision by himself/herself.
- *Buyer:* the person who actually makes the purchase, whether in person, by mail, or on the telephone.
- *User:* whoever consumes the purchased product.
- *Gatekeeper:* the gatekeeper role is usually attached to one of the other five, particularly the initiator or buyer. The gatekeeper is concerned with controlling a buying decision by choosing whether or not to let crucial information through the 'gate'. For example a mother might choose not to mention to her teenage children that the Screams in the Night record shop is having a CD sale (initiator), or she might buy her husband a fat-free dessert from Tasteless Foods despite the fact that his favourite ice cream from OD Inc is back in stock again (buyer).

The role that family members adopt at any given time may also depend on which spouse is dominant and for which product. There are four possibilities here, based on the relative influence each perceives. Either (1) *husband* or (2) *wife* may be dominant, or an equal number of individual decisions may be made by each spouse, known as (3) *autonomic*, or (4) decisions may be *joint* (or syncratic).[13]

The most likely situation for a given product will depend on the nature of the product, the situation in which it is being considered and the particular stage in the decision-making process. Findings for specific products are as follows:[14]

- Husband dominant: lawn mowers, hardware.
- Wife dominant: women's and children's clothing, kitchenware, groceries.
- Autonomic: sports equipment, cameras, lamps, toys and games.
- Joint: holidays, television sets, refrigerators.

■ Resolving Conflicts

Any group of two or more people that has to make decisions continuously over many years is bound to have disagreements at some time. Different families will have a different number of disagreements of course. They will also differ in extent, from the most trivial difference of opinion to the most ferocious psychological (or even physical) conflict. We have already seen how families are the repositories of the deepest emotions; we will now consider the various strategies they may use in the face of conflict between members, particularly husband and wife.

There are perhaps four major strategies that families use, which I will label coercion, persuasion, bargaining and manipulation.[15]

- *Coercion*: this is invariably used by the husband. It can involve a wide variety of behaviour including:
    - expertise ('I know more about digitized widget blockers than you do');
    - authority ('I'm the head of this family and I demand respect');
    - threats ('If you don't agree to buy it I won't take you out to Grease Boy Burgers for a nice dinner');
    - punishment (thump).
- *Persuasion*: the use of reasoned argument, presented in a reasonable manner.
- *Bargaining*: this strategy is one of 'give and take' and involves the spouse making a concession in order to obtain a more desirable goal ('If I agree to see this play will you try that new Albanian restaurant?') Sometimes the concession required looks suspiciously like bribery ('If you'll try that new Albanian restaurant I'll pay for the meal').
- *Manipulation*: this is a purely psychological strategy that may be used by any family member. It can include sulking, hurt silence, the withdrawal of affection and so on in an attempt to pressure the other party into agreement. These strategies are, of course, a childish way of dealing with conflict. They are therefore deeply ingrained in someone's personality, fairly easily triggered, difficult to eradicate and often unconsciously used.

■ **Changing Roles**

While consumer decision-making conflicts of interest are very common to most families, it also seems that most families go to great lengths to avoid *open* conflict, especially when it comes to important decisions. A study of couples buying a house, for instance, found that they tended *not* to follow a rational and orderly approach to what is, after all, the most important purchase a couple can make. What people tended to do instead was described, appropriately enough, as 'muddling through'.

It was found that people were often unsure of their partner's preferences, or even their own, until the process of buying the house was underway. It was difficult, therefore, to bring any of the above strategies into play. That helped the couple focus on their feelings and the implications of the purchase as they gradually groped their way towards a joint decision.[16] It is hardly surprising that moving house is one of the most stressful things that people can do.

Recent research has suggested that the joint agonizing pattern found in house buying may be growing more common as family roles change. It has been argued that, with the shift towards greater social equality between the sexes, various areas of decision-making are becoming rather less husband- or wife-specific, with more and more areas of consumer decision making being up for discussion and negotiation.[17]

Many have also argued that, with as many women out working as men, the household chores and the products that go with them are one of these areas of consumer behaviour, and therefore of particular interest to marketers. Before we get carried away with this line of argument, however, I would like to inject a note of caution.

As recently as the early 1980s men in full-time employment usually saw their domestic contribution as merely *helping out* with the chores, even when their wife was also working full-time.[18] This attitude may well be changing though. In a recent British survey 91 per cent of men agreed with the proposition that 'when both partners work full-time, the man should take an equal share of the domestic chores'.

Is this not good evidence that New Man has really arrived and is busy weighing up the merits of the various toilet cleaners? Sorry. Although their *attitudes* may have changed, men's *behaviour* lags far behind: less than 20 per cent actually did the chores on an equal basis.[19] This striking discrepancy between expressed attitudes and actual behaviour – of crucial importance to marketers and advertisers – is an issue we will explore further in Chapter 13. In this context though we can single out one household situation where the gap has closed between men's attitudes and behaviour as regards domestic chores.

With so many women now earning, some of them will inevitably earn more than the men they live with, especially perhaps in the United States. It has been found there that women who earn more than their partner can translate this into an advantage in the domestic 'balance of power' by demanding – and usually receiving – more practical help and acceptance of responsibility from him.[20] Thus the behaviour of the men involved has changed not because their attitudes towards housework have changed (though they often have) but because the objective financial situation in the family household has changed and they have had to adapt to it, painful though it may have been.

■ Life Cycle Effects

A convenient and often-used way of summarising family effects on consumer behaviour is to trace the various stages in a family's life cycle. The concept of life cycle is a sociological one and is a way of looking at families from the outside, as it were, and placing them within their society. This external view is a useful contrast to the internal view of family relationships that has been our focus up to now.

Figure 8.3 gives us an overview of the family life cycle and its relation to the formation of households over time. It follows the individual lives of three generations of one family: G1, the grandfather, born in 1920, G2, the son, born in 1945, and G3, the granddaughter, born in 1970. The grandfathers' family of procreation is the son's family of origin, of course, and both are part of the one household. When the granddaughter is born the parents and grandparents decide to share one large household as an extended family. This ends when the grandparents move into a retirement home in 1980. Then in 1992 the grand-daughter leaves college and sets up home on her own, from which point each of the three generations has formed a separate household.

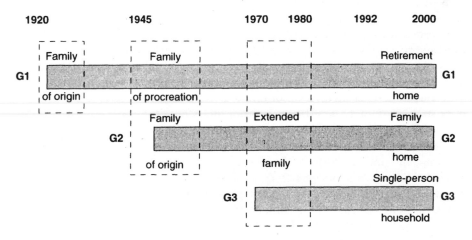

Figure 8.3 Households and the family cycle

Within this framework there are many ways of categorizing the different stages of a person's *consumer* life cycle. The most elaborate of these categorizations lists some 18 stages, though the authors concede that their long list has no more predictive value than the shorter ones from a previous generation.[21] It is the most widely accepted of these more traditional lists that we will use here:[22]

- *Bachelor*: unmarried person under 35.
- *Newly married*: under 35, no children.
- *Full nest I*: married, youngest child under 6.
- *Full nest II*: married, youngest child 6 –12.
- *Full nest III*: married, youngest child in teens.
- *Empty nest I*: married, children left home.
- *Empty nest II*: married, children left home, retired.
- *Solitary survivor*: widow(er), children left home, still working.
- *Retired solitary survivor*: as above, but retired.

■ Stage 1: Bachelor

People at this stage usually have relatively low incomes because they are just entering the world of work. But as they also have relatively few financial burdens, a relatively large part of their income is available for personal spending. This money will typically be spent on cars, entertainment, food, drink, travel, clothes and, in particular, audio-cassettes and records.[23]

■ Stage 2: Newly Married

Despite a growing trend for couples to live together without getting married the vast majority of people do so at some point in their lives. The current figure in the United States, for example is about 90 per cent. Moreover many marketers and advertisers have a vested interest in them continuing to do so, for marriage is a readily identifiable and important event. It is also an enormously lucrative industry, worth about $32 billion *a year* in the United States.[24]
This is sometimes called the 'honeymoon' stage because newly married young couples are often in a relatively good financial situation with two full-time incomes and no children. However, much of their income is transformed into outgoings because of the cost of setting up a new household. Apart from housing, the manufactures of furniture, appliances, kitchenware and so on all have newlyweds as a prime market, Nevertheless some disposable income is often left over, and the use of this income usually follows the bachelor spending pattern, though perhaps at a reduced level.

■ Stage 3: Full Nest I

This is the stage at which couples have their first child and it marks the end of the honeymoon phase of marriage. It has by far the largest number of people in it – about 25 per cent of the population. Not surprisingly this represents a major change in the pattern of consumer behaviour. Even today many young mothers stop working (or at least working full-time) outside the home and the resultant drop in income coincides with the hugely expensive new arrival.

A lot of the disposable income of previous stages is therefore lost, and in any event the opportunity to spend it is drastically curtailed by the demands of parenthood. And even if the opportunity remains the *pattern* of consumption may be different, for instance visits to junk food restaurants instead of real ones. The highest level of debt is incurred at this stage and it is the prime market for financial products such as insurance and investment plans. However the greatest outlay (at least in the United States) – far more than on any other item at any stage – is on milk and disposable nappies.[25]

■ Stage 4: Full Nest II

By this stage the family's youngest child is at least six years old and in school. As a consequence the mother has probably returned to paid employment, at least part-time, and the husband may be earning more. They therefore have a larger income and more of it may be disposable. Food is a heavy expense at this stage, and savings are often made by buying 'family' packs. A lot of income also goes directly on the children's interests in, for example, music (instruments and lessons) and sport (clothing and equipment).

■ Stage 5: Full Nest III

This is really a progression of the previous stage. The family finances continue to improve and there may even be contributions from teenage children, still living at home but on the lookout for their own sources of income. Patterns of expenditure are also similar to the previous stage except that, with wear and tear, the time has arrived to replace a lot of household durables, often with more expensive versions than the originals, which were probably purchased with relatively lower incomes. Extra items may also be considered at this stage, such as second (or third) cars, boats and new forms of home entertainment.

■ Stage 6: Empty Nest I

This stage may well be the most favourable financially for the couple. The children have grown up and left the nest, while the parents are still working and at the peak of their earnings. Necessary expenditure is relatively low and disposable income is at its highest level. The pattern of spending and consumption at this stage tends to become more luxurious in terms of travel, recreation and gifts. In recent years there seems to have been a trend for the nest to be occupied again by the occasional returning child, usually because of unemployment, separation or divorce.[26]

■ Stage 7: Empty Nest II

With retirement from the world of paid employment there is usually a fairly drastic fall in a couple's income. This is the point at which people may consider moving out of their family dwelling into a smaller retirement home, perhaps in a warmer climate. If they stay in the same place they usually curtail activities that take them out of the home. They are now a primary market for medical and health care goods and services.

■ Stage 8: Solitary Survivor

People enter this stage if their spouse dies and they are still in the world of paid employment. As well as the medical and health care products of the previous stage, their relatively high income keeps them in the market for luxury travel, recreation and gift giving.

■ Stage 9: Retired Solitary Survivor

Someone in this category has the same health needs as anyone else of their age, but with a greatly reduced income there will be little discretionary expenditure. Financial stringency may also lead to a general dwindling of life's pleasures, marked by insecurity and loneliness. This is not a category that gets marketers salivating.

■ Non-Family Households

Marketers have generally found the consumer life cycle helpful in segmenting target markets and predicting where high and low demands for their products are likely to be.[27] But this model doesn't cover non-family households. In Figure 8.3 we saw one common example of a non-family household, where the granddaughter lived on her own.

But the father (G2) could easily have come into this category as well. With almost half of all marriages in Western countries now ending in divorce we might well have included him in that same single-person category. Or if he had got divorced because he was gay and went to live with a male partner he would form a different type of non-family household. In the United States non-family households now comprise about 30 per cent of the total, whereas married couples with children (the McTypicals) are now about 27 per cent.[28]

Clear differences have been found in the spending and consumption patterns of single people under 40 and married people of the same age. Apparently, for instance, they feel more anxiety and insecurity about their self-image and their appearance and the way they present themselves in public.[29] Some marketers have attempted to reduce these pressures by 'legitimizing' the single state as just as honourable and worthy of respect as the married state. Everything, from single-serving prepared foods to smaller but more luxurious new dwellings, has met with success.

■ Further Reading

Bartos, R., *Marketing To Women Around the World* (Cambridge, Mass.: Harvard Business School Press, 1989). A global survey of the changing role of women as consumers and the practical implications for marketers.

Cheal, D., *The Gift Economy* (London: Routledge, 1988). An analysis of family holidays and the implications of exchanging gifts.

Furstenbert, F. and G. B. Spanier, *Recycling the Family* (Beverly Hills: Sage Publications, 1984). An analysis of the spending implications for divorced consumers.

Ihinger-Tallman, M. and K. Pasley, *Remarriage* (Newbury Park, CA: Sage Publications, 1988). Examines the complexity of consumer decision making among households of remarried people.

Keilman, N., A. Kuitsten and A. Vossen (eds), *Modelling Household Formation and Dissolution* (New York: Oxford University Press, 1988). A survey of the life cycle of households throughout the world.

Olson, D. H. *et al.*, *Families: What Makes Them Work?* (Beverly Hills: Sage Publications, 1983). Outlines a way of classifying families of all types as an aid to marketing.

It is also worth browsing through the latest issues of the following periodicals: *Advances in Consumer Research, American Demographics, Journal of Consumer Research, Journal of Marketing Research*.

■ Questions for Discussion

1. What are the advantages and disadvantages of using the family rather than the individual as a focus of consumer behaviour?
2. Illustrate the differences between a 'family' and a 'household'. What implications do these differences have for marketers?
3. What have been the most important changes in Western families/households since the Second World War? How have they affected consumer behaviour?
4. What effects can parents and children have on each other's consumer behaviour?
5. What do couples do about resolving conflicts over consumer decisions?
6. What is meant by the consumer life-cycle effect? How does it apply to (a) families, (b) non-family households?

CHAPTER 9

Social and Developmental Influences

■ Introduction

How does our psychological development affect our consumer behaviour?

In our discussion of family influences in Chapter 8 we took a brief look at the process of socialization, the way people become social, as opposed to individual, human beings. We saw that the complex and powerful emotional life of the family has a general but very important influence on the kind of social beings that children become, their basic orientation to the outside world. Part of this process involves learning how to be a consumer by coshopping with parents and by parents acting as role models.

In this chapter we will examine the socialization process more closely. We will be concerned primarily with the process of individual development, both mental and emotional, in children and adolescents and how that process is affected by the various social influences that children encounter as they grow up. Our goal is to understand consumer socialization, of course, and we will approach it through a study of *maturation* processes: the development of *the economic mind* and *the psychology of money*.

The general socialization process was illustrated in Figure 8.1. The particular aspects of socialization that we are interested in here are shown in Figure 9.1.

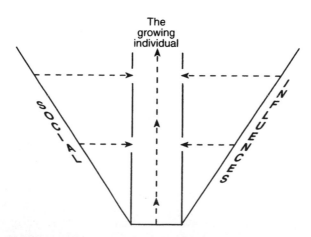

Figure 9.1   Socialization and individual development

Figure 9.1 illustrates the fact that while everybody develops psychologically as part of growing up - though in different ways and at different rates - everybody is also open to influences from their external social environment as well as their family. This is not something that parents can shield children from, even if they want to, and it is important because it interacts with the individual process of development and inevitably makes it more complex.

■ Maturation

In psychological terms *maturation* is usually defined along the following lines: 'The processes of growth and development which are common to all the members of a species and appear regardless of individual heredity or environment.[1] It is through these processes that all human beings are able to walk and talk and think, regardless of who their parents are, where they live, or how much money they have. These aspects of being human are therefore quite different from ones that are genetically transmitted (such as eye colour and skin colour) or ones that are due to the environment (for example which of the world's many languages is being spoken where the child lives).

Abilities connected with maturation will therefore appear in the growing child according to an inborn biological timetable. If children are not maturationally ready to walk or talk, no amount of doting parental encouragement will enable them to do so. Their brains have to grow to the point where the activity is neurologically possible. At that point parental encouragement will then be helpful in the acquisition and mastery of these skills.

■ Stages of Development

The same argument seems to hold true for the ability to think, which is what concerns us most. There is a maturational process that every child has to go through in order to acquire adult mental abilities. As the brain grows and develops the child is able to think and reason with ever-increasing complexity. Thanks to the work of the great Swiss psychologist Jean Piaget four different stages have been identified in the child's progress. The term 'stage' in psychology is used to describe, 'a developmental process taking place in a series of non-arbitrary, sequential, and progressive steps, each of which subsumes all the preceding steps.[2] In order to have adult thought processes every child will achieve the same sets of mental abilities, in the same order and at roughly the same age. Every new stage of development will not only include all previous learning but will also transform it, so that the same world will be understood differently. Understanding how this process worked was Piaget's contribution to psychology.

Piaget worked in Paris at the start of his career, in the early years of the twentieth century, administering intelligence tests to school children. The work was routine and unstimulating to a man of his ability and imagination, until he noticed something that aroused his curiosity. When children gave wrong answers to his test questions they seemed to do so in a particular manner. It wasn't just that some children gave more wrong answers than others, but that all children of a certain age seemed to give the same kind of wrong answers to the same questions.

By simple and systematic experimentation Piaget was able to demonstrate that children perceive things in a different way than adults do. The nature of the child's world, the one he or she has to make sense of, is quite different from the world of the adult. Before Piaget's discoveries these worlds were cut off from each other. Children could not convey their perceptions to adults in ways (that is, by language) that adults could understand, and adults themselves – having crossed into the adult world of adult perception – could no longer perceive the world as they had when young.

Piaget's insight lay in not taking for granted that children perceive the same world as adults. Instead, with the wrong answers to intelligence tests as his clues, he asked them how they *did* perceive and was rewarded with some fascinating answers. For example an adult knows that if two small, fat jars contain the same amount of water and the contents of one jar are then poured into a tall, thin jar, the amount of water remains the same (Figure 9.2).

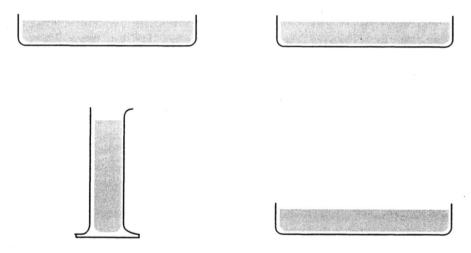

Figure 9.2 Understanding conservation

If you ask seven-year-old children about this procedure they too will understand it. But four-year-old children, no matter how intelligent, will tell you that the tall, thin jar contains more water because it is higher, or less water because it is thinner. But there is no way they will believe that the amount of water has not changed – even when they themselves do the pouring. Their intellectual equipment has simply not matured to the point where they can understand the *principle of conservation* involved.

Seven-year-old children seem to understand this principle intuitively. In fact they may look at you in amusement, wondering why you are asking them such an obvious (such a childish) question. They may only have acquired this ability a few months ago, but they now can't imagine the world being any other way. It is clear, therefore, that between the ages of four and seven some very important developments take place in the way children view the world around them.

The process of development from child to adult is not a gradual increase in knowledge, said Piaget, but rather a progression from one way of organizing the world to another, more complex, way. Human infants do not so much grow from small people into larger people, as from childlike people into adultlike people. In doing so they seem to pass through what Piaget claims are several well-defined and typical stages of development.[3]

■ Sensory Motor Stage (birth to two years)

At this stage language, and therefore symbols, play a very small part in children's development. They are concerned with discovering their own bodies and investigating their growing power to act on their environment, shaking rattles and kicking and thumping in their cots.

The major achievement at this stage is the discovery of *object constancy*. By the end of the first year of life, objects that are removed from children's field of vision no longer cease to exist for them, as they had before. They realize that objects have a separate existence from them, and they can hold images of the objects in their minds.

■ Preoperational Stage (two to seven years)

The acquisition of language and the use of symbols characterize this stage of development. In fact words, and especially the names of things, come to have a magical quality for children. They believe that the name of an object is part of the object, and that it couldn't exist without its name. They call a stick a rifle and treat it as if it were. And they become very upset if someone calls them 'a bad name'.

At this stage children do not yet understand the principle of conservation illustrated in Figure 9.2. This lack of understanding also extends to social relationships. For instance a small boy doesn't understand that if he has a brother, then so does his brother, or that someone can be Catholic and American at the same time. He hasn't yet grasped that people and objects can belong to more than one category.

■ Concrete Operations Stage (seven to eleven years)

After the age of seven children can understand conservation and are able to classify things and people into more than one category. This achievement marks a crucial point in children's cognitive development. They have begun to grasp the fact that the physical properties of things – their quantity, number, weight and volume – remain the same even if their appearance changes.

They learn that there is order to the physical world and that there are rules they can learn to find out what that order is. They are thus in a position to *know* what the world is really like even when it does not agree with their *perceptions* of it. Children who have not yet completed the stage of concrete operations are tied to the perceptual cues they receive from the environment when trying to make sense of it. However, as the name of the stage implies, children can only apply the new rules they have learned to concrete objects in their environment. Abstract thinking is still beyond them.

■ Formal Operations Stage (eleven years onwards)

The ability to form concepts and to think abstractly is the final achievement in children's intellectual development and this appears some time after the age of eleven. The use of logical reasoning to solve problems is the particular accomplishment of this stage. No longer are the children dependent on the physical presence of objects that they can see and manipulate. Now they can work things out in their heads and come up with the answers to problems. By late adolescence they are cognitively adults.

■ Assimilation and Accommodation

As children mature they have to adapt to a more and more complex world that presents them with new information all the time. Piaget suggests that there are two parts to this process of adaptation. In one part children assimilate new information about the world into their cognitive system, their existing way of thinking. This is called *assimilation.*

The other part comes into play when children's existing way of thinking is insufficiently complex to allow them to make sense of some new information. They are then forced to reorganize their cognitive system to adapt to this new situation. This is called *accommodation.* When a particularly important accommodation has been achieved they may be ready to move on to the next stage of development.

We should note that Piaget's stages of development seem to hold true in a wide variety of cultures and not just in his native Switzerland. It appears that children mature intellectually at roughly the same age in roughly the same way in Europe, America, Hong Kong and Africa. There are of course individual differences between children in all these cultures. Some children understand the principle of conservation at the age of six and others at the age of eight.

Piaget, however, despite (or perhaps because of) his early work in intelligence testing, was not very interested in individual timetables of.maturation. He thought it might be possible to speed up childen's passage through the stages of development by training them to do certain things, but he didn't see much point in doing so. In fact it could be harmful. Sooner or later, he reasoned, everybody goes through all the stages of development and as a biologist he perhaps felt that there may be a good reason for letting this process take its course. Perhaps we need the experience of maturing at our own pace to prepare us adequately for the adaptations we will have to make for the rest of our lives.

■ **From Egocentric to Reciprocal**

During the earlier stages of development the children's world centres around themselves. They know how the world looks to them but cannot visualize how it looks to other people. Piaget called this view of the world *egocentric.* To a five-year-old child, for example, a foreigner is always somebody else, never the child. People from another country are foreigners even in their own country, but the child is not a foreigner no matter where he or she goes.

As children develop they acquire the ability to 'decentre' themselves and put themselves in someone else's place. They learn to play games by fixed rules, even if it means they will lose. They acquire what Piaget calls *reciprocity*, a cognitive achievement that forms the psychological basis for adult social behaviour in all organized human societies. With reciprocity we are able to deal with concepts of equity, impartiality, justice and fairness, concepts that have a bearing on our economic life and our role as consumers.

■ **Differences Make More Sense than Similarities**

Although Piaget was not very interested in the educational implications of his work, they are nonetheless of far-reaching importance. Perhaps one of the more simple yet striking derivations of his findings is that children can understand *differences* between people and things much more easily than they can *similarities*. Questions about similarities and differences are a standard feature of the commonly used intelligence test, the Stanford-Binet. In this test six-year-old children, for instance, can usually tell us that summer is hot and winter is cold. But not until they are much older can they tell us that summer and winter are both seasons.

The ability to see similarities as well as differences is often a difficult intellectual task even for adults, and there is a suggestion that it may require more cognitive complexity than is needed to identify differences alone. It is thus easier to learn and to teach differences than similarities, a factor that is reflected in the curriculum of any school system. Differences of dress, manner, language, customs, behaviour and appearance are very evident and are frequently stressed by all the social institutions (for example family, school, church and play group) that children have to deal with. Similarities have to be sought out, and even when children are intellectually capable of handling such concepts there is little reward in doing so.

■ Language and Culture

Earlier in this chapter we noted that thoughts are expressed in language. However this is just one aspect of the intimate relationship between thought and language. Children develop their intellectual abilities using the symbols and concepts of the language spoken by the people they grow up with. They learn one set of symbols and concepts if the people speak Navajo; another if they speak English.

A language reflects the things that are important to the people who speak it. To people who speak English, time is of great importance. Time flies for us; to people who speak Spanish, it walks. We surround ourselves with clocks and watches and divide the passage of time into hours, minutes and even seconds. We need to know what time trains leave, classes start and programmes end. We usually know what day of the week it is and we certainly know whether our holiday started last week or starts next month. Imagine how disoriented we would be if our language did not have separate words for past and future.

Yet such is the case with the African language of Schambala, in which there is only 'today' and 'not today'. Evidently the people who speak Schambala, don't have many trains to catch. Time plays a different part in their lives. It is perceived and thought about differently. If they speak only Schambala they will never understand what it's like to live in our kind of culture. The language they speak affects the way they perceive the world and how they make sense of it. Thus the thought and culture that is reflected in a language is also shaped by the use of that language.

We will explore the effects of language on the consumer more fully in Chapter 12, and its use in advertising in Chapter 14. However this is a good place to note that the particular words used in any context are always important, rarely neutral, and often come with an emotional charge. The debate on abortion, for instance, is between those who believe that a certain medical procedure should be readily available and those who oppose it. But this is expressed by campaigners as either 'freedom of choice' or 'the right to life'. This is a pretty stark example, of course, but it does have some resonance for the consumer. How would our children regard cars and air pollution when they grow up if engine exhaust was referred to as 'carfart'?

The manipulation of language in this way by marketers is such a pervasive feature of our consumer environment that we have been socialized not only to accept it but perhaps not even to notice it. Table 9.1 offers a few reminders.

■ Development of Economic Concepts

As with the case of general cognitive or mental development, the development of understanding specific economic concepts also follows some fairly clear stages. However unlike Piaget's work on *basic* mental capacities, specifically *economic* concepts such as prices, wages, profit and loss, investment, savings, credit and so on are largely learned.

Table 9.1 Marketing manipulation of language

Message	Meaning
Ladies' intimate apparel	Women's underwear
Tourist class	Second class
Economy class	Second class
Standard class	Second class
For your convenience	For our convenience
Farm fresh eggs	Battery eggs
Train timetable revision	Reduction in services
Train fare revision	Increase in prices
Compact residence	Small house
Bijou residence	Tiny house
Imposing residence	Ugly house
Another opportunity to see...	TV repeat
The best of...	Ancient TV repeat
A classic programme of...	Prehistoric TV repeat
De luxe product	Expensive
Premium product	Expensive
First-class service	Expensive

To take one obvious example, not so long ago words such as profit, investment, credit and rent had virtually no meaning for children growing up under communism in Eastern Europe. Indeed this is at the root of the difficulties being experienced by those countries in changing to a market economy. The same holds true for children of different backgrounds and experiences in the same country. If they have experience of handling money, buying things, going to the bank and so on they will understand economic concepts earlier and better than children who don't. That is, the basic mental equipment must be there, but unless it is used appropriately the concept will be more difficult for children to grasp.[4]

Whereas Piaget's developmental stages dealt with concepts of the physical world such as time, place and number, psychologists working with economic concepts have found that the *interaction* of this basic cognitive maturation with specific learning about and experience of buying and selling, profit and loss and so forth has made their work more complex. It is extremely difficult, if not impossible, in this context to disentangle the effects of maturation and learning. So the stages of development in a child's understanding of economic concepts do not exactly parallel Piaget's stages.

Instead most researchers in this field have come up with a three-phase model that can only be loosely applied to particular ages.[5]

■ Phase I: Pre-Economic

I have called this phase pre-economic because the children in it, while they may well have some experience of money, do not *by themselves* understand the key role it plays in economic exchange. As we will see later in the chapter, though, *specific teaching* of the economic concepts involved can make a difference. These children would be under seven years of age.

■ Phase II: Micro-Economic

In this phase children understand the concepts of economic exchange – for example buying and selling – on an individual local level but not on a societal level. That is, they don't understand where the goods in the shop and the money to buy them with come from, or how these networks are related to each other. These children would be aged 7–8 to 12–14.

■ Phase III: Macro-Economic

By this phase of development children understand most, though not all, forms of economic exchange and the networks and institutions (for example banks) that link them. They have achieved the level of understanding of most adults, in other words, though they may be as young as 14–15. In one study, for example, some 89 per cent of children that age understood how a large and sudden increase in the availability of money in the economy would lead to rising prices and a shortage of consumer goods.[6]

■ External Influences on Consumer Socialization

As well as the extensive effects that children have on family spending (for both their needs and their preferences) that we discussed in Chapter 8, they also form a huge market in their own right because of the money they spend themselves. Children under 12 spend about $4 billion a year in the United States for instance. So how they come to understand and fulfil the role of consumer is a process of obvious importance. Studies in this field reveal a broadly similar series of phases to the learning of economic concepts. Their findings have been summarized as follows:

> They show the child at age 4 and 5 to be entering the consumer role with enthusiasm, but limited knowledge. But by ages 9 and 10 young people are performing as consumers with at least as much confidence and expertise as they display in any other societal roles. A child sees consuming as a logical role to assume, and recognises that basic needs such as affiliation and self-esteem can be fulfilled in the market-place with ease. How does the young person (say 10–18 years old) differ from the average adult consumer? Mainly s/he is younger![7]

Much of the rest of this chapter will examine the different influences on children as they go through these phases.

■ Parents

We saw in Chapter 8 how parents provide the psychological framework for a child's view of the world and how to deal with it. We also noted how children may receive their first consumer 'training' by coshopping trips with their parents and by the parents acting as a general role model of how consumers behave. The most casual survey of your local supermarket will show that this form of socialization begins shortly after birth.

The parent in question is usually the mother, who still takes primary responsibility in most cases for shopping, and certainly for food shopping. The mother–child relationship is therefore of specific consumer importance and it is likely that more educated mothers are better able to help their children understand the economic concepts that surround the role of being a consumer.[8]

There is another specific way in which parents can influence their children's consumer socialization: the use of pocket money. Most children receive pocket money and it is either given without strings attached or in return for some form of domestic labour. For younger children it usually represents their entire income. For older children (from about 12–13 years onwards) this is often supplemented by paid work outside the home, so the socializing effect of the allowance is therefore diluted.

As might be expected there are often differences between families, depending on their circumstances, though not always in the way you might expect. In the United Kingdom, for instance, one study found that working-class parents gave their children *more* pocket money than middle-class parents.[9] Another found that Scottish parents gave their children more money – in some cases a lot more – than English parents (sorry, I couldn't resist that).[10]

Having an allowance does seem to help children develop the basic skills necessary to use money as a consumer from an early age in such things as pricing, budgeting and judging relative value.[11] However children do different things with their allowances, and the kind of social class differences that we will discuss in Chapter 11 have their origins here.

We've already seen that middle-class children tend to receive less pocket money than working-class children, but they also tend to *save* more of it than working-class children.[12] Middle-class children are already learning the prime middle-class virtue of 'delayed gratification'; working-class children are already learning that there's no point to it.

■ School

There are three ways in which children's school experiences contribute to their consumer socialization: via the influence of peers, teachers and courses.

☐   *Peers*

The influence of peers begins at the start of school life. Peer group acceptance is desperately important to children, and this importance only increases with age. It is therefore vital to play the right games, eat the right food, have the right toys and, especially, wear the right clothes.

Peers' opinions of these products are far more important than parents', whose judgement is simply not to be trusted. To a large extent children's fashions, foods and crazes are fostered and channelled by marketing and advertising, particularly American marketing and advertising, which have been passed on to the global market, usually without local resistance – how else can we explain the sight of British boys in baggy Bermudas and turned-around baseball caps?

There is another way in which peers contribute to a child's consumer socialization: through what has been described as the 'playground economy'.[13] Children use some form of currency other than cash in this economy, for example marbles, but they can still do some rather sophisticated things with it. Marbles have different values for instance with, say, three of one kind being equal to one of another, but these values are determined by the supply and demand of the playground economy and not the price in the shops. Children can handle such concepts much more readily, and at a younger age, in what to them is the 'real world' than they appear to do when asked about the same concepts in the more remote and abstract world that adults inhabit.

☐   *Teachers*

Being adults the consumer judgement of teachers is not to be trusted any more than that of parents. By the time children reach adolescence teachers, like parents, are no longer looked to as role models – unless it's a model of what to avoid. They do have an influence, however, and that influence is in the form of helping children make connections from specific subject lessons to the wider consumer environment. This might take such forms as a discussion of cars and pollution in chemistry, or the food chain in biology, or the language of advertising in English lessons, or risk taking in mathematics.

☐   *Courses*

Specific courses in consumer behaviour are not usually taught in schools. But some schools do teach economics, and as we saw earlier in the chapter, an understanding of economic concepts is a useful background for older children in their future role as informed consumers. However there is some evidence that specific teaching of economic concepts that takes account of the child's maturational level can be successful even with children in what we called earlier the pre-economic phase (Piaget's pre-operational stage).[14] With the right teaching it does appear possible for children as young as five or six to grasp at least some economic concepts that developmentally (according to the theory) they are not supposed to be ready for.

One crucial condition for this kind of programme to work is parental support, and in fact parents tend to be very supportive of this kind of focused teaching, even when it sometimes shows up their own ignorance of the topic! There seems to be little doubt that courses in economics for children and teenagers at all stages of the school curriculum result in a greater understanding of how the economy works, and therefore in better-informed consumers. So why is the subject not more widely taught?

■ Social Norms

A social norm is simply the behaviour that is *expected* of people in a society. It is what people usually think of as 'normal' behaviour. As children grow up and go through the process of socialization they learn that certain kinds of social behaviour are approved of in their society while others are not. By the use of these norms a society ensures that most people do what is expected of them most of the time. By learning the norms of their society people can predict the behaviour of others with a high degree of accuracy.

Such *prediction* is absolutely essential for social life to exist. Unless everybody in the United States followed the social norm of driving on the right-hand side of the road the country would fall into chaos. These kinds of norm are obviously very practical. Everyone unquestioningly accepts them as right and proper standards of behaviour – without even being aware of them. But there are other norms that are subject to social change over time, and therefore to a great deal of debate and controversy. Until fairly recently it was the unquestioned norm in our society for men to go out to work while women stayed home with the kids.

This norm still remains (and to a large extent still remains unquestioned), but for a much more limited period of time – when the children are very young. As well as varying over time social norms also vary from place to place. Driving on the left-hand side of the road is just as important a norm in the United Kingdom as driving on the right is in the United States.

Social norms are reflected in a similar fashion in the consumer socialization of a society's children. Because different countries emphasize different areas of economic and consumer life, their children will have a different level of familiarity and understanding of different concepts. Zimbabwean children have been found to have a better understanding of the concept of 'profit', and to acquire it earlier, than British children.[15] Trading plays a much greater part in the life of the African children and this is expressed in their cognitive development.

Similarly the concepts of 'profit' and 'banking' were studied in Hong Kong, where it was found that Chinese children understood them better, and at a younger age, than either European[16] or American[17] children. It is presumably the very powerful and active business ethos of Hong Kong, permeating the entire society at every level, that makes it a crucial social norm and therefore vital in the socialization of its children.

■ Marketing and Advertising

We have seen that children are a very important market, whether in their own right, as an influence on their parents' buying behaviour or as future adult consumers. As a group they are therefore extremely important to marketers and advertisers. But this is a politically sensitive area and for many years now governmental bodies and groups of concerned parents have expressed alarm at the effects that marketing and advertising may be having on their society's children. Indeed in the United Kingdom and part of Canada direct advertising to children is forbidden, and there have been many attempts to impose a similar ban in other countries, including the United States.

How justified is this concern? In part it stems from an outmoded view of what socialization is, which we discussed earlier in the chapter. Socialization is not simply about doing things *to* children. As we have seen in connection with consumer behaviour, as well as more generally, there is a complex process of interaction and *mutual influence* between adults and children. This is not to say that the relationship is an equal one in every respect – adults obviously have a lot more physical power, money and authority – but there are always (at least) two parties to any psychological relationship and it is never just a simple one-way process.

Just as children are not merely passive recipients of adult influences, neither are they just passive recipients of messages from the adult world, including advertising messages. The most recent research on the effects of television advertising on children has emphasized this judgement. It used to be thought, for instance, that preschool children were unable to distinguish between advertising and programmes. But there is now evidence that very young children, perhaps as young as the second year of life, are able to make this distinction.[18]

This is not to suggest, of course, that television advertising has no effect on young children; it very clearly does. But as we saw in Chapter 4 with subliminal perception, and again in Chapter 7 with consumer motivation, the influence that advertising has on consumer behaviour of whatever age must be understood, certainly, but not feared as a mysterious or uncontrollable power.

Children do watch a lot of television, however, and they do see a lot of advertising. It is estimated that American children watch 3–4 hours television a day, on average, and that would add up to viewing about 20 000 advertisements a year. Whatever the product being sold, when directed at children advertisments are invariably fast and frothy and relentlessly 'fun', rather than providing information on the product itself.

In many cases this is quite understandable. Why would junk food manufacturers want to tell children, or their parents, what their product is really made of and what it will do to them? And there is little doubt that the sheer volume of junk food advertising influences children's choices, with kids who watch the most television being most heavily influenced.[19]

This is a set of issues we will return to and examine in greater detail in the final part of this book when we discuss consumerism. Before ending the present chapter, though, it might be appropriate to look at a few more research findings of particular relevance to consumer socialization.

Advertisers are fond of arguing that messages aimed at children are viewed in the context of the home and that they will therefore be interpreted and processed within the framework of parental guidelines. However most parents don't watch children's television, nor do they teach their offspring specifically about advertising.[20] While even young children may be able to distinguish advertisements from programmes, what they have a lot more difficulty in doing below the age of 12, and especially below the age of 7, is *evaluating* the advertising message being aimed at them.

As we saw earlier when discussing Piaget's stages of development, their brain has not matured sufficiently for them to have acquired the necessary cognitive equipment for clear and rational judgment. There is a limit to any young child's resistance to persuasion. No matter how intelligent or sophisticated they may be for their age, the mental capacities of young children may simply be overwhelmed.[21]

As children grow up and have personal experience of the products, especially toys, being marketed and advertised to them, this experience, combined with their growing maturation, strengthens their resistance to persuasion. Indeed by adolescence personal experience may well be more important than television advertising when making consumer choices.[22]

As well as advertising aimed directly at them, children can also be affected by advertisements for adult products. Television advertisements for lipstick, for example, made a favourable impression on 10-year-old girls, who associated the product with adulthood and the enviable status of being grown up.[23] It may be that such exposure influences future brand and product choices when adult patterns of consumption are eventually adopted.

■ Further Reading

Danziger, K., *Socialization* (Baltimore: Penguin, 1973). A brief account that manages to be both scholarly and stimulating. It is now out of print, but good libraries should have a copy.

Garbarino, J. and F. M. Stott, *et al.*, *What Children Can Tell Us* (San Francisco: Jossey-Bass, 1990). Outlines the development of children as consumers and the research techniques used to study them.

Moschis, G., *Consumer Socialization: A Life-Cycle Perspective* (Lexington, MA: Lexington Books, 1987). A thorough account of the topic that deals well with adult as well as childhood socialization.

Piaget J. and B. Inhelder, *The Psychology of the Child* (New York: Basic Books, 1969). Piaget's own account of his life's work.

Ward S., D. B. Wackman and E. Wartella, *How Children Learn to Buy* (Beverly Hills: Sage, 1977). A good early account of childhood consumer socialization.

It is also worth browsing through the latest issues of the following periodicals: *Advances in Consumer Research, Journal of Advertising Research, Journal of Consumer Research, Journal of Marketing Research.*

■ Questions for Discussion

1. How does Piaget's theory of developmental stages relate to the consumer socialization of children?
2. What is the role of language in children's interaction with the world of advertising? Give examples from current campaigns.
3. In what ways does the development of economic thinking affect a child's exposure to the marketplace?
4. Contrast the different influences of parents, teachers and peer groups as a child becomes a consumer and grows into adolescence.
5. How vulnerable are children of different ages to the influence of marketers and advertisers?

CHAPTER 10

The Influence of Small Groups

I wouldn't belong to any group that would have me as a member (Groucho Marx).

■ Introduction

What are the effects of group pressure on the individual consumer?

We opened Part III: (The Social Perspective) with an examination of the effect that the family has on our consumer behaviour. Our family is, of course, our first experience of group life and forms the psychological prototype for our dealings with any other group. Its psychological importance cannot be overestimated, yet in terms of consumer behaviour its influences are probably much more general than specific. If we are interested in the specific consumer choices of adults we also need to consider the influences of all the other groups that we come into contact with, and that is the subject of the present chapter.

It is very difficult to give an all-inclusive definition of the word 'group'. A concept that can be applied to entities as diverse as a couple of room mates and a world-wide religion – both of which can have an effect, as we shall see, on consumer behaviour – can only be surrounded, rather than explained, by a definition. However 'two or more people who regard themselves as a collectivity and interact with each other while sharing the same norms' is perhaps as good a working definition as we can get. It will allow us to unpack the most important ways in which groups influence their members as consumers.

■ Types of Group

There are several useful ways in which the vast diversity of groups can be categorized.

■ Primary and Secondary Groups

Primary groups are also known as 'small groups' or 'face-to-face' groups. That is, these are groups small enough for members to sit round a table and see each other directly, and where everyone gets to know everyone else quite well. Typically, such groups have about four to eight members. Most of us belong to several groups of this size at any given time in our family, school, social and work life. It has been discovered over many years of research that there are psychological forces, or *dynamics*, that are particularly prominent in these small groups, and we will examine some of these later in the chapter.

Secondary groups are those whose membership is too large for them to be classified as primary. There is no hard-and-fast number that marks a definite cut-off point. Sports teams of eleven people may still form a primary group, for instance. This kind of size does get close to the upper limit of such a group, however, and a membership of, say, 20 would probably not be a primary group. What groups of this size might do, however, if they are sufficiently close-knit, is split up into two or more primary groups.

If someone does not know all the people in a particular group, only interacts with them infrequently and is not immediately or intimately involved with them when he or she does so then that group is only of *secondary* importance to him or her. This group may be a transnational company, a professional association or a religion.

Though far more research has focused on the influence of primary groups than secondary groups, it is worth noting that secondary groups can still have a direct effect on their members' consumer behaviour. Members of a dental association for example, are not only a ready market for advertising on the latest instruments of torture peculiar to their trade but also for group discounts on life insurance. Catholic newspapers will have advertising on package deals to Rome, Jewish ones to Israel and Moslem ones to Mecca.

■ Formal and Informal Groups

These groups differ in terms of the degree of structure and organization they have. If a group has a membership list, office bearers, levels of authority and clearly defined roles for its members then it is probably a *formal* group, for example a political party or a trade union. A group of business school graduates who meet for lunch once a month would be an *informal* group.

As with primary and secondary groups though, there is no absolute cut-off point between formal and informal groups and there are plenty of grey areas. *Ad hoc* groups are probably the most common of these in-between groups, where a group of people meet for a specific purpose and then disband. Environmental protection groups fighting a proposal for a motorway through their community would be one example, and groups protesting the transportation of live animals for slaughter would be another.

When the reason for the *ad hoc* group's existence no longer exists, neither will the group. Yet as these activities are usually locally based they will probably involve families and other primary groups whose existence *will* continue. Moreover membership of such groups and the publicity often given to them may well have an effect on attitudes towards car ownership and usage or towards the consumption of meat, for example.

■ Membership and Reference Groups

A *membership group* is simply any group that someone belongs to or qualifies for membership of. In every human society babies are born into the same social groups as their parents. They are automatically members of their social class or language or religious group, for instance. People's group memberships are therefore of great importance, as we have already seen, in shaping their psychology.

Adults, however, have some choice. Thus market researchers may choose whether or not to become members of the Market Research Society, if they are professionally qualified to do so. Even for adults though there may not be a real choice. Thus for people who wish to practice law or medicine in most countries membership of the appropriate professional association is usually mandatory.

Nonetheless as children grow up they will reach a stage of development where they are able to compare the groups of which they are members with other groups in their social environment they don't belong to. When this happens their group membership may no longer be automatically acceptable to them. Girls may realise, for instance, that they're not allowed to do all the things that boys do, or that boys seem to get preferential treatment in school and in preparation for the world of work.[1]

This particular form of dissatisfaction with one's membership group is very difficult to deal with, particularly as such basic membership groups are actively fostered by parents and all other adult social influences, including advertising and marketing. Adult expectations of appropriate gender differences in behaviour are communicated very quickly to children. As early as age one boys tend to play more vigorously and aggressively than girls.[2] Children are already acting out what their parents consider to be the masculine and feminine roles in their society, by following their lead and responding to their encouragement or discouragement of various activities.

We find, therefore, that small boys are typically encouraged to play with building blocks but not with dolls, and vice versa for girls.[3] And the marketing strategies and advertising campaigns for these and similar products enthusiastically endorse these gender differences. Girls are typically encouraged to seek help and to offer help to others, but boys are not. By the age of two girls have apparently learned that their membership group is supposed to be dependent and conformist while boys know that theirs is supposed to be ruggedly independent.

Only in recent years have marketers and advertisers caught up with the idea that quite a few frilly little girls grow up to be ruggedly independent young women with lots of money to spend. The resultant contortions that have appeared in the advertising messages of a vast array of products, from cars to trainers to life insurance, has been fun to watch.

In comparison with a membership group, a *reference group* is a group with which people identify, and whose group norms on values, judgments and behaviour they follow (refer to), *whether they are accepted by the group or not* and whether they are physically part of it or not. In the past, when the self-image of black people was more negative, some light-skinned blacks rejected their blackness and tried to 'become' white. One means of doing this was to straighten their hair, using products developed for just that purpose. Their membership group was black but their reference group – the group with which they compared themselves and whose norms they referred to for guidance in their behaviour – was white. With an increasingly positive black self-image the bottom fell out of the hair-straightener market.

To the extent that black people, or any other group of people, feel positive about their membership group and value its particular qualities, their membership group will also be their reference group. The relationship between membership and reference groups is illustrated in Figure 10.1. However it is the consumer effects of having *different* reference groups and membership groups that have most interested both marketers and social scientists.

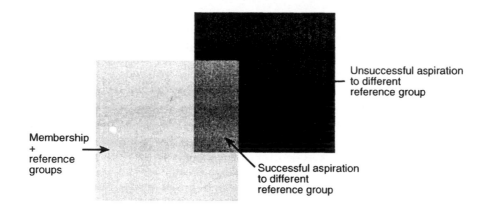

Figure 10.1   Membership and reference groups

Reference groups are also known as *aspirational* or *symbolic groups* because individuals aspire to leave their membership group and be accepted by their reference group, or at least to identify with people who symbolize the values or behaviours they admire.   Reference group theory and its applications have become so important to the study of consumer behaviour that we will devote a separate section to this field later in the chapter.

■ Properties of Group Life

There has been a vast amount of research on the way people behave in groups, and particularly small groups, and we can do no more here than attempt to catch a flavour of this work. It is important to do so however because the effects of *group influence* on the individual can be quite far-reaching with regard to his or her consumer behaviour. In Chapter 10 we will deal specifically with the process of making a buying decision, and how that is affected by group influences.   In this chapter we are concerned more with the general relationships between group members.

■ Unintended Group Influence

Some of the most powerful influences on individuals are exerted quite unintentionally, simply by the conditions under which the group lives. It was discovered many years ago that one of the most important ways of predicting whether two people will get married is to find out how far away they live from each other.

One study of 5000 couples in Philadelphia found that a third of them had lived within five blocks of each other, and more than half of them had lived within twenty blocks of each other.[4] At least in Western societies people like to feel that their spouse has been freely chosen without any arbitrary outside influence, but the truth appears to be a little less romantic. This is also why couples tend to have similar patterns of consumer behaviour, patterns that are systematically different from those of couples who met in different kinds of neighbourhood.

The development of friendship between people is often similarly based on their physical proximity to each other. A study of friendship patterns between student couples in an apartment block in Boston revealed that next-door neighbours were listed as best friends by 41 per cent of the couples, while those living at the far end of their floor were listed only 10 per cent of the time. People living in between were chosen 22 per cent of the time.[5] Friendship patterns at work can also be affected by physical proximity. For instance it has been found, that small, closed offices produce far more friendships than large, open-plan offices.[6]

■ Word of Mouth and Opinion Leadership

Friendship patterns are important to consumer behaviour because one's friends and neighbours are often the source of advice on goods and services.[7] This process is known as *word-of-mouth* contact, or the working of a *referral network* when it deals with services, for example finding a plumber. Word-of-mouth operates within small, informal groups and takes place on such a continuous basis that we may not even be aware of how often we receive – or give – advice. It is difficult to overestimate how influential this process is, however, and indeed estimates of the number of buying decisions affected range as high as 80 per cent.[8]

People who seem to have a particular influence on the buying decisions of a group have often been called *opinion leaders* in studies of consumer behaviour. We came across this term in Chapter 3, where we considered the importance of opinion leaders to the success of new products and innovations. We noted there that they seem to have higher self-esteem and self-confidence than the average consumer and are respected for their judgment about when it is appropriate to try out a new product.

Outside this area, though, when we are dealing with established products, it probably doesn't make much sense to look for personality characteristics as a way of identifying opinion leaders. Their 'leadership', in other words, is largely situational and depends mainly on the type of product being considered. Everybody consumes some products; nobody consumes every product; everybody is probably capable of being an opinion leader – that is, exerting influence – about something at some time in their lives, (indeed this is probably true of any kind of leadership).[9]

This way of thinking about opinion leadership highlights two facts: (1) that it is usually specific to a particular product category or categories, and (2) that what is involved is a relationship between at least two people, where the influence often goes in both directions. Your neighbour's spotty adolescent son will probably not be in a position to influence you about fashionable clothes, life insurance or discreet aftershaves, but try him on personal computers and you may strike oil. You, on the other hand, may be his guru on college courses (or discreet aftershaves).

The above example of looking for a personal computer encapsulates the major conditions necessary for someone to exert influence within a group context:

- There is an ongoing personal relationship.
- The other person (the spotty one) is a handy computer expert.
- You do not personally have the information/knowledge/experience to evaluate different models.
- You don't entirely trust the sales pitches on such a complex and expensive item

Computers are the kind of product that seem to attract particularly knowledgeable and enthusiastic opinion leaders. Electronics and car mechanics appear to have a similar effect. These opinion leaders are sometimes known as *market mavens* (*maven* being the Yiddish word for an expert), and they may be unusually influential in buying decisions for these products.[10] It is probably not true, however, that they *all* wear nylon anoraks and write in green ink.

We will consider both word-of-mouth communication and opinion leadership in more detail in Chapter 14 when we discuss the effects of advertising on consumer behaviour. It is worth noting here, though, that this form of influence has more impact on consumer behaviour than any form of marketing strategy or advertising campaign.[11]

■ Group Norms and the Power of Conformity

In Chapter 9 we saw how crucial are *norms* of behaviour – what is expected of people and what is considered normal – to the functioning of a society. We noted there how children quickly and efficiently learn the norms their society considers appropriate. As adults we have usually completely internalized these norms so that we are not even conscious of them.

This internalization of social norms is, psychologically, an indication of how important and powerful they are. It is only when we are placed in the position of having to go against a norm that we become aware of this. This kind of situation has been extensively studied in laboratories with small groups and from this work has emerged our understanding of how a social norm of behaviour operates.

Because so much of our life is lived in groups they provide us with our psychological sustenance, sense of belonging, meaning and even our very identity – with the contents of our self-image. And our membership of a number of small groups (family, work, social, political, sporting and so on) is largely what links us to the broader society. Maintaining the group norms is thus the paramount objective of any group. Without them the group would cease to exist. There is therefore a constant pressure on members to conform to the group norms, a pressure we only become aware of when something unusual happens. People usually conform to group and social norms. Conformity *is* the norm. Several classic studies will help illuminate the psychological mechanism that makes this social engine work and the many different forms it can take.

In the early 1950s Solomon Asch did a series of studies on the effects of group pressure on the individual that startled other psychologists, and even Asch himself.[12] The typical Asch experiment had seven people seated around a table judging lengths of lines. Only one of the seven subjects in Asch's experiment was a real (that is, naive) subject. The other six were paid confederates of the experimenter, and it was their job to produce the group pressure that was to be directed at the naive subject. The study was billed as an exercise in visual perception and the subjects were supposed to compare the length of a line on one card with three lines on another card, as in Figure 10.2.

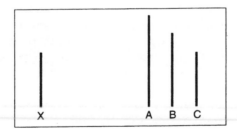

Figure 10.2 Asch conformity experiment

The experimenter then asked the subjects whether line X was equal in length to lines A, B or C. Asch deliberately made the task very easy so that when they were alone the subjects would always give the right answer. What Asch wanted to find out was what would happen if his six confederates all gave the same wrong answer. Would the naive subject say what he really saw, or would he be influenced by the unanimous judgment of the group to conform and give the same wrong answer as everyone else?

In each of the experiments Asch had arranged things so that the naive subject was seated in the number six position where he would hear five other judgments before his own turn came. In fully a third of the cases the naive subject succumbed to the group pressure he felt and gave an answer he knew to be wrong. Three quarters of the subjects did so at least once, with only a quarter of the subjects sticking to their own judgments throughout.

Asch's experiments have been repeated many times by other psychologists and the findings have usually been the same. A great deal of work has also gone into studying the various factors involved and these are commonly divided into individual factors and group factors.

A study of the people who yielded to group pressure found that they were much lower in self-esteem and had a poorer image of themselves than the people who did not yield. The most important group factor is whether or not the majority making the wrong judgment is unanimous. If even one other person agrees with the naive subject, his likelihood of yielding to group pressure is greatly reduced. In this situation there was only 5–10 per cent conformity.

Other psychologists interested in the same phenomenon adopted a somewhat different approach.   Richard Crutchfield, for instance, developed a technique that dispensed with the need for confederates and gave him a great deal of control over the conformity situation.[13]

In Crutchfield's experiments, five people each made their individual judgments of the stimuli. The subjects were seated side by side, each person seated in his own cubicle facing a switchboard and out of sight of the others. Verbal communication was not allowed, and the only way a subject could communicate with the others, or with the experimenter, was by flicking a switch in front of him that lit up lights on everyone else's switchboard.

Each subject was asked to indicate in this way whether he agreed or disagreed with various statements that were presented to the group. The switchboard in front of him registered the answers of the other group members. Unlike the Asch situation, however, each of the people in the group was a naive subject whose responses to group pressure were being studied. In fact there was no communication between the subjects in the group. Crutchfield systematically controlled the situation by providing each subject with false information on his switchboard about the judgments of the other four people.

At certain points each subject found himself faced with that looked like a unanimous group choice supporting the wrong answer to a particular statement. When the statements dealt with the same level of difficulty as in the Asch study – that is, easy perceptual comparisons or arithmetical problems – Crutchfield obtained about the same level of conformity as Asch, about one third of the subjects,

But when Crutchfield made the arithmetical problem difficult, up to 80 per cent of the subjects were persuaded to conform to the false group consensus and agree with an answer that was clearly wrong. In this situation Crutchfield also induced bright college students to agree with a great number of odd statements: for example that most Americans are over 65 years old, that the average person only has a life expectancy of 25 years, and that this same average American eats six meals a day – perhaps accounting for the fact that he or she only sleeps four hours a night.

Most striking of all perhaps was the reaction to the statement 'Free speech being a privilege rather than a right, it is proper for a society to suspend free speech whenever it feels itself threatened'. In the control group free of group pressure, only 19 per cent of the subjects agreed with this statement; in Crutchfield's situation of group pressure, 58 per cent agreed.

A different type of conformity in a group setting was the object of research by Stanley Milgram.[14] In Milgram's work the conformity studied was not compliance with a norm set by a group of people in the same room as the subject, but compliance to a general norm of society – obedience to authority.

Like Asch, Milgram was interested in observing the behaviour of one naive subject at a time, in a controlled setting. The subjects thought they were taking part in a learning experiment where they were to play the role of a teacher, while another person (Milgram's confederate) took the part of a learner. The learner was supposed to memorize lists of nonsense syllables which the teacher was supposed to help him learn by giving him an electric shock whenever he made an error. The more errors the learner made, the stronger the voltage he was given – up to 450 volts, at which point the switch was marked 'Danger! Severe Shock XXX'.

In fact no electric shocks were actually given although the subject thought they were. The situation was rigged. Communication between teacher and learner was by means of an intercom, for the confederate was supposedly strapped into an impressive-looking electronic apparatus in the next room, out of sight of the teacher. The responses the subject thought he was getting from the learner were actually a tape recording with prearranged right and wrong answers. As the errors increased, and the punishment along with it, the subject heard howls of pain, demands to be let out, and finally silence from the room next door. The real purpose of the experiment was to see how far the subject would go in giving someone electric shocks when prompted to do so by an authority – the experimenter.

When people are asked to guess how many subjects continued up to the 450-volt mark, the usual estimate is about 1 per cent. In fact some 65 per cent, almost two thirds of the subjects, did so. Milgram is careful to point out that the subjects in his study were not sadists who enjoyed inflicting pain on other people. Far from it – they were extremely uncomfortable about the whole situation and often expressed a desire to terminate the experiment. Yet only a third of the subjects were willing to defy the experimenter's authority and refuse to continue.

As with the subjects in the Asch experiment the people who did not succumb to the pressure to conform tended to have higher self-esteem than those who did. The most important situational factor was the amount of personal responsibility the subject had to accept for his or her actions. In one part of the study the subject had to force down the learner's hand on to a shockplate in order to deliver the maximum 450 volts. Under these conditions the amount of conformity was more than halved; less than one third of the subjects were willing to go that far.

■ Conformity and Consumer Norms

Later in this chapter, when we consider reference groups and consumer behaviour, we will look at some specific findings of the effects of conformity. Based on the foregoing discussion, though, it would be reasonable to draw the following general conclusions with regard to consumer behaviour:

- Most of us feel somewhat uncomfortable if our consumer behaviour is out-of-step with those around us, for example not owning a television set would be non-conformist behaviour in most groups. So would smoking cigarettes at a dinner party – the opposite would have been true a generation or two ago.
- People who don't mind so much being out-of-step are likely to be opinion leaders, especially of new products or innovations such as personal stereos, or ceasing to be a meat eater.
- Even though it's hard for most people to resist the pressure to conform it may take the support of just one other person to enable them to do so.
- Most of us will accept some transparently silly opinions if they are a norm of our group, for example that Bermuda shorts are attractive. Indeed the fashion industry, especially for women, seems to be largely based on this phenomenon. Thus hemlines go up and down and shoulders go in and out, and each time a change occurs people seem to accept it and change their wardrobe accordingly.

This last example of the fashion industry highlights one of the basic dilemmas of consumer behaviour, at least in Western societies: how do we reconcile the prevailing ideology of individual consumer choice with the reality of the enormous pressure to conform? Ever since Henry Ford and the advent of mass production, with its highly profitable economies of scale, it has been in a producer's interest for all consumers to want – or at least to accept – the same product, marketed perhaps with a few trivial variations such as colour, size and styling to maintain the fiction of free choice. Few producers nowadays are willing to show Ford's open contempt for the consumer.

When there is no real competition in product provision it is difficult to know how conformist, as opposed to manipulated, consumers really are. This has been particularly true of the automotive industry, with its oil and steel cartels and its price-fixing car manufacturers, and of the fashion industry. Try shopping for an electric car, for instance, or a long skirt when hemlines are short. It has something of the remorseless logic of Aristotle's famous syllogism:

All men are mortal,
Socrates is a man,
Therefore Socrates is mortal.

or
All suits are baggy,
I need a suit,
Therefore I will buy a baggy suit.

To highlight this issue, consider the difference between the car industry and the home entertainment industry. The cars that we drive today are recognisably the same product that came off Henry Ford's assembly line in 1913. They may have acquired a lot of wire and plastic and lost a lot of steel, but they are controlled, powered and used in just the same way.

Now compare the home entertainment industry. In 1913 the state-of-the-art of home entertainment was probably the piano. Today it is satellite television with stereo sound, and soon it will be virtual reality. Why the difference? Unlike those in the automotive industry, producer cartels in this new field were not able to get a firm grip on the manufacturing process, and the Japanese entered the field relatively early. Indeed it was only when Japanese car sales overtook the big three of Detroit in the 1980s that a little competition began to creep into that product too.

It does appear as though most consumers are conformist enough not to question how the range of products they are presented with comes to be, though as we'll see in Part V there are hints that this might be changing. It is ironic that the most advanced manufacturing companies in the world are the ones that regard the consumer as a valued colleague to be closely consulted rather than a mug to be conned and manipulated. We saw in Chapter 2 how the Japanese company Matsushita achieved great success with a traditional mass market product – the bicycle – by customizing it; tailoring it precisely to each individual customer's dimensions. I wonder if they've considered making suits?

■ Power

Another way in which group life may affect individuals' consumer behaviour is through their perception of the power the group has to influence them. A widely accepted classification of group power lists five forms of power: reward, coercive, legitimate, expert and referent.[15] Though this classification was first presented in relation to work organizations, it has since been applied to consumer behaviour as well.[16] Examples of group power operating in each of these ways might be as follows:

☐ *Reward Power*

This is the ability the group has to give people something they value. The 'reward' may take either the material form of services and goods or the psychological form of acceptance or recognition for certain behaviour, increased status and so on. Bonuses, sales commissions, office parties and presentations, sporting the colours of a local football team, or having a key role in group purchasing decisions are all examples of reward power.

☐ *Coercive Power*

This is largely the opposite of reward power. It is the ability to punish, or withhold rewards from, the individual. The feeling that one *has* to wear the colours of a certain football team or lose the acceptance of one's group would be an example of coercive power. Indeed this particular sanction is probably exercised through large swathes of our society. How many thrusting young executives would wear jeans and tee shirt rather than a baggy suit?

☐   *Legitimate Power*

A member's perception that his or her group has a right to influence him or her as a consumer would be considered legitimate power in action. This power is often exercised through group representatives, such as parents deciding on appropriate pocket money, or doctors and health educators urging people to give up smoking and eat more fruit and vegetables.

☐   *Expert Power*

This power is based on the possession of knowledge or skills that the individual consumer values. Opinion leaders are obviously in this category, but as we have seen this category can include virtually everybody and anybody at one time or another.

☐   *Referent Power*

The source of this form of influence lies in the emotional identification that the individual has with a particular group or with some prominent person who *represents* the group to the individual. The closer the identification, the more influential the referent power. This form of power is extensively exploited in marketing with the use of endorsements from sporting and showbiz celebrities. The idea is that identification passes from the group the celebrity represents, via him or her, to the product. We will examine this process more closely in Chapter 14, but next we will look at the topic of reference groups in general.

■ Reference Groups and Consumer Behaviour

Earlier in this chapter we briefly compared reference groups with membership groups. We noted that although people's reference group could also be their membership group, what interested us particularly was those instances where this wasn't the case and they aspired to be accepted by a different group.

■ Conformity Pressure and Specific Influences

☐   *Direct Influences*

The Asch[17] study discussed above (Figure 10.2) is generally considered the classic study in this field. It was precisely because the group was a new reference group for the naive subject that he felt under so much pressure to conform. Had the group's opinions and judgements not mattered to the naive subject he would have come up with the correct answer every time. The same was true of the Crutchfield[18] study of social and political opinions as well as arithmetical problems.

These findings inspired a wide variety of work on groups in a wide variety of situations, including purchase decisions. In one study a group of young men, only one of whom was a naive subject, were invited to choose the best out of three suits, labelled A, B and C. The suits were in fact identical. The naive subjects were asked to evaluate the suits by themselves and then as part of a group. By themselves the subject's choices were randomly distributed over the three possibilities. In the group setting the naive subjects heard the other members give the unanimous judgment 'B', and sure enough they yielded to group pressure.[19]

Like the Asch and Crutchfield studies this group was formed in the researcher's laboratory. Other work has shown that the direct influence of pressure to conform can also be identified in actual buying situations where the members of the group know each other, and the need for social approval will therefore be particularly powerful. Women's fashions (oddly enough) was one clear example of this influence at work.[20]

☐ *Indirect Influence*

As we saw earlier in this chapter with Milgram's study on conformity to the norm of obedience,[21] our behaviour can be strongly influenced by a reference group that is not physically present. We are very concerned what people whose opinion we consider important will think of us. A classic marketing study conducted in 1950 had already found that this effect was operating in consumer behaviour.[22]

The subjects in the study were asked to judge what a person was like by looking at her shopping list. Using a form of projective technique two groups were each given a shopping list, identical except for one product. One group was given the list of a shopper who bought instant coffee, the other group's shopper had ground coffee on her list.

This was shortly after instant coffee had been introduced in the United States and people felt guilty about using convenience foods. The instant coffee group decided that its shopper was a lazy housekeeper and a poor wife, in contrast with the competent housekeeper and good wife who used ground coffee. Of course instant coffee later became widely accepted as group norms changed, and a follow-up study 20 years later found no negative associations whatever with the product.[23]

■ **Variability of Products**

It has been found that reference groups can have different degrees of influence over the buying and consumption of different kinds of products. Two dimensions seem to be particularly important: how exclusive the product is and where it is used. These dimensions have been operationalized as *luxury–necessity* and *public–private*.[24]   Reference group influence should be strongest when the product is a luxury good that is used publicly (for example a sailing boat), and weakest when it is a private necessity (for instance a refrigerator).

It is also possible to use these two dimensions to distinguish between reference group effects on a particular brand or model as opposed to the general product:

- *Public necessities.* As most of the market has this product (for example a suit) reference group influence will be weak, but because the product is highly visible the particular brand chosen will be subject to strong influence (though not, in this case, the style – which at the time of writing will of course be baggy).
- *Public luxuries.* As noted above, reference group influences should be strongest in this segment because it is both visible and relatively exclusive (for example a set of golf clubs). Thus influence would be exerted to own the product in the first place and then to buy a particular brand.
- *Private necessities.* Again as noted above, reference group influence should be at its weakest here because more or less everyone uses the product and uses it privately. Influence on both product (for instance a mattress) and brand should be minimal.

■ Differences in Consumer Susceptibility

□ *Group Factors*

A study conducted in the late 1970s compared the effects of reference group influence on the consumer behaviour of students and 'housewives'.[25], and found that students tend to be the more susceptible group. There are probably several reasons for this, the most important being that students probably have much more frequent and continuing contact with other members of the peer reference group that is so important to them. We have already seen in this chapter the effects of sheer proximity on group formation and influence. Students would also be less experienced and less specialized consumers than 'housewives'.

In general terms the more cohesive and integrated the reference group, and the more an individual feels that he or she belongs to the group, the greater the group's influence will be.[26] The practical difficulty for marketing is that it is extremely difficult to link specific individuals with specific products and specific reference group influences, unless a great deal is known about each.

□ *Individual Factors*

When we discussed the psychology of group conformity earlier in the chapter we noted that those who are most resistant to conformity pressure are generally self-confident and high in self-esteem. That is, when placed in a situation of conflict between denying their own perceptions or value judgments on the one hand

and going against the group norm on the other, they have the strength of personality to stand by what they believe.

While very few areas of consumer behaviour induce that level of psychological tension, the relationship between individual and group is probably very similar. Such people, as we have seen more than once already, will include the innovators. What that may mean in practice is that at any given time the potentially non-conforming consumer is the one who must be enlisted by marketers who want to *change* reference group norms and, through that, patterns of consumption.

■ Further Reading

Aronson, E., *The Social Animal*, 6th edn (New York: Freeman, 1992). The best and most readable introduction to the study of small groups and their implications for society.

Clausen, J. (ed.), *Socialization and Society* (Boston: Little, Brown, 1968). A good overview of the way individuals are linked to their society via small group membership.

Rogers, E. M., *Diffusion of Innovations*, 3rd edn (New York: Free Press, 1983). Includes an account of the way group life influences the diffusion of innovations. Rogers is one of the leading researchers in this field.

Robertson, T. and H. Kassarjian (eds), *Handbook of Consumer Behavior* (Englewood Cliffs, N J:Prentice-Hall, 1991). The authoritative guide to theories and concepts in consumer behaviour. This edition contains some useful articles on the influence of group life.

Swap, W. C. and Associates (eds), *Group Decision Making* (Beverly Hills, CA: Sage, 1984). A detailed and technical overview of the way groups arrive at decisions in a wide variety of situations.

It is also worth browsing through the latest issues of the following periodicals: *Advances in Consumer Research, Journal of Consumer Research, Journal of Marketing Research.*

■ Questions for Discussion

1. What is the difference between (a) a primary and a secondary group, (b) a formal and an informal group?

2. What is the difference between a membership group and a reference group? Which reference group is most important to you and how does it influence your consumer behaviour? What are the most important factors in reference group influence?

3. Why are your friends so important to your consumer behaviour? Illustrate this in reference to (a) goods, (b) services.

4. What is 'opinion leadership'? Give some examples from your own experience of giving and receiving leadership in consumer behaviour.

5. What are group and social norms of behaviour? Why are they so powerful? How is non-conformity to these norms expressed in consumer behaviour?

CHAPTER 11

The Influence of Social Class

F. Scott Fitzgerald: 'The rich are really different from you and me.'
Ernest Hemingway: 'Yes, they've got more money.'

Introduction

How does our social class affect what we buy?

In the above dialogue between the two famous American writers both are obviously correct, but in different ways. We do have less money than rich people, but if we had more money it would not necessarily make us more like them. When we discussed market segmentation in Chapter 2 we saw that consumers could not be put into market segments by virtue of their income alone. For instance college professors and used car salesmen may have the same income but they will probably spend it in quite different ways. The same probably holds true for rock stars and Rockefellers.

What Hemingway was talking about was a *quantitative* difference. But what Fitzgerald had in mind was a *qualitative* distinction: the Great Gatsby was rich, while a poor person who wins the lottery simply has a lot of money. It is the qualitative dimension that will concern us in this chapter.

We noted in Chapter 2 that one way of segmenting a market is by socio-economic status (SES), which is determined by education and occupation as well as income. While there are many individual exceptions, of course, these three factors are often in alignment. Thus more highly educated people tend to do the kind of managerial and professional jobs that bring with them a relatively high income, and we can be pretty sure that most people with a high income have received higher education and work in high-status jobs. Quite a lot of what is meant by *social class* is actually contained in the concept of SES, but not all of it as we shall see below.

Social Stratification

The term 'class' comes from the Latin word *'classis'*, which was used by the Romans when classifying the population by wealth for administrative purposes. But the division of a society into different rank-ordered classes – a process known as *social stratification*[1] – existed long before the Romans; it is as old as human society itself.

Every country in the world has a socially stratified society. Even countries with an egalitarian ideology, such as the United States, have clear social class differences that may actually have increased over the nation's history. In fact these differences might even be more pronounced than in countries more associated with class differences, such as the United Kingdom, and which do not have the same egalitarian ideology.[2] Indeed even the former Soviet Union and other communist countries that were officially classless, or rather where everyone was the same (working) class, still showed clear signs of social stratification.

A stratified society, like a stratified cliff face, implies the existence of a hierarchy between the top and bottom strata. In geology this stratification denotes earlier or later laying down of a layer of molten rock or sediment. In sociology it denotes social groups that are either more or less highly valued. Thus we talk about the 'upper class' (or indeed the 'upper crust') the 'lower class' and the 'middle class'. Social stratification therefore implies the existence of a fundamental inequality in the way the resources of a society are distributed.

As well as the different levels of SES mentioned above, social stratification also highlights differences between the sexes and between ethnic groups. We will take up this topic in more detail in Chapter 12 but we should note here that just as income, education and occupation often go together to form SES, so do SES level, gender and ethnicity. Thus in most Western societies black females of low SES occupy the bottom stratum of society (and are treated accordingly) and white males of high SES occupy the top stratum.

Social stratification also implies that the people in each stratum tend to interact largely with others in the same stratum. They tend to live in the same kind of neighbourhood, have the same kind of friends, have the same kind of colleagues at work and even, as we saw in earlier chapters, be likely to meet their life partners in this way. It is not that the strata are cut off from each other deliberately – though in the case of the Hindu caste system they might be – but rather that they tend to conform to the group norms of social behaviour that we studied in the last chapter.

■ Social Status and Symbols

In any hierarchical system, where different levels are rank ordered, a person's *status* depends on his or her rank. In social stratification a high rank is accorded in different ways, for example through the *power* of being a legislator, through the *wealth* of being a successful entrepreneur, through the *prestige* attached to sporting talent or to creativity in the arts and sciences.

Different societies ascribe the same groups different degrees of social status, and in different ways. Writers have a higher social status in, say, France than in the United Kingdom. Managers have a higher social status in the United States than in Japan. As a society changes, social status may change accordingly. In the former Soviet Union poets, gymnasts and scientists had high status. In Russia today their stock has slumped dramatically, in favour of entrepreneurs – who didn't exist a few years ago.

The words 'status' and 'class' are often used interchangeably in practice. What usually catches the eye are the *symbols* that denote someone's status in society and the class that he or she is placed in. We have already seen in previous chapters that consumers buy products because of what they stand for as well as for their practical use. This symbolic use of products is the most visible way in which people claim status for themselves.

This kind of buying behaviour has been called *conspicuous consumption* at its most visible, where people are laying claim to membership in the highest social class.[3] Driving a Rolls or wearing a Rolex would fall into this category. But status symbolism is usually much more subtle than that.

If you accept the prevailing norms depicted in the advertising then the use of money itself reflects status. Only lower-class people use cash. Middle-class people use plastic, such as the American Express card which 'says more about you than money ever could'. But those with the highest status do neither – they have employees to take care of such things for them. The Queen, for instance, never carries cash and it's difficult to imagine her using a credit card.

Similarly, if you carry a briefcase to work you are automatically placed in the middle classes. The slimmer and more elegant the case the higher your status. But people of the very highest status don't carry a briefcase at all, they have somebody to walk behind and carry it for them.

Status symbols are also a very potent force in the life of organizations. Having a carpet on your office floor or a key to the executive lavatory can be a matter of great importance to people. It is also a cheap way for organizations to reward their employees. Any attempt to change an organization has to take this factor into account. That is why Japanese companies caused such a stir in their Western factories when they insisted that everyone from the chief executive to the office boy wore the same uniform, ate in the same canteen and used the same facilities.

What these Japanese companies were doing was removing the element of competition from status symbols. After all the most important aspect of status symbols is that very few people have them. If everybody drives exactly the same company car and parks it in the same building it can not be used as a status symbol. If everybody has a Rolex, or a good imitation thereof, there's no longer any point in owning one.

It is therefore the *exclusiveness* of a status symbol that is its attraction. But a symbol, whatever it is, is only a symbol. That is, it stands for something else. Psychologically, what a status symbol represents is being respected and accorded honour by other people. That is why the leaders of the world's fastest growing consumer industry, organized crime, are so concerned with gaining respect, both from their peers and from the non-criminal world. Their money can buy them any goods or services they want, but what they want most of all can't be bought. So they settle for the symbols of it. And the symbol is not always one of luxurious consumption. It might well be a large donation to communal or charitable causes.

The rest of us also value respect above anything else that society can offer us and as consumers we are tempted to purchase it whenever we can in the form of a status symbol.[4] The effectiveness of a product or service as a status symbol seems to rest on five factors:

- Exclusivity – only a few people should be eligible to acquire it.
- It should be relatively expensive.
- It should be of good quality.
- It should be of limited supply.
- It should be used by honoured and respected people.

Some status symbols endure for a long time – Rolls Royces, Havana cigars and vintage champagne, for instance – but times change and with them the meaning of certain symbols.

Gucci leather goods were accepted status symbols from the 1920s until the 1980s, when they came to be seen by many as hackneyed and déclassé after Gucci went downmarket and tried to broaden its appeal. Many of the electronic goods and household items that were status symbols when they were first introduced, and were relatively expensive, are now within the reach of most people with a middle-class income and middle-class tastes – even if others might classify these people as working class.

■ Life Chances and Lifestyles

We noted in the last chapter that the primary group membership of people is the family they were born into. The social status of that family is therefore the social status that the individual will have. As adults these individuals may become socially mobile, either upwardly or downwardly, and move into a different stratum of society. We have already seen the great psychological effect the family has on the development of its members and this is allied to its social effect. Put briefly, families at different levels of the social hierarchy afford their new members different *life chances* for their future in society.

These life chances cut across the psychological development, the emotional relationships, within a family. For example what would you think of the life chances of a boy who did poorly at school and left without any qualifications, whose father was a heavy drinker and died of a sexually transmitted disease, and whose mother ran around with other men? Not a lot I suspect. But what if I told you the boy was born and raised in a palace, was the son of a lord and prominent politician, went to one of the fanciest schools in England, and his name was Winston Churchill?

A person's future socioeconomic status is therefore dependent to a considerable extent on the social hand he or she is dealt at birth. Of course there are many individual exceptions to this trend, but the overall pattern is clear in countries all over the world. A person's future level of education, occupation and income depends more than anything else on the social status of the family he or she is born into. And this relationship is something that marketers and advertisers, themselves largely middle-class in origin, may not be sufficiently aware of.[5]

The differences between higher and lower social strata are even greater than is shown by the future SES level of their offspring however. It is widely accepted that the morbidity and mortality rates also differ between the strata. In other words the higher your social status the longer are you likely to live and the healthier will you be.[6] In addition you have a greater chance of finding a job and are less likely to lose it, either through being made redundant or by suffering a stress-related illness.[7]

The life chances of an individual therefore have a powerful bearing on his or her *lifestyle*. As we saw in our discussion of market segmentation in Chapter 2, a lot of work has been done by consumer researchers in trying to identify consistently different lifestyles. This research used psychological factors such as motivation and personality to come up with a set of consumer (or psychographic) profiles. You will no doubt recall *Thelma* 'the old-fashioned traditionalist', *Candice* 'the chic suburbanite', *Mildred* 'the militant mother', *Cathy* 'the contented housewife' and *Eleanor* 'the elegant socialite'. Let's look a little more closely at the lifestyles of Thelma and Eleanor:

- *Thelma*: devoted to husband, children and home ... socially and politically conservative ... keen churchgoer ... no higher education ... watches a vast amount of television.
- *Eleanor*: highly educated and sophisticated ... career-oriented big city dweller ... aware of social and political issues ... reads newspapers and magazines ... watches little television.

Even in these very short descriptions we can get a flavour of the very different lives these two women lead. They are clearly in widely separated social strata, probably based on the different life chances they were born with. It obviously follows that their patterns of consumption will probably be vastly different too.

We would also have to presume that Eleanor and Thelma see themselves as having different lifestyles and being in different social classes. In other words they will have some *class consciousness*. This term refers to people's *subjective* awareness that they might *objectively* be placed in a certain class because of their SES or lifestyle. Indications of class consciousness can be seen in some of the various interest groups to which people belong, for example political parties, trade unions, pressure groups and so on, though these are rarely watertight and there are always exceptions, for instance one or two rich people supporting the Socialist Workers' Party or poor people supporting the Republican Party.[8]

■ Measuring Social Class

■ Methods Used

Three main forms of method are used to measure social class: *objective, subjective* and *reputational*.

□   *Objective Methods*

These methods use the three readily quantifiable SES measures of occupation, income and education, which we have already discussed.   It is also possible therefore to quantify the close links between these three measures.[9] In addition to SES measures marketers sometimes add information obtained from geodemographic segmentation, as discussed in Chapter 2. You will recall that this form of segmentation is based on the idea that people who live in the same neighbourhood will tend to be similar on the three measures of SES. They will thus tend to have similar needs, wants and preferences and a similar amount of money to spend on them. This is therefore a way of objectively identifying ready-made *clusters* of households with similar lifestyles and patterns of consumption.

Objective methods of measuring social class may be separated according to the type of index used: those that use a *single variable* and those that are *multi-variable* in content.

Single-variable index   This type of index uses only one of the socio-economic and other variables listed above. *Occupation* is generally regarded as the best single measure of social class because it infers a lot of other factors as well. If someone tells you she's a corporate lawyer you will know she's had extensive formal education and will have a relatively high salary. If someone says he's a cleaner the reverse will probably be true.

But occupation is even more important than that when judging social class, and in ways that make the process more complex. A society accords differential status to the occupations of its members. That is, the amount of respect with which people treat each other is based on the type of work they do. A job is a very important part of a person's self-image – when people are asked to describe themselves they invariably do so in terms of their occupation. When people meet each other for the first time it's quite normal to ask 'what do you do?' (meaning 'what do you do for a living?') This process begins in early childhood, when children are often asked 'what are you going to be when you grow up?' (that is, 'what will you work at?') It is not therefore surprising that losing a job can be psychologically devastating.

Scales of occupational prestige tend to bear out some popular perceptions. Doctors and college teachers are usually top or near the top, labourers and car salesman (and advertising executives) at or near the bottom.[10] Status accorded to individuals on the basis of their job may cut across the other SES factors of income and education, with people rated similarly on occupational prestige having very different incomes, for instance, or living in different areas.

Multivariable index   This type of index uses more than one variable in combination to form a composite and more complex measure of social class. We have already seen how a single-variable index, though convenient and easy to use, does not capture all the subtlety contained in the concept of social class.

In America in the 1960s the United States Bureau of the Census developed a *socio-economic status score,* which combines all three SES variables of occupation, education and (family) income. This measure was intended primarily for use in the compilation of official research and statistics.[11] Richard Coleman has developed a measure intended for commercial use called *Coleman's Computerized Status Index* (CSI).[12] The CSI includes information on occupational prestige and area of residence as well as the usual SES variables of occupation, education and family income.

☐   *Subjective Methods*

A subjective method of measuring social class is one that asks people to rank *themselves* in the class hierarchy. In a sense this is a measure of class consciousness because it really invites people to say which class they identify with. This usually tends to create a great bulge in the middle of the hierarchy as respondents, especially in the United States, are reluctant to describe themselves as either lower class or upper class.

Most Americans, therefore, seem to regard themselves as middle class even when in terms of their SES they would be classified differently. This obviously reflects the prevailing egalitarian ideology. I remember in the 1970s seeing Nelson Rockefeller, an enormously wealthy man by any standards, trying to persuade Congress that he was fit to be vice-president of the United States because he was really just an ordinary middle-class guy like them. While one's reference group identification probably influences one's consumer behaviour, as we saw in the last chapter, there ccouldn't have been many middle-class people with the same consumption patterns as Nelson Rockefeller.

☐   *Reputational Method*

With the reputational method people are asked to rate *each other* on the social class hierarchy. This method is obviously limited, therefore, to small communities where everyone is fairly aware of everyone else's lifestyle. This method, like the subjective method of measuring social class, is of much less practical use to the marketer than the objective methods we considered above, although it has helped social scientists achieve a richer understanding of the way social classes are formed and how they relate to each other.[13]

☐   *Interpretive Methods*

More recently a method of gauging and understanding social class has been proposed in consumer research that is sometimes described as *interpretive.* As the name implies it involves researchers interpreting the written and visual products of a society to find clues about its attitudes and norms regarding social class behaviour. Fiction, as well as non-fiction such as social commentary and advertising material, is examined in a manner similar to literary criticism. Though this method is not as readily quantifiable as the use of objective indicators such as SES, it is a systematic study that is attracting some interest from consumer researchers.[14]

■ Social Class Categories

■ How Many Classes are There?

When we discussed market segmentation in Chapter 2 we saw that the same population can be divided in many different ways depending on what aspect of people's lives one is interested in. The same is true of social class. Researchers with different interests have divided the population into anything from two to nine different social classes.

Those interested in social research, for example, often divide a sample of the population into lower/working class and middle class only, and ignore the upper class. (People who are *really* upper class are rarely available for study.) Those who study aspects of the world of work frequently divide their sample into blue collar (manual workers) and white collar (office workers). At the other end of the scale sociologists who focus on the phenomenon of social class itself may be interested in identifying the smallest gradations in the hierarchy and end up with something like the following:

- Upper-upper, Middle-upper, Lower-upper.
- Upper-middle, Middle-middle, Lower-middle.
- Upper-lower, Middle-lower, Lower-lower.

Even a hierarchy as elaborate as this, however, conceals wide variations of SES factors *within* each level. For our purposes here we will consider the classification systems used most often by marketers and market researchers in the United States and the United Kingdom.

■ American Classification

The most widely accepted classification in the United States is that of Richard Coleman and is derived from his Computerized Status Index (CSI) which we looked at earlier in the chapter. Use of the CSI produced the classification depicted in Table 11.1

Table 11.1   Coleman's CSI classification

Classification	Percentage of population
Upper-upper	0.3
Lower-upper	1.2
Upper-middle	12.5
Middle class	32.0
Working class	38.0
Lower class	9.0
Lower-lower	7.0

Source. Coleman, R. P. 'The Continuing significance of social class to marketing', *Journal of Consumer Research*, 10, 267, December 1983.

We can see from Table 11.1 that just two of these social class groups – middle class and working class – between them represent 70 per cent of the total population. The people in these two classes are often referred to as 'Middle Americans' and what they are thought to want, like and believe in now sets the agenda not only for producers, marketers and advertisers, but for all social, economic and political decision makers. Let us look in a little more detail at these groups, as well as the more marginal ones above and below them on the status hierarchy.

☐   *Upper-Upper Class (0.3 per cent of the population)*

This is by far the smallest of all the social class groups. The people in it are regarded as the American aristocracy, and that's a pretty accurate description. Like all aristocrats the key to their wealth, power and position is *inheritance,* dating back for five or six generations in most cases. Likewise they are very homogeneous in background: they are all white, for instance, and mainly Protestant. And like all aristocrats they are a difficult group to penetrate: they tend to frequent the same few schools, universities and clubs where they meet – and marry – people like themselves. Nelson Rockefeller was a good example of this class.

In percentage terms this class is a minuscule fraction of the population, but in terms of what it owns it is extremely important. It is generally considered to control over a fifth of America's wealth directly (that is, personally) and indirectly to exert some influence over the remainder through its interpersonal networks among economic and political decision makers. People in this class generally have conservative lifestyles, including their consumer behaviour: they tend towards the 'tweedy' rather than the 'trendy', and they usually patronize long-established, up-market retailers.[15]

☐   *Lower-Upper Class (1.2 per cent of the population)*

This group is also a very tiny fraction of the population, though about four times the size of the aristocracy. Individuals may be as rich as, or even richer than, members of the upper-upper class but their wealth is not inherited. Either they or their parents are the first members of their family to reach this level of the status hierarchy. They represent 'new money' as opposed to the 'old money' of the aristocracy. '

The members of this group have therefore been very successful in what they do for a living, notably in business and the professions but also in less traditional wealth earners such as sport, the arts, the media and show business. Their consumption patterns tend to be less conservative and more expressive than those of the aristocracy; that is, they are more inclined to buy particularly fashionable and expensive goods and services because of the effect these have on their social standing.[16] This is the *conspicuous consumption* we encountered earlier in the chapter.

☐   *Upper-Middle Class (12.5 per cent of the population)*

The members of this group are generally high in all SES indicators, but especially education. They are often professionals who can exploit their expert knowledge financially as consultant physicians, specialist lawyers, computer designers and so on. Senior corporate managers and successful self-employed business and professional people would also be in this group. They tend to be active and visible in their local community, to be child-centred and particularly interested in their children's schooling, and to be especially concerned about 'the quality of life', including environmental and ecological issues.

This group, though affluent, has less disposable income per household than the two upper-class groups, but often has just as much interest in quality and 'good taste' on the one hand and conspicuous consumption on the other. Because of their frequently child-centred orientation much of their consumption patterns for both quality and 'show' are often connected with the home.

☐   *Middle Class (32 per cent of the population)*

The people in this group are the more comfortably off members of Middle America, though not affluent, and represent nearly a third of the population. In occupational terms they tend to be white-collar workers, junior or perhaps middle managers, or skilled blue-collar workers. But they have a lot less job security than the groups above them in the hierarchy.

Respectability is important to them, as is living in a 'nice' house in a 'nice' area and sending 'nice' children to a 'nice' school. Their consumption patterns tend towards the conformist rather than the colourful. Their most important psychological characteristic is a willingness to 'delay gratification', to forego present consumption for investment in the future, for example their children's schooling.

☐   *Working Class (38 per cent of the population)*

This is the largest social class, representing nearly two fifths of the population, and it comprises the less-well-off members of Middle America. The people in this group are mainly blue-collar workers and job insecurity is an ever-present shadow, especially as they are usually dependent on their income to meet regular expenses. Jobs are regarded mainly as a a source of income rather than a career, and they are therefore oriented more towards the present than the future.

The people in this group are also very family oriented but perhaps more traditionally than other classes, often with a dominant father sporting unreconstructed macho behaviour. Consumption patterns also tend towards the traditional, but with heavier consumption than other groups of cigarettes and alcohol.

☐   *Lower Class (9 per cent of the population)*

The people in this group are usually in work, but only just. The work they do may be unskilled, part-time, temporary, seasonal or any combination thereof. It will certainly be poorly paid with little in the way of fringe benefits such as holidays or sick pay, and there will be no job security at all. What they earn will just about keep them off the breadline and no more. Their lives are very much oriented towards the present out of sheer necessity.

The members of this group have little disposable income and usually have to buy as cheaply as they can. However it has long been recognized that one contradictory aspect of buying behaviour seems to be particularly prevalent among this group: they tend to spend a far greater proportion of their income than other groups on luxury items such as jewellery, clothing and electronic equipment – particularly those with famous brand names. This has been interpreted psychologically as *compensatory consumption*, where people try to compensate for the awful financial grind of their lives by treating themselves and their loved ones well.[17]

☐   *Lower-Lower Class (7 per cent of the population)*

The people in this group are similar to those in the lower class group except that they are usually *out* of work rather than in it, and living in even direr poverty. They tend to own even less, and disposable income is virtually non-existent as they are likely to be receiving some kind of welfare benefits – unless that is they have actually fallen through the net and are living rough.[18]

■   **British Classification**

The standard British classification used in social and market research has always been somewhat different from the American, as might be expected in a country with a different class structure. It uses six categories of social class, designated by the letters A–E (Table 11.2):[19]

Table 11.2   British social classes

Classification	Percentage of households
A (upper-middle class)	3
B (middle class)	10
C_1 (lower-middle class)	24
C_2 (skilled working class)	30
D (unskilled working class)	25
E (lower class)	8

- *A (upper middle class)*: the head of the household is in a senior position in business or the professions, and usually lives in a town house or a large detached house in the suburbs.
- *B (middle class)*: a less senior version of the 'A' household. Middle managers.
- C_1 *(lower middle class)*: small tradesmen, white-collar workers, junior managers.
- C_2 *(skilled working class)*: blue-collar workers.
- *D (unskilled working class)*: normally in work but as labourers or in other jobs at the bottom of the occupational ladder.
- *E (lower class)*: people whose employment is only casual, part-time or temporary, the unemployed, widows, people living on the state retirement pension or welfare benefits.

Comparisons between different social systems and different rating scales are always difficult to make and rarely exact, but if we look at Tables 11.1 and 11.2 one important distinction does seem to emerge: the American middle class seems to be larger than the British, and the British working classes larger than the American.

The American system also seems to identify a wider continuum, with a greater disparity between the top and bottom of the classification than the British system. This is partly because there probably is a greater disparity in class structure. But partly it is because the British system of classification does not identify the tiny group of people, known as the upper-upper class in the American system, whose wealth and power are also based on inheritance and social–interpersonal networks (known as 'the old school tie').

British market researchers using this system often divide their samples into two groups for comparison purposes: A, B, C_1 (middle class) and C_2, D (working class). In 1992 an attempt was made to bring this classification more into line with recent changes in lifestyles and patterns of disposable income.

Previous surveys of social class, both public and private, had taken for granted that the 'head of household' was male and that his occupation should define his household's place in the status hierarchy. Henceforth the 'chief income earner' would do so, whatever the source of the income.[20] As in the American classification system, this helps researchers form a better idea of how people in a particular group are likely to spend their disposable income.

■ Changing Social Class

There are two questions to consider here, both of which are important for marketers. First, is the categorization of people into social classes undergoing change? Second, to what extent can individuals change their social class?

As we noted in the preceding section, systems of social classification need to be updated periodically as social, economic and political changes occur in a society. But while the changes made to the British system of classification probably produced a more accurate categorization of householders in terms of disposable income and suggested a certain blurring of the lines between neighbouring classes, there is no evidence that the class system as such has changed very much. People's lifestyles, and therefore consumption patterns, must still be greatly affected by their social status.

In the United States the issue of changing social classes has been studied in some detail by consumer researchers. As reflected in our comparison of the British and American classification systems in the preceding section, one conclusion is that the middle class is expanding while the working class is contracting, and another is that the gap between the top and bottom of the status hierarchy is growing.[21] There is little evidence, however, that differences between the various classes in terms of occupational status and lifestyle have decreased significantly.

The issue of *individual* social mobility is a little different. Western societies, and especially the United States, have long prided themselves on the extent of upward mobility they have fostered. The expansion of the American middle classes would seem to support this ideology, though with the savage levels of white-collar unemployment and small-business failure in recent years *downward* mobility would also seem to be a distinct possibility for an increasing number of people.

There is some evidence that the extreme ends of the American status hierarchy are most susceptible to movement, both upward and downward. A study reported in the mid 1980s showed that over a ten-year period only about half of the people in the very highest and the very lowest brackets stayed there. People stuck in poverty and dependence on welfare amounted to no more than 2 – 3 per cent of the population.[22]

■ Marketing and Consumer Behaviour

There is an obvious temptation for marketers to target people in the higher social classes. In per capita terms consumers in these classes have the highest amount of disposable income. They also tend to be the social classes that marketing managers come from or identify with, especially in the United States. However even in the United States the working classes form an enormous market – accounting for almost a third of total income – and they may display greater brand loyalty than more upmarket consumers.[23]

Related to this factor is the kind of 'class consciousness' we have noted before in this book where people are very aware of the 'appropriate' kinds of places for them to shop. A change in marketing strategy that is intended to appeal to a significantly wider audience can result in the alienation of a retailer's traditional market, especially if the move is upmarket.[24]

We have seen at various points in this book how the different lifestyles of the different social classes means that they have quite different consumption patterns (theatre tickets and expensive wine versus lottery tickets and cheap beer, for instance). But perhaps more important than this difference is the less obvious one of differences in attitudes towards money, and its use.

We have seen that the higher social strata tend to be more future-oriented and therefore more inclined to invest in things such as stocks and bonds, life insurance and pensions. Richer people tend to use their credit cards as a substitute for cash while poorer people tend to use them for instalment purchases of things they couldn't otherwise afford.[25]

In any society, only a relatively small proportion of the population can afford to live a rich, luxurious lifestyle. But many more people may aspire to it, or enjoy partaking of it wherever possible. Few people drink vintage champagne on a regular basis, but many people will do so on a celebratory occasion. Marketers will naturally try to increase the number of such occasions. But perhaps the most astute form of class marketing is one that encourages people to associate a rich lifestyle with an everyday product – such as soap. 'A little luxury every day' is the slogan and selling point of Cusson's Imperial Leather.

■ Further Reading

Coleman, R. and L. Rainwater, *Social Standing in America: New Dimensions of Class* (New York: Basic Books, 1978). A thorough discussion of social class in the United States by two leading researchers.

Jowell, R., S. Witherspoon and L. Brook (eds), *British Social Attitudes: The Seventh Report* (Aldershot: Gower/SCPR, 1990). An annual series of large-scale surveys. The 1990 edition has information on the development of a classification system based on occupation.

Kriesberg, L., *Social Inequality* (Englewood Cliffs, N: Prentice-Hall, 1979). A wide-ranging review of all the factors related to classifying social class in the United States.

Lapham, L., *Money and Class in America* (London: Weidenfeld and Nicolson, 1988). Makes the argument that money has almost a religious significance in the United States compared with other countries.

Ries, A. and J. Trout, *Positioning: The Battle for your Mind* (New York: McGraw-Hill, 1981). Analyses the concept of a 'pecking order' in the way social status influences consumer behaviour.

It is also worth browsing through the latest issues of the following periodicals: *Advances in Consumer Research, Advertising Age, American Demographics, Journal of Social Research.*

■ Questions for Discussion

1. What is 'social stratification' and how does it affect consumer behaviour?
2. What are 'status symbols' (give some examples)? What factors are present in effective status symbols?
3. What is the relationship between income and social class? Under what circumstances might marketers target only a consumer's income level?
4. How do 'life chances' affect lifestyles?
5. How many social classes are there? How much does the number of classes identified matter to marketers?
6. How would you classify large local retailers in terms of the social class of their customers? Do marketing strategies differ?

CHAPTER 12
Cultural Influences

■ Introduction

How does our culture and the sub-cultures we belong to affect what we buy?

The word 'culture' is popularly used to refer to certain kinds of leisure activity, like going to see a Shakespeare play or listening to classical music. People who engage in this kind of behaviour are referred to as 'cultured'. They form a small percentage of the population and their interests and activities are often depicted in the British and North American mass media as being somewhat unworldly and rather elitist.

However the word 'culture' also has a social scientific meaning that is quite different from its popular usage and encompasses every person on earth. My favourite dictionary of management puts it this way:

> In anthropology a culture is usually defined as the shared beliefs, values, attitudes and expectations about appropriate ways to behave that are held by the members of a social group. This term is also important in psychology where the *unquestioned assumptions* people share about the world, about the human condition, about what is right, wrong or normal are perhaps even more important.[1]

As we saw in Chapters 8 and 9 the most dominant social grouping is the nation-state, and therefore the dominant form of culture will be a national one: French, Egyptian, Chinese or Indian culture for instance.

There are, however, clear and systematic differences between each of the national cultures, and these differences are reflected in consumer behaviour.

The most obvious differences are language, religion, dress, food, social customs, history and geography. But within each of these national cultures there may be large variations. Every nation has a dominant culture – be it statistically and/or socially and/or politically – and every nation has one or more less-dominant subcultures.

If we take India, for example, a representative of the statistically dominant culture would be a Hindi speaker of the Hindu religion. But hundreds of languages are spoken in India, the half-a-dozen or so major ones each being spoken by millions of people. There are also large Muslim, Buddhist and Christian communities, and representatives of several other religions. Even a small and relatively homogeneous country such as Switzerland is divided into French, German and Italian speakers (though in Switzerland most people speak more than one of these languages – reflecting an important aspect of the *national* Swiss culture).

We will return to the issue of subcultural differences later in the chapter, but it is worth reminding ourselves here that everyone in a given country is socialized into the national culture – a process sometimes called *enculturation* – regardless of the subcultures they also belong to. As we noted in Chapter 8, there is some evidence that even nations with such similar institutions as the United States and Canada can produce people who regard the world, and their own place in it, in very different ways. Nation states form the boundaries within which the psychological development of the person takes place, and they select from the vast range of psychological possibilities those aspects of behaviour that they consider most valuable.

We have already considered the socialization process in Figures 8.1 and 9.1. With the help of a similar diagram (Figure 12.1) it might be useful to consider the socialization of people from different countries into their own national culture.

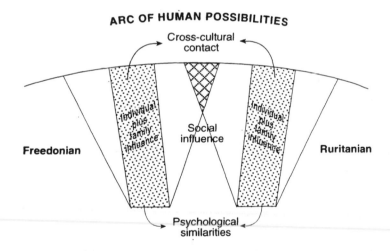

Figure 12.1   Socialization into national culture

We saw in Chapters 8 and 9 how the most important institutions in society, for example family and school as well as religious and political organizations, normally present the same message about the same beliefs and values to the growing child. These beliefs and values are the ones chosen by the dominant national group from what is sometimes called *the arc of human possibilities.*

Figure 12.1 shows that different national cultures may inhabit different points along this arc (though at the same time they will have many things in common). When our Freedonian and Ruritanian children become adults, therefore, they will not deal with each other simply as one human being to another but as a Freedonian to a Ruritanian, bringing with them to the encounter all the accumulated psychological and social baggage of their time on earth. Given that patterns of consumption are a crucial part of this baggage, the implications for marketing beyond one's own national culture are enormous. We will consider this issue, and the related one of subcultural differences, in some detail later in the chapter.

Our culture, then, is normally something we learn as we grow up, whether formally in history and civics lessons at school, or informally at home. What we learn are the norms of our society and we learn them so well that we consider them to be the normal and even natural way to think, feel and act. Indeed it may only be when we meet people from another country who have had a different process of enculturation that we even become aware of our own particular experience. And if we go to live in another country we will have to learn to adapt to a new culture – a process known as *acculturation*.

■ Similarities across Culture

We noted, as portrayed in Figure 12.1, that different cultures may choose to emphasize similar aspects of being human. In fact, though it may not look like it, different national cultures have a great deal in common with each other. Social scientists interested in identifying universal aspects of culture have listed as many as 73 of them, all the way from age-grading and athletic sports to weaning and weather control, which are found in every known society.[2] Here are a few of the more important universals:

- Calendar making
- Courtship
- Forbidden food
- Gift giving
- Joking
- Music
- Myths
- Personal names
- Religious rituals
- Status ranking

When we add to these the basic foundations of any society such as education, government and law we can see that every culture has had to grapple with all the universal questions that arise whenever large groups of people wish to live together. It is the specific *answers* to these questions that may be different. These differences, which we will deal with below, are easy to spot – much more easily than the similarities – and that, as we noted in Chapter 4, may be an inevitable outcome of the way in which we perceive the world. As you read the next section, though, it might not be a bad idea to reflect on this point occasionally, and consider whether you may be more similar to, than different from, your counterpart in another culture.

Before leaving the issue of cultural similarities it is worth noting that in recent years – particularly with the advent of satellite broadcasting and, most recently, the Internet – many commentators have noted a *convergence* between different cultures in their patterns of consumption. But while the new media of communication may have provided the means for some shared cultural experiences (most notably in watching sport, for instance the World Cup or the Olympic Games) the reason that most of the world drinks Coca Cola and eats McDonald's hamburgers is perhaps due more to the strength of American marketing and advertising.

Much of the cultural convergence in consumer behaviour, in other words, may take the form of local adaptations to American products. There is nothing new about this. Hollywood movies have been seen around the world for most of this century, and with them their depiction of American cultural values. With some notable exceptions (such as Japanese electronics and Scotch whisky) this is not true of products from other countries.

■ Differences between Cultures

■ Language

The playwright George Bernard Shaw once quipped that the English and the Irish were two peoples divided by a common language. Speaking the same language is no guarantee against differences in national culture. Thus the differences in the use of English between the United States and Britain may reflect important differences between their two cultures.

Some of the differences are merely amusing (although they may illustrate a problem in communication), such as the phrase 'I'm mad about this flat'. In New York, if you said this you'd be angry about a punctured tyre, but in London you'd be delighted with the place you live in. And what do you make of the following differences?

American	British
He ran for office	He stood for office
They took a vacation	They went on holiday
I took a shower	I had a shower
She took an exam	She sat an exam
Coffee break	Teatime
Movies	Pictures

Here is an example that periodically causes problems at international meetings. When a Briton and an American wish to table an item on the agenda for discussion they do not want to do the same thing – in fact, they want to do opposite things. The American wants to take the item *off* the agenda, but the Briton wants to put it *on* the agenda.

The gap in communication becomes wider, of course, when the people trying to communicate in the same language come from very different cultures. An Arab psychologist named Shouby studied the Arabic language and culture and concluded that in comparison with the use of English by English speakers, Arabic was full of overassertion and exaggeration, flowery and unrealistic.

Thus, Shouby notes, 'If an Arab says exactly what he means without the expected exaggeration other Arabs may still think that he means the opposite. This fact leads to misunderstanding on the part of non-Arabs who do not realize that the Arab speaker is merely following a linguistic tradition'.[3] The corollary of this is also true, Shouby argues – namely that an Arab finds it hard to take a simple statement at face value.

Shouby reports an encounter that gave him a chance to observe his conclusions in action. The people trying to communicate with each other were both friends of his, an English woman and an Arab man. The woman told . Shouby that the man persisted in declaring his amorous intentions toward her despite unequivocal refusal on her part. The man told him that the woman was leading him on but that he hadn't really shown much interest in her. Both were quite sincere, Shouby argues, and both were being true to their cultures. The resultant meeting between Arab exaggeration and British understatement produced something less than perfect communication.

On the other hand different nations that share a common language may also share a great deal in terms of culture; even a sense of humour. Thus a New Zealand beer called Steinlager ran an advertisement in the United Kingdom with the following copy: 'What do you call a sophisticated Australian? A New Zealander'.

When communication is attempted between two different languages there are, of course, much greater opportunities for miscommunication. This is a problem of immediate concern to overseas marketers and several classic mistakes have passed into marketing legend. Pepsi Cola's slogan 'Come alive with Pepsi' became 'Come out of the grave' in German and 'bring your ancestors back from the grave' in Chinese.[4]

The Ford Motor Company had some interesting problems in Latin America. The Caliente did not do well in Mexico, for instance, where the word is slang for prostitute. And calling another model 'a small male appendage' did little for the sales of the Pinto in Brazil. But my all-time favourite comes from the prepared foods market, where Frank Perdue (North America's answer to Bernard Matthews) had the personally and proudly announced slogan 'It takes a tough man to make a tender chicken'. In Spanish this turned into 'It takes a sexually stimulated man to make a chicken affectionate', which might well be true but somewhat misses the point of the original.[5]

■ **Non-Verbal Communication**

While the use of language is enormously important to us, it is not the only way in which we communicate. There is a wide variety of *non-verbal communication* in everyday use such as style of clothing, gestures, facial expressions, amount of eye contact, tone of voice and body postures. Members of a given culture learn to communicate with each other in these non-verbal ways just as much as (or perhaps even more than) they do verbally.

People whose work requires them to be alert to nuances of meaning when dealing with other people – such as salesmen and psychotherapists – are more conscious of non-verbal forms of communication (sometimes called 'body language') than most people, and perhaps more adept at interpreting it. People from a different culture may find it much harder to tune into different patterns of non-verbal communication than into a different language. Making eye contact in Western cultures, for instance, is usually interpreted as a sign of friendliness and interest, but in some Eastern cultures it is considered rude. These differences are, of course, reflected in business and sales contacts and in advertising.[6]

■ Cultural Values

Language and body language are the most visible and immediate ways in which cultures differ from each other. But these are primarily the *means* by which members of a culture communicate with each other. What we will now consider is what they are communicating about, the *content* of the communication.

This content is often referred to as *cultural values*, a term that includes the shared beliefs and the unquestioned assumptions about what is important and right and normal in the way people behave, which was at the heart of our definition of culture at the beginning of this chapter. A nation derives its cultural values from 'the arc of human possibilities', which was illustrated in Figure 12.1. To the extent that the members of a culture share these values and are guided by them, they can be expected to behave in similar ways when they are in similar situations, including buying and consuming. This kind of predictability is crucial to a marketing strategy.

It is important for marketers to understand a national culture in broad general terms and to be aware of its most basic values. Only then can they really hope to be aware of the kind of attitudinal differences towards individual products that can mean the difference between successful marketing and complete failure. Most of the examples of poor marketing across cultures that are quoted above are by American firms operating overseas, but the problem is by no means unknown the other way round.

The German manufacturer Miele, for instance, produces high-quality, front-loading washing machines that sell well in various European countries but not in the United States. The difference is that a washing machine in Europe is generally regarded as a consumer durable and is expected to give many years of highly efficient service. In the United States washing machines are generally of the more convenient, but less efficient, top-loading kind. They also cost about a third of the price of the Miele machine.

Therein lies the difference in cultural values. The washing machine (or indeed any other machine) as a consumer durable is a largely alien concept in the United States, where it is regarded as more of a disposable item. The greater physical mobility of American society leads to convenience and disposability being valued more highly than durability, or even efficiency.[7]

There are also times when a company's attempt to reflect the values of a target market can backfire – and times when it deserves to. As I draft this paragraph in February 1996 there are reports in the British media about such a case involving the Ford Motor Company. As part of its 'everything we do is driven by you' advertising campaign the company used a photograph of 25 smiling workers from its Dagenham plant.

Then five of the smiling workers noticed that, with the wonders of modern computer technology, they'd been given a change of skin colour, from black to white. After being threatened with an all-out strike the company explained the 'oversight'. Apparently this version of the advertisement had been intended for Poland, where – it was thought – punters would buy more cars if they perceived them as an all-white product.

The particular set of cultural values that have been studied most in consumer behaviour is that of the United States. Many commentators have come up with many different lists of such values but there is a wide measure of agreement about the importance of certain factors. These factors seem to fall into two fairly distinct types that we may refer to as 'ideals and actualities', as follows:

Ideals	Actualities
Individualism	Materialism
Equality	Progress, achievement and success
Humanitarianism	Efficiency and practicality
Youthfullness	Activity
Social conformity	Mastery of environment

■ Ideals

Each of these represents an ideal state of affairs that is not usually, or always, attained in practice.

Individualism

One of the most prominent American ideals highlights the importance of individual (as opposed to group) fulfilment. This is exemplified by the highly popular personality theory of Abraham Maslow, which we encountered in Chapter 5. At the apex of Maslow's pyramid of human needs was that of *self actualization*, where an individual strives to become all that he or she can be. The popular emphasis here is very much on self-reliance and independence which may not be entirely what Maslow had in mind. After all emotional maturity also includes the ability to trust and be dependent on other people in forming human relationships.

In consumer terms the value of individualism is promoted by all those products, such as clothes, cosmetics and even cars, whose sales pitch is that they enhance the unique or distinctive aspects of the user's personality. The role model used in advertising is that of the rugged individualist who goes his (and increasingly her) own way. It is based on a deeply rooted heroic image of people who stand up for what they know is right, regardless of the odds against them. Think of Gary Cooper in 'High Noon', for instance, or Gregory Peck in 'To Kill a Mockingbird'.

☐ *Equality*

'We believe these truths to be self-evident', begins the American Declaration of Independence, 'that all men are created equal'. This noble sentiment has informed American values ever since 1776. It is, and always has been, both an ideal aspiration for the American society and a source of great contention.

In addition to the fact that the declaration excluded approximately half of the human race – females – its author and some of its signatories owned black male slaves, men whose *inequality* was self-evident. What Jefferson and company really meant, of course, was 'that all free white men of property are created equal'. or as George Orwell put it in *Animal Farm* a couple of centuries later, 'all animals are equal but some are more equal than others'.

Yet it would be quite wrong to deny the power of the egalitarian ideal in influencing the behaviour of Americans. The last two generations have been deeply concerned with the effects of inequality between blacks and whites and then between men and women – and, for that matter, between homosexuals and heterosexuals.

The belief in a meritocracy is perhaps stronger than ever before and few Americans would disagree with the Declaration of Independence that everyone has 'an equal right to life, liberty and the pursuit of happiness'. Equality of *opportunity* to achieve success and material prosperity (rather than equality of treatment) is therefore the primary form that this cultural value now takes and this is echoed in product advertising. Taken together with the previous core value of individualism, this helps account for the hero worship of self-made billionaires such as H. Ross Perot as opposed to those with inherited wealth such as the Rockefellers.

☐ *Humanitarianism*

Americans have a world-wide (and well-deserved) reputation for helping other people in need. In the United States itself Americans give somewhere between $100 and 200 *billion* dollars a year to charity. This cultural value of generosity is also recognised by business and government, but at that level the motivation for giving may not be quite the same as it is for individuals or families.

People seeing television reports of an African famine may be moved spontaneously to write a cheque to an aid organization, but large organizations do not usually act on the basis of impulse. This is not to doubt the personal humanitarian values of the people who run American business and government, but simply to point out that in their professional lives they have to cope with other interests, such as shareholders or influential lobbyists.

It is not entirely unknown, for instance, for companies whose products have been criticized on humanitarian grounds to buy themselves a little favourable publicity by sponsoring good works in the local community. Nor has the government always resisted the temptation to tie international aid to business deals with American companies. This is a topic we will explore in some more detail in Part V.

☐   *Youthfulness*

This value refers to the widespread desire to look and act young (which is open to everyone), as opposed to actually *being* young (which is obviously limited to a minority group – and a relatively poor one at that). Advertisements for skin creams and hair colouring are obviously appealing to this value, and it is also found with detergents, perfumes, vitamins and even package tours.

There are probably two sources of this value. One is the generally accepted belief that the United States is a 'a young country' in comparison with the rest of the world. As it is only some 69 years younger than the United Kingdom and almost two centuries older than, say, Zimbabwe and Pakistan there is clearly a mythical element to this belief.

The other source of this value is the importance attached to 'the new' as opposed to 'the old'. Technological development and product innovation is widely seen as good by definition and of course it forms an essential basis for the consumer society to exist and thrive. Being seen as 'old' therefore implies that one is not just likely to be unfashionable, but also outmoded and given to using inferior products.   Moreover this is not tempered by a cultural respect for the aged, as there is for example in an even more technologically advanced country like Japan.

☐   *Social Conformity*

A set of cultural characteristics, as with a set of individual personality characteristics, need not be entirely consistent. Just as most of us display contradictory aspects of our personalities so do most national cultures. That is why Americans value not only the individualism with which we began this section, but also social conformity.

In the previous two chapters we saw how social life would simply not be possible without general and continuous conformity by people to group and societal norms. However the American cultural value goes further than this and makes a positive *virtue* of conformity. In consumer terms this usually takes the form of trivia such as hair length or clothing, where people who buck the norm might be considered odd and unreliable, though usually pretty harmless.

The dark side of this cultural value is seen when it comes up against other core values such as individualism and equality. The classic case is the story of the House Un-American Activities Committee of the 1950s and 1960s. The very name says it all. Can you imagine a House Un-Canadian Activities Committee, or a House Un-British Activities Committee?

What was considered Un-American in this case was support for 'left-wing' political ideas (such as 'all men are created equal'). Even today it is difficult to imagine a rugged individualist who happens to be, say, an avowed atheist, running for political office in the United States, despite a constitution that proudly proclaims the separation of church and state. Advertising plays it very safe, of course, and errs on the side of conformity when values clash. The nearest it gets to rugged individualism is the 'Marlboro Man', who reserved the right to smoke himself to death with the brand of his choice (literally in the case of the actor concerned, who tried to sue the manufacturer after contracting cancer).

■ Actualities

These perhaps represent more of the everyday lives that people actually lead than the preceding set of ideals, which act as a more general guide.

□ *Materialism*

Americans are probably the world's most enthusiastic consumers. They account for about a quarter of all manufactured exports *in the whole world,* and this with about 4 per cent of the world's population. Increased material comfort, luxury and pleasure are the major goals that drive the consumer economy and it is systematically encouraged by advertising[8] and marketing.[9] Success is usually measured in terms of acquisitions such as houses, cars and electronic goods, and people devote an enormous amount of their lives to acquiring these things.

However it is not only the pursuit of material comfort that is important but the *enjoyment* of it, and indeed the *necessity* for many people of having a lifestyle that the rest of the world might regard as luxurious. For many non-Americans this is exemplified by the quality and quantity of American plumbing – a source of wonder and admiration for most of us. Indeed the bathroom is to America what the kitchen is to France.

I once ran a Junior Year Abroad Programme for American students in London. While most of the students were generally appreciative of the educational experience provided for them, this was a matter of trivial importance compared with the *absolute necessity* of having at least one long hot shower a day. As the Victorian accommodation had not been built with this need primarily in mind, there were times when it simply wasn't possible. My feeble attempts to explain that no one would actually die as a consequence were met with incredulity and outrage.

□   *Progress, Achievement and Success*

Commentators are generally agreed that most Americans are usually much more influenced by their view of the future than the past. Many people would subscribe to Henry Ford's famous view that 'history is bunk' – or if not 'bunk' then perhaps irrelevant, for the most part, to their own lives in which 'new' is self-evidently better than 'old'. This linear view of time, that it becomes more important as it goes from past to present to future, is closely allied to that of *progress*, that the present is better than the past and the future will be better than the present. As I have suggested elsewhere, 'This view is heavily influenced by the development of science and technology, where steady progress over time in understanding and knowledge is self-evident'.[10]

From the founding of the Republic it was generally accepted – largely unconsciously – that the American society was *progressing*, that people were getting healthier and wealthier and more materially comfortable all the time. But this implicit belief in the inevitability of progress is, I think, beginning to falter:

> For the first time, perhaps, since the Industrial Revolution this unconscious assumption of continuous progress over time is being widely questioned. The effects of political and economic policies leading to unemployment and lack of job security (or work alternatives), as well as social upheavals and environmental concerns, have forced upon many people throughout the world the conclusion that not only is the present worse than the past but the future for their children may be even worse than the present.[11]

Needless to say these concerns are not usually reflected in product advertising, which remains relentlessly upbeat. And Americans do still enjoy a greater average spending power than the citizens of any other country. The per capita gross domestic product in the mid 1990s is about $22 000 a year compared with $19 000 for Japan and $16 000 for the United Kingdom. However this position may not last indefinitely. A country that was the world's largest creditor in 1980 was by 1995 the world's largest debtor, owing other countries something like $5 *trillion*.

The individual correlate of this materialist social environment is the need for *achievement* that it fosters. This is seen at its clearest in entrepreneurial business activities, and while not, of course, exclusive to Americans it perhaps accounts for more of the American motivation to work hard and achieve worldly success than any other factor.[12] This driving force is often traced back to the early Puritan days and what came to be known as the 'protestant work ethic', as famously redefined by President Richard Nixon on Labor Day 1971: 'The "work ethic" holds that labor is good in itself; that a man or woman becomes a better person by virtue of the act of working'.

The signs of being a successful achiever lie in the ownership of widely desired and immediately apparent consumer goods such as a Jaguar or a Mercedes or a big house in an expensive neighbourhood. We saw in Chapter 11 that the more successful people become materially, the more oriented they are towards concern with the future, thus reinforcing the links between progress, achievement and success, and at the same time fostering these in their children. We also saw in that chapter how appealing it is for less successful people to comfort or reward themselves whenever possible with a *taste* of the 'good life'.

☐ *Efficiency and Practicality*

Along with the idea of progress there has long been an American cultural value of efficiency, of doing things as well as they can be done, and then doing them even better. Continuous technical improvement and invention of machines, processes and services has been the expression of this value, and its heroes have been entrepreneurs such as Edison and Ford who could transmute such increased efficiency into gold.

This concern for efficiency was also applied to the management of time at work, where the ability to get as much as possible out of people during their working day became a guiding principle of American management, and a source of conflict with workforces who objected to being treated like machines. This form of 'time and motion study' was invented by Frederick W. Taylor at the end of the nineteenth century and in many workplaces is as important now as it was then.

It was the *practicality* of a machine or a method that always appealed to Americans, rather than the concept or the ideas behind them. It was a 'how to' approach to back up a 'can do' philosophy of society. Most domestic labour-saving devices and services, from sewing machines to microwave ovens and fast food outlets, originated in the United States and have invariably found a more receptive and enthusiastic market there than in other countries. Of course 'labour saving' implies 'time saving', and the value of that is in freeing people to engage in leisure activities.

☐ *Activity*

Related to the work ethic we have already discussed is the value of *activity*. Old Puritan sayings such as 'the Devil makes work for idle hands' still have a lot of mileage left in them. The value of working hard goes without saying, but there is also a cultural value in *playing* hard in one's leisure time. Modern clichés such as 'no pain, no gain' are now applied to efforts to maintain fitness – an enormous industry in the United States.

The reward, in other words, is not in the activity itself (whether it's a competitive sport such as tennis or a solo pursuit such as jogging) but in the sense of *achievement*, presumably at having survived the ordeal. Any suspicion of having fun is, of course, severely frowned upon.   The idea is that if you don't take it seriously it's not worth doing. Of course this attitude may just be related to the fact that the more seriously you take the activity the more money you're going to spend on equipping yourself to do it.

By thus equipping yourself, of course, you are also demonstrating to the world what a seriously active person you are, one of the 70 per cent of Americans who engage in one or more athletic pursuits daily.[13] This is why no self-respecting Manhattanite will go out for the *New York Times* on a Sunday morning in anything less than the most fashionable jogging gear.

□   *Mastery of the Environment*

The United States has a powerfully emotive cultural myth, and indeed history, of 'taming the wilderness' and pushing the frontier westwards. The development of the transcontinental railway system in the nineteenth century and the high-way system in the twentieth gave Americans immediate visual evidence of their mastery over the environment. Of course the price for this mastery was paid by the Native American peoples whose lands were seized and whose way of life was destroyed.

That way of life emphasized the cultural value of living in harmony with nature rather than seeing it as a hostile environment that had to be tamed, mastered and plundered for its mineral wealth and other resources. To the growing nineteenth-century economy, Indian cultural values were either incomprehensible or outmoded, and in any event could not be allowed to stand in the way of 'progress'.

In modern consumer terms mastery of the environment has been most noticeable in the food chain from field to table. Intensive farming has turned a predominantly agrarian society into an urban one over the course of the twentieth century. At the beginning of the century most Americans still lived on the land. By the end of the century that figure was down to about 1–2 per cent of the population.

With the extensive use of irrigation and chemicals this tiny fraction of the American population is able to feed the rest and to engineer fruits and vegeta-bles that *look* attractive (whatever they taste like) and have an ever-increasing shelf life in the retail outlets. In recent years the ecological and health costs of this agribusiness have increasingly exercised the consumer, an issue we will return to in Part V.

■   **Differences in Cultural Values**

We have already seen that even national cultures as similar as those of the United States and Canada can contain significant differences. It is worth taking a brief look at some of those differences as they shed a different light on the meaning of cultural values.

At the height of the Cold War in 1970 I studied two samples of bright upper-middle-class-children, one in Detroit, Michigan, and the other just a few miles away across the border in Hamilton, Ontario. Among the findings of this study were the following:[14]

- The American children had a much greater awareness of their country's international power .
- They understood political concepts such as 'foreigner' much earlier than the Canadian children.
- These concepts had a much more ideological content for the Americans than for the Canadians (for example 'freedom' for the American children meant something like not being under the heel of a communist commissar; for the Canadians it was more likely to be the ability to go out and play ice hockey when you felt like it).

Thus the cultural values of the two countries were clearly evident in the different ways their children perceived the social world, even as early as age six.

A later study of the whole range of national values also found many differences between the two countries, including the following:[15]

Table 12.1 Differences between the cultural values of Canadians and Americans

Canadians	*Americans*
More law-abiding	Less law-abiding
Emphasize *community* rights and obligations	Emphasize *individual* rights and obligations
Slightly suspicious of success	Worship success
Value achievement less	Value achievement more
Less committed to work ethic	Highly committed to work ethic
Value social relationships more	Value social relationships less
Great concentration of banks and corporate ownership	Great diversity of companies and banks
Much more in favour of government intervention in business and welfare issues	Much more *laissez-faire*
Canadian labour union membership double that of United States	

These are general cultural values and any given individual in either country might not conform to them of course. One important reason for this is that every dominant national culture has one or more *subcultures* that might be of more influence in shaping a given person's behaviour.

■ Subcultures

A subculture may be considered a culture within a culture, one that shares many of the values of the dominant or parent culture while retaining its own special characteristics. There are many examples of subcultures in the European and North American national cultures, some of which are more easily identifiable than others.

Psychologically, subcultures that are important to people and their sense of identity can have an influence on their behaviour. But only the individual can really give us that information. Thus a black woman may be put into the categories of skin colour and sex by a marketing observer but what might be more important to her are her membership of the medical profession and her humanist beliefs, two quite different subcultures. However in many cases the more obvious subcultures that people belong to *are* important to their sense of identity and are therefore relevant to marketing.

We considered a number of subcultures under the heading 'Market Segmentation' in Chapter 2 - age, geography and lifestyle, for example – but in this context I think it more appropriate to examine the other major subcultural factor in our society – ethnicity.

■   Ethnicity

Different national cultures contain different degrees and types of ethnicity. In the United States the figure is about 25 per cent of the population. It is about the same in the United Kingdom if the Scots, Welsh and Northern Irish are included (if not, the figure falls to about 5 per cent). Ethnicity has two components, *national origin* and *race*.

□   *National Origin*

One deviation from a national culture in consumer terms may be found in the case of smaller nations that are part of larger political groupings, for example Scotland and Wales within the United Kingdom. We have already noted that Scots consume more confectionery than other Britons and they presumably account also for most of the haggis eaten in the United Kingdom! But these food products are relatively minor variations in the overall pattern of British consumer spending and of interest largely to speciality or niche markets.

A somewhat more important reflection of different cultural values may be found in the different rates of home and car ownership in Scotland and England. Scots have long had much lower rates of ownership than the English and this difference has not appreciably altered in recent years. It may well be founded in different cultural values regarding support of community and public ownership in Scotland as opposed to individualism and private ownership in England.

Another influence of national origin is attachment to a national culture outside the boundaries of the country one lives in. This kind of subculture has been extensively studied in the United States, where most of those who are not actually immigrants themselves can trace their ancestry back to someone who was.

Thus many people are aware of their roots in an Irish, Italian, Japanese or Mexican national culture, for example – to the point where their consumer behaviour might be affected by it. Food is the most obvious market, of course, but there are many others, such as travel to the country in question, clothing, cultural and linguistic products, or subscription to ethnic newspapers and magazines that contain advertising for *general* usage products and services as well as more specialized ones.

However strong the bond that Americans have to a national subculture it is usually placed within the framework of the American national culture. One can see this most easily in food consumption patterns, and it has often been remarked how the American version of a dish is different from the original.

This observation has been studied in the case of Mexican-Americans living in the south-west of the United States. A group of Mexican-Americans were compared with Anglos and with people in Mexico City of the same socio-economic status. A pattern of consumption emerged that reflected a new cultural style, rather than simply a merging of the two, that was formed by the process of assimilating the different national cultures.[16] This is one small example of the way in which 'hyphenated' Americans form distinct subcultures while adhering to the basic values of the parent culture.

There are also knock-on effects in buyer behaviour. Hispanic-Americans generally tend to be more conservative food shoppers than their Anglo counterparts. They tend to follow the buying patterns of their parents, for instance, buying familiar brands and not being tempted into impulse buying, and preferring to shop at smaller, often ethnic, stores despite their prices being higher than those of supermarkets. And they also seem to prefer fresh food to frozen or prepared foods.[17]

☐ *Race*

What is usually meant by 'race' is skin colour. The word only has meaning insofar as people classify *themselves* as belonging to a certain racial group, because objectively some people who consider themselves 'white'may have darker pigmentation than some who consider themselves 'black'.

Racial categorizations also cut across national origins, of course, as in the case of Jamaican immigrants to the United Kingdom or Korean immigrants to the United States. And the situation becomes even more complex with the native-born children of these immigrants, who are British or American citizens.

However the racial group that has been most studied in the research literature on consumer behaviour is unique to the United States, with no cross-affiliation to any other national culture, black-Americans. At 12 per cent of the population they are the largest ethnic group in the United States (although they have a much lower birth rate than Hispanic-Americans who, on present projections, will overtake them in number early in the twenty-first century).

Estimates of black-American spending range widely from $150–270 billion per year. Whatever the true figure it is clearly substantial. While on average blacks have a lower socio-economic status than whites, their sheer number makes them an important market and there is also a sizeable and growing black middle class with a considerable disposable income.   Finding and reaching this market requires some thought, as blacks tend to read different magazines and watch different television shows than whites.   This is a point we will consider in Chapter 14 when we discuss communication and persuasion.

The history of black consumption patterns in the United States has been affected by the historical position of black people in relation to whites; that is, one of systematic prejudice and discrimination.   Where blacks could live, work, travel, be educated or eat was (and in some cases still is) related to factors other than their ability to pay.

Blacks are now spending more money in these areas of historical discrimination, encouraged by marketing campaigns specifically targeted at them by leading companies, yet differences still remain.   There are some clear differences in the investment spending pattern of the black and white middle classes, for instance, though their spending on consumer goods may be quite similar.

Thus only 9 per cent of blacks, compared with 24 per cent of whites, own stocks or mutual funds and only 4 per cent (as opposed to 11 per cent) have equity in a business.   The net result is that even when they earn comparable salaries whites have over three times the median net worth of blacks.[18]   These patterns are possibly exacerbated by the tendency for blacks to engage in the kind of *compensatory consumption* we noted earlier, whereby people reward themselves with socially visible luxuries they can enjoy in the present (such as Scotch whisky or expensive clothes) rather than delaying gratification and planning for the future.

☐   *Regional*

Finally in this section it might be appropriate to say a word about religion, which of course is another cultural factor related to ethnicity.   The difficulty for students of consumer behaviour is that there is not a great deal of research on the specific effects of religion as opposed to nationality or race.[19]   Although the more obvious issues are familiar enough in marketing, such as not targeting Moslems for alcohol or pork products for instance, or Christian Scientists for proprietary drugs.

■ Changes in Culture

While basic cultural values, such as those we have outlined, may endure for many years, no culture anywhere is static and unchanging.   In fact the converse is nearer the truth, cultures are *always* in the process of changing.   But sometimes what is required to see the changes taking place is a longer-term view than we are accustomed (or encouraged) to take.   I'm reminded of the historian who was asked recently what he thought was the most important effect of the French Revolution (in 1789).   He replied 'it's too soon to tell'.

For those people who can't take our historian's view of events, various researchers have tried to capture changes in cultural values (particularly in the United States) as they happen, and to predict what their impact on consumption patterns might be. One important method used to track such change is called *content analysis*. As its name suggests the method analyzes the contents of various cultural products – for example newspapers, magazines, films and advertising – and compares them at different times. If this is done systematically, certain new themes and patterns of behaviour will be identified.[20]

Among the most important changes identified in recent years are the following:

- 'Baby boomers' (born between 1946 and 1964) believe in many of the core American values noted above, but along with that goes a more relaxed attitude towards the sexual behaviour of others and a certain uneasiness with the crasser aspects of material consumption.[21]
- Time is becoming an ever-scarcer and more valued commodity (for people in work, that is). Products and services that save time – microwave ovens, fast-food outlets, cleaning services and so on – are being more heavily used. Money, in other words, is being traded for time.[22]
- People are spending more time in, and money on, the home, with a great increase in home entertainment and do-it-yourself improvements. This trend is sometimes known as *cocooning*.[23]
- There is great interest in all aspects of health, from individual fitness programmes to the long-term effects of pollution and environmental degradation. This includes all aspects of farming, fishing and the rearing of livestock and all the points along the food chain, as well as smoking, drinking, drugs and alternative medicine.[24] We shall take another look at this issue when we discuss consumerism in Part V.

■ Further Reading

Browne, R. B. (ed.), *Rituals and Ceremonies in Popular Culture* (Bowling Green, Ohio: Bowling Green University Popular Press, 1980). An interesting series of studies that includes an interpretation of consumption as the essential ritual of modern life.

Caplan, N., J. K. Whitmore and M. H. Choy, *The Boat People and Achievement in America: A Study of Family Life, Hard Work, and Cultural Values* (Ann Arbor, MI: University of Michigan Press, 1989) An influential anthropological approach to the North American market that deals in cultural boundaries rather than the political ones of country, state and region.

Rokeach, M. (ed.), *Understanding Human Values: Individual and Societal* (New York: Free Press, 1979) A useful overview by a leading researcher in the field of identifying values and constructing instruments for measuring them.

Spradley, J. P. and M. A. Rykiewich (eds), *The Nacirema: Readings on American Culture* (Boston: Little, Brown, 1980). An interesting set of readings on the origins of American cultural values.

It is also worth browsing through the latest issues of the following periodicals: *Advances in Consumer Psychology, Advertising Age, Journal of Consumer Marketing, Journal of International Consumer Marketing, Journal of Consumer Research, Marketing World.*

■ Questions for Discussion

1. What is meant by 'culture' in the social scientific sense? What is its importance to the marketer?
2. Are similarities or differences between cultures more important to the marketer?
3. How might language difference be important in marketing? What non-verbal behaviour might be relevant?
4. What is the relevance of 'cultural values' to marketing? What are the differences between ideal and actual American values?
5. What are the major subcultures that marketers should be aware of? What opportunities and problems do they present?

CHAPTER 13

Attitudes

Introduction

Where do our attitudes about products come from and how do they change?

If someone were to ask you 'do you like Coca Cola?' they would be trying to find out your *attitude* towards the product. If you answered 'yes' to that question you would have a lot of company as Coca Cola is generally considered the most powerful brand image in the solar system.[1] Many people, therefore, must have a favourable attitude towards the product.

But simply answering 'yes' or 'no' to a question about liking something gives us only a very general understanding of a person's relationship with the product. In relation to Coca Cola, for instance it doesn't tell us *how much* they like it or *how often* (or even whether) they actually drink the stuff. If I was asked 'do you like vintage champagne?' my answer would be an enthusiastic 'yes!' But that doesn't mean I have it with dinner every night – even if I could afford to do so.

Expressing an attitude in this form is therefore not a *comprehensive* answer to anything but rather a quick and convenient way of *summarising* a lot of information about the relationship between a person and an object – whether it's a country, a religion, a political belief or a breakfast cereal. Attitudes therefore have a very important part to play in our lives and in our consumer behaviour. Attitudes towards specific products, as expressed by target consumers, are at the heart of market research, of course, and as we'll see in Chapter 14 people's attitudes towards advertisements are an important aspect of the advertisement's effectiveness.[2] But what exactly *are* attitudes? That is the first major question we will look at in this chapter. Then we will consider how attitudes change and the relationship between attitudes and behaviour.

What are Attitudes?

The study of attitudes is one of the most intensively researched areas of psychology. Although there are over 100 different definitions of the term, a widely accepted definition of attitude would be something like the following: 'A stable, long-lasting, learned predisposition to respond to certain things in a certain way. The *concept* has a cognitive (belief) aspect, an *affective* (feeling) aspect, and a *conative* (action) aspect'.[3] Let's unpack that a little:

- 'Stable' implies that an attitude, once formed, will keep that form and remain identifiably the same over time. If you detested spinach last week you won't be any more inclined to eat it this week – even if you've since discovered how good it is for you.

- 'Long-lasting' is essentially stability over a period of years. Your spinach aversion may well date back to your childhood, along with your highly favourable attitude towards chocolate ice cream.
- 'Learned', as we saw in Chapter 6, is the basis of nearly all human behaviour. I know it's hard to believe, but nobody is born with a negative attitude towards spinach – or any other food – it has to be learned. Like most powerful food preferences it is probably formed very early in life. Take the case of chili peppers, for instances, which can blow your head off when you come upon them for the first time as an adult. Yet five-year-old Mexican children will eat them happily.[4] They have no idea how good chili peppers are for them, of course, though their mothers do. They eat them because of the positive emotional association they have with them. Learning to associate mother love with a particular food produces a combination of unbeatable psychological power, which is why advertisers try to manufacture it all the time.
- 'Predisposition to respond' is a way of describing the link to a consumer's actual *behaviour*. If we see chili peppers on sale at the supermarket we might expect Mexican consumers to buy more of them than Anglos because of their predisposition to respond positively to that particular stimulus.
- 'In a certain way' emphasizes the *consistency* of an attitude over time. Given my stated preference for vintage champagne you might expect me to buy it whenever I visit the wine shop. It is as well to note, though, that situational factors (such as lack of money) can frequently intervene between attitude and actual buying behaviour, though the attitude may be just as strongly held as ever.

■ Characteristics and Components of Attitudes

Like a proprietary pain killer, attitudes contain not one, not two, but three active ingredients, as listed in the definition above. These are depicted in Figure 13.1.

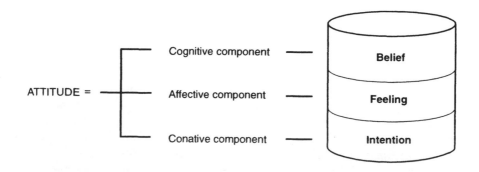

Figure 13.1   Attitude components

- The *cognitive component* deals with questions such as 'what do you *think* of Aloparc's new freeze-dried offalburger?' This attitude component is therefore mainly concerned with a consumer's *opinions* about the product's properties, for example whether it's crunchy, chewy or smoky, whether the price is reasonable, or whether the packaging is informative.
- The *affective component* deals with the question 'how do you *feel* about Aloparc's new freeze-dried offalburger?' This attitude component is therefore mainly concerned with a consumer's feelings about the product's properties, for example is it appealing or unappealing; is it liked or disliked?
- The *conative component* relates to the question 'do you *intend to buy* Aloparc's new freeze-dried offalburger?' This attitude component is therefore mainly concerned with a consumer's *likely behaviour* in relation to the product.

Market researchers have developed a variety of ways, using detailed questionnaires, to tap into each of these components of consumers' attitudes towards a product. Some examples are shown below.

1. *Measuring Beliefs*
   (a) How would you rate the smokiness of Aloparc Offalburgers?
       Very __   __   __   __   __   __   __   Not at all

   (b) How strongly do you agree with the following statement: 'Aloparc Offalburgers taste smoky?'

Strongly agree	Somewhat agree	Slightly agree	Neither agree nor disagree	Slightly disagree	Somewhat disagree	Strongly disagree
()	() •	()	()	()	()	()

2. *Measuring Feelings*
   (a) How much do you like Aloparc Offalburgers?
       Like very much __   __   __   __   __   __   __   Dislike very much

   (b) Compared with other burgers, Aloparc Offalburgers are:
       Appealing ()   ()   ()   ()   ()   ()   () Unappealing

3. *Measuring Intentions*
   (a) What is the probability that you will buy Aloparc Offalburgers?
       0% 10% 20% 30% 40% 50% 60% 70% 80% 90% 100%

   (b) How likely are you to buy Aloparc Offalburgers in the next month?
       – Very likely
       – Likely
       – Unlikely
       – Very unlikely

Although we need to isolate these three components of an attitude in order to study them, a measure of one component by itself may be quite misleading.

Even an accurate measure of a consumer's intentions doesn't predict to buying behaviour – I've been *intending* to buy a new pair of gloves for years. Nor does it tell you *why* someone has certain likes and dislikes, a crucial piece of information when trying to predict their actual behaviour.

Attitudes and action are, of course, interdependent. One important implication of this interdependence is that there is a powerful tendency for these components to be *consistent* with each other. In other words if your opinion of Aloparc Offalburgers is that they have a very smoky flavour and you just love smoky flavours, then you will probably like the product and be likely to buy it, other things being equal. Of course other things may not be equal – you may decide to become a vegetarian for instance.

It is also clear that human beings have the ability to live with a certain amount of psychological discomfort if they feel that, on balance, they gain more than they lose. There cannot be anyone left on the planet, for instance, who is unaware of the health risks associated with smoking cigarettes. Yet millions of people continue to smoke. Indeed I have a friend who flourishes his cigarette pack with the cheery line 'anyone like a cancer stick?'

We will explore the psychological processes involved in more detail later in the chapter. For the moment let us just note that while I *know* that Aloparc Pizzas are junk food that won't do much for me nutritionally, I may *like* the taste of them so much that I eat them anyway.

■ Forming Attitudes

In Chapter 6 we saw how crucially important the learning process is to human beings. Other than physiological reflexes and abilities that depend on maturation of the brain (such as language), virtually all human activities are learned. This is perhaps most evidently true of the attitudes we hold. Nobody is born with an attitude about anything.

The two major theories of learning we discussed in Chapter 6, the behaviourist and the cognitive approaches, provided us with many clear examples of consumer attitudes being formed:

- In *classical conditioning* the goal is to associate a product (unconditioned stimulus) with a particular image (conditioned stimulus) that is thought to be attractive, for example alcoholic drinks and soft drinks paired with golden beaches, about which people are assumed to have highly favourable attitudes.
- In *stimulus generalization* an existing association is extended to a new version of the existing brand or product, for example Heinz 57 varieties or Baskin Robbins' ice cream flavours.
- In *stimulus discrimination* the opposite effect is sought by market leaders, who want the favourable consumer attitudes already established by their products to be distinguished from those of their competitors. 'Me too' products, on the other hand, take advantage of stimulus generalization.

- In *operant conditioning* the reward or 'reinforcement' that consumers receive from a positive experience of a brand or product is the essence of the attitude we recognize as brand loyalty. It may take only one negative experience to change this attitude and destroy the brand loyalty, like the time I found a dead fly in my favourite mineral water.
- *Cognitive learning theory*, involving the search for and processing of information that lies behind the formation of many attitudes, is concerned with relatively complex, infrequent and important consumer decisions, such as buying a house or a car.

■ Sources of Attitudes

□ *Family*

We noted in Chapter 8 (and elsewhere throughout the book) how early family influences have an enormous impact in the formation of our attitudes about everything, including our consumer attitudes and even our attitudes towards particular brands and products.

□ *Peers*

We followed up the study of family influences by examining, in Chapter 9, the growing influence of friends, and the peer group in general, on the consumer preferences of young people and their fast-changing fads and fashions in many product areas. Opinion leaders, as we noted in Chapter 3, have an important influence, even on adult consumers, particularly with regard to the adoption of new products and innovations.

□ *Direct Experience*

Despite the important influences that other people may have on our attitudes towards certain products, the influence of direct personal experience is usually considered to be even greater. There is no substitute for actually trying something yourself and evaluating the experience, which is why marketers frequently offer free trials, discount coupons and other inducements to consumers.[5]

Consumer attitudes formed through direct experience of a product are apparently held with greater conviction than those based on other sources, especially advertising.[6] Nonetheless we must, as ever, be careful of the ambiguous links between attitudes and behaviour. I have a very positive attitude towards Rolls Royce cars for instance, but I have never bought one, and am never likely to either, no matter how much I may have enjoyed riding in them.

■ Theories of Attitudes

The most popular way of finding out people's attitudes towards anything has been to ask them how much they liked X, or whether they preferred X to Y. As we discussed earlier in the chapter this kind of question taps into someone's *feelings* about an object, which is useful as a global evaluation, as far as it goes, but limited. That is, it only deals with one aspect of an attitude and tells us nothing about beliefs or intentions to act in relation to the object.   This approach to understanding attitudes is therefore known as a *single-attribute model.*

■ Multi-Attribute Models

In the 1970s a number of *multi-attribute* models of attitudes were developed which tried to overcome the problems of single-attribute models and provide a greater understanding of the complexity in the construction of many attitudes. One such model was suggested by Martin Fishbein and his colleagues, and as it became very popular with marketers and researchers in consumer behaviour we will consider Fishbein's work as our representative of the multi-attribute approach.[7]

Multi-attribute models of attitudes are primarily interested in the cognitive aspect of Figure 13.1, the beliefs that people have about something. In terms of consumer behaviour this takes the form of beliefs about the different attributes of a product or service. In practical terms this is calculated as one belief per attribute and is expressed symbolically in the following formula:

$$A_0 = \sum_{i=1}^{n} b_i e_i$$

where A_0 = someone's global attitude towards the object (for example a product, service or store); b_i = the strength of his or her belief that the object has attribute i (for example a mauve nose stud is the ultimate in high fashion); e_i = his evaluation of attribute i (for example how good or bad it is to be fashionable); n = the number of salient beliefs/attributes for that person; and $\sum$ = the sum of...

The Fishbein model therefore pays particular attention to the cognitive aspect of attitudes by focusing on consumer beliefs about a product and attempting to combine these beliefs with the strength of feeling in the consumer's evaluation of the product. Let's take a hypothetical example to see how this measure might be applied in practice. Table 13.1 shows the results of a comparison between two canned lagers: Bozo and Plonker. Let us suppose that a sample of appropriate consumers has been surveyed and five major attributes of the products have been identified as important in making an assessment, as follows:

- Price (perceived as low?)
- Flavour (any discernible?)
- Fizzy (how fizzy?)

- Alcoholic content (how much?)
- Design of can (how attractive?)

The *evaluative* component (e_i) might be measured as follows on a seven-point scale from 'very good' to 'very bad':

A lager with a discernible flavour is
very good $\underline{\quad}$ $\underline{\quad}$ $\underline{\quad}$ $\underline{\quad}$ $\underline{\quad}$ $\underline{\quad}$ $\underline{\quad}$ very bad
 +3 +2 +1 0 -1 -2 -3

This would also be done for each of the other four attributes identified.

The *belief* component (b_i) might be measured as follows on a seven-point scale from 'very likely' to 'very unlikely' according to how strongly respondents believe that a particular lager possesses a particular attribute. For example:

How likely is it that Plonker lager has a vast amount of fizz?
very likely $\underline{\quad}$ $\underline{\quad}$ $\underline{\quad}$ $\underline{\quad}$ $\underline{\quad}$ $\underline{\quad}$ $\underline{\quad}$ very unlikely
 +3 +2 +1 · 0 -1 -2 -3

Consumers' beliefs for each attribute of each of the two brands would be measured in this way

Table 13.1 Hypothetical illustration of Fishbein's Multi-attribute Model

| Attribute | Evaluation (e_i) | Belief strength (b_i) | | | |
| | | Bozo | | Plonker | |
		(b)	(be)	(b)	(be)
Price	+3	+2	+6	+1	+3
Flavour	+3	+3	+9	+2	+6
Fizz	+2	-1	-2	-2	-4
Alcohol	+3	+1	+3	+3	+9
Design	+1	0	0	0	0
Total $\Sigma b_i e_i$			+16		+14

A summary of the information contained in Table 13.1 would be that price, flavour and alcoholic content are particularly important to lager drinkers. They were most attracted by low price, high alcoholic content and no discernible flavour, and in their overall judgement Bozo was marginally better than Plonker. However the differences between the products contained within the total score would be of greater interest to market researchers and their clients, for it is the differences recorded on the individual attributes that provide the scope to suggest changes to the product.

The Fishbein model and other multi-attribute models of attitudes was enthu-siastically taken up by market researchers and consumer behaviourists in the 1970s. But it soon became apparent that even knowing consumers' detailed beliefs as well as their feelings about a product did not always enable one to predict whether they would actually buy it. There were still too many other factors affecting the links between attitude and behaviour.

Fishbein and his colleague Ajzen responded to these findings with a revised model, the *behavioural intentions model*.[8] The aim of this model was to reduce some – though not all – of the predictive uncertainty between expressed attitudes and actual behaviour by adding a measure of the consumer's *intention* to act in a particular way. The focus of the behavioural intentions model is not so much the attitude of the person (consumer) towards an object (product) as his or her attitude towards *behaving in a particular way* towards the object (that is, buying the product). The formula for the behavioural intentions model is therefore as follows:

$$A_B = \sum_{i=1}^{n} b_i e_i$$

where A_B = the individual's overall attitude about indulging in a particular behaviour (for example buying and consuming a six-pack of Plonker); b_i = the strength of the belief that indulging in the behaviour will result in the consequence i (for example that Plonker will get him or her drunk more quickly); e_i = the evaluation of consequence i (for example how favourably does he or she look upon getting drunk as soon as possible); n = the number of salient behavioural beliefs; and Σ = the sum of...

Table 13.2 illustrates a hypothetical example of this model using the same products as Table 13.1.

Table 13.2   Hypothetical illustration of Fishbein's behavioural intentions model

Beliefs about behaviorural consequences	Evaluation (e_i)	Belief strength (b_i) Bozo		Plonker	
		(b)	(be)	(b)	(be)
Drinking Bozo/Plonker will:					
Make me a more interesting person	-1	-2	+2	+2	-2
Get me drunk fastest	+3	+2	+6	+3	+9
Get me drunk cheapest	+2	+3	+6	+2	+4
Improve my status with my friends	+2	+3	+6	+2	+4
Make me feel more manly	+3	+2	+6	+2	+6
Total $\Sigma b_i e_i$			+26		+21

With the revised model we can see that a slightly larger gap has opened up between the two products, largely because of a greater fear among consumers that drinking Plonker is likely to make them a 'more interesting' person than drinking Bozo – an outcome that would seriously damage their peer group status. We can now predict with somewhat greater confidence that consumers prefer Bozo to Plonker and are more likely to buy it.

Fishbein argued further that fully understanding people's behavioural intentions also requires a measure of the *subjective norms* that influence them. These norms are represented by the 'significant others' (family, friends, and so on) in a person's life, and what his or her view is of how they would want him or her to behave. This might be operationalized by a market researcher as follows:

My best friend thinks that I

should ( ) ( ) ( ) ( ) ( ) ( ) ( ) should not

drink Plonker

Just as with the attitudes towards behaviour formulation, researchers are interested in what lies behind the subjective norms individuals express. That is, they are interested in their beliefs about the perceptions of the significant others in their lives and in their motivation to comply with them. A measure of this motivation might be constructed as follows:

I usually like to follow my best friend's suggestions:

always __ __ __ __ __ __ __ never

These factors would then yield the following equation:

$$SN = \sum_{i=1}^{k} b_i m_i$$

where SN = the individual's subjective norm about indulging in a particular behaviour; b_i = the strength of his belief that person i thinks he should or should not indulge in the behaviour; m_i = his motivation to comply with his belief about what person i would want him to do; k = the number of significant others; and $\sum$ = the sum of...

Fishbein's models have had a considerable impact on psychology and marketing, and attempts to predict the behaviour of consumers have undoubtedly improved as a result.[9] Nonetheless some important problems and shortcomings remain.[10] The model is good at explaining and predicting *reasoned*, calculative behaviour of the straightforward problem-solving variety – 'What's the most useful personal computer for my consulting business?' and 'What kind of refrigerator would fit best in this kitchen?' are relevant examples.

However the Fishbein model is unhelpful in explaining *unreasoned* behaviour,

for instance 'Why do I go out for a loaf of bread and come back with two
magazines and a jar of pickles?' or 'Why do I buy a newspaper on my way
home from work every night, even though I never read it?' The workings of
unconscious emotions, which by definition can't be entered into a calculation,
influence a lot of our behaviour in general and consumer behaviour in particular,
as we saw in Chapter 7. That's why so many shops put carefully selected items
just next to the check-out till to encourage us to pick them up on impulse.

Moreover there is not necessarily a neat progression from forming an
attitude, to developing an intention, to acting on that intention. Attitudes can
sometimes be followed directly by behaviour while many things – as we have seen
more than once already – can come between an intention and actual behaviour.
We will explore these issues further in the final section of this chapter. For the
moment we will turn our attention to the ways in which attitudes change.

■ Changing Attitudes

To a large extent the psychological processes we have studied in the formation
of attitudes are also relevant to the changing of attitudes. But some other
important factors are also involved. For many years the study of the way attitudes
change has been one of the most important areas of psychological research.
This research has taken three main forms in recent years, as follows:

- *Mere exposure.* In Chapter 4 we saw how merely exposing a subject to a
  stimulus (a name, face or object, for instance) may be enough for the subject
  to form slightly positive attitudes towards the stimulus in question. Thus in
  relatively unimportant decisions such as the purchase of washing-up liquid or
  detergent the most heavily advertised brands will become most familiar to
  the consumer and therefore most likely to be picked off the supermarket
  shelf. Similarly, we saw how an American insurance company was able to
  change consumer attitudes with a two-week advertising campaign: $1 million
  worth of television exposure increased its familiarity among consumers from
  thirty fourth in a list of insurance companies to third.[11]
- *Persuasive communication.* The longest tradition in the study of the way
  attitudes change is to treat the process of change as a form of information
  processing that is being subjected to persuasive communications. This
  tradition is of particular relevance to consumer behaviour because of its
  crucial role in trying to understand the effects of advertising. For that reason
  we will consider it separately and in detail in Chapter 14.
- *Cognitive dissonance.* The theory of cognitive dissonance states that, because
  people have a powerful drive to be consistent, if they hold two *psychologically*
  inconsistent cognitions (beliefs, idea, values or attitudes) at the same time, or
  if their behaviour contradicts these cognitions, they will need to find a way of
  reducing the resultant tension. This has been a very influential theory in
  psychology, and like many such theories it sounds deceptively simple. It has

been particularly useful in teasing out the complex links between attitudes and behaviour, and for that reason we will deal with it in detail in the final section of this chapter.

■ Attitude Change and Marketing

For the remainder of this section we will consider some of the practical applications that have been attempted by marketers employing the psychology of attitude change. In general terms market leaders are much more interested in strengthening consumer attitudes towards their products than in changing them. Their competitors usually have more to gain by changing consumer attitudes away from their existing brand loyalties.

■ Strategies

□ Low Consumer Involvement

We have already seen on several occasions that if a buying decision is a relatively unimportant one consumers are less likely to spend time and effort on making a deliberate, conscious, rational, calculating choice of product – or what is known in the trade as a *systematic processing strategy*. This means that their attitudes are more open to *peripheral* influences, for example the mere exposure effect discussed above. So perhaps the most obvious strategy for a marketer faced with low consumer involvement is simply an advertising blitz.

There is another strategy that might be used with low consumer involvement, one that we've encountered several times already in this book: classical conditioning – one of the simplest forms of learning there is. You will recall that classical conditioning involves the association of a neutral stimulus (the product) with one that produces a positive response in the consumer (glamour, power, success, popularity and so on). This association is made, of course, without the intervention of any rational thought processes.

An experimental study of attitudes towards facial tissues showed how this might be done as a marketing strategy. There were four groups of subjects in four different conditions, each one showing a mock advertisement for a fictitious brand. One condition had only text and no picture; the other three had colour photographs with the brand name but no text. One of the photographs was of an abstract painting, another was of an ocean sunset and the third was of a cute fluffy kitten.[12]

Guess which of the four groups rated the tissues as softest? That's right, the abstract painting group. (Just seeing if you were awake; it was of course the fluffy kitten group.) A similar effect has been found for advertisements with background music that consumers find appealing.[13] The implications are that associating the product with fluffy kittens or appealing music, or similar positive stimuli, will be more effective in changing consumer attitudes in a low involvement situation than an appeal to consumer *beliefs* via verbal messages.

□   *Increasing Involvement*

A second major strategy for changing consumer attitudes involves the attempt to increase the consumer's level of involvement in the decision and then direct it towards the product. One popular form of this technique is to associate a product with a currently prominent cause or social issue, such as healthy eating or the environment.

There must be few food manufacturers that haven't tried this one and their ingenuity can be quite impressive, for instance claiming that a certain yoghurt has more potassium than a banana. Similarly, some recent advertisements for major oil companies would lead a Martian to assume that the companies are actually in the business of caring for the environment. For both these products, normally there is very little agonizing between brands before a purchase decision is made.

□   *Involvement and the Multi-Attribute Model*

The third major strategy relates to decisions in which consumers normally have some involvement and are consciously trying to choose the best option. Techniques used with this strategy may be discussed in terms of the Fishbein multi-attribute model of behavioural intentions, which we met earlier in this chapter.[14]   These include changing beliefs and evaluations about the consequences of purchasing a product.

- *Changing beliefs* (b_i)   This involves changing the consumer's beliefs about the benefits that will result from purchasing the product. This is perhaps the most common attribute appeal found in advertising. Anything that claims to 'last longest', be 'most reliable' or give 'best value for money' would use this technique.
- *Changing evaluations* (e_i)   Changing consumer evaluations would require people who might already be aware of the product's characteristics to place a higher value on one or more of them. For example cans of baked beans have always sold well because consumers find them cheap and convenient. But when people discovered that they were also high in fibre, and therefore good for them, sales took another quantum leap.
- *Changing beliefs and evaluations* (b_ie_i)   Adding or removing an attribute can change the combination of beliefs and evaluations, for example adding fibre to bread or removing caffeine from coffee. Sometimes both can happen with a single product, such as adding vitamins to milk and removing fat. A product might even be rewarded with a favourable change in consumer attitudes by adding and removing the same attribute, but at different times, as in the case of fluoride and toothpaste.

■   Attitudes and Behaviour

The commonsense notion that knowing someone's attitudes towards a product will inform you of the likelihood of their buying it is quite a useful rule-of-thumb for practical purposes. It is certainly a useful starting point in our attempt to understand the relationship between attitudes and behaviour. There is, after all, good evidence for the links between consumers' positive attitudes towards particular brands and their decision to buy them.[15]

However, as we have seen throughout this chapter, there are many occasions when a positive attitude towards a product does not predict to its purchase. Indeed the research mentioned in the preceding paragraph linking positive attitudes to buying behaviour also found that about a quarter of the respondents who had stopped using a given product still retained very favourable attitudes towards it.

If attitudes and attitude changes do not always predict behaviour it has been found, conversely, that behaviour can sometimes predict attitudes and attitude change. The mechanism by which this happens can be explained by the cognitive dissonance theory we encountered earlier in the chapter.

In 1957 Leon Festinger proposed a simple but far-reaching theory.[16] Noting the powerful drive towards consistency, or *consonance*, Festinger suggested that if an individual holds two psychologically inconsistent cognitions (beliefs, attitudes, values, ideas) at the same time, he or she will be in a state of *cognitive dissonance*. Because cognitive dissonance is a state of psychological tension it is inherently unpleasant, Festinger argued, and we are strongly motivated to reduce it. It is important to note here that dissonance theory does not deal with *logical* inconsistency but *psychological* inconsistency. In other words people are not so much concerned with actually *being* consistent as *feeling* consistent; not so much with *being* rational as with *rationalizing*.

Festinger tested this theory experimentally in the key study of what has become a huge body of research on cognitive dissonance theory and its ramifications.[17] His student subjects worked at some very boring and repetitive tasks for a long period of time and were then placed in a situation of cognitive dissonance. They were asked to tell other students waiting to participate in the study that the tasks were very interesting and enjoyable. Some of the subjects were paid twenty dollars (a sizeable sum in the late 1950s) for telling this lie and some were paid only one dollar.

The subjects were then asked to report how they themselves felt about the tests. The group that had been paid twenty dollars found it boring and dull, just as it was. But the group that had been paid one dollar claimed the task was interesting and enjoyable. The first group had reduced dissonance by an external justification – it was worth twenty bucks to tell someone that a boring task was enjoyable. But they didn't believe it themselves, of course, and so their attitude towards the task didn't change.

The other group had no such external justification for their behaviour so they had to look internally to make sense of what they had done. Their cognition 'I told someone a boring task was enjoyable' was dissonant with their cognition 'I am an honest person'. One of these cognitions had to give, and as self-image is deeply felt and strongly implanted it was easier to change the other attitude.   So these people *persuaded themselves* that the task had been really enjoyable, just as they had told the other students it was.

There are a couple of points of particular interest to us here.   One is that these findings run contrary to commonsense, which would presumably argue that if you want people to adopt a certain attitude, the more you pay them the more likely they are to do so.   In this study the *less* people were paid the more readily they changed their attitudes.

The second point again concerns the relationship between attitudes and behaviour.   We've already seen that a person holding certain attitudes doesn't necessarily act on them; there are many other factors involved.   Similarly a change in behaviour will not necessarily follow from a change in attitude. However the cognitive dissonance studies have shown that if the appropriate *behaviour comes first* then it's more likely that a change in *attitude will follow.* Behaviour is usually a lot more resistant to change than attitude, as any heavy smoker who's decided to give it up can tell you.

One of the earliest findings of the cognitive dissonance studies is also of particular importance for the world of the consumer.   It deals with the dissonance that arises as a result of making a decision.   A decision costs us time and effort and it leads to a choice.   By definition we then have to forgo whatever it was we didn't choose.   But choice usually implies that each alternative has at least something positive in its favour, and the closer the alternatives are in attractiveness the harder the decision will be to make and the greater the dissonance experienced afterwards.   What do you do about the negative points of the alternative you chose and the positive aspects of the one you didn't?

It is particularly clear how we cope with this dissonance when consumer choices are involved.   Take buying a new car for instance.   The evidence is that as soon as we've made the decision and bought the car we'll be especially attentive to advertisements that extol the virtues of that particular model – and we'll carefully avoid advertisements for competing models.[18]   In fact even when people were offered a reward, to take part in a study, of the two electrical appliances they previously considered equally attractive, a few minutes after making their choice they rated the one they had chosen more highly than the one they had rejected.[19]   We will return to these issues in a different context in Chapters 15 and 16.

■ Directionality of Cause

We have now seen that the direction of causality between attitudes and behaviour can be either way, thus:

Attitudes ⇌ Behaviour

Is there anything we can conclude about the conditions under which one direction or the other can be predicted?   Earlier in the chapter we discussed the importance that the degree of consumer involvement in the purchase decision has on marketing strategies, and that factor appears to be the key to the question of directionality as well.[20] The relationship may be summarized as follows:

- With high involvement: Attitudes → Behaviour
- With low involvement: Behaviour → Attitudes

■ Further Reading

Eagly, A. and S. Chaiken, *The Psychology of Attitudes* (Chicago: Harcourt Brace Jovanovich, 1993). A very good survey of an enormous amount of research and thinking in this field.

Kuhl, J. and J. Beckmann (eds), *Action Control: From Cognition to Behavior* (New York: Springer-Verlag, 1985). An authoritative overview of the links between attitudes and behaviour.

Mitchell, A. (ed.), *Advances in Consumer Behavior: Ad Exposure, Memory and Choice* (Hillsdale, NJ: Lawrence Erlbaum Associates, 1992). An overview of the attitude–behaviour links with specific relevance to consumer behaviour.

Robertson, T. and H. Kassarjian (eds), *Handbook of Consumer Behavior* (Englewood Cliffs, NJ: Prentice-Hall, 1991). The authoritative account of the most important concepts used in research on consumer behaviour. The 1991 edition has some particularly useful articles on attitudes.

It is also worth browsing through the latest issues of the following periodicals: *Advances in Consumer Research, Journal of Consumer Research, Journal of Marketing Research.*

■ Questions for Discussion

1. What are the constituent part of a consumer's attitude towards a product? How can each part be measured?
2. What are the sources of such an attitude?
3. Why is Fishbein's multi-attribute model (Table 13.1) considered so useful by consumer researchers, and what are its limitations?
4. How did Fishbein's later revisions to his multi-attribute model try to overcome these limitations, and how successful have they been?
5. What strategies have marketers used to strengthen existing consumer attitudes (for market leaders) and change them (for challengers)? Show how such strategies might be implemented for a particular product that has a clear market leader and challenger.
6. Even if you know a lot about a consumer's attitude towards a particular product, why might it still be difficult to predict whether he or she will actually buy it? Under what circumstances might it be easier to predict the other way around; that is, from behaviour to attitudes?

PART IV
Consumer Decision-Making

■ Introduction

Parts II and III gave us complementary views of the consumer and provided us with a basis for tackling the core issue of consumer behaviour in Part IV – of decision-making.

Chapter 14 looks at the effects of advertising communications on the decision-making process. Chapter 15 analyses the way consumers approach that process and in Chapter 16 we analyse the actual taking of the buying decision and the consequences that continue to affect both consumer and marketer. Finally, in Chapter 17 we look at how these processes work for organizational purchasers.

Communication and Persuasion

I know that half of my advertising is effective. I just don't know which half (American businessman).

■ Introduction

How does advertising affect our behaviour?

We noted in the previous chapter that the longest research tradition in the study of attitude change has been to regard it as a form of information processing that is being subjected to persuasive communication. For consumer behaviour the most obvious kind of persuasive communication comes in the form of advertising, whose primary aim is to persuade people to form or increase positive attitudes or intentions towards a particular product.

It is therefore essential for us to have some idea of *how* we process advertising information. Only then can we understand how the persuasive element of advertising affects us and try to gauge how effective these attempts at persuasion may be. A lot of psychological research has been carried out on all aspects of both communication and persuasion and we will summarize the most relevant findings for consumer behaviour.

In doing so we will see how the forms of advertising we are familiar with are actually reflections of our dominant culture, and as we learned in Chapter 12, cultural influences have deep roots in the way we make sense of our lives, roots that extend far beyond the consumer behaviour that is our particular concern.

■ The Importance of Advertising

The presence of advertising in our lives is universal and pervasive. We have all been living with advertising since we were born. Mass advertising started well over a century ago with the development of the mass press and has become more and more extensive over the course of the twentieth century with the invention of films, radio and, especially, television. There has also been increasingly intensive use of local outlets for advertising, such as sporting venues, billboards and buses (and even bus stops and bus tickets).

Advertising is now an enormous global industry. In the United States alone over $130 billion dollars a year is spent on it and many more billions on sales promotions in retail outlets, brochures, discount coupon schemes and so on. For that kind of money you get an awful lot of advertisements. A typical estimate is that the average American is exposed to several hundred advertisements a day, or over 100 000 a year.

Our attitude towards advertising in general seems to be ambiguous. On the one hand advertising is regarded with some suspicion, which at its most extreme is sometimes expressed as a fear of being helpless to avoid the sinister manipulations of clever and devious marketers. We came across this fear in Chapter 4 in our discussion of subliminal perception, and again in Chapter 7 when we dealt with the issue of whether needs could be created by advertising. In both these cases we saw that the fears were largely unfounded and the inference of manipulated powers greatly exaggerated.

At the same time there also seems to be a widespread attitude that, presumably because we are so familiar with advertising, we can 'see through it'. We tend to regard ourselves as pretty sophisticated when it comes to dealing with advertisements and so we're confident that we can see the pitch coming and won't allow it to influence our buying behaviour. Alas, as we'll see below, this confidence is just as misplaced as our opposite fear of being helplessly manipulated!

■ The Process of Communication

The various steps in the process of communication can be represented in a simple diagram (Figure 14.1).

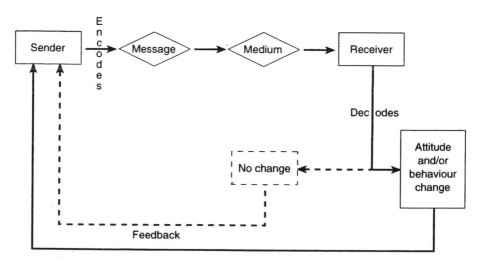

Figure 14.1   The process of communication

In this model a sender encodes and transmits a message, via a recognised medium of communication, to a receiver, who decodes it and may or may not be influenced by it to change his or her attitude and/or behaviour towards the object of the communication. In either event feedback from the receiver to the sender is essential if the process of communication is to continue. This is done by the sender evaluating the response to his or her communication and deciding whether to continue transmitting the same message via the same medium or to change one or both in some way.

This is a general model of the communication process. The sender and receiver could as easily be husband and wife, two office colleagues or a double glazing salesman and his prospective punters, as a household brand name and its potential consumers. However because of our interest here in the specific effects of advertising we shall concentrate on the latter.

The *sender* initiates the process by transmitting a *message* about its product. This message may be encoded verbally or non-verbally, or often in a combination of the two that combines words and pictures if the *medium* of communication is print or poster. Different media may combine these with music, and perhaps animation, as in film and television. The intended *receiver* is one of a target market audience that has been selected for this particular product. The receiver then *decodes* the message in a way that makes sense to him or her.

The sender's goal is for the receiver to perceive the precise message that was encoded and for it to influence the receiver's attitude and/or behaviour in a positive direction. Of course there are many potential pitfalls along the way. We came across some of the most graphic of these in Chapter 12, where we examined the effects of cultural differences. You'll recall how the American slogan 'It takes a tough man to make a tender chicken' emerged south of the border as 'It takes a sexually stimulated man to make a chicken affectionate'.

As with all the other psychological processes we have studied, we will examine the constituent parts of the process of communication individually. But in real life, of course, they interact with each other all the time. We will then consider, the *source* of the communication, the *communication itself* and the *audience* for that communication.

■ The Source (Sender)

Two important factors determine the persuasiveness of a communicator (the source of a communication aimed at changing people's attitudes): *credibility* and *attractiveness*.

☐ Credibility

What makes a communicator credible is being perceived by the target of the communication as *expert* and *trustworthy*. The more a communicator seems to know what he or she is talking about and appears to be trustworthy, the more effective her or his communication will be.[1]

Arguing against one's own apparent interests is a particularly effective way of gaining the target's trust, as when a gangster argues for a tougher criminal justice system.[2] Thus it has been suggested that the heir to the R. J. Reynolds tobacco fortune, who urged sufferers from smoking-related illnesses to sue the tobacco companies, will be the most persuasive advocate for the anti-smoking lobby.[3]

Historically there are powerful examples of the effect of sources arguing the opposite of what their position is popularly supposed to be. In a 1955 broadcast Winston Churchill, the aristocratic Conservative prime minister, declared that 'Trade unionism in Britain has done a good job for our people and our nation'. Similarly in 1960, at his farewell address President Eisenhower warned of the growing power of the 'military–industrial complex' in the United States. This would have been a striking enough statement for any Republican president to make, but from one of America's most celebrated generals it was positively startling.

It has been found that smooth, fast-talking communicators tend to be more credible than slow, hesitant ones.[4] In an era when public discussion consists of television soundbites this seems a particularly depressing finding. However it has also been found that under certain conditions communicators with low credibility can be just as effective as those with high credibility – not at the time of the communication but a few weeks later. What seems to happen in this *sleeper effect* is that the message is important enough for people to remember, but they forget who gave it to them.[5]

☐   *Attractiveness*

But why then are sports stars paid a lot of money to advertise razor blades on television, or showbiz stars to advertise washing-up liquid? Do they really know all that more than the rest of us about shaving or washing-up? And it's not as though we think they are touting the stuff for free, out of a great sense of conviction. On American television it is even quite common for actors to advertise products on the basis of the fictitious parts they play in a series. Thus Karl Malden, who has played a detective, has reassured punters worried about theft on holiday of the advantage of using a particular brand of traveller's cheque, and Robert Young, who has played a doctor, has given them valuable advice on health care.

In the case of sports and showbiz stars, trustworthiness and expertise does not come into it. Their *attractiveness* as popular celebrities is their selling point. In the case of actors it's the attractiveness of the fictitious characters they play. It has also been established that in various ways we are inclined to favour attractive people and to try to please them.[6] And the way to please the celebrities in the television advertisements is, of course, to buy whatever it is they're trying to flog to us.

Of course if the *wrong* celebrity is chosen for a product the results can be spectacularly embarrassing for the marketer. Take the case of the American beef producers who hired the lovely film star Cybill Sheppard to tell consumers how great their product was. Then people discovered that the lovely Cybill was a vegetarian. Publicity like this affects the whole advertising industry because it gives the game away to an already sceptical audience.

The accepted wisdom in social psychology is that this technique does often work, but only up to a point. That is, it only applies to *trivial* issues such as choosing an aspirin or a detergent, but not for really important issues like choosing a president.[7] Well, I suppose it depends what you mean by 'trivial'. After all our entire consumer economy rests on the assumption that people will continually make these – essentially mundane and non-rational – kinds of decision. And why are presidential and other candidates so keen to have celebrity endorsement if they don't affect voter behaviour? (I suppose you could argue that the choice of candidate people are usually faced with *is* pretty trivial and this is good evidence of it.)

■ The Communication (Message)

The nature of the communication itself, and the manner of its presentation, are also influential factors in its effectiveness. Several key questions are often considered here.[8]

- Should the appeal be to reason or emotion?
- Are images or statistics more persuasive?
- Should the message be one-sided or two-sided?
- The primacy or recency effect.
- The size of the discrepancy in attitude being addressed.

□ *Reason or Emotion*

This is a particularly difficult distinction to draw. We have seen throughout this book how pervasive emotional influence is on what appear to be rational mental processes. Modern research in this area no longer tries to make a distinction between reason and emotion but looks rather at the effects of different levels of emotional arousal, and particularly the arousal of *fear*. Is it more persuasive to present a mild threat to the target audience or should you really try to scare people?

Such a question is of interest to insurance companies and people running public health and safety campaigns for instance. Do you persuade people more effectively not to drink and drive by hitting them with pictures of broken bodies and machines in gory detail, or do you soften the impact with less explicit images and more reasoned argument?

The answer seems to be that the more fear you arouse in people the more likely they are to be influenced by the communication, *provided* you give them clear and practical ways of dealing with the fear you have aroused.[9] It is the combination of high emotional arousal plus specific instructions for dealing with it that produces the effect. Either factor on its own is ineffective.

However it also looks as though this effect is context-specific. It can be used to increase the take-up of inoculation against a particular disease, for instance, but it doesn't seem to work if the problem and the solution are more diffuse and relate to a change in lifestyle. In particular it doesn't seem to work in the fight against AIDS.[10] But then there is no inoculation at present, or any other medical procedure, that can prevent AIDS or the acquisition of the AIDS virus HIV. It is a matter of changing sexual and social behaviour and not a medical matter at all.

☐   *Are Images or Statistics More Persuasive?*

The old Chinese proverb about one little picture being worth a thousand words seems to make intuitive sense and is widely quoted in many contexts. Can we extend 'picture' to include mental picture and 'words' to include numbers? When we face a buying decision about a stereo system or a car do we consult the appropriate consumer reports and make a rational decision based solely on the statistical findings from painstaking tests and surveys?

Well we might like to think so but it appears that we find personal anecdotes about a particular brand or model somewhat more persuasive, even if it's (say) just one negative instance of a car falling apart as opposed to many hundreds of positive instances to the contrary. Apparently the vividness of the individual image is more persuasive than a string of statistics.[11] The psychological 'hook' is more powerful.

Elliot Aronson and his colleagues have applied this effect to energy conservation in the home. They trained representatives of local power companies to use vivid images rather than facts and figures when recommending energy saving measures to home owners. Thus they did not recommend weatherproofing by pointing out gaps around doorframes and measures of heat loss but by suggesting that these gaps added up to the size of a basketball, 'and if you had a hole that size in your wall, wouldn't you want to patch it up?' Before this image was introduced into the communication only 15 per cent of home owners had accepted the recommendations; afterwards the figure rose to 61 per cent.[12]

☐   *One-Sided or Two-Sided Arguments*

Is it more persuasive to present only one side of an argument in your communication or to mention the opposing side (before demolishing it of course)? Like so many simple-sounding questions in psychology the answer is 'it all depends'. This issue was first studied by social psychologists interested in the indoctrination of American servicemen during the Second World War.[13] There were two major findings from this research:

- For people who held the same opinion as the communicator the one-sided approach was more effective; for people who held the opposing opinion the two-sided approach was more effective.
- If people were uninformed they responded best to a one-sided argument; if they were well-informed a two-sided argument was more persuasive.

These findings were replicated in the 1960s and are still generally accepted as valid.[14] The findings imply that marketers should target different messages at different audiences. If people know nothing about a product, or are already sold on it, they should respond best to a one-sided argument; and vice versa for a two-sided argument.

☐ *The Primacy and Recency Effect*

It has been found that the order in which messages are presented to an audience can have an effect on how favourably they perceive them, with the first communication possibly benefiting from the *primacy* effect and the last from the *recency* effect, depending on the circumstances. These order effects were first teased out in an experiment that simulated a jury trial, where the subjects (the 'jurors') received the arguments of both the prosecution and the defence.[15]

The key factor is time. The recency effect is found when there is a relatively large gap between the two arguments and a small gap between the second presentation and the jury's verdict. The primacy effect is found when there is a small gap between the two presentations and a large gap between the second one and the verdict. There is obvious relevance here to scheduling television and radio advertisements to appear at the time when a buying decision is likely to be made for a given product.

☐ *Size of Attitude Discrepancy*

The final aspect of the persuasiveness of a communication that we will consider is the size of the discrepancy between it and the attitude of the target audience. Generally speaking people are more inclined to change their attitude if there is only a relatively small discrepancy between them and the message. However if the source of the communication is a particularly credible one, the *greater* the discrepancy between the message and the attitude of the audience, the more likely they are to change their attitude.[16] If you want to send a health message to heavy drinkers, for instance, an unknown entity might get them to cut down a little, but a famous heavy drinker might persuade them to give it up completely.

■ **The Audience**

The final set of factors we will deal with concerns the characteristics of the target audience. We have already seen how the pre-existing attitudes of an audience and the extent to which they are informed about the relevant issues can affect the persuasiveness of a given message. We will take a quick look here at some other factors: *self-esteem*, the need for *social approval*, the *prior experience* of the audience just before the communication is made, whether the audience is asked to make a *public commitment*, and *mood*. These factors affect the way members of an audience decode and perceive a message, and how they respond to it.

☐ *Self-Esteem*

Though there are differences of interpretation here, there is some evidence to suggest that people with low self-esteem may be more easily persuaded by a given communication than people with high self-esteem.[17] Certainly there is a lot of evidence from the conformity studies of Asch and Milgram, which we discussed in Chapter 10, that people with low self-esteem are more susceptible to the implicit attempts to influence encountered in those situations. It should make at least as much sense in situations when the attempts are explicit.

☐ *Social Approval*

Allied to the issue of self-esteem is the finding that people with a deeply felt need for social approval tend to be more affected by social influence than other people.[18]

☐ *Prior Experience*

As we noted in the last chapter, this is probably the most important audience factor in attitude change. There are two aspects to it. Generally speaking we may be persuasible when a belief we take for granted is questioned, for instance the value of democracy. The reason for this is apparently that we are unused to defending this belief and lack the time to marshall the arguments in its favour.

One way of defending against such an attempt at persuasion is to be 'inoculated' against it by prior exposure to a mild form of the argument. In medical terms an inoculation consists of importing into the body a weak form of the disease in question, which stimulates the body's natural defences to deal with it. So if the full-blown disease attacks the body at a later time the defences that have already been stimulated provide it with immunity.

Something analogous to this process of inoculation may take place in resistance to attitude change. In an experiment by William McGuire, a group of people were faced with arguments against their previously unchallenged assumption that the regular brushing of teeth prevents decay. This was followed by a refutation of the arguments that supported their original beliefs. A week later this group, and a control group who had not received the 'inoculation', were presented with another challenge to their belief about tooth brushing. The 'inoculated' group in this situation were not nearly as susceptible to persuasion as the control group.[19]

Even when counter arguments cannot be mustered, simply *forewarning* people of a communication that will challenge their beliefs can have some effect. When people are strongly committed to a particular belief they find the communication less persuasive.[20] However if people are not strongly committed in their belief they seem to become more persuasible.[21]

☐ *Public Commitment*

In Chapter 7 we discussed the relationship between individuals in small groups and the way in which group dynamics affected the behaviour of group members.

There is an important study in the group dynamics tradition that throws some useful light on audience factors in the communication process. This study was conducted in the United States during the Second World War by Kurt Lewin, who was taking part in a government campaign to persuade people to eat less popular (though quite nutritious) cuts of meat rather than steaks and other choice cuts, which were less plentiful and whose prices had risen sharply.

In particular the American government was interested in persuading people to eat offal – brains, hearts, lungs and kidneys. Most Americans found offal quite unappealing (as indeed they still do), and certainly unfamiliar to cook, so the campaign had a difficult task to perform.

Lewin's view was that mass advertising techniques would not be very effective in reaching individuals because eating behaviour was largely governed by group norms. So if you wanted to change people's eating behaviour you would first have to change the norms of their group. As the most important group member (of the family) in this instance was the housewife, Lewin designed a study using groups of housewives to see how this might be done.[22]

Six groups were used in the research and they were studied under two conditions. Half the women were given a lecture on the influences of nutrition on the health of the family, the war effort and saving money. The lecturer then handed out recipes using offal. In the other condition the study utilised group discussion, based on a group leader's introduction of the same topics, which tried to elicit the specific contributions that the members of the group could make when they went home.

In particular the participants were encouraged to discuss the reasons for resistance to change in eating behaviour. The recipes were then distributed and the group members were asked who would be willing to try out one of the recipes during the following week.

A week later all the subjects of the study were interviewed at home. The findings were striking. Only 3 per cent of the lecture group had tried one of the offal recipes but 32 per cent of the discussion group had done so. The difference was that the discussion group members had participated in making the group decision and then made a *public commitment* to try out the new recipes – that is, to change their attitudes and their behaviour towards eating cheaper cuts of meat. The people in the lecture group could only make a private commitment to change in response to the communication they received.

Since Lewin's initial work the discussion technique has been widely used by change agents in organizations.[23] It has also been used very successfully in direct marketing to groups of consumers via product agents. A wide and ever-increasing array of goods have been sold in this way, from kitchen Tupperware in the 1950s to naughty nighties in the 1990s.

□ *Mood*

The final audience characteristic we will consider is that of mood, or 'feeling state' as it is sometimes called in the trade. In other words what kind of mood consumers are in when they are exposed to the advertisement – good, bad, cheerful, depressed, serious, whimsical or whatever – and how this might affect their response.[24]

Content   Mood can, of course, be affected by many things over which advertisers have no control, such as a sudden change in the weather or the cat chewing a favourite plant. Where an advertiser can exert some control, though, is on the *content* of an advertisement. As we've seen several times already in this book, evoking positive feelings by the use of attractive visuals and music is now standard practice. The hope is that the consumer will associate the positive feelings evoked with the featured product. And there is indeed some evidence that the persuasiveness of an advertisement might thereby be increased.[25]

Context   It is also in the advertiser's interests to place an advertisement in the most effective place, and it does appear that different types of television programme affect the moods of viewers – and therefore their response to the advertisements it contains – in different ways.[26] A programme may have the (predictable) effect of making viewers temporarily sad or happy, for example. It also appears possible that when the mood of the programme and the mood of the advertisement are congruent, viewers will have a particularly positive reaction to the message.[27] So it's probably not a good idea to have a frothy upbeat advertisement for a soft drink during a programme on famine or earthquake devastation.

It is obviously very important, given the audience characteristics we have been discussing, for marketers to choose the right, or the most important, audience for their product's advertising. This is most readily done on the basis of the market segmentation approach we discussed in Chapter 2 and again in Chapter 5. No product can appeal to every consumer at any given time so attempts to devise universally applicable messages are inevitably doomed.

Finding a group of audience characteristics – whether lifestyle, demographic, cultural or whatever – is generally considered a more fruitful approach. Concentrating on a particular market segment may then dictate the medium used to transmit the message. It will also dictate *how* the medium is used. As we have seen elsewhere, soap operas were originally devised as vehicles for selling soap powder and detergent to housewives. These kinds of advertisement tend not to appear when football is being televised.

■ Feedback and Evaluation

■ Elaboration Likelihood Model (ELM)

The Elaboration Likelihood Model (ELM) suggests that there are two different 'routes to persuasion' for communications aimed at consumers.[28] These are the *central route* and the *peripheral route*. The central route is followed when the consumer's involvement and motivation to assess the product are high, and vice versa for the peripheral route. We encountered this approach in the previous chapter when we considered the ways in which attitudes are formed.

The difference between the two routes is seen when consumers process the information in an advertising message. The nature of the difference lies in the amount of *elaboration* (thinking about) the message that the consumer engages in. So when the consumer elaborates on the message, persuasion will come via the (rational) central route. When the consumer is not highly motivated by or involved in the advertisement, and therefore elaboration is low, the advertisement may still be persuasive but if it is it will be via the peripheral (non-rational) route.

That is, the receiver of the message may respond to cues – such as background music or the attractiveness of the source – that do not involve much conscious thought about the information being transmitted. Attitude change by this route will not be as powerful in its effects as attitude change by the more elaborated central route.

■ Attitudes towards the ad

Related to the ELM research is that which is often described as studying 'attitudes towards the ad'.[29] This work suggests that when consumers are exposed to an advertising message they might not only have attitudes about the message and the product it describes but about the advertisement itself. There is a lot of evidence that these attitudes towards the advertisement can have a significant effect on a consumer's attitudes towards the product, and like or dislike of an advertisement often transfers to the product being advertised.[30]

However, we've already noted many times that psychological processes are rarely that straightforward. It is perfectly possible for a consumer to enjoy an advertisement as entertainment (hardly surprising given the amount of money and creative ability that go into many of them) yet still be left cold by the product, or even be unable – as we've seen in the case of Campari/Martini/Cinzano – to remember which brand is which.

But the opposite effect is also possible. That is, an advertisement may be quite effective in terms of the product's sales and market position yet be cordially disliked by the consumer. That was apparently the case with Procter and Gamble's advertisements for its Charmin brand of toilet tissue. Between 1968 and 1982 the company ran a series extolling the 'squeezably soft' nature of its product based around the character of a store manager called 'Mr Whipple'. Mr Whipple was forever trying to stop the (female) customers from squeezing the irresistible Charmin and ending up succumbing himself.

Anyone who saw it would agree that it would be difficult to imagine a more cringe-making advertisement (I still remember it with sickening clarity twenty years later). And that was just the point. The advertisement was deliberately designed to be irritating so that it would stick in people's minds.[31]

■ Feedback

So far we have been largely concerned with the communication process, as outlined in Figure 14.1, up to the point where the receiver of the message decodes it and reacts to it. This reaction might involve a change of attitude and/or behaviour, or it might not. That process describes a *one-way* mode of communication from sender to receiver, and it seems to fit the way mass-communication advertising operates, with its emphasis on the importance of the message, the medium by which it is sent and the nature of the target market.

This form of persuasion is often contrasted with personal selling, whether in retail outlets, door-to-door sales, telephone sales or wherever. This process is a *two-way* mode of communication, and what makes it two-way is the availability of *feedback* from the prospective customer. We have seen in several parts of this book how important the feedback process is to many areas of our psychology. Think of how we perceive the world (Chapter 4), how we learn (Chapter 6) or how we become members of society (Chapter 9), to take just a few of the major examples.

There is no question that a salesperson in a two-way interaction with a consumer can have a very important impact on his or her decision to buy.[32] This stems from the fact that the two form, however fleetingly, a personal relationship where both personality factors and the salesperson's expert status can come into play.

This is the kind of relationship that advertisers try to recreate with the use of celebrity endorsements and other techniques that we discussed above, but it can only ever be a pale imitation of the real thing. On the other hand personal selling is obviously a very labour-intensive method, while mass-media advertising can reach millions of people simultaneously.

While the immediate feedback of personal selling is not available to the advertiser – though with interactive technology it may be on the way – there are still ways in which feedback can be communicated from receiver to sender (as depicted in Figure 14.1). Indeed if there is to be any attempt to assess the persuasiveness of the communication, feedback has to be an integral part of the process.

Routine post-testing and debriefing measures are carried out by many advertising agencies to assess consumer attitudes towards both the advertisement and the product being advertised. This information is then used to modify the advertisement if desired. However, as we noted above, consumers may hate a particular advertisement but still buy the product – and vice versa. Similarly, samples of television viewers are routinely tested on both recall and recognition of advertisements (see Chapter 6). But here again there may be a lot of slippage between attitudes and buying behaviour.

The use of new technology might help close this oft-noted gap between attitude and behaviour. Computerised data from supermarket scanners, for instance, may be combined with detailed media advertising data, particularly in a local area, to provide some correlation between advertising exposure and sales at a given time. By selecting panels of consumers and linking the feedback on their television viewing behaviour to that of their supermarket buying behaviour, it is possible to track a marketing campaign over time and change elements of both advertising and in-store promotion as required.[33]

With correlational data such as this it is still not possible to say definitely that Mrs Gadgett bought a jar of Aloparc's new pickled prunes *because* she saw them advertised on television (there are many other possible factors that are not being controlled) but it may be a good working hypothesis, and it is about the best we can do at the moment.

■ Cultural Factors in Advertising

In Chapter 9 we examined the ways in which children in a society are socialized to be consumers. We saw that there are differences in the way this occurs in different national cultures so that, for example, Chinese children in Hong Kong understand the concepts of 'profit' and 'banking' better, and at a younger age, than either European or American children. We also noted (both here and in Chapter 12) that there are many sub-cultural differences within any national culture that also have an important effect on a child's consumer socialization. Thus we saw how working-class Western children tend to receive more pocket money than middle-class children and are more inclined to spend it than save it.

Though these particular kinds of cultural factor are not usually taken into account by advertisers, the cultural differences involved are quite evident when pointed out. So American advertisers now quite routinely segment their campaigns between blacks, whites and Hispanics, for instance, because they have learned how important cultural differences are to the consumers involved.

However other, less visible cultural factors are involved in advertising. I said at the beginning of this chapter that cultural influences have deep roots in the way we make sense of our lives, roots that extend far beyond the consumer behaviour that is our particular concern. When we are socialized into our society there are many things about it – the social norms – that we take for granted. As we noted in Chapter 9, concepts such as profit and loss, credit and rent, all of which we take for granted, didn't really exist in former communist countries and this is one of the basic problems these national cultures are facing in their change to market economies.

In terms of consumer behaviour, therefore, the idea of customer services is quite alien to these cultures, as anyone who has ever visited one can tell you. Supermarkets as we understand them don't really exist for the local populations either, as the concept of consumer choice is also a new one. How far this is necessarily always a bad thing for the *culture*, as opposed to the economy, is something we will explore in part 5.

Because they are an intrinsic part of our culture, advertisers reflect back to us these unquestioned assumptions about being a consumer and in so doing they imply (as we noted in Chapters 10 and 11) that these social norms are also *normal* – that is natural, right and proper.[34] By implication, therefore, anything different is, at least to some extent, abnormal, unnatural, wrong and improper. Here we will consider two of the most important cultural aspects of advertising: the use of *humour* and the use of *sex*.

■ Humour in Advertising

It is difficult to put a figure on it, but I have seen estimates that over 40 per cent of all advertisements employ humour. A review of this field came to the following conclusions about the use of humour in advertising:[35]

- It attracts attention.
- It may increase comprehension.
- It can enhance the attitudes towards the advertisement.
- It may not increase source credibility.
- It does not increase the persuasiveness of the message.
- It is more effective if related to the product rather than unrelated.
- It is more effective with existing products than new ones.
- It is more effective with low-involvement products than high-involvement ones.
- Its effectiveness varies with the kind of product.
- Its effectiveness varies with the kind of audience.

Because humour is so allied to likeableness and pleasant situations in our perception of the social world it is obviously a very tempting device for advertisers to employ. 'Disneyland' is not only very big business but a state of mind that many people find very appealing (for instance, 'Cathy' and 'Thelma' in Chapter 2). 'Ronald McDonald' and even 'Mr Whipple" would fit into this view of the world.

But, fortunately, not everyone has the same sense of humour and I suspect that this may be the kind of lifestyle factor that segments the market. Something with a little more irony than the world of Walt McWhipple might be more to the taste of young urban professionals for instance. So humour can still not be relied on by advertisers to reach a universal audience. They still need to target their market carefully. The evidence is that the wrong kind of humour, or indeed any attempt at humour, can backfire if the product and/or the context and/or the audience are not right for it.

■ Sex in Advertising

If anything the use of sex in advertising is even more prevalent than humour. Erotic appeal, using models of both sexes, has always been widely used in Western advertising. The *way* it has been used has varied with the general social and cultural climate. It became noticeably more explicit – especially visually –

during the 1960s and 1970s, but because of public fear of AIDS and other sexually transmitted diseases it has (generally speaking) become a little more subtle since then.[36]

The success or failure of sex in advertising follow similar lines to that of humour. Like humour, erotic appeals are very good at grabbing the consumer's attention. Even more than with humour, though, the consumer may simply find this distracting, particularly the male consumer (so perhaps those car advertisements with beautiful women hanging all over them are just a waste of money). Women are much more likely than men to recall the product and its brand name in advertisements they find sexy[37] In general, nudity can have a negative effect on most people when (as you might have predicted) a model of the same sex is used[38]

As with humour, the predisposition of the viewer is an important factor in its effectiveness, and the apparent relevance of the product to this form of treatment is also important. Products specifically concerned with sex appeal, such as lingerie or aftershave, are generally most acceptable. However that hasn't stopped notable attempts in recent years to shift products such as ice cream (Haagen Dazs) or mustard (Grey Poupon) using sexual imagery and innuendo.

■ Further Reading

Bryant, J. and D. Zillman (eds), *Perspectives in Media Effects* (Hillsdale, NJ: Lawrence Erlbaum Associates, 1986). A thorough and authoritative compilation of social scientific research into the effects of the media (especially television) on audience behaviour.

Cialdini, R. B., *Influence: How and Why People Agree to Things* (New York: William Morrow, 1984). An interesting and accessible account of influence techniques and the psychology involved.

Davis, H. and A. Silk (eds), *Behavioral and Management Sciences in Marketing* (New York: Ronald Press, 1978). A useful overview of how a variety of disciplines contribute to marketing. Includes some key contributions.

Patzer, G., *The Physical Attractiveness Phenomena* (New York: Plenum Press, 1985). A thorough exploration of physical attractiveness and communication by one of the leading researchers of the issue.

Pratkanis, A. R. and E. Aronson, *Age of Propaganda: The Everyday Use and Abuse of Persuasion* (New York: W. H. Freeman, 1992). A study of the methods of persuasion used in an American election year to market politicians.

Sternthal, B. and C. S. Craig, *Consumer Behavior: An Information Processing Perspective* (Englewood Cliffs, NJ: Prentice-Hall, 1982). A general overview of persuasive communication from an information processing perspective.

It is also worth browsing through the latest issues of the following periodicals: *Advances in Consumer Research, Advertising Age, Journal of Advertising Research, Journal of Marketing Research, Journal of Consumer Research.*

■ Questions for Discussion

1. What makes the source of a communication particularly credible? Give examples from current advertising campaigns.
2. Give examples of a one-sided and a two-sided advertising message and suggest why the particular strategy was chosen in each case.
3. Give an example of an advertising message using an appeal to fear. How effective is it and why?
4. What does the mood of an audience have to do with the content and context of an ad?
5. What is the relationship between an audience's attitudes towards an ad and the ad's effectiveness?
6. Give examples of the use of (a) humour and (b) sex in advertising. How effective is this strategy?

CHAPTER 15

Approaching a Decision

Introduction

In a sense our whole lives are the sum of all the decisions we have ever made. Some decisions seem large to us (who to live with and what house to live in) and others small (what movie to watch and what soft drink to buy). The financial and psychological investment is much greater in a large decision, as are the potential rewards of making a good decision and the penalties of making a bad one.

Yet all the decisions we make have some things in common. They each involve the existence of more than one possibility to choose from, for instance (or there would be no decision to make), and they all bring into play the same psychological processes. In this chapter we will examine the ways in which we go about making a decision, and then focus on consumer decisions and how we go about deciding what to buy.

How People Make Decisions

The first point to make about making a decision is that we don't know the outcome of choosing each of the alternatives we are faced with. This is blindingly obvious, of course, but it is worth pointing out nonetheless because it gets to the heart of the decision-making process and why we find it so difficult.

Not only are we operating (as we do for much of our lives) in a state of some uncertainty about the future, but the smaller the differences between the competing alternatives the harder is it for us to make a decision. It is *evaluating the probabilities* of these different outcomes that is particularly difficult – very often more difficult than the actual decision itself.

The other obvious point about decisions that is worth spelling out is that we are constantly making them. From the moment we get up in the morning we are faced with deciding what to wear and what to have for breakfast and we make decisions throughout the rest of the day. Indeed we normally make so many decisions in the course of a day, every day, that only rarely do we realise that we are in fact making a decision. Decisions are just part of the business of living our lives, and are taken for granted.

Rationality

Rationality is what you and I would like to think we use when making a decision.

Moreover we like to believe that we are rational in both the *psychological* and the *economic* senses of the word. Psychologically we make objective, dispassionate choices that are not influenced by prejudice or other· irrational influences. Economically we find out all the information there is on each of the alternatives, assess the advantages and disadvantages of each, then choose the best one on the basis of a cost–benefit analysis.

The odd thing is that, very occasionally, we actually do make decisions like that. It is important to realise this because when we consider the vast number of decisions that are not made in that way it might seem that we're not capable of rational decision making at all. We certainly are, but because we are real people living in the real world the odds are very much against us.

For a start most decisions are made in a state of *incomplete information*. The Western romantic myth has it, for instance, that there is only one boy or girl in the whole world for you and it's just a matter of finding Ms or Mr Right. If we tried to operationalize a decision-making process on that basis we'd all be dead long before we could find a partner. Yet most of us in fact do so. Are we all making the wrong decision? With the divorce rate heading for one in two it *appears* that many of us might be. On the other hand many of us clearly are making the right decision. And even in the case of partners who do split up, getting together may have been the best decision at the time.

Furthermore, as we have seen throughout this book, much of our behaviour is not really thought about consciously. It may be influenced by habits learned when we were very young or unconscious motivation that we'd rather not know about. How do smokers decide when to have a cigarette for instance? Or how do drinkers decide when to have a drink – when they're thirsty?

Often, therefore, we are not really trying to find the *best possible* alternative; what we are really looking for is a *good enough* alternative. This is sometimes known as *satisficing*, a term introduced into modern economics by theorists who were concerned that a model of decision-making that simply assumed perfect rationality on the part of consumers was, to put it mildly, a trifle unrealistic. Indeed apart from traditional economists, Treasury officials and of course politicians, few people take it seriously any more. So how *do* we go about making decisions in the absence of complete rationality? The answer seems to be *heuristics*.

■ Heuristics

A *heuristic* is simply a procedure or method or strategy for solving a problem or making a decision. It is similar to an *algorithm*, a procedure widely used in science, except that an algorithm is guaranteed to find the solution, or the best solution, whereas a heuristic is not. Perhaps then it would be better, for our purposes, to think of a heuristic as a rule-of-thumb. That is, a heuristic may be a good place from which to start if we're faced with a decision and it may provide a reasonable guide in the search for a solution, but no more than that. A heuristic may therefore be helpful, but it may also lead us totally astray.

The reason we need heuristics when making decisions is simply that the world we live in turns us into misers – *cognitive misers*. We have already encountered this phenomenon in several forms. In Chapter 4 we saw how the constant stream of sensations that arrive at our sense organs are turned into recognisable images of the physical world by the process of perception. In Chapter 6 we learned how we fashion new knowledge and skills out of a constant stream of information. And in Chapter 10 we observed ourselves judging the behaviour of other people by pigeonholing them into a few categories or stereotypes.

What we are trying to do in each of these cases is to make sense of the situation we are in in the simplest possible way and with the least amount of rational, mental (cognitive) processing. We do this by selecting a rule-of-thumb and applying it to the situation. We therefore guard our cognitive capital carefully and spend it reluctantly.[1] As we have seen time and again in this book, we simply have no choice. The amount of information we have to deal with, the number of decisions we have to make, would simply overwhelm us if we didn't take short cuts and use rules-of-thumb to navigate our way through the world.

We will consider three forms of heuristic that psychologists have identified in the way people make decision: the *representative* heuristic, the *attitude* heuristic and the *availability* heuristic.

■ The Representative Heuristic

In the representative heuristic we pick out something familiar in a new object and then equate its similarity with one we know.[2] The halo effect we first came across in Chapter 5 is an example of this heuristic. If someone is perceived as 'warm' or 'beautiful' we attribute all sorts of unrelated positive characteristics to them, for example intelligence or honesty. The classic use of this heuristic in consumer behaviour is judging quality on the basis of price.

We know that luxury goods, famous brand names and celebrated retailers are usually more expensive than their competitors. So when faced with a decision about buying a product we will often use the price as the representative characteristic for choosing between alternatives: an expensive bouquet of flowers for someone we love, a cheap and nasty bottle of Ruritanian Riesling for someone we detest.

■ The Attitude Heuristic

We saw in Chapter 12 how an attitude is formed with a belief and an evaluative component to it. It can therefore contain a global judgment of someone or something that saves us the cognitive effort of considering the situation all over again each time we come across them. Indeed there is evidence that we can use our attitude as a heuristic in deciding what the objective fact is of a situation.

Thus when faced with the alternatives that Ronald Reagan obtained either an 'A' or a 'C' average in college, people who liked him believed 'A' to be true and those who disliked him believed 'C' to be true.[3] ('C' is in fact correct.) In consumer terms I suspect you'd find similar attitudes differences over the beneficial effects of marijuana (or alcohol) between people who like it and people who don't. Starting off with liking or disliking a product then believing what we *want* to be true about it is probably more common in our decision making than we care to admit.

■ The Availability Heuristic

The final heuristic we will consider is the one we use when estimating the likelihood of something occurring, using relevant data from our memory. The more available this information is to us the more likely we are to think the event will occur. Try this example yourself. Are there more English words beginning with the letter 'k' (for example 'kilt') or ones with 'k' as the third letter (for example 'like')? Most people will say the former, which is wrong.[4] The reason we get it wrong is that we can remember words beginning with 'k' *more easily* ('kith and kin', 'kitchen' and 'kindergarten') than words with 'k' in third position ('rake', 'woke'). As a result we assume, wrongly, that the greater availability of examples in our memory means that a greater number of instances exist – such as the number of coffee creams in a box of chocolates per-haps.

This also helps to explain the great trust we have in the validity of *hindsight*. Once an event has actually occurred we can easily convince ourselves, not only that it was inevitable, but that we always knew it would happen. The reality may have been quite different, but once the event has actually happened it becomes available to our memory as an example of something we are certain about. Maybe this is why after an election more people claim to have voted for the winner than could possibly have done so. In consumer terms, you always *knew* you'd have trouble if you bought that car.

Having sketched the psychological background to the way people generally approach decisions, for the rest of this chapter we will focus our attention on widely used models of the entire consumer decision-making and the purchasing process that follows it.

■ The Consumer Decision-Making Process

A widely accepted model of the consumer decision-making process is outlined in Figure 15.1. We will deal with stages 1, 2 and 3 of the process in this chapter, and stages 4 and 5 in the next.

■ Stage 1: Recognizing a Problem

The first stage of the consumer decision-making process is when consumers perceive a need, something that is missing from their lives, and this perception triggers off the process. The consumers' 'problem' in this model is therefore to close the gap between their *actual state*, the one they are currently in, and the

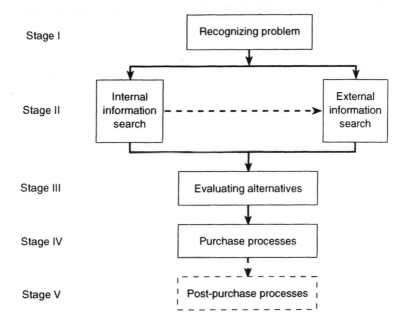

Stage I — Recognizing problem

Stage II — Internal information search · · · · · · · · · ·> External information search

Stage III — Evaluating alternatives

Stage IV — Purchase processes

Stage V — Post-purchase processes

Figure 15.1   The consumer decision-making process

desired state they would like to be in. But if no need is actually perceived then there is no problem, and the process doesn't start. So there might be a discrepancy between the consumers' actual and desired states but one that is not great enough to register with them because it has not crossed their *absolute threshold* of awareness (as we discussed in our study of perception in Chapter 4).

However, even if consumers do recognize a need the right conditions may not be in place to trigger the decision-making process. There are two reasons for this:

- The consumers might not consider the recognised need sufficiently important to act on it (I may be in need of lunch as I write this sentence but not sufficiently so [yet] for me to break my train of thought).
- The consumers might not be able to satisfy the need (I recognize that I need a long break in the sun but my piggy bank is empty).

There are however many situations in which consumers can and are prepared to act on the problem of need recognition, and we will now consider these.

The process that brings consumers to this point is depicted in Figure 15.2.

☐ *Acting on Problem Recognition*

There are many antecedent causes that lead people to act on the recognition of a problem. They may be divided into the following five groups:

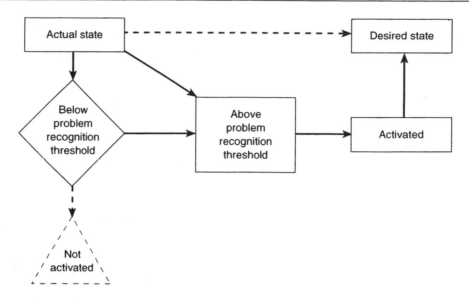

Figure 15.2   Problem recognition

- Changing circumstances.
- Depleted stock.
- Dissatisfaction with stock.
- Marketing influences.
- Product add-ons:

Changing circumstances   This group of causes is one of the largest, and it may in turn be divided into three:

- Changes in finances.
- Changes in needs.
- Changes in wants.

A *change in finances* may be positive or negative, of course, but either way it can affect consumer decision-making behaviour. An increase in income may lead to the purchase of previously unconsidered luxuries, for example. A decrease will usually lead to reduced spending and consumption, probably in discretionary areas such as entertainment and holiday travel, and perhaps a reassessment of needs as opposed to wants.

Needs may be activated by the sheer passage of time, whether it is the consumption of food and drink on a daily basis or the kind of life-cycle effects we discussed in Chapter 8. When a couple have a child they immediately have a need they didn't have before – a need for baby products. As people get older they often have a greater need for health care.

Wants, while not being necessities, are also often linked to the life-cycle. Not many children want 10-year-old malt whisky, though lots of adults do. In this instance the new want depends on the physiological maturity of taste buds and capacity for alcohol, as well as social factors such as increased opportunities, fashion, peer group norms and so on.

There are also times when the differences between wants and needs may be blurred by changing circumstances. Think of the question 'does he *need* a haircut?' applied to men in different occupations, at different stages of the life-cycle and in different eras.

Depleted stock   This is also a frequent and regularly occurring cause of problem recognition and is also linked to the passage of time. Our stock of goods and services is simply *depleted* by regular consumption. Running out of milk is a frequently encountered trigger for problem recognition. So is writing a letter then realizing you don't have a stamp for it.

Dissatisfaction with stock   Even when our stock of something is not depleted enough to need replacing we may often be dissatisfied with its continuing ability to fulfil its function. This is the effect of time again and it is most obvious in the case of clothes fashions, where hemlines may now be too high/low or ties too broad/narrow. The problem recognition in this case is, of course, triggered by social norms. If we don't care how unfashionable we look then we won't recognize a problem.

Here's an alternative though. I've discovered through empirical observation that fashions go in cycles and if you keep your clothes long enough (on average about 12 years ± 3) they will duly come back into fashion. This is what social scientists call a curvilinear relationship and is illustrated in Figure 15.3.

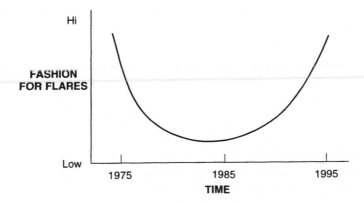

Figure 15.3   Fashion cycles

So if I'd kept my flares from the 1970s I could have worn them in the early 1990s (provided I could still get into them that is, which may on second thoughts have led to a different cause of dissatisfaction).

Marketing influences   In one sense most attempted *marketing influences* have the goal of persuading consumers to recognize (and take steps to close) the gap between their actual current state of not owning a particular product and the desired state of owning it. We have seen throughout this book how difficult it can be for marketers to be successful in this goal.

Perhaps the point at which marketers and consumers focus most clearly on problem recognition is when new products and innovations are introduced, which we considered in Chapter 3. We noted there that what seems to make for successful innovation is the ability to satisfy a demand that consumers were perhaps unaware they had. This can be seen most clearly in spectacularly successful innovations such as fast food outlets, photocopiers, word processors, portable telephones, personal stereos and, most of all, supermarkets. What each of these innovations did was to change the way that people related to each other in large ways and small.

Product add-ons   Buying one product can often activate a problem recognition of the need for *product add-ons.* New owners of CD players are immediately in the market for CD records. First-time home buyers are obviously in need of furniture and appliances.

■   Stage 2: Searching for Information

Once a problem of need has been recognized and the consumer is willing and able to act on it, the second stage of the decision-making process is activated: the *search for information.* We should note here that while this seems to be an eminently objective and rational part of the decision-making process it is not quite as straightforward as it looks.

The main reason for this lies in the fact that decisions do not always become easier as we accumulate more information on the alternative brands available. Indeed the process often becomes more difficult as new information reveals other aspects of the product that we hadn't previously been aware of. Certain brands (of computer, mobile phone, VCR and so on) may have some of the features that you would like; other brands may have other features.

Until you started the search for information you were happily ignorant of these complexities. Because of our tendency towards cognitive miserliness, discussed earlier in this chapter, we may perhaps curtail our search at the earliest opportunity rather than carry it through to its logical conclusion.[5]

Bearing this psychological dimension in mind we can now turn to the search process itself. This may be either *internal* or *external.*

□   *The Internal Search*

The internal search for information is the first step and it may be undirected or directed.

Undirected internal search behaviour occurs when we learn things without intending to and add them to our long-term memory bank. Psychologists call this *incidental learning*. Perhaps the first information we acquire from incidental learning is that mother is soft and warm and the source of food and comfort.

As adults we may, for example, learn the names of all the shops on our way home from work or college, not because we deliberately set out to do so but because we see these landmarks every day and our brain registers that information without our being aware of it. A number of studies have examined this process at work in the way consumers behave in shopping malls and how it affects their buying decisions.[6]

Directed internal search behaviour occurs when we *deliberately* try to retrieve relevant information from memory. If this process turns up sufficient information there is no need for the consumer to search any further. There is some evidence, in fact, that for many (perhaps most) consumer situations a simple memory scan provides sufficient information for people to make a decision. This has been found, for instance, in choosing retail outlets[7] and car repair services.[8]

The adequacy of internal search can be affected by several factors. Brand loyalty and satisfaction with previous similar purchases will obviously enhance it. Being a first-time or very infrequent buyer will detract from it, as will the temptations of impulse buying in supermarkets, during sales or while on holiday.

☐ *The External Search*

There are times for all of us when an internal search is insufficient, we don't have direct experience of the product and we must turn to some form of *external* search, all of which are directed. As we have seen in previous chapters the most important sources of consumer information for most people are family and friends, retail sales staff and advertisements. If someone wants to make a more thorough search they will then turn to specialist or technical magazines or consumer reports.

A lot of work has been done on the amount of external searching people engage in to acquire information on a product, and several general conclusions may be drawn:[9]

- Many consumers do very little external searching, even for major purchases such as houses, cars and appliances – a sizeable number only consider a single brand or retailer.
- As we noted earlier, a search among the alternatives may obtain only a limited amount of information before being curtailed.
- For fast-moving consumer goods the time taken for an external information search may be counted in seconds. One study of supermarket shopping found that on average shoppers take less than 12 seconds to make a choice, with 42 per cent taking 5 seconds or less.[10] The great majority of shoppers in this study only inspected or handled one brand and one size of product. Less

than a quarter of shoppers made a price comparison between the brand they chose and competing products, and 40 per cent didn't even check the price at all![11]

There are two sets of specific factors that can affect external information search: *situational* and *individual* factors. These may lead to an increase or decrease in search activity.

Situational factors that *increase* search:

- Social pressure to search from family or peers.
- High cost of product.
- Shopping is convenient..
- Information easy to obtain.
- Clear differences in price or quality of product alternatives.
- Long-lasting product.

Situational factors that *decrease* search:

- Time pressure.
- Ease of returning/exchanging goods.
- Low cost of product.
- Difficult shopping conditions.
- Influential salesperson.

Individual factors that *increase* search:

- High involvement in decision.
- Ability to access, process and use information.
- Confidence and enjoyment in learning.
- High socio-economic status.
- Enjoyment of shopping in general.
- Enjoyment of variety and new experiences in shopping.
- High perceived benefits/low perceived costs.

Individual factors that *decrease* search:

- Low involvement in decision
- Brand loyalty
- Difficulty coping with information
- Difficulty coping with salesperson
- General dislike of shopping
- A lot of past experience
- Low perceived benefits/high perceived costs

☐ *The Risk Factor*

You may recall that when we discussed the psychology of perception in Chapter 4 we ended the chapter with a section on 'perceiving risk'. We saw there that, to the extent we are consciously aware of uncertainty in making a decision, we are perceiving *risk* about the consequences of that decision. Therefore risk should always be qualified by the adjective 'perceived' because it is always subjective and may bear little relation to any assessment of objective reality, or to someone else's perceived risk.

In Chapter 4 we identified six kinds of risk that consumers perceive: performance, financial, physical, time, social and psychological. We looked at the ways in which people coped with perceptions of risk and found that brand loyalty was the most popular strategy for reducing risk. In this chapter we have discussed a psychological mechanism that might account for the popularity of this strategy – cognitive miserliness. Brand loyalty, after all, is a good way of not having to make a decision about a new alternative.

There is a related way of using this mechanism to reduce uncertainty and risk. It involves our building up a collection of basic beliefs about the market that are really stereotypes but also allow us to navigate our way more confidently through a vast sea of information without foundering on the reefs of difficult decisions.

These beliefs cover the whole range of shopping behaviour in dealing with advertising, retailers, different brands and so on. Some typical examples would be:[12]

- All brands are basically the same.
- Locally owned stores give the best service.
- The more salespeople there are in a store, the more expensive its products.
- The most heavily advertised brands are normally among the best.
- One of the best ways to decide which brand to select is to look at what everybody else is buying.

There is, of course, at least a grain of truth in all these beliefs, but the important point is that they are used as *generalizations* in all situations, as if they were always true. A moment's thought will reveal exceptions to each of them, of course. But they do have the function of helping us feel psychologically more *comfortable* in a shopping situation, which – as we've seen more than once in this book – may be more important to us than the money saved by applying a rational cost–benefit analysis to the decision.

■ **Stage 3: Evaluating the Alternatives**

Having recognized the problem of need and searched for information about possible alternatives, the consumer arrives at the third stage of the decision-making process: evaluation of the alternatives.

□   *Criteria of Evaluation*

What criteria are used by the consumer to evaluate product alternatives? The answer to this question varies from product to product, and different features are considered for each one. Someone buying a new car will usually consider engine performance, safety, reliability and mileage. Someone buying a new colour television may consider picture quality and size of screen.

The criteria chosen for evaluation will vary from one consumer to another. A car buyer may be more concerned with its social status or luxurious fittings than any of the criteria mentioned in the last paragraph, for instance. Some criteria are widely used across product categories especially – as we have seen in this and other chapters – *price* and *brand name*.

At the same time we have also seen in this chapter that consumers can be remarkably unaware of price; in supermarket shopping for instance.[13] A well-known brand may be used on many occasions as a substitute quality criterion as well as a status symbol. This has long been known about the purchase of aspirin and other products where the consumer is normally unable to assess the quality of the product.[14]

A number of criteria may therefore be important or *salient* to any given consumer for any given product. This is not to say, however, that they will necessarily be acted on. If all the brands of a given product are unfamiliar to a customer, or if all the alternatives have the same price, then despite their salience to the consumer they will not influence her or his evaluation. That is, they will not be *determinant* attributes because they do not differentiate between alternatives, the consumer's most important task.

□   *Arriving at the Alternatives*

Having settled on the appropriate criteria for evaluation the consumer must then decide which alternatives to choose from. These alternatives are known as the *evoked set* (or sometimes the *consideration set*). The brands contained within the evoked set are a subset of all existing brands of a particular product.

The size of the evoked set to be considered varies by consumer, of course, ranging from one (for brand-loyal customers) upwards. However the size of the evoked set also varies by product. Thus one study has found that the average size can vary from 2.2 alternatives for air fresheners to 6.9 alternatives for beer.[15]

□   *Assessing the Alternatives*

Generally speaking consumers assess alternative possibilities in terms of brands or product attributes. In the former, different attributes of a given brand would be considered; in the latter, different brands would be compared on a given attribute. It seems likely that we start with a consideration of attributes (for example price, quality, size and so on) then move on to assess particular brands.[16]

In line with our cognitive miserliness we tend to use various techniques to restrict the amount of assessment we do. One of these is to have a cut-off point beyond which an attribute is unacceptable to us. The obvious example is price, but it may be any product attribute from the bagginess of a suit to the dryness of a wine.[17]

☐ *Choosing a Decision-Making Rule*

The process of choosing a decision-making rule is sometimes described as following a *decision strategy*, an *information processing* strategy or, as we discussed at the beginning of this chapter, *heuristics*. In this section we will look specifically at buying heuristics and classify the different kinds of decision-making rules chosen and under what conditions. The heuristics we looked at earlier were concerned mainly with purchases that did not demand a great deal of motivated, involved behaviour, and consequently not a great deal of cognitive activity. The heuristics we will now consider generally demand more motivation and involvement and more cognitive activity.[18]

Consumer decision-making rules are usually divided into two broad categories: *compensatory* and *noncompensatory*.

Compensatory decision rules As the name suggests, people selecting this rule compensate for a perceived weakness in one attribute of the product by offsetting it against perceived strengths ('Reek' aftershave numbs your taste buds but it's cheap and drives women wild). By definition, therefore, the consumer is using more than one criterion to evaluate the product. In the simplest version of this rule the consumer simply adds up the pluses and minuses of each alternative and the one with the most pluses wins. In the more complex version the relevant attributes are weighted according to their importance to the consumer. This is a very similar process to the multi-attribute attitude models we discussed in Chapter 13.

Noncompensatory decision-making rules With a noncompensatory decision-making rule a consumer cannot offset the negative attributes of a brand or product with positive ones (If your sense of taste is very important to you and 'Reek' aftershave anaesthetizes it, you'll just have to find some other way of driving women wild.) Four kinds of noncompensatory decision-making rules are often identified: *conjunctive, disjunctive, lexicographic,* and *elimination.*

In using the *conjunctive rule* the consumer establishes a minimum acceptable standard for each attribute. This standard acts as a cut-off point for rejecting alternatives. This is often used as the first way of reducing a large number of alternatives. If *all* the alternatives are rejected the consumer must decide whether to change the cut-off point of the decision-making rule – or remove her- or himself from the market.

The *disjunctive decision-making* rule also employs a cut-off but in this case if an alternative achieves the minimum standard it is acceptable. If only one alternative achieves the standard that is the one that is purchased. If a number of alternatives make it past the cut-off point then another decision-making rule must be selected.

One of the decision-making rules that may be chosen if the disjunctive rule is insufficient is the *lexicographic rule*. With this rule, criteria are assessed in their order of importance to the consumer. So if several of the alternatives meet the cut-off point on the most important attribute (price) the next most important attribute (ease of use) will be considered, and so on until a decision can be made.

The *elimination rule* is very similar to the lexicographic rule except that here the consumer establishes acceptable minimum standards for *all* the attributes to be considered rather than rank ordering them one at a time. Any alternative that doesn't reach acceptable standards is eliminated.

Finally, we should note that these decision-making rules may also be used in sequence: that is, conjunctive → disjunctive and so on until a decision is made.

■ Marketing Implications

Before ending our discussion of consumer decision-making processes we should take a brief look at their implications for marketing. Three issues seem to be particularly important: (a) knowing the *decision-making rules* used by consumers of a given product, (b) the *cues* that consumers use when assessing alternatives and (c) the *presentation* of appropriate information to the consumer.

■ Knowing the Decision-Making Rules

It makes obvious good sense for marketers to know which decision-making rules are used by the consumers who buy their products. Ideally the marketing and advertising strategy for a product should not cause customers to re-evaluate their choice of the product or to change their decision-making rule.

The most obvious change factor to avoid is price. For example if a consumer's decision-making rule is 'buy the cheapest', a price increase relative to competing products might well rule this particular brand out of contention. On if the decision-making rule is 'eliminate anything costing more than £x' and the price increase brings it above this cut-off point, the brand will no longer be considered.

■ Consumers' Use of Cues

In earlier chapters we saw how people constantly make use of cues to make sense of the world, whether they are in the form of sensory information and perceptual cues or interpersonal behaviour and social cues, for instance. When people are in consumer mode they will use a range of cues in the same way to form a coherent image of goods and services.

One study considered the use of these cues in relation to four kinds of service, those of a doctor, a dentist, a hairdresser and a bank.[19] The cue most relied on (out of eight possibilities) for the first three services was 'personal referral'. With banking it came second only to 'physical location'. One of the least important cues was 'advertising'. It was only of any importance in choosing a bank, and even then it was only fourth on the list.

In this study 'price' was only important in choosing a hairdresser. Obviously different services (plumber, caterer, accountant) might well generate a different rank ordering of cues relied on. What is worth thinking about though is the relative importance of 'personal referral' and the unimportance of advertising. Moreover non-cognitive cues such as novelty or curiosity might also play an important part in many decisions, a point we will explore in the next chapter.

This echoes similar findings we have noted at various points in this book and seems to suggest that the usual marketing strategies might, in some situations, have a rather limited influence on buying decisions. Once more we have an illustration of how complex the psychological processes behind consumer behaviour are, and how difficult it may be for the marketer to intervene intelligently and effectively in these processes on behalf of a particular product.

■ Presentation of Consumer Information

What information should be presented to the consumer, how much and in what form? are the questions at the heart of any marketing and advertising strategy. There has been a lot of research on this issue and there is of course no easy answer to what looks like a series of straightforward questions.[20] For example how much information should a product's packaging contain? In our discussion of visual perception in Chapter 4 we noted that package designers are aware of the fact that many people who need reading glasses don't always use them when they are shopping, so they make their packages as easy as possible to recognize, identify and read.

This seems to suggest that less information on a package is better than more. However this seems to reduce the marketer's scope to convince those consumers who are undecided about whether the product meets conditions of their decision-making rules. But too much information might lead to cognitive overload, where the consumers' processing capacity is overwhelmed and they become confused. Yet unless the information is provided the consumers can't use it even if they want to, and there is also some evidence that different segments of the market will be responsive to different kinds of information.

Having considered the background to human decision making and examined the techniques people use, and how they actually operate, we are ready to deal with the purchasing process itself and what happens after a purchase is made. These form stages 4 and 5 of our model, as outlined in Figure 15.1, and we will deal with them in the next chapter.

■ Further Reading

Bettman, J. R., *An Information Processing Theory of Consumer Choice* (Reading, MA: Addison-Wesley, 1979). An account of a widely used theoretical model by one of the leading researchers in the field.

Howard, J. A., *Consumer Behavior in Marketing Strategy* (Englewood Cliffs, NJ: Prentice-Hall, 1989). An analysis of consumer decision making by a leading researcher.

Sternthal, B. and C. S. Craig, *Consumer Behavior: An Information Processing Perspective* (Englewood Cliffs, NJ: Prentice-Hall, 1982). A good general review of this approach.

It is also worth browsing through recent issues of the following periodicals: *Advances in Consumer Research*, *Journal of Consumer Research*.

■ Questions for Discussion

1. Why can't the decisions we make always be entirely rational? What does 'satisficing' have to do with this problem?
2. What is the relationship between being a 'cognitive miser' and using heuristics?
3. What factors determine whether consumers recognise that they have a particular need? How did need recognition trigger your last clothing purchase? Was the process any different from your decision to buy your last book?
4. Give examples of how a consumer might use internal as opposed to external search before making a decision?
5. How do consumers go about assessing competing alternatives? How do they go about choosing a decision rule?

CHAPTER 16

The Decision and its Consequences

■ Introduction

In the last chapter we examined the first three stages of our model of consumer decision-making processes (Figure 15.1): stage 1 – recognizing a problem; stage 2 – searching for information; stage 3 – evaluating the alternatives. In this chapter we will deal with the remaining two stages: stage 4 – purchase processes; and stage 5 – post-purchase processes. The division of these five stages between the two chapters is largely arbitrary and the reason for the division is simply size. So you should really treat Chapters 15 and 16 as though they were one long chapter.

■ Stage 4: Purchasing Processes

Purchasing processes are what the consumer experiences at the point of sale, wherever and whenever that may be. We will examine these experiences as they occur in the two main situations, *in-store* and *at-home*.

■ In-Store Purchasing

In-store purchasing refers to goods and services bought in retail outlets such as supermarkets, city-centre shops, shopping malls and car showrooms.

■ Why Do People Go Shopping?

You may recall that we addressed this question in the course of our discussion on motivation in Chapter 7. We noted there that the obvious answer – 'people go shopping because they need to buy things' – is only the tip of the psychological iceberg. Apart from the home and workplace, Americans probably now spend more time in shopping malls than anywhere else.[1] And they do not just go there to buy things. Some of the other reasons that have been identified for going shopping include the following:[2]

- It gets you out and breaks up the routine.
- It provides you with information on what's available.

- It is a form of entertainment and recreation.
- It enables you to meet friends and other people.
- It can make you feel important and needed in your role as household provider.
- It can provide exercise.
- It can provide sensory stimulation (sights, sounds, smells and so on).
- Being waited on by deferential and attentive assistants can give you a sense of being important, or even powerful.
- It gives you the opportunity to exercise your hunting and bargaining skills, and success can provide a feeling of achievement.

It has indeed been argued that the buying process may even be an end in itself for many people, providing a psychological gratification that is quite removed from the process of consumption.[3] Instead of shopping in order to buy, in other words, people may buy in *order to shop*. This phenomenon does seem to be reflected in popular slogans such as 'born to shop' and 'shop till you drop'. It is clearly important for retailers to be aware of the psychology of the shopping trip when presenting consumers with their goods and services.

■ How Do People Choose a Shop?

The picture we have been painting of enthusiastic and dedicated shoppers is of course a generalization. It may be true of some people all of the time and most people some of the time, but there are also quite a few people – who may be described as *antishoppers* – who don't like shopping any of the time.[4] In the United States they have been estimated at 15–25 per cent of all consumers. Antishoppers include large numbers of married couples with children who simply find shopping a stressful chore for which they have less and less time and patience.[5]

Few people can actually avoid shopping trips altogether, however, and even the most reluctant antishoppers have a lot of potential business to give to a retail outlet. So how would they go about choosing one? The evidence seems to be that the process of making a decision about where to shop is very similar to making a decision about which product or brand to buy, as discussed in the previous chapter. And this is apparently true of all shoppers, however reluctant or enthusiastic.[6]

Thus consumers will select appropriate decision rules and evaluate alternative stores on that basis. As with brand and product choice, many of the decision-making rules will be framed to expend the minimum psychological effort. If 'go to the nearest supermarket' results in a satisfactory shopping trip it will become part of a routine. It will therefore be extremely difficult for a rival supermarket to intervene, no matter how energetic and imaginative its marketing, advertising and sales promotion strategies are. The more reluctant the shopper, the more true will this be of course.

But at least half of all consumers are generally thought to be open to persuasion by retail outlets and these are usually the heaviest purchasers.[7] We will therefore consider the major factors that influence their choice of shop. These are *location, layout, merchandising* and *service.*

☐ *Location*

The most obvious influence on choice of shop is perhaps that of location. Retailers are very fond of telling us that only three things matter in their business; location, location and location. In Chapter 10 we noted the effects of sheer proximity on such an important psychological issue as the development of friendship patterns. It is no surprise, therefore, that the closer a shop is to our home then, other things being equal, the more we are likely to shop there.[8]

At the same time we have seen throughout this book that, psychologically, others things are often not 'equal', that there are individual and lifestyle differences between consumers that have the effect of making their behaviour patterns more complex and difficult to understand. Research has found, for example, that those who are more likely to shop outside their own area have different characteristics from other consumers.[9] They tend to be younger, more upmarket and more adventurous consumers who are willing to invest the extra time, money and energy required. Fifteen minutes driving time appears to be an important cut-off point in decision-making rules that include proximity.[10]

At least in the United States, a trend seems to be developing away from use of out-of-town shopping malls towards a return to closer, if less attractive, shopping centres.[11] The main reason for this appears to be the increasing pressure of time on people in the world of work. Between 1987 and 1991 the number of people who *never* visited shopping malls went from 12 per cent to 18 per cent.

☐ *Layout*

In Chapter 4 we saw how people match their self-image to shops they feel are 'appropriate' for them to frequent. Apart from famous department stores such as Bloomingdales and Harrods, whose names evoke a particular image in everyone's mind, shoppers tend to judge the appropriateness of lesser known places by their external and internal layout, and the overall physical impression they present.[12] Design, decor, furnishings, carpeting and so on all contribute to the mood in which the consumer approaches the shopping experience and therefore the purchase decision-making process itself.

In Chapter 4 we also considered the effects of sensory *ambiance* on shoppers. We noted how the conditions provided by retailers might affect buying behaviour by stimulating all the senses, but especially hearing and vision. As well as the shop layout noted above, the way in which merchandise is arranged and the way the shop and its displays are lit can present an image of cheapness or luxury to consumers.[13]

Music in shops has been used, and studied, for many years now. We saw in Chapter 4 that people spend less time shopping (but the same amount of money) when the music is loud. They also walk more slowly and spend more when the music is slow in tempo. Shoppers also spend more if the music is to their taste.

☐　*Merchandising*

Changes to the way goods and services are offered to the consumer can also have an impact on buying patterns. The old city-centre pattern of shopping in specialised outlets (bakers, fishmongers and so on) changed for many people with the opening of suburban supermarkets that supplied the same goods and services in a single place. This trend has continued in recent years with developments such as dry cleaners and newsagents also being sited in supermarkets. At the same time pharmacies may now sell food and drink. As the pattern of product specialization becomes increasingly blurred, price and convenience become more important factors in choosing where to shop.

☐　*Service*

Quality of service is obviously important to shoppers. As we've noted several times in this book, salespeople can be very influential and shoppers with relatively low self-confidence can be intimidated from using a particular retail outlet by sales behaviour they perceive as aggressive or patronizing. What shoppers respond to, therefore, are salespeople who are open and approachable, as well as helpful and knowledgeable.

Retail outlets also offer a variety of consumer services to try to reinforce store loyalty and build a relationship with customers. Moving in this direction is widely held to be the path of success (and indeed survival) in the future.[14] Services offered might include a charge card, interest free credit, gift wrapping or the provision of a crèche.

■ Buying Behaviour

Having chosen a shop, our consumer can now start to buy things. What factors will influence his or her buying behaviour at the point of sale? In a sense this is the most crucial aspect of the consumer decision-making process because it is where the consumer, the retailer and the product all come together. We will consider two major factors: *merchandising* and *price*.

☐　*Merchandising*

However reluctant some people may be to shop, the great majority do so, especially in supermarkets where much of the relevant research has been focused. There are two related aspects of retail buying behaviour that the marketer needs to be aware of when planning the merchandising of products: the *time* people take to make a decision and the amount of *planning* that goes into it.

One well-known study of the *time* taken to make buying decisions in a supermarket came up with some intriguing findings:[15]

- The time taken varied from less than a second (people whisking things off the shelf as they passed) to a rather more reflective five-and-a-half minutes. The latter was highly unusual: a matter of seconds was the general rule.
- There were, as you might expect, differences between products. Those that required label reading (such as tuna and washing powder) took longer – about 30 seconds – than products that didn't.

It has been found that only a minority of shoppers *plan* to buy a particular product when they enter a retail outlet. Estimates vary from a fifth to a third of all shoppers.[16] Of the remainder, some have a general idea of the product they want to buy, but not the brand, and a few change their mind when they are in the shop and buy something different. But that still leaves more than half of all shoppers making *unplanned* purchases in a retail outlet.

Unplanned purchases are therefore an area of buying behaviour of great interest to retailers and marketers. It would be wrong to assume, though, that all these purchases are what is often called *impulse buying*. An unknown number of unplanned purchases occur when something in the shop, perhaps a sales promotion or even just the product itself, stimulates the customer's memory and enables him or her to recall that she or he needs a new X or some more Y. Nonetheless a very sizeable number of in-store purchases *are* the result of impulse buying.

While impulse buying is obviously an area of shopping behaviour where marketers and retailers can influence the consumer, this is more difficult than it may seem. The reason for this is that impulse buying probably has nothing to do with the decision-making model we have been discussing here and in Chapter 15.[17] This kind of behaviour has strongly emotional, and probably unconscious, roots (such as we discussed in Chapter 7). It may take the following forms:

- An unexpected and spontaneous urge to make an immediate purchase of something that catches the eye.
- An intense and irresistible motivational pressure that is strong enough to override all other considerations.
- A feeling of excitement.
- Disregard of possibly harmful consequences.

There is no way that marketers and retailers can know what will turn on a given shopper at a given time. What they do therefore is to use merchandising techniques that maximize the number of opportunities for impulse buying, in particular the analysis of *traffic patterns* and the use of *point-of-sale promotions*.

Regarding *traffic patterns* it is not entirely a coincidence that all supermarkets this side of Alpha Centauri have fresh fruit and vegetables prominently displayed just as you enter. Or that the in-store bakery is in a certain location. Or that there are all sorts of little consumable items displayed at the checkouts to catch your eye as you unload your trolley. The layout and location of products in any retail outlet is used to lead shoppers along a particular route that will give them optimum exposure to what is on sale and maximum encouragement to buy it.

The height at which products are shelved can also affect their sales.[18] Eye-level shelving is most influential, followed by waist level and floor level. Not everything can be shelved at eye level and part of a retailer's strategy might therefore be to boost certain items for limited periods.

Point-of-sale promotions are the most focused forms of advertising there are. Particular brands or products are specially displayed in a particular shop to a ready-made audience. There is no question that sales of the products are often increased as a result of these displays.[19] What is less clear is whether, or to what extent, these increased sales are simply being diverted from normal sales areas. It does seem, though, that not only are the combined sales on these occasions still well above normal, but sales tend to return to normal once the display is removed.

☐ *Price*

Our discussion of point-of-sale promotions did not mention price, but of course promotions often make use of pricing to encourage sales. One frequently used technique is *multiple-pricing*, where a discount is given when more than one of the item is purchased. Another is discount coupons; and a straight reduction in price might be offered for a limited period.

Consumers seem to like these kinds of offer and respond to them, but it's not at all clear how effective a strategy promotional pricing is for the retailer. Thus people will often switch brands or even shops to take advantage of a special offer, but there is not much evidence that they will stay with the brand or shop when the promotion ends and the price rises again.[20]

The idea of 'getting a good deal' is of course a very attractive one to shoppers generally, but rather than encouraging brand switching it seems more likely simply to encourage bargain hunting, which – as we have seen more than once – is an important psychological benefit that people can get from shopping.

Yet for many shoppers it is the *idea* rather than the actuality of the 'good deal' that seems to be important. You'll recall how we discovered, in the previous chapter, a study where 40 per cent of supermarket shoppers didn't even check the price of the goods they chose. In the same study less than half of the sample knew the correct price of the goods they had just put into their trolley.[21]

■ **At-Home Purchasing**

Though the great majority of purchases are made in retail outlets there does seem to be a growing trend in recent years towards home shopping. Reliable information is difficult to find though, and estimates in the United States of this kind of activity range from 2 – 16 per cent of all retail sales. This involves *direct marketing* to the consumer and takes various forms, such as:

- Items advertised in newspapers and magazines.
- Printed mail order catalogues (about 25 *billion* a year are distributed in North America alone).
- Door-to-door selling (more frequent outside North America – less chance of getting shot).
- Party plans (such as Ann Summers parties in the UK for ladies' lingerie and sex aids).
- Telecommunications (including interactive shopping channels on cable television, teletext and video cassettes).
- Advertising inserts in local newspapers.

All these methods give marketers the advantage of precise market segmentation if they know exactly who they are targeting.

Most commentators seem to agree that the trend towards direct marketing, especially via telecommunications, will become more significant in terms of consumer behaviour. There are a number of reasons for this:[22]

- Our identity as consumers is being emphasized increasingly in our society, and encouragement to express individuality in terms of consumption has led to an ever-greater demand for goods and services that has outstripped the display capacity of retail outlets.
- There are more women than ever in paid employment, and as their domestic responsibilities are largely unchanged they have less time to go shopping.
- The increased pursuit of 'serious' leisure, which also leaves less time to go shopping.
- An increasing demand for specialized or unusual products that are not easily available in retail outlets.
- The increased level of technological sophistication and use of electronic equipment by consumers.
- The increased level of psychological sophistication among consumers about innovative ways of shopping.

One might also add to this list:

- Offers of interest-free credit for a period of months.
- The easy availability of credit and plastic forms of payment.
- The avoidance of shopping hassle.
- The increased tendency towards focusing on home life (home entertainment, take-away meals, do-it-yourself improvements, and so on).

However I don't think there is any danger of retail outlets going out of business just yet – or at all. While there certainly will be an increase in the volume of home shopping I can see no evidence that this will inevitably be at the expense of retail outlets, except when it comes to those who think of their home as a fortress. But I would argue that the blurring of lines between retail outlets that we have already noted is echoed by the relationship between in-store and at-home shopping.

Not only do many home shoppers also visit retail outlets, but there is some evidence that retailers may be moving into both locations. Some of the most famous retailers in the United States, for example Saks Fifth Avenue, are moving into direct marketing as a way of *complementing* their in-store operation. Selfridges are doing something similar in the United Kingdom. Fears that this would compete with in-store sales are apparently unfounded. Moving in the other direction, the famous Fuller Brush Company has opened retail outlets to attract the upmarket part of its traditional American clientele who can no longer be reached by door-to-door selling.[23]

But I think there is another reason why home shopping will never seriously challenge the dominance of in-store shopping. As we've seen several times in the past two chapters, the most important benefits consumers get from going out shopping are social and psychological. Indeed a 1985 survey of consumers found that only 10 per cent of them had any interest in shopping by interactive television. While this number will probably increase as the technology becomes more familiar and easy to use, my hunch is that it may not increase by much.

■ Consequences of the Decision

We have followed consumers through the decision-making process outlined in Figure 15.1. The first four stages have taken them up to the point of purchase, so why do we have to go any further? Well if you turn back to Figure 15.1 you will see that stage 5 is represented by a broken line.

That is because it represents a new phase in the decision-making process. The point of purchasing (normally) is consumption and in the process of consumption the product is being assessed. This assessment will then be used when new buying decisions have to be made, so it is crucial for the marketer to understand how it is done. It is these post-purchase psychological processes that we will now consider in the final stage of our model.

■ Stage 5: Post-Purchase Processes

The experience the consumer has with the product purchased is fed back into an early stage of the decision-making process: stage 3, as illustrated in Figure 16.1. What is particularly important is the amount of *consumer satisfaction/ dissatisfaction* (CS/D). This addition provides us with a model of a continuous decision-making process.

☐ *Consumer Satisfaction/Dissatisfaction (CS/D)*

Since the late 1970s the study of consumer satisfaction has become a major area of research in consumer behaviour.[24] The issue is of course a little more

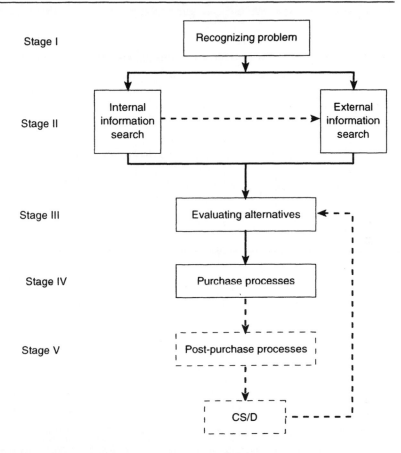

Figure 16.1 Continuous decision-making process

complex than it might at first appear. It is certainly clear that both consumers and marketers want to maximize consumer satisfaction. It also *seems* fairly clear what constitutes satisfaction: an evaluation, after consuming a chosen alternative, that it meets expectations.

However the use of the word *expectations* in this definition inevitably makes the issue more complex. The reason for this, it has been suggested, is that satisfaction is not so much an emotion as the *evaluation* of an emotion. It is the *comparison* between what we expect and what we actually experience that is important.[25]

Hence, even though we enjoyed eating the Aloparc Offalburger, if we didn't enjoy it *as much as we expected to* our experience could still be categorized as dissatisfaction. This is sometimes known as *negative disconfirmation*. Of course disconfirmation in a *positive* direction is also possible, where our enjoyment of the product is greater than expected, and that would result in an experience of satisfaction. Figure 16.2 illustrates the operation of CS/D on the consumer decision-making process.

Research on consumer evaluation of various products seems to confirm that CS/D does operate in the decision-making process. Indeed the more the consumer is satisfied with a product the greater the expectation raised when it is purchased again. Failure to meet that expectation can result in at least mild dissatisfaction. One can understand why market reputations based on quality are so jealously guarded.[26]

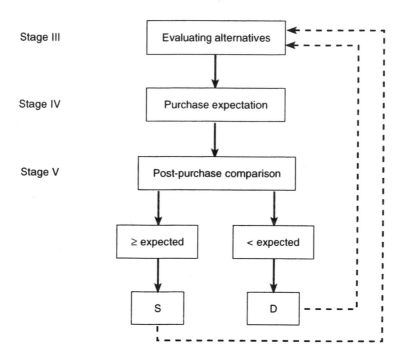

Figure 16.2   CS/D and the consumer decision-making process

Conversely it has been found that consumers who have formed a low expectation of an item may be so pleasantly surprised by a favourable repeat purchase that they express greater satisfaction than people who liked the product at the first encounter.[27]   The issue of *how much* satisfaction/dissatisfaction it takes to influence a consumer's buying behaviour is of course a crucial one for the marketer. Given the complexity of the decision-making process, though, it has to remain largely a matter of the marketer's judgement and experience.

☐   *Dealing with Consumer Dissatisfaction*

The consumer   Although we noted above that there are situations where consumer dissatisfaction with a first purchase might change to satisfaction with a subsequent purchase, the problem for the marketer is how to persuade the consumer to make that subsequent purchase. People who are not fully satisfied with the initial purchase are less likely to repurchase a product than those who are. And what's more they may be twice as likely to tell other people about their negative experience than consumers who were satisfied.[28]

I think it is vital for marketers to realize that – because of the psychology of decision-making – consumers will do whatever they can to feel satisfied with their purchases. As we saw when we discussed the phenomenon of cognitive dissonance in Chapter 13, this extends to people routinely convincing themselves that they have made the right choice.

You will recall that, according to this theory, if someone holds two psychologically inconsistent cognitions (beliefs, attitudes, values or ideas) at the same time, she or he will be in a state of cognitive dissonance. Because of the psychological tension involved this is an inherently unpleasant experience that we are strongly motivated to resolve. In the case of evaluating a purchase it might take the following form:

- *Cognition 1*:   'I am a competent shopper'.
- *Cognition 2*:   'I have just paid a lot of money for a new car that is unreliable, expensive to run and ugly to look at'.

These two cognitions are likely to be dissonant with each other: competent shoppers don't waste their money on poor products. As buyers are stuck with the results of their decisions, what can they do to feel better? As self-image is very resistant to change it is hard for people to achieve consistency by saying 'Actually I'm not a competent shopper at all'. So they will probably work on the other cognition.

This may take two forms. One is to admit the purchase was a mistake and do whatever can be done to rectify it. But that is also difficult to do psychologically and uses up a lot of emotional and mental energy. So what is most likely to happen is that people will change the cognition by changing their attitude towards the product. They will re-evaluate it upwards until it becomes a good purchase, such as a competent shopper would make, and one that they are quite *satisfied* with.

There are, of course, limiting factors to the operation of cognitive dissonance reduction in consumer behaviour: if their cars refuse to start every other morning the consumers will probably be forced to accept that they made a bad purchase. The important point is though that as long as they can *convince themselves* that the decision was a good one they will be prepared to put up with the car's defects.

Cognitive dissonance reaches its height when the decision to be made is important to us (when we are very involved in it) and when the alternative choices are close to each other in attractiveness, making the decision a difficult one to make. As this is perhaps the most common purchase situation with expensive items, understanding it is of great importance to the marketer.

As we noted in Chapter 13, if we have a difficult decision to make when buying a new product, say a stereo system, there are certain behaviours we are likely to engage in to reduce dissonance. In forgoing the option we didn't choose we have to deal with our perceptions of the negative points of the alternative we chose and the positive features of the one(s) we didn't.

As soon as we have made the decision to buy a Woofmeister stereo we will be especially attentive to advertisements that tell us how wonderful it is – and we'll carefully not notice all the advertisements for competing models.[29] This process really does start immediately. As we noted earlier, as a reward for taking part in a study the participants were offered one of two electrical appliances that they had previously perceived to be *equally attractive*. But a few minutes after choosing one of the appliances, they rated the one they had chosen *more highly* and the one they had rejected *less highly*.[30]

The marketer   As we saw in the case of the dissatisfied car buyers, sometimes the postpurchase experience is so negative that, however motivated buyers are to adapt to it, they simply cannot do so. At this point the relationship between purchaser and marketer comes sharply into focus. It is very difficult to measure the amount of general dissatisfaction there is among consumers. There is great variability by product, by individual and perhaps by culture. Estimates range from less than 20 per cent to more than 50 per cent. The key question here is will consumers make the marketers aware of their dissatisfaction. In other words, *will they complain?*

The general findings of studies on this topic are that most dissatisfied consumers do *not* complain to the seller.[31] As we saw above, they are more likely to complain to friends and relatives. They are also liable to avoid the brand or product in question in the future. Sometimes they will even take legal action rather than complain directly to the seller.[32] This should be a matter of great concern to the marketer, who has had the chance to persuade the consumers to be loyal to a brand or product, but failed.

As you might expect, people who complain when they are dissatisfied tend to be different in many ways from people who don't. They tend to be younger, have a higher socio-economic status and the self-confidence that goes with it.[33] (I suspect they also tend to live in New York rather than London.) But are their complaints dealt with by the seller? The evidence is not too encouraging. Typically, less than 60 per cent of written complaints receive a response.[34] Apparently junk food purveyors are most responsive and clothing companies least.

This finding does not quite fit in with all the portentous company waffle about 'total quality management', 'staying close to the customer', 'every customer complaint is an opportunity' and all the other marketspeak they constantly bombard us with. This is one issue upon which there is no lack of research evidence. There is now a large body of literature on all aspects of quality of customer care.[35] But the very fact that so many business gurus make a nice living out of presenting these slogans to companies as radical new ideas shows how reluctant the great majority of product and service providers are to take customer complaints seriously.

The most successful marketers do so, however, and consumers respond to it with appreciation – and repeat business.[36] The form that a complaint system takes (money back, goods exchanged, letter of apology/explanation or whatever) doesn't matter very much. What matters to the consumer in his or her relationship with the seller is simply *to be taken seriously.* That need is as psychologically important in this relationship as it is in any other kind of relationship, and marketers who find it difficult to accept are treating their customers with contempt and may soon (one hopes) find themselves out of business.

■ Further Reading

Foxall, G. R., *Consumer Choice* (London: Macmillan, 1983). An overview of the consumer buying process, including situational effects and the role of the marketer in influencing consumer choice.

Howard, J., *Consumer Behavior in Marketing Strategy* (Englewood Cliffs, NJ: Prentice-Hall, 1989). Outlines the different levels of effort involved in consumer decision making and their marketing implications.

Percy, L. and A. G. Woodside (eds), *Advertising and Consumer Psychology* (Lexington, MA: Lexington Books, 1983). Contains useful articles on consumers' evaluation of both advertising and products.

It is also worth browsing through the latest articles in the following periodicals: *Advances in Consumer Research, Journal of Consumer Research, Journal of Retailing, Journal of Marketing Research.*

■ Questions for Discussion

1. Why do people go shopping?
2. What factors influence their choice of a place to shop? How do marketers reach them?
3. What is meant by 'consumer satisfaction/dissatisfaction' (CS/D) with a purchase? Why should marketers be concerned with it?
4. What does cognitive dissonance have to do with a consumer's post-purchase experiences?
5. What can marketers do to increase post-purchase satisfaction and decrease dissatisfaction?

CHAPTER 17

The Organization as Purchaser

Introduction

In the previous sixteen chapters we have reviewed consumption and buying behaviour as these processes applied to individuals. However, in terms of financial outlay far more money is actually spent on goods and services by the world's organizations than the world's individual consumers.

This is hardly surprising when we consider that we're talking about government departments and public bodies of all kinds, as well as businesses and private institutions; everything from the U S Department of Defence or the National Health Service to a corner pizzeria or a small consultancy. The cost of their single purchases can range from billions for nuclear submarines to pennies for coffee filters.

Organizational buyers are therefore of enormous potential importance to all marketers and we will round off this part of the book with a review of that market. In order to understand the similarities to and differences from the individual consumer markets, we need to start with a very brief discussion of the nature of organizations and their place in our consumer society.

The Context of Organizational Behaviour

What is an Organization?

This is a simple enough question, you might think, but like many simple questions in the behavioural and social sciences it does not have a simple answer. 'Organizations are difficult to define' says a leading British textbook on the subject.[1] 'It is surprisingly difficult to give a simple definition of an organization' says a leading American text.[2] Why this should be so may become clearer if we start off with a few preliminary definitions and see where that leads us.

The British textbook quoted above has the following definition, 'Organizations are social arrangements for the controlled performance of collective goals',[3] while the American one says 'An organization is the planned coordination of the activities of a number of people for the achievement of some common, explicit purpose or goal...'[4] and *The Penguin Management Handbook* defines an organization as 'A social group deliberately created and maintained for the purpose of achieving specific objectives'.[5] There seems to be a large measure of agreement in these definitions. They all include three main factors:

- *Social Identity:* an organization is composed of people who all share a sense of belonging to it in some way.

- *Coordination*: the activities of these people are arranged so that they will inter-act with each other in what is intended to be a supportive and complementary fashion.
- *Goal-directed behaviour*: the reason for the arrangement of these activities is to accomplish the stated goals of the organization.

It is very important to note at the outset that although an organization is composed of individual people, these people are not (with rare exceptions) what the organization is supposed to be about. That is, an organization is interested only in what its members do, not who they are, what they want or how they feel about things. Organizations exist independently of any and all individual members.

As far as organizations are concerned individual members are interchangeable. Indeed from an organizational point of view they have no individual existence at all. What the organization – any organization – is concerned with is the *role* that a given person plays, whether the role is floor sweeper, assistant production engineer, marketing manager or chief executive. Whether the role is performed by Tom, Dick or Harriet is immaterial to the organization.

Although organizations are not about the people in them they do not, of course, run themselves. This is one source of the difficulty in defining an organization and understanding how it works, for everyone brings his or her individual personality to the role that they play, and the interlocking pattern of roles that looks so neat on an organizational flowchart is a lot more messy in real life.

The organizations we belong to, and therefore our fellow members, will have a set of expectations of us depending on what role we are supposed to fulfil. We in turn will have certain expectations of other people, and it is in the network of these interlocking sets of expectations that organizational life – and indeed all the organized life of a society – occurs.

■ Types of Organization

Organizational theorists usually distinguish two forms of organization: formal and informal. The simple definitions of an organization given above are usually applied to what are called *formal organizations*. Formal organizations, sometimes known as 'bureaucratic' organizations, represent the earliest scientific thinking about organizations that appeared at the beginning of the twentieth century. The bureaucratic model of organizations is associated primarily with the German sociologist Max Weber.

The term 'bureaucratic' has a negative ring to our modern ear. We tend to use it in everyday speech to describe an organization that is obstructive, rigid, ineffective and wasteful both of its own staff time and resources and those of its customers. But the bureaucratic model that Weber suggested was intended to combat nepotism, favouritism, corruption and personal whim in the running of organizations – a central problem of his time – and to encourage a more professional and efficient administration. Weber proposed that organizations should ideally contain four essential features:[6]

- A hierarchy of authority with power flowing from the top down.
- A division of labour into specialised tasks.
- The existence of written rules and procedures.
- The rational application of these rules and procedures.

The formal bureaucratic model represents the way organizations are *supposed* to run, and the behaviour that is officially expected of people. This is encapsulated in the public face that organizations present to the world via their annual reports, brochures, rulebooks, organizational charts and so forth.

But as most people who work in organizations have swiftly realised, what is supposed to happen is not always what does happen and research has revealed the great extent and diverse nature of this gap.[7] People form their own groups within the organization based on friendships and common interests as one way of overcoming the rigid, impersonal nature of the formal system. These groups can sometimes cut across both functional and hierarchical lines and indeed may even be used in preference to the formal system as a more efficient way of giving and receiving information.

These groups make up what has been called *the informal organization* and this is a universal feature of formal organizations. Indeed there are times when they could not function without the informal organization, for instance when staff voluntarily do far more than they are officially contracted to do in order to help the organization through a crisis. However there are also times when the needs and values of the informal organization may be different from or even opposed to the formal one, for example if a new method of working is imposed from above without prior consultation.

Though a great deal of research has been done since the 1920s on the way the informal system can affect the output and productivity of an organization, the formal system still remains the basic model for work organizations – to many of the people who are supposed to run them as well as to organizational theorists.

One important outcome of using this model is that organizations and the people in them tend to be treated as if they are two distinct entities, each with a separate existence of their own. Behavioural scientists see this as the most practical way of studying something very complex, and it is also in line with general managerial thinking and practice. This has led to great stress being laid on studying *either* the individual *or* the organization. In the former case individual behaviour and personality and the motivation behind it is regarded as paramount and the organization is regarded as a static, fixed background. In the latter case, how the organization is structured and the way it functions are seen as all-important while the behaviour of any given individual within it is regarded as simply the product of these organizational forces.

These two approaches have been described respectively as the 'individualistic fallacy' and the 'culturalistic fallacy'.[8] What is sometimes added to this model, to link it to society in general, is a third entity: the *environment.* This results in what has been characterised as a 'Russian doll' approach, where each entity is contained within a larger one and is treated as if it can be removed without affecting the shape of the others,[9] as illustrated in Figure 17.1.

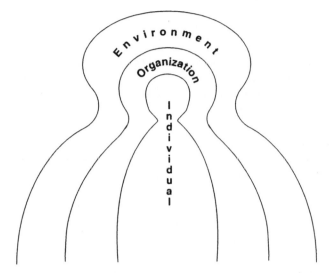

Figure 17.1 The 'Russian doll' approach to organizational behaviour

While the Russian doll model may be of some use in studying behaviour of enormous complexity by focusing on one entity and holding everything else constant, it has one crucial flaw: nothing about human behaviour is static. It is now generally accepted that what makes us human is our social existence, our relationships with other people. And all human relationships are a two-way process. Whether the relationship is between husband and wife, worker and boss, teacher and student or customer and salesman, each always affects the other – however equal or unequal that relationship may be.

■ Organizing Rather than Organization

It is often remarked by business gurus discussing the importance of staff that 'an organization is its people', and this sentiment is usually received with pious nods of approval by the people who run organizations. But despite its modern status as a megacliché, it is literally true nonetheless. When behavioural scientists talk of 'organizational behaviour' they are not referring to the actions of some mysterious creature hidden away on the top floor. Organizations do not, of course, behave. What we are being asked to look at are the actions of various members of the organization at certain times and places and in certain ways. Their collective actions, when purchasing goods and services for instance, represent organizational behaviour.

Thus although the Ford Motor Company continued to exist while it experienced a fourfold turnover of staff with the introduction of the assembly line in 1913, the nature of the organization inevitably changed with the changing membership. Indeed the Ford Motor Company at the end of the twentieth century is a very different organization from the one that Henry Ford started at the beginning of the century. Similarly the experience of being a member of that organization has been a very different one over the course of the century.

Within the continuity of a company over time there is also (though it may not be apparent) constant change, and that of course is the nature of the human condition. A man may have the same name for 100 years but he will look – and be – a quite different person at different points in that century. Why? Because as he goes through life he not only changes physically, he also changes psychologically as he interacts with the people around him. He affects them and they affect him and in the process he comes to be the unique individual he is. It is the same with organizations. An organization is the product of the interrelationships that its members have with each other, including their individual views of what the organization is about. And each member therefore affects, and is at the same time affected by, the organization and its environment.

This is a much messier model to deal with than the neat Russian dolls but it's also much closer to what actually happens in real life. It also has two other important aspects:

- It emphasizes the fact that individuals always have some sort of relationship with each other within the organization.
- It discards the managerial viewpoint.

By emphasizing relationships between people we are drawing attention to the *process of organizing* rather than to an entity called an organization that has no separate existence. This process is continuous and ever-changing whereas the entity is an idealized snapshot at any given point in time. The process is really the way in which people make sense of their work environment by comparing, discussing and modifying their individual views and understanding of the organization.   Making sense of ourselves and our lives is the most basic psychological process there is and it is not something that we can do alone: it has to be done in conjunction with other people.[10] At times of stress or crisis, when the identity and *raison d'être* of the organization becomes salient – reorganization, takeover bids, mergers and so on – this process will become quite overt. But normally it proceeds in an unspoken, even unconscious, manner.

■ Conflicts of Interest

It has been clear for a long time that members of work organizations do not always share the same goals and values. The differences between management and workforce, and the turbulent history of industrial relations in many countries, are the most obvious examples.

The specialization of jobs and division of labour found in large organizations also led to the emergence of special interests and divisions within the organizations along functional lines. This is an inherent conflict in work organizations to this day and it remains largely unacknowledged. For example a company's research and development division might promise the appearance of a world-beating widget if only their budget was doubled and they had ten years to work on it, while the sales and marketing people would be happy with a bog standard widget that works, just as long as they can hire extra salesmen and show it to the customers by next Tuesday. What does the organization do? Does it decide whether its goals and values imply a long-term or a short-term strategy and act accordingly (leaving one group of staff very unhappy) or does it fudge the issue? I'll give you three guesses.

Even the basic, and apparently obvious, issue of just deciding who the members of an organization are throws up serious difficulties of definition. Everyone would presumably agree that the staff of a company are members, but does that apply to all staff, including part-time or temporary people and people on fixed-term contracts? How about consultants on long-term contracts? Or people who work in the field offices on the other side of the world? How about retired employees with a company pension and company shares? In fact how about shareholders in general who might legally own the company but who have no other contact with it whatsoever? Other than wanting the company to stay in business, what possible agreement could all these people reach on its particular goals and values, let alone the everyday running of the organization?

So not only is organizational life untidy and difficult to predict and deal with, it has the potential for internal conflict built into its normal pattern of working, quite apart from the particular stresses caused by unusual situations,

■ Power and Political Behaviour

One of the most striking aspects of our everyday experience of organizations is that some people seem to have a greater influence over what happens than other people. The exercise of this influence is often referred to as having power. This is another of those complex terms in social and behavioural science that we need to unpack for a closer look. However it has been suggested that the common-sense view of power – I have power over you to the extent that I can get you to do something you wouldn't do otherwise – might be a good place to start.[11]

There is more than one source of power and various writers in this field have attempted to identify and catalogue them, notably French and Raven[12] who distinguished five kinds or bases of power. They called these *reward, coercive, legitimate, referent* and *expert* power.

- *Reward power* is the ability to give people something they value, such as promotion, more money or a bigger office.
- *Coercive power* is a kind of negative reward power, the ability to punish, for example by demotion or the withholding of a salary increase, and these two kinds of power are usually held by the same person.

- *Legitimate power* usually mean the authority one has as a consequence of one's position in the organization and, very importantly, the willingness of people of inferior position to accept that authority.
- *Referent power* is often thought of as the possession of charisma, such that people identify with someone because of his or her personal qualities and are then happy to be his or her followers.
- *Expert power* depends on the possession of knowledge or skills that other people happen to value particularly highly, for example in areas such as law, finance, science and technology.

The most obvious source of power we encounter in an organization is, of course, legitimate power. The more hierarchical the organization the more evident this type of power becomes. In the army or the civil service one may encounter a dozen or more different levels in the hierarchy, each with its own carefully defined amount of authority over the levels below it. This is sometimes described as a 'tall' organization. (See Figure 17.2.)

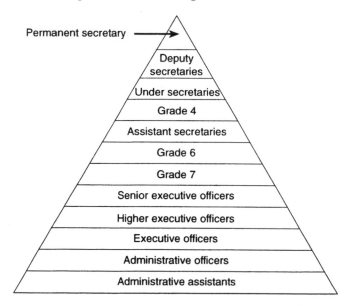

Figure 17.2 Tall organization (British Civil Service)

In the late nineteenth century, when the factory system was coming to its peak, the tall organization was regarded as a model for the running of a large commercial enterprise. The focus was on hierarchy, discipline and control. By the late twentieth century the widespread decline in heavy industry and traditional forms of manufacturing, together with the rise of professional specialization in organizations, may have resulted in a certain shift in power, with an increase in expert power at the expense of the legitimate power of management.

This shift has been particularly pronounced for two groups of experts: those in *computing* and *accountancy*. It has been argued that personnel managers are a third such group. In the second half of the twentieth century the world of work has seen a relatively slow but steadily increasing degree of computerization. This is true of the manufacturing sector as well as the service sector and administration. Consequently many organizations may well become more and more dependent on their computer systems and the people who design, install, run and maintain them. However people do not give up power willingly in organizations and senior management will often try to undermine the computer experts' power.[13]

The source of experts' power within the organization actually comes from outside it, from their professional skills, knowledge and experience. Indeed their first loyalty may be to their profession, which is the source of a lifelong form of identity, and means of employment, as opposed to their particular work organization, of which they may be members for only a few years. Experts are not part of the hierarchy of line management and may even report directly to the chief executive. To the extent that an organization is dependent on its expert members, and is sometimes built round their expertise, its reliance on the traditional use of legitimate power is correspondingly curtailed. Thus it is not surprising that, for example, computer software companies and design consultancies tend to have very few hierarchical levels and are 'flat organizations'.

If anything the position of accountants in organizations has become even more powerful than that of computer experts, for they now exert a great influence on the daily life of many organizations and indeed the very of organizational discourse. Regardless of the organization's purpose, goals language and values, in the main the cost of its current operations and future activities has been accepted as the dominant factor in its decision- making process since the recessions and restructurings of the 1980s. Often 'the bottom line' is the only factor that really matters, irrespective of whether the organization is providing a public service, making washing machines or producing films. And as 70 – 90 per cent of an organization's costs typically are staff salaries, the implications of the accountant's expertise for an organization's members are obviously profound.

When power of this kind is found in an organization it suggests something much more important than simply a victory for expertise. The ability to set an organizations' agenda, define the issues it should deal with and the language used to discuss these issues, confers on the group in question the power to see off any potential opposition without a fight, perhaps even without the opposition being aware of it. In these circumstances the controlling group has succeeded in identifying its own interests with those of the organization as a whole.[14]

So, far from being something unsavoury or a distracting annoyance, the way power is distributed and used in an organization is at the very heart of organizational life. It is integral to the way people behave in organizations that they will use whatever power they have to further their own interests.[15]

Sometimes these uses of power will be in line with the formally stated interests of the organization and sometimes they won't. But there need be nothing cynical or reprehensible about this, and if we are to understand the psychology of organizational behaviour we need to take a dispassionate look at what people actually do and why they do it.[16]

As well as behaving in an individual capacity, members of organizations usually belong to a particular section or department of the organization. Often the political behaviour they are involved in concerns the interests of their department. But just as individuals are unequal in power, so are departments: 'Some may be involved in most major decisions, others only in a few. ... Production, sales and finance, by whichever titles they may be known in different forms of organization, are a core trio through whose hands most decisions must pass'.[17]

In both their individual and representative capacities, members of organizations will form alliances and coalitions with each other to further mutual interests. The pattern of these coalitions will shift over time and with changing circumstances. This behaviour takes place within the informal network that underlies every formal organization and exists alongside the more static distribution of power described by French and Raven.[18]

Just as the distribution and use of power in society is the stuff of politics, the same is true of life in the organization. When people exercise power over others and over resources by virtue of their formal authority, their expertise, their personal qualities or the coalitions they join, they are acting politically. Political behaviour is thus an integral and routine part of organizational behaviour and not a flaw (usually described as 'office politics') that detracts from the otherwise smooth functioning of the organization.[19]

■ Communicating and the Use of Information

Another, related key area of our experience in organizations is that of internal communication, and there is widespread concern about the way the transmission of information takes place. Some organizational theorists think that this aspect of an organization's life is the most important and most problematic one it has. The old cliché that 'information is power' is widely believed in organizations, and the use of information – who has access to what and when – is often regarded as the organization's power structure in action.

In traditional, formal organizations, information usually mirrors the legitimate power structure of authority by flowing downwards from the top of the organization. A serious problem with this form of communication is that over 80 per cent of the contents of a message may be lost during its journey from the top to the bottom of a hierarchy comprising five or six levels – which is only about half the distance it would have to travel in the civil service.[20]

It has been suggested that attempts to communicate in the reverse direction are even more problematic because people are very aware that the recipients of their messages have power over them and often use information to control them, and they may be afraid of presenting their boss with bad news or unwelcome information. While people may be very keen, indeed desperate, to communicate upwards they often feel that they have to tailor their presentation of the information very carefully, to such an extent that the essence of the message may very well be lost.[21]

Such distorted communication on the formal level invariably leads to increased reliance on informal communication. The information that members of an organization receive verbally via the 'grapevine' is transmitted far more quickly, is often regarded as more trustworthy and, as we have seen, is unlikely to be any less accurate. Although the grapevine usually operates horizontally, via people at more or less the same level in the hierarchy, it can be used quite effectively to pass messages up and down the line in cases where formal, written communications might be seen as more rigid or threatening and lead to fixed positions being taken on either side of a conflict of interests.

There can also, of course, be too much communication or, more usually, too much of the wrong kind of communication, where people are snowed under with information they do not really want or need while the information they are most interested in may not be given them. Management consultants are fond of telling organizations that they generate far too much paper and too much of it is marked 'Secret' or 'Confidential', thus clogging up the arteries of communication.

■ Organizational Culture(s)

The term 'organizational culture' has become very widely used in recent years but it is also used in a wide variety of different ways in both the popular and the scientific literature. A leading management scientist has identified ten different usages.[22] To my mind the most helpful use of the term is one that combines the anthropological idea of shared beliefs, values, attitudes and expectations with the psychological notion of the unquestioned assumptions that everyone has about the organization's ways of doing things, its traditions and so on.

As we saw earlier in this chapter, however, there is often very little that *all* the members of a work organization can agree on and I would therefore suggest that we really need to use the plural and talk about *cultures*, and indeed subcultures, in organizations. Thus as well as interaction and relationships at the individual level, in any organization there seems to be a parallel process involving the different cultures to be found there. Seen from within there may be as many different cultures in an organization as there are interest groups. These are often determined by function (for example marketing or research) or hierarchy (senior management or shop floor) although they may arise through other factors such as location (headquarters or field office) or even length of service (old timers or new hands).

When looking at an organization from outside we are often likely to be struck by a broad, general set of characteristics that forms what is usually referred to as a 'corporate culture'. We can see immediately that the civil service has a vastly different corporate culture from a small market research firm for instance. Even in the same field there may be great differences between two corporate cultures, such as the traditional buttoned-down image of IBM compared with the laid-back Californian image of Apple.

With the growing importance of multinational organizations we should also note that there are many differences of *national* culture at work, as we discussed in Chapter 12.[23] Japanese companies do not operate in New York or Glasgow in quite the same way as they do in Tokyo. Differences in national culture can show up quite strikingly in an organization's everyday functioning. For example:

> The readiness to joke even about business matters is distinctively British ... take the production director who reacts to the suggestion that the firm manufacture rather than buy-in a simple component with: 'Let's stick to what we're good at ... losing vast sums of money.' This is not a universal phenomenon. Such irreverence in the business context from American lips is unthinkable. In the American case, corporate humour is constrained by the intensity of feeling and seriousness of organizational purpose.[24]

■ Individual and Organizational Buying

Keeping in mind this brief overview of organizations and how they operate, we will turn now to the specific *purchasing* function within organizations and how this differs from purchasing by individuals. But we should first note the similarities between the two.

Similarities:

- The most important similarity is that the model of individual consumer decision-making processes that we detailed in the last two chapters can be equally well applied to organizations. As we saw earlier in the chapter decisions are made on behalf of the organization by individuals. For purchasing decisions research has found that organizational buyers go about their task as though they were shopping for themselves.[25]
- Though relatively rare, a buying decision on behalf of an organization may be made by a single individual; conversely, as we discovered in Chapters 8, 9 and 10, a purchase by an individual consumer might be the result of family, household or group actions.
- Organizational sellers are increasingly targeting organizational buyers via the advertising techniques used for individual consumers.[26]

Differences:

- There are far fewer organizational buyers and they purchase much larger quantities than individual buyers.
- The organizational buyer is not usually the final consumer or end user of

what is bought. This is partly true of individual consumers, for example when they buy for others in their household or when they buy gifts, but usually the individual purchaser is also the end user of the product.

- Organizational buyers and sellers tend to operate in a much smaller market, where they may actually know each other. With very specialized and expensive products, indeed, the buyer and seller may even be in a symbiotic relationship on a one-to-one basis, for example makers of advanced weapons systems and government defence departments.

- The demand for industrial products, for instance cloth or steel or cardboard containers, is mainly dependent on the final consumer or end user. This is known as *derived demand* and may be several steps removed from the raw material, as in wool → cloth maker → tailor → clothing store. So if baggy suits go out of fashion there may be repercussions all the way down the line.

■ The Process of Organizational Buying

■ Who Does the Buying?

The people who do the buying on behalf of organizations generally do so as their full-time occupation. In large organizations, both public and private, they are often called *purchasing agents*; in smaller organizations and in the retail trade they are usually referred to as *buyers*. In large organizations there is usually a purchasing department or function that may employ quite a few people.

It is often assumed that, because of the professional role of the people doing the buying on behalf of organizations, the buying process is entirely objective and rational – unlike that of individual consumers. Having read this book, however, you will know better. We have already pointed out in this chapter how the same decision-making model may be applied to both individual and organizational buyers. A key element of that process is individual feelings and preferences, often based on needs that are quite unconscious and perhaps irrational.

While professional buyers may not be the end users of the products they purchase, they are still human beings whose professional objectivity will inevitably be tempered by their emotional life. For example they will have some kind of relationship with each of the salespeople they deal with. And they also have their own position in the organization to consider, with *its* complex web of relationships, stresses and obligations.

■ How is the Buying Decision Made?

There is another reason why the picture of rational and objective organizational buying may be somewhat inaccurate. In many organizations the buying decisions are made by a group of people representing different parts of the organization, of which the purchasing/buying department is just one. This is obviously particularly important (as we saw earlier in the chapter) with an expensive and infrequent purchase decision such as a new building or a computer system. Such a group is known variously as the *buying centre* or the *decision-making unit.*

Six different roles (some perhaps played by more than one person) have been identified in the working of this group:[27]

- The *initiator*, who identifies the need for a given product.
- The *influencer*, who is able to affect a buying decision, either directly or indirectly.
- The *gatekeeper*, who is able to control the flow of information reaching the group.
- The *user*, who will actually consume the product within the organization.
- The *decider*, who has the ultimate authority to make the final decision.
- The *buyer*, who will actually do the purchasing.

The role of the professional buyer is therefore only one input into the decision-making process, and it may not be the most important one. The organizational politics that we discussed earlier in the chapter will be much in evidence throughout the process, with the representatives of the more powerful departments having a disproportionate influence on the final decision.

We would therefore expect just as many poor buying decisions to be taken by organizations as are taken by individuals. Usually they are well-hidden from external sight but occasionally a spectacular purchasing disaster gives the game away – for example the system installed when the London Stock Exchange was computerised had to be scrapped and replaced, at enormous cost.

Moreover, once a decision is taken by the organization we would expect the same post-purchase processes to operate that we examined in the last chapter. This is especially true of the need to reduce the cognitive dissonance that arises when a difficult choice has to be made. As we have seen, people go to great lengths to justify their decision, talking up the alternative chosen and talking down its competitors.

It is extremely difficult for people to admit that they may have made the wrong choice. So individuals and their organizations can find themselves locked into a spiral of justification, which guarantees that the more uncertain they were at the time of the decision, the more energy and ingenuity they will exert to prove themselves right. If the decision *was* a bad one, this can only end in tears and a huge amount of money will be wasted before the organization corrects its mistake or cuts its losses.

Neither fixed procedures, nor form filling, nor formal negotiations with buyers will remove the psychological needs that the decision-making group has. Only an increased awareness of those needs and their influence will help.

There is one final psychological process that organizations would benefit from knowing about, and it arises from the working of the group itself. When we examined some of the psychological dynamics of small groups in Chapter 10 we found that the *cohesiveness* of a group, and the extent to which its members conform to the norms of behaviour expected from them, are absolutely crucial to the survival of the group. Unless everyone knows what to expect of everyone else and they all pull in the same direction the group will never go anywhere.

However there is such a thing as *too much* group cohesiveness and conformity to group norms. This has been illustrated by a famous case study of political decision-making, the decision of the group chaired by President John Kennedy to invade Cuba at the Bay of Pigs in 1961. The invasion went disastrously wrong for the American government, with serious political consequences. President Kennedy himself later referred to the decision as 'stupid', but neither he nor any other member of the group could be described as a stupid person.

The explanation for the bad decision lay in the group's dynamics rather than the personalities of its members. These members had such a high regard for each other's ability that as a group they acted as though they were invulnerable to error. It became unthinkable to them that such bright, professional, objective people could get it wrong.

Their cohesiveness meant that they treated outsiders with contempt. Their conformity meant that great pressure was put on those who dissented from the prevailing norm, or even expressed doubts about it. Such views were regarded as disloyal. Information that didn't fit the emerging view made the group uncomfortable and so it was usually discredited or ignored, resulting in a premature closure of the group's options. Also ignored were the various ethical issues surrounding the invasion of another country.

Closed off from other influences and turned in on itself, the group thus decided that some 1400 Cuban exiles could successfully invade the island and defeat a highly motivated and popularly supported army a hundred times stronger. The result was a fiasco that was all over in two days.

This kind of process has been called *groupthink*.[28] The Bay of Pigs crisis and its analysis has become a case study for foreign service officers and others in avoiding the dangers of groupthink. It was a particularly dramatic example of the process, and therefore lends itself to study. A more recent example in this vein is the suggestion that groupthink by the operators may have been responsible for the terrible nuclear accident at Chernobyl.[29]

But every organization in daily life has decision-making groups that are capable of falling into the same traps. One industrial example that has been studied looks at the decisions leading up to the introduction of unsuccessful models of new cars onto the market.[30] There is no way that organizational purchasing decisions can be exempt from the dangers of groupthink. The only antidote to it is an awareness of the psychological factors involved.

■ Further Reading

Bonoma, T. G. Zaltman and W. Johnson, *Industrial Buying Behavior* (Cambridge, MA: Marketing Science Institute, 1977). Contains a model for analyzing the exchanges that take place between a buying and a selling organization.

King, R. (ed.), *Marketing: Perspectives for the 1990s* (Richmond, VA: Southern Marketing Association, 1992). A recent and authoritative review that includes work on organizational buying and the building of relationships between different organizations in the buying process.

Webster, F. E. and Y. Wind, *Organizational Buying Behavior* (Englewood Cliffs, NJ: Prentice-Hall, 1972). A classic overview of the field by two pioneering researchers.

Woodside, A. (ed.), *Advances in Business Marketing* (Greenwich, CT: JAI, 1987) An authoritative overview of the field that is particularly useful on the nature of relationships between people in different organizations who are part of the buying process.

It is also worth browsing through the latest issues of the following periodicals: *Advances in Consumer Research, Journal of Consumer Research, Journal of Marketing, Industrial Marketing Management, Sales and Marketing Management.*

■ Questions for Discussion

1. What is an organization? How might an organizational culture affect it as a consumer?
2. What are the major similarities and differences between individual buying and organizational buying? How would this be reflected when (a) you and (b) the organization you know best buy tea or coffee?
3. How is a buying decision made in a large organization?
4. How can factors external to the organization affect its purchasing decisions?
5. Why is it so important to understand the psychological factors that influence (a) individuals and (b) small groups in the organizational buying process?

PART V
Consumerism

■ Introduction

In this final part we draw on all the work of the foregoing four parts to deal with a related series of issues often called 'consumerism'.

In Chapter 18 we analyse the process by which consumers have come to be aware of themselves as a separate interest group and the effects this has had on producers and marketers. In Chapter 19 we extrapolate these trends into the immediate future. In both chapters we note how the effects of consumerism is changing the social context in which individual consumer behaviour takes place, that was our starting point for understanding the consumer in Part I.

CHAPTER 18

Consumer Awareness

Introduction

The twentieth century has been the century of 'the consumer'. I have put quotation marks round the term because it has been used in many different ways by many different people. In this book we have adopted a largely psychological perspective on consumer behaviour, but the consumer has also been claimed by:[1]

economists, sociologists, cultural critics, postmodernists, Marxists, conservatives, advertisers, journalists, pop-semioticians, marketers and marketeers, historians of ideas, environmentalists and activists.

In this chapter we will unpack the term 'consumer'. We will examine how the awareness people have of themselves as consumers arose and developed over the past century and where it now stands.

Images of the Consumer

Each of the theoretical approaches mentioned above has interpreted buying and consumption from the perspective of its own specialised concerns with the result that 'the consumer' has been pictured in many different guises and as having very different kinds of relationships to producers and the rest of society – some of these mutually contradictory. Each of these conceptions has shed a different light on what it has meant to be a consumer in the twentieth century. A recent overview of this field has distinguished nine different views of the consumer, each of which we will consider briefly.[2]

The Consumer as Chooser

This is perhaps the most prevalent image of the consumer. It embodies the key value of a capitalist consumer-oriented society that having a choice of goods and services is, in and of itself, *a good thing*. Not only that, but the more choice there is for consumers the more business there will be for producers and the better it will be for the economy, and therefore (it goes without saying) for society in general. The consumers' role is therefore crucial: they have to keep choosing between the alternatives presented to them and do so with ever-greater frequency and enthusiasm.

■ The Consumer as Communicator

In this role consumers use the acts of buying and consumption to communicate non-verbally with others (and indeed with themselves). It is a way of expressing one's feelings, social status and lifestyle. The products and services bought and consumed thus have meanings over and above the fulfilment of an immediate need.

■ The Consumer as Explorer

This consumer role emphasizes the importance of shopping as an act of exploring, but in a user-friendly environment carefully designed to reassure and comfort while it stimulates. Hunting for bargains and discovering new products are not pleasures the Western consumer usually pursues in a hot, noisy, smelly, over-crowded and possibly dangerous bazaar. They are indulged in spacious air-conditioned shopping malls with no immediate sales pressure and convenient restaurants and toilets. Indeed with the growth of home shopping they may be indulged in the comfort and security of one's own electronic fireside.

■ The Consumer as Identity-Seeker

Identity is now a central concept of social and behavioural science. Defining who he or she is and what he or she values by the goods and services he or she buys, consumes and gives as gifts, is widely regarded as one of the most important roles the consumer enacts.

■ The Consumer as Hedonist

Enjoying pleasure – especially physical pleasure – without feeling guilty about it is the essence of *hedonism*. It is therefore the antithesis of the Protestant work ethic, which instead emphasizes the primacy of work, earning and sacrifice as the way to individual fulfilment. It is this work ethic that drives the production of goods and services in a capitalist society and provides the ideology within which people are encouraged to make sense of the inherently mind-numbing, soul-destroying, exhausting and stressful jobs that so many of them have to do for a living.

Yet this society, through its marketing and advertising, also encourages people to be eager, avid, guilt-free, pleasure-seeking consumers, because ever-increasing consumption is deemed necessary for producers to maintain a prosperous economy. The psychological contradiction produced in people by these mixed messages is the result of what has been identified as a central paradox in our society.[3]

■ The Consumer as Victim

This is obviously not a role that anyone would consciously seek for themselves, but since at least the 1950s it has been argued that every consumer, to a greater or lesser extent, may be a victim of manipulation and exploitation by producers and the marketers and advertisers who serve them. The type of victimisation the consumer might experience can range from being relatively trivial in its effects (being overcharged for goods, despite the pretence of competition, because of price cartels) to the life-threatening (badly made toys or inadequately tested drugs). What all such experiences have in common is the producer's contempt for the consumer.

■ The Consumer as Rebel

In this role the consumer uses products to make a critical statement about the values of the consumer society. It is possible for any consumer to adopt this role at any time, but it is most noticeable among young people where acts of rebellion may coalesce into a more-or-less coherent movement. The disfiguring of blue jeans has been identified as a popular act of youthful rebellion in Western culture. Tearing one's jeans, it has been suggested, is a way in which the consumer can deliberately assert a different cultural meaning and use to that given by the producer.

■ The Consumer as Activist

Consumer activitists are people who consciously and actively promote the interests of consumers as a group, in relation to producers and to society as a whole. These activities can cover a very wide spectrum, from the Consumers Association's testing of product quality to political movements (for example the American Revolutionaries) that use consumer boycotts as a weapon against foreign oppression.

■ The Consumer as Citizen

The concept of 'citizen' is a political one; it denotes someone who is linked into a community and a nation-state by a web of rights that he or she can claim (freedom of speech, for instance) and responsibilities that he or she is expected to discharge (such as voting in an election or serving on a jury). As we have seen, the concept of 'consumer' arises from the economic activity in a society, and in particular the market place in which producers sell their goods and services. Consumers, on this account, are individual, self-contained units without reference to a wider social grouping than their household.

The attempt to marry the two concepts of consumer and citizen has been most fruitful when the need for social awareness by the individual has been stressed. The consumer as citizen is therefore conscious of how the market operates, the way producers operate and the effects that marketing and advertising have on buying and consumption. Such a consumer will also be aware of the behaviour of other consumers and will be ready to respond to activists by joining boycotts, writing letters, changing consumption patterns, and so on, where she or he believes that the greater good of her or his community is concerned as well as her or his own immediate interests.

In the course of discussing research on consumer psychology in this book we have come across instances of the consumer acting in each of these roles. In this chapter and the next we will highlight the last two perspectives, the consumer as *activist* and the consumer as *citizen*. We will begin by examining the history of consumer advocacy in Western society.

■ The History of the Consumer Movement

Consumer advocacy, which is often referred to as 'consumerism' in the United States, is not new. The Book of Proverbs in the Old Testament, for instance, deals with the sins of deceiving and defrauding the consumer. This is quite a different emphasis from Roman culture with its famous legal maxim *caveat emptor* (buyer beware). The Roman view has invariably been the dominant one in Western civilization: that it is up to consumers to protect their own interests while producers are entitled to treat consumers in any way the law does not specifically forbid.

The cards, therefore, have traditionally been stacked against the consumer throughout the history of Western civilization. Advocates of consumer interests have invariably been seen as radicals who want to upset the *status quo* (and the vested interests that benefit from it). This was as true of the Protestant reformers Martin Luther and John Calvin attacking shady selling techniques in the sixteenth century as Ralph Nader taking on the car industry in the twentieth.[4]

In more recent times several distinct periods of consumer advocacy have been identified.

■ The Co-operative Movement

Most accounts of organized consumer movements begin with the work of American radicals at the turn of the twentieth century, but the co-operative movement in the north of England predated this by about 50 years.[5] Set up in 1844, this movement was a response by industrial workers to the effects of the rapacious, virtually unfettered 'robber baron' capitalism that was then at its peak in Britain.

The world of work went through a radical transformation after the industrial revolution, which began in Britain. Small workplaces run by master craftsmen and their extended families were replaced by factories, owned by the new entrepreneurs, which eventually contained hundreds of people crammed into them alongside noisy, dirty and dangerous machinery – the 'dark satanic mills' described by the poet William Blake.

However there is some evidence that the new technology of work was of secondary importance to the change in the psychological relationship between employers and employee. The factory system predated the introduction of steam-powered machinery, and indeed even flourished in its absence. The impetus behind the rise of the factory system seems to have been the desire by employers to control the working lives of their employees as rigidly as possible, in the interest of maximizing their profits.[6]

Given the physical existence of the factories it made economic sense to site the new technology in them. E. P. Thompson, the well-known historian of the English working class, has shown how employers used their factories to control, for the first time, every aspect of the production process and, more importantly, the working life of their employees. This involved the use of impersonal forms of regulation, for instance the clock to measure punctuality, the imposition of a detailed system of discipline, and the close *visual* supervision of each worker's behaviour.[7]

Working conditions in these early factories were indeed as hellish as Blake suggested, for men, women and even children. A report on child labour in 1832 gave examples of children starting work at the factory at 3.00 am and working until 10.00 pm or even later. During these nineteen hours they had a 15 minute break for breakfast, 30 minutes for dinner and a further 15 minutes to have something to drink.[8] These children were also liable to receive corporal punishment for any 'transgressions'. Sanitation was, of course, rudimentary. The work itself was so hard and dangerous that many children died.

We think of these working conditions now as 'Dickensian' and Dickens was, after all, writing largely from his own observations of mid-nineteenth century England. In fact the conditions of work in the early factories were virtually slave labour. Indeed people were often legally bound to their employers and unable to take their labour elsewhere. Psychologically their condition may have been even worse than slavery. There was no guarantee whatsoever of employment and if there was a slump in demand they could be dismissed at any time, a difficult enough fate now but quite calamitous then. While slaves could hope for a benevolent master, some kind of personal relationship (however subservient) and a permanent place in the household, the factory worker was usually denied even these meagre psychological comforts.

Psychologically the co-operative movement was therefore an attempt by groups of workers (beginning in 1844) to take back from the factory owners some control over their own lives. They based this attempt on a new understanding of their position in the economy. Not only did their labour produce the goods that went out of the factories into the market but they themselves were also the consumers who largely propped up that market. So by acting together – by *co-operating* – there was no reason why the consumer could not be king and take precedence over the people who owned the means of production and operated them solely on the basis of self-interest.

The movement began with a single shop, in Rochdale, to sell goods only to its members. The profits made on these sales were then shared out among the members. The co-operative ideology was thus directly opposed to that of the prevailing market orthodoxy that prosperity could only be achieved by fostering self-interest and the pursuit of private profit. Given the extent and power of the vested interests ranged against it, it is hardly surprising that the co-operative movement did not seriously threaten to take over from the prevailing ideology.

Yet the movement had (and is still having) considerable success in some areas. Local co-operatives were very important to many working-class consumers throughout Britain for nearly a century after the Rochdale pioneers. Indeed in a sense the movement may have been a victim of its own success, as the following summary suggests:

> The hard work, zeal and commitment of the pioneers who built the local societies, who saved and invested in new shops, factories and land to serve working people, all this brought good quality goods and services to those who hitherto had lacked them. But as the movement has grown in size and influence and its affairs have inevitably come to be conducted by professional managers, its vision has become more pragmatic, though it has never collapsed into quite the ethos of other retail organizations.[9]

Yet the co-operative movement is still alive, and indeed thriving in situations far removed from mid-nineteenth century Rochdale, such as the many thousands of Japanese consumer groups (*seikatsu*) that were formed to buy food in bulk for their members.

■ American Consumerism

□ *Before the Second World War*

The process of industrialization occurred later in the United States than in Britain, as did the organization of consumer interests. The first Consumers League was formed in New York in 1891. But it was not until 1906 that the first American consumer movement had any notable success. This was due to the work of Upton Sinclair, a socialist writer with a similarly radical view of production and consumption as the co-operative pioneers in Britain.

Sinclair had been sent as a journalist to investigate the dreadful working conditions in the Chicago stockyards, the largest meat processing centre in the United States. He published his exposé in the form of a novel called *The Jungle* with the intention of attacking the profit-oriented capitalist system and bettering the lot of the American worker.

Sinclair expected that his account of workers and rats falling into the machinery and being minced up into hamburger meat would produce a public outcry for safer, more humane working conditions. But he had misjudged the American psyche. Sinclair's audience did not live up to his expectations. There was an outcry, all right, but it had little to do with the plight of the workers. It was for better food hygiene laws. In 1906 Congress passed the Meat Inspection Act and the Pure Food and Drug Act.

This outcome set the direction in which American consumerism would travel for the next 60 years. Appeals to fair trading and value-for-money for the consumer found a much wider and more receptive audience than a full-frontal attack on the evils of the capitalist system. The American public was particularly exercised by the trend towards the concentration of capital with the creation of monopolies and other business practices that restricted competition. In 1944 the Federal Trade Commission was established to deal with this issue.

After the First World War returning American servicemen formed the advance guard of a new consumer army eager to enjoy the fruits of the rapidly expanding American economy. In 1927 another book played an important part in galvanizing public opinion on consumer issues. This was a bestseller called *Your Money's Worth*, which attempted to show how consumers were systematically exploited by producers and deceived by advertising.

The book also attacked the lack of standards for, and testing of, products which would arm consumers with the necessary information to make informed buying decisions. One result of this publicity was the establishment of the Consumers Union in 1936. This organization launched *Consumer Reports*, a magazine that now has about 5 000 000 subscribers. By the end of the 1930s the Federal Trade Commission had been given some legal teeth with which to defend consumer interests.

☐ *Fordism and the Fordist Deal*

During these thirty years of American consumerism the influence of Henry Ford on both production and consumption was quite enormous. We noted in Chapter 1 that Ford's invention of the moving assembly line in 1913 marked the real start of the trend towards the mass production of goods, as well as that of the dominance of the producer over the consumer.

To get people to work on his assembly line Ford paid them about twice as much as his competitors. What he demanded in return was complete devotion to the job and, even more importantly, an individual relationship with the company. No hint of his workers seeing themselves as a group with their own particular interests was tolerated. Ford passionately hated trade unions and any display of worker solidarity.

However what Ford did understand and encourage was the dual identity that workers had as both producers and consumers of goods – goods such as his phenomenally successful Model T. This meant that the high wages he paid not only encouraged workers to produce more, but also to *consume* more.[10] As he himself put it, 'If you cut wages you just cut the number of your customers'. Thus Ford offered his workers an unspoken 'deal': 'if you keep your mouth shut and work hard you will enjoy an ever-increasing standard of living'.

Many commentators have argued that this 'deal' formed the basis of the economic relationships that have governed consumer behaviour throughout the twentieth century. The widespread view that the Fordist deal has now broken down is something we will deal with in the next chapter when we consider the likely future of the consumer.

□ *After the Second World War*

In 1962 the American consumer movement received a major boost with the presentation to Congress by President John F. Kennedy of a 'Consumer Bill of Rights'. These rights were four in number:[11]

- T*he right to safety*: that is, protection against products hazardous to health and life.
- *The right to be informed*: that is, protection against fraudulent, deceitful or misleading information, in advertising or elsewhere, by providing people with the facts necessary to make an informed choice.
- *The right to choose*: that is, the assurance of reasonable access, where possible, to a variety of products and services at competitive prices, or governmental regulation to assure satisfactory quality and service at fair prices.
- *The right to be heard*: that is, the right of redress, with the assurance that consumer interests will receive full and sympathetic consideration by government and fair and expeditious action.

As we will see below, other rights have since been added to this list by consumer activists. Taken together these rights form a useful framework for a discussion of consumer issues.

The right to safety   This is the most basic and the least contentious of all consumer rights. It is one that both producers and consumers can readily agree upon. As we noted earlier in the chapter, this concern goes back to the beginning of the twentieth century and the work by Upton Sinclair that resulted in stringent food hygiene laws. The importance of this right is underlined by the number of people injured each year by goods and services they have purchased. In the late 1970s the Consumer Product Safety Commission estimated this figure for the United States at about 20 million people, and that figure did not include injuries from cars, guns, drugs and many other potentially harmful products.[12]

The name most associated with the right to safety, and indeed with the American consumer movement in general, is that of Ralph Nader. Nader became a national hero in 1965 with the publication of his book *Unsafe at any Speed*, an exposé of how safety was systematically endangered by the production methods of the American car industry. He was eventually successful in having these methods changed.[13]

Unlike the prewar American consumer movement, Nader was interested in much more than simply getting the consumer a better deal from the producer. He was really interested in changing the way the market economy worked and altering the relationship between producer and consumer. In this he had a lot in common with both his countryman Upton Sinclair and the earlier British pioneers of the co-operative movement.

Nader took the view that the consumers are largely defenceless in the face of the giant corporations that produce the goods and services they use. Moreover the kind of stand taken by President Kennedy on behalf of the consumer is rare. Governments and state officials normally side with the powerful. As a lawyer Nader believed that existing laws had to be used proactively in defence of consumers' rights. Consumer organizations therefore had to be tough-minded and imaginative in their work and assiduous in publicizing it through the mass media. There are now 29 organizations in the United States pursuing Nader's type of consumerism.[14]

The right to be informed   This right has been much more vigorously and openly contested by producers than that of consumer safety. The point of it is to protect consumers from deliberate attempts to deceive them with false information conveyed by the advertising or labelling of goods and services. The point of advertising has always been to present a product in the most favourable light possible, which invariably involves *exaggeration* ('Krapulike Kup Kakes are orgiastic!'). But is this *deception*? Can it edge into deception? And most importantly, can it affect our buying behaviour and persuade us to use the product?

The relevant regulatory body in the United States, the Federal Trade Commission, has usually taken the position that consumers will not be deceived by such advertising because they will recognize exaggeration when they see it and discount it accordingly. However research evidence suggests a different conclusion, as we learned in Chapter 14. A leading social psychologist, Elliot Aronson, summarizes it thus:[15] 'Simply because we *think* we are immune to persuasion does not necessarily mean we *are* immune to persuasion. In the case of many consumer products, the public will tend to buy a specific brand for no other reason than the fact that it is heavily advertised (emphasis in original)'.

Moreover, unlike you and me, not all consumers are able to recognize exaggeration when they see it and may take advertising claims at face value.[16] And gullible consumers need at least as much protection as sceptical ones. This is particularly true when advertisers stretch the meaning of the words they use into new and exotic shapes. Take the word 'fresh', for instance, a highly desirable description for a food product. If you pick up a box of eggs in a supermarket you will often find it labelled 'farm fresh'. But you know the eggs came from battery chickens used as egg-laying machines in cages (or it would say 'free range'), so what does 'farm fresh' actually *mean*?

In 1991 in the United States there was a test case involving the use of the word 'fresh' in advertising.[17] Procter and Gamble had decided to use the word to describe one of its orange juice brands, a product made from concentrate. The Food and Drug Administration (FDA) asked the company to stop describing the stuff as 'fresh', but was rebuffed. So the FDA used its legal powers to confiscate the product and ban all future use of the word 'fresh' in its advertising, packaging and production.

This was certainly a (small) victory for consumer rights but it also highlights what major transnational corporations try to get away with in one of the world's most sophisticated consumer nations. Had Proctor and Gamble not been challenged by the FDA there is no doubt that many consumers of the product would have accepted it as fresh orange juice. I have seen for myself that this bastardization of the language does work. While doing market research for food manufacturers in the United Kingdom I heard consumers using the word 'fresh' for products they had just defrosted – or even taken out of a tin!

Ralph Nader sees the provision of free and fair information as being absolutely crucial to the defence of consumer interests. In describing the relationship between producers and consumers of food, for example, he says:

> Making food appear what it is not is an integral part of the $125 billion food industry. The deception ranges from the surface packaging to the integrity of the food products' quality to the very shaping of food tastes ... there has been an overwhelmingly dominant channel of distorted information from the food industry to the consumer.[18]

A large part of the problem from the consumers' point of view is that they cannot rely on any trusted short cuts when buying products (or heuristics as we noted in Chapters 15 and 16), not even brand loyalty. Many consumers have had their faith shaken in the most reputable of companies, as when Volvo was found to have reinforced the cars used in those famous advertisements that demonstrated how uncrushable its products are.

This seems to be a particular problem with food products. A car, especially an expensive car, is a rare purchase and subject to relatively greater scrutiny by prospective purchasers. But regardless of income everybody has to eat every day and that is where brand loyalty is particularly important – for both producer and consumer.

Yet you find a household name like Quaker Oats willing to claim, untruthfully, that its bran cereals reduce the risk of heart attack. So not only do buyers have to 'beware', they really have constantly to scrutinize and assess all the advertising, labelling and packaging of virtually everything they pick up in the supermarket – and a PhD in nutrition would be of great help too.

The burden of wading through all the information and misinformation to find out what they really want to know about a product may be why so many shoppers, as we saw in Chapter 4, close their eyes and just toss things in the trolley. Moreover if you have lots of money you can employ clever people to help you get round the rules. Carlsberg changed its advertising from 'the best lager in the world' – an impossible claim to substantiate – to '*probably* the best lager in the world', thus keeping within the rules and gaining the consumer's attention at the same time.

The right to choose   This would appear to be one right that is absolutely guaranteed by a market economy. Free competition between producers of goods and services is the very essence of the capitalist system is it not? Well yes, but only up to a point. There are really two questions at issue here:

- How much choice does the consumer have?
- How real is the choice?

With regard to *how much*, everyone would presumably agree that the centralized economy of the former Soviet Union, where there was little or no producer response to consumer demand and little or no choice of brand per product, was the antithesis of the consumer market economy. If you are going to have such an economy you need *some* choice to provide the stimulus of competition. However the very existence – and use – of antitrust legislation in the United States and the Monopolies and Mergers Commission in the United Kingdom demonstrates that while competition may be a desirable practice from the consumer's point of view it lacks a certain appeal when looked at from the producer's perspective.

Indeed the history of Western business has been one of ever-increasing attempts by producers to *reduce* competition because it made life for each competitor tougher, more uncertain and less profitable. The ideal was to dominate a given market, if possible with a monopoly position, or failing that to be part of an oligopoly, cartel, price-fixing ring or 'gentleman's agreement' that would maximize profits and share price and minimize future uncertainty. These activities are not usually considered as being in the consumer's best interests.[19]

A prominent example of this conflict of interests in recent years concerned the American car industry. The 'Big Three' of Detroit (Ford, Chrysler and General Motors) were ardent proponents of the bracing virtues of free trade until Japanese imports began to outsell their own products in the 1980s because they were cheaper and better made. Then they began screaming for trade restrictions against their Japanese competitors.

Indeed the history of the car industry (as we noted in Chapter 10) is a good example of the way in which restricted competition hinders the creativity that can go into product development. The cars that we drive today are recognizably the same product that came off Henry Ford's production line in 1913. They are powered, steered and used in exactly the same way. Plastic and electrical wiring has been added and a lot of steel subtracted, but that's about it.

Now consider the home entertainment industry. In 1913 the state-of-the-art was probably the piano. Today it's satellite television with stereo sound, and tomorrow it'll be virtual reality. Why the difference? The small groups of oil, steel, rubber and car manufacturing companies had a firm grip on the car market that served their interlocking interests. The last thing they wanted was innovation and competition rocking their very comfortable boat.

Largely because of the nature of the product, this was much more difficult to arrange with home entertainment. When the Japanese developed their expertise in electronics after the Second World War and entered the field in a big way there wasn't much the rest of the world could do about it. The consumer benefited from the ensuing competition and the increased choice.

So do we have more choice now than we used to? Oddly enough the answer is both 'yes' and 'no'. Compared with previous historical periods there clearly is more choice – for the average consumer in a rich country that is.[20] In more recent times, since 1960 say, the picture is more mixed. We have more of some things (confectionery, cosmetics and books) less of others (brands of television sets, cinemas and food shops).[21] And at the end of the twentieth century there are, of course, far fewer car manufacturers than there were at the beginning.

With regard to *how real*, the existence of a number of product brands to choose from is one thing: the *nature* of that choice is quite another. In one sense what appears to be a wide choice, made possible by a modern consumer economy, may be nothing of the kind. In Britain, for example, nine varieties of apple are available in the shops. A considerable choice indeed.

Yet the number of varieties that have actually been produced in Britain is about 2000.[22] And this tendency to present the appearance of abundant choice while in fact drastically narrowing down the options available to the consumer is found throughout the food industry. Consider, for instance, the cornucopia of tomatoes in your local supermarket – but try to find one that tastes of anything.

We have also seen at various points in this book how trivial and unimportant many of the choices are that people make. Being faced with umpteen brands of detergent or margarine constitutes a choice only in the most limited and technical sense.

The crucial issue is that while the choice between virtually identical brands matters little to the consumer, it matters a great deal to the producer. And that is why so much attention is lavished on this form of choice as opposed to more important alternatives such as having electric cars or different news sources. Moreover we should never lose sight of the fact that most real choice is exercised, everywhere, by those consumers with the most money.

The right to be heard This is the most problematic of the four consumer rights announced by President Kennedy. One central problem lies in the way consumer behaviour is usually thought of. You will recall that in Chapters 15 and 16 we examined the research on how consumers make buying decisions. These studies, and the models of buying behaviour that have emerged from them, are certainly useful but they have the effect of focusing entirely on the consumer in what is really an interaction between consumer and producer.

It is as though the market situation consists entirely of consumers making good or bad decisions. There is no room here for the possibility that the consumer's choices might be irrelevant because they are made in all innocence of the fact that producers are trying to cheat, deceive or swindle them. Gabriel and Lang put this very well: 'In marketing terms, the notion of being a victim does not exist. When things go wrong, there is the language of consumer irrationality. Business is rational, its customers unpredictable'.[23]

The unquestioned assumption that the goods and services provided will be satisfactory means that the burden of consumer protection falls mainly on consumers themselves, on consumer organizations and on those governmental agencies that are meant to act on the consumers' behalf. Ways of protecting the consumer are usually listed under the headings *prevention, restitution* and *punishment.*[24]

1. *Prevention.* Preventing the need for consumer redress by listening to consumer interests before problems appear is obviously ideal. Some industries and professions (for instance medicine and advertising) have *codes of conduct*

for their practitioners and, very occasionally (as when a doctor is struck off the register for malpractice), these may actually be enforced. However there is probably no substitute for genuine self-regulation by companies, which means paying real attention, and not just the usual lip service, to *quality*. If a company does this then, in its dealings with its customers, this would imply it has a conscious policy never to rip them off.

2. *Restitution*. Once a consumer has been wronged in some way the focus of attention should be on the producer's side of the market place. If a consumer has been deceived, or sold a defective product, all that he or she can do about it is to complain and make sure the supplier of the goods or service knows what has happened. It is then up to the company in question to provide restitution by apologizing and replacing the item, or paying compensation and so on.

Often a producer has a legal obligation to do this, but even when there is no such formal requirement it is always in the company's best interests to do so. As we noted in Chapter 16, dissatisfied customers are twice as likely to tell other people about their experience as people who are satisfied; and who is more likely to be dissatisfied than a customer who feels cheated?

And it really doesn't take all that much to convert a dissatisfied customer into a loyal fan. As we also noted in Chapter 16, people will go to great lengths to persuade themselves that they have made the right choice, and most dissatisfied customers do not in fact complain to the seller. Yet many companies are still reluctant to make the necessary restitution if it means admitting culpability and often don't even respond to letters of complaint. They would rather lose the customer.

3. *Punishment*. The final source of redress for consumers faced with unresponsive producers is legal. But this is often a hugely expensive and time-consuming business. In rare cases companies may be fined if their infraction is particularly blatant, but this is rarely effective in changing the behaviour of the company in question, or any other that might find itself in a similar position.

Slightly more effective is the threat of company officials going to jail and – at least in the United States, where lawsuits (known as "class actions") are possible on behalf of *large groups* of wronged consumers and the government regulations have teeth – this does occasionally happen. Fraud in the stock market is a recent case in point.

But probably the most important form of punishment for a company is bad publicity. And the bigger the company the greater the loss of reputation (and potential profits). As we will see in the next chapter this is one way in which an otherwise powerless consumer can exact some restitution from a giant corporation.

☐ *Other Consumer Rights*

Both consumer awareness and the nature of the marketplace (and indeed the world) has changed considerably since the Kennedy pronouncement on the four consumer rights. Each of these rights is as vital to the consumer now as it was in the early 1960s, but most consumer movements would add the desirability of two further rights based on more recent commercial developments, *the right to a clean environment* and *the right to privacy*. Therefore consumers should have the right to:

- Safety
- Be informed
- Choose
- Be heard
- A clean environment
- Privacy

The right to a clean environment   One of the by-products of ever-increasing consumption that Western consumers have become more aware of in recent years is environmental pollution. Many people are now concerned about the quality of the air they breathe, the water they drink and the food they eat, as well as less immediate threats such as the depletion of the ozone layer and the poisoning of the world's oceans. Most people, when polled, express deep concern about many of these issues.[25] For example an American study found that:

- 62 per cent think that environmental pollution is a very serious threat.
- 55 per cent think that regulations to control environmental pollution are not strong enough.
- Most importantly for producers, only 36 per cent think that business is doing enough to alleviate pollution.

When it comes down to actual buying choices though, consumer behaviour is a little more complex than the figures suggest. Thus over 80 per cent of American consumers are convinced of the importance of buying only environmentally sound products[26], yet if such a product costs a little more than competing products, or is a little less convenient to use, most of these concerned consumers will not choose it.[27] This is not the first time in this book that we've noted a large gap between expressed attitudes and actual behaviour, a theme we will pick up again in the next chapter, together with a closer look at the future of environmentalism.

The right to privacy   This is the most recent concern of the consumer movement. It refers to the consumer's right to keep his or her personal information private, whether biographical, medical, financial or whatever. This has always been of some concern to most consumer movements, but it has achieved much greater salience since the early 1970s when developments in microelectronics meant that it became possible to computerize personal data previously held on cards or files, thus making their storage, transmission and accessibility much easier.
    Of course much of the normal daily business of a modern society is depen-

dent on just this kind of information technology, both in the public and the private sector. Taxation, electoral rolls, welfare benefits, medical history, credit records, insurance policies and, of course, direct marketing are just a few of the more obvious activities involved.

What worries people most is the *unauthorized* transmission and use of this data.[28] It is one thing for a hospital consultant to have your medical records, quite another for a life insurance company to have them – or a medical supplies company that might want to target you for its products. The average British citizen in 1995 was listed on some 200 different databases, all of them potentially transferrable elsewhere.[29]

Most industrialized countries now have legislation to prevent unauthorized access by organizations, both public and private, to personal data. This is regarded as the essential minimum by consumer groups, but the basic problem for the consumer, and indeed for society as a whole, is one of *trust*.

The average consumer, even if she or he knows what her or his legal rights are, has no way of knowing which organization holds what information about her or him, and has to take it entirely on trust that the data protection laws are being obeyed, and enforced if necessary. Given all that we have learned about public and private abuses of privacy in recent years (which we have to assume is just the tip of the iceberg) it should not be too surprising that consumers everywhere remain extremely uneasy about the issue.

■ Further Reading

Aaker, D. A. and G. S. Day (eds), *Consumerism: Search for the Consumer Interest*, 4th edn (New York: Free Press, 1982). An overview of the history and theory of consumerism in the United States.

Birchall, J., *Co-op: The People's Business* (Manchester: Manchester University Press, 1994). A recent history of the co-operative movement in Britain.

Davidson, M. P., The *Consumerist Manifesto: Advertising in Postmodern Times* (London: Routledge, 1992). A look at the effects on consumers of recent hard-edged advertising. Written by a former advertising executive in Britain.

Dittmar, H., *The Social Psychology of Material Possessions* (Hemel Hempstead: Harvester Wheatsheaf, 1992). An examination of experimental and other research evidence on the psychological meaning in our society of owning things.

Penz, P. G., *Consumer Sovereignty and Human Interests* (Cambridge: Cambridge University Press, 1986). Suggests how increased consumer self-knowledge could play an important part in consumer protection.

Velasquez, M. G., *Business Ethics: Concepts and Cases*, 2nd edn (Englewood Cliffs, NJ: Prentice-Hall, 1988). A detailed examination of theory and practice that includes the major ethical and philosophical systems, as they affect the rights of the consumer and the obligations of the producer.

It is also worth browsing through the latest issues of the following periodicals: *Advances in Consumer Research, Harvard Business Review, Journal of Consumer Research.*

■ Questions for Discussion

1. Why are there so many different images of 'the consumer'? Which ones are most important to the marketer?
2. Why should marketers be aware of the history of the consumer movement?
3. Do you think consumers should have any legal rights? What would be the effect on marketers if consumers had no rights?
4. Give two examples of deceptive advertising. How would you correct them?
5. If no deception at all was allowed in advertising what would be the effects on (a) consumers, (b) advertisers, (c) marketers?

CHAPTER 19

The Future Consumer

■ Introduction

In the previous chapter we examined the growth of consumer awareness in recent years and saw that it built on a long history of organized movements for and government legislation on consumer interests. In this final chapter we will consider the current position of the consumer and (cautiously!) attempt to extrapolate future events from the most recent trends in the consumer behaviour dealt with in this book.

■ The Changing Consumer Experience

The one thing we know for sure about the consumer environment is that it is changing. In the largest sense change is endemic, of course, to all human affairs (and indeed to the universe). But in trying to study the psychology of consumer behaviour we are inevitably led into seeing patterns and building models that may, as a by-product, give the impression of stasis, and therefore predictability, about certain aspects of the consumer experience.

The reality (as you had already guessed) is a little more complex than that. In the near future a lot of our present consumer behaviour will continue in the same way – or at least it will look as if it is. But there will be considerable changes too. To try to chart these likely continuities and discontinuities we will approach the consumer experience from three distinct perspectives: those of *the producer*, *the market place* and *the consumer*.

■ The Producer

■ Customer Responsiveness

One trend that first became apparent in the 1970s and will continue into the foreseeable future is that of focusing on the needs of the customer. This approach to marketing has become something of a gospel over the past generation, preached enthusiastically by celebrated business gurus such as Tom Peters.[1] But, like any other gospel, though it receives widespread lip service it is not actually practiced all that much.

The original impetus for the customer-centred approach was provided by Japan as European and North American producers began to realize that they were losing huge amounts of market share to Japanese competitors. They simply couldn't cope with the superior quality of Japanese goods and services. This quality was not achieved by Japanese workers putting in more effort than their European or North American counterparts, but by more enlightened *management* of the producer organizations.

Two factors in particular were critical. One is often referred to as 'Management By Wandering About' (MBWA) and it is particularly important for senior management, both as a way of staying in touch with the workers at the productive end of the business and also as a way of staying in touch with the consumers of their products at the point of sale – a form of market research in other words.

By staying in touch with those members of the organization who actually produce the goods and services Japanese senior management were able to ensure that quality was built in as part of the manufacturing process and not, as in most Western companies, added on at the end, if at all. They called this process *kaizen* or continuous improvement. It gave every worker the responsibility of making the product better as a normal part of the job, as opposed to the 'quality supervisors' of Western companies whose job was simply to reject defective items *after they had been made.*

By staying in touch with their customers they were able to feed a stream of ideas back to the people working on production. Apart from their highly successful penetration of Western markets this approach meant that Japanese companies were able to take market share away from Western companies in their home market too. For example in less than ten years, between the mid 1970s and the mid 1980s, they reduced Procter and Gamble's share of the disposable nappy (diaper) market in Japan from 90 per cent to 8 per cent.

In self-defence Procter and Gamble was obliged to invest heavily in local consumer research and marketing advice. One of the important lessons it learned was that Japanese consumers are much more concerned than Americans with product quality and much less concerned about price. As a result Procter and Gamble stopped losing money in its Japanese markets in 1987.[2]

We encountered another example of customer responsiveness pioneered by the Japanese when we discussed market segmentation in Chapter 2. We noted there that the policy of customizing products as far as possible to meet the buyer's specifications is as old as the market place itself. But while Western producers have always regarded customizing as relevant to high-quality low-volume services such as tailoring and cabinet making, the Japanese innovation was to apply it to manufactured products that are traditionally found in high-volume markets, for example bicycles.

One of the most important trends in the future of the producer, therefore, will be this attempt to marry what was previously seen as polar opposites: *mass production*, which had its classic expression in Henry Ford's black (only) model T, and *individual customizing*. The line between the two will probably never again be as distinct as it has been throughout the twentieth century.

This post-Fordist form of niche market manufacturing is known as *lean production*. It combines:

> the advantages of craft and mass production, while avoiding the high cost of the former and the rigidity of the latter ... lean producers employ teams of multiskilled workers at all levels of the organization and use highly flexible, increasingly automated machines to produce volumes of products in enormous variety.[3]

As well as emphasizing quality of product, this system also emphasizes quality of labour in terms of skill, learning ability and flexibility of the work role. But the emphasis on quality inevitably implies a sharp decline in *quantity*, in labour just as much as product. This is the antithesis of the mass production system pioneered by Henry Ford, with consumer consequences we will explore below.

■ Business Ethics

Many people – especially producers – regard the term 'business ethics' as an oxymoron, a contradiction in terms. They would argue that the basic goal of being in business, and the only one that really matters, is to make as much money as possible. Ethics is simply irrelevant. And in support of their argument they could probably cite most of the history of business practice. As we saw in the last chapter the uphill struggle for consumer rights and protection has high-lighted the non-ethical, or even unethical nature of standard business practices.

In modern times the issue of ethics in business was sharply highlighted in the 1980s and early 1990s when the prevailing goal of business throughout much of the world seemed to be short-term financial gain. In practice this often involved cutting what were identified as 'costs' – which turned out to be mainly staff salaries and benefits – which in turn meant firing people. This goal was usually underpinned by an extreme individualist ideology. So when the stock market manipulator (and soon-to-be convicted crook) Ivan Boesky famously announced at a graduation ceremony at Stanford Business School that 'greed is good', he was applauded wildly.

While the fast-buck merchants presumably cared little about the millions of people whose livelihood they removed, what they also failed to appreciate was that they were also reneging on the Fordist deal that we discussed in the last chapter. The essence of this deal, you will recall, was that 'the producer is also the consumer; the consumer is also the producer'. In other words if people have jobs they will spend much of their income on consumption; if they don't they can't, and production will therefore suffer.

The severe recession of the 1980s, followed by the lack of consumer confidence in the 1990s, may have helped to stimulate the current discussions on business ethics. If a large number of people are prevented from doing much consuming and all the rest are worried about their job security, then consumers will, ironically, be guided by the same short-term considerations that ruled the producers who helped bring about this state of affairs. People will therefore be markedly more reluctant to enter into long-term financial commitments such as mortgages or to purchase new consumer durables such as cars.

The activities usually referred to as 'business ethics' are of three varieties:

- *Codes of ethics*, such as those we noted in the last chapter, where organizations, professions and sometimes industries have more or less explicit guidelines for their members about what constitutes acceptable behaviour towards consumers, clients, other organizations and other staff members. The number of American corporations with in-house codes and workshops on applying them has grown rapidly in recent years and these now constitute nearly half of the largest 1000 companies.[4]
- *Changes in the board of directors* to include external appointees from outside the business world who reflect broader social concerns. Occasionally these appointments even extend beyond the token woman or black person.
- *Social marketing* awareness by an organization, meaning it modifies the traditional marketing concept we have observed throughout this book by being socially responsible in the marketing of its goods and services as well as trying to make a profit.

Employees of an organization will only follow these business ethics in practice if senior managers encourage them and act on them themselves. Indeed when employees are found guilty of unethical business practices it is invariably the result of pressure on them from higher up in the company hierarchy.[5]

■ The Market Place

■ Political Changes

Like every other aspect of our society, the nature of the marketplace in which producers and consumers interact is greatly affected by political changes. The most visible political changes in industrialized countries result from government actions. These often occur when the political party in office changes, and with it official policy, as well as the less tangible but perhaps even more important *ideology* about what constitutes the most important values of society.

As we saw in the previous chapter there has been a general trend over the course of the twentieth century, particularly in the United States, for successive governments to enact legislation designed to protect consumer interests. Between the Pure Food and Drug Act of 1906 and the Magnuson–Moss Warranty Improvement Act of 1975 some 15 pieces of legislation were passed to protect the American consumer.[6] And during this time 10 independent regulatory agencies were set up to deal with virtually every area of consumer interest: the Federal Trade Commission, the Food and Drug Administration, the Consumer Products Safety Commission, the Environmental Protection Agency, the Federal Communications Commission, the Interstate Commerce Commission, the Federal Maritime Commission, the Securities and Exchange Commission, the Commodity Futures Trade Commission and the International Trade Commission.

In the 1980s the political mood changed in the United States with the election of Ronald Reagan, and in the United Kingdom with the election of Margaret Thatcher. Both these administrations fostered a sharp swing to the right politically in which a passionate free market ideology formed the background for a policy of *deregulation* wherever possible. What deregulation meant in practice was the reduction of governmental activity in the market place in favour of a 'self-regulated' market, where all producers and consumers are supposed to follow their own best interests.

Given the obvious and enormous disparity in the wealth and influence of the average producer as opposed to the average consumer – along with widespread public concern about that fact – even the most right wing of governments has had to admit the need for *some* form of consumer protection. But while laws may remain on the statute books they will be quite ineffective if they are not actively enforced. And while consumer protection agencies may remain in existence they will not do much protecting unless the government gives them the resources to do the job. In the United States, the United Kingdom and other parts of the world during the 1980s and into the 1990s legislation was less than zealously enforced and agencies routinely suffered debilitating cuts in budgets and staffing.

However the early 1990s also witnessed the beginning of a swing away from this deregulatory stance, fuelled largely by the increasing consumer awareness and concern that we charted in the last chapter and which have now appeared on the agendas of the major political parties. In the United States this seems to be particularly true about environmental issues, price fixing and, to a lesser extent, product safety and honesty in advertising.[7]

■ Shopping Trends and Buyer Behaviour

Over the course of the twentieth century the relationship between mass production and mass consumption, which we have considered in this chapter and the previous one, has had the effect of increasing the level of mass prosperity. One effect this has had on marketing and advertising has been to switch the emphasis from providing information on products that satisfy a few basic fixed needs to the identification and satisfaction of new 'needs' that are really *wants* rather than necessities for living. Nobody 'needs' a television set, for instance, and in 1930 nobody had one. Yet not having one today would be considered a sign either of severe deprivation or rebellion against the cultural norm.

Once an innovation like this has become accepted, the focus of marketing and advertising is fixed on the competition between brands. That is, when the price of a product is low enough to be affordable to most potential consumers

they are able to choose whether or not to own it. The next aspect of choice –
and the one that mainly concerns marketers and advertisers – is which *brand* the
consumer will choose. So for most people in the market place most of the time,
what 'choice' means is *brand choice*.[8]

In Chapter 14 we saw the tremendous importance that producers place upon
their brands, spending vast amounts of money to develop brand personalities
and secure brand loyalty. In recent years, however, changes in the market place
have suggested radical transformations in brand choice and its effect on the
consumer. Now that famous marques of British car – Rover and Jaguar – are
owned by and have been absorbed into companies in other countries, what does
brand loyalty (or even 'buying British') mean? And what can 'brand value'
mean to the consumer when companies such as IBM can plunge from being one
of the highest ever brand values in 1993 to near worthlessness in 1994?

In addition to this organizational volatility there has been a retailing trend in
recent years that may well have an important effect on consumer choice in the
future: *own-brand* or private label products. It has been standard practice for a
number of years for most leading retailers to buy in generic products such as
food or clothing from the same group of suppliers – often in cheaper labour
markets – and then putting their own label on the product. This trade has
usually formed a relatively small but steady share of retailers' profits. There have
recently been signs, however, that with the effect of widespread job insecurity
consumers are not only buying these generic products, but are increasingly
buying a wider range of cheaper own-label products rather than the more
famous brands. The advantage for the supermarket is that, even allowing for the
discount, their profit margin is greater. My local Safeway is currently urging its
customers to 'cut your shopping bill in half' by choosing its 112 own-brand
products instead of the most popular alternatives.

Two of the best-known brands in the world are Coca Cola and Pepsi Cola, who
for many years have been deadly rivals at the top of the soft drinks market. But
both have recently been losing market share – heavily – to own-brand colas.
Consumers apparently see little difference in taste between the giants and the
own-brands, and value for money now seems to be overcoming brand loyalty and
brand image here as well.[9]

If this trend continues to grow – and the foreseeable economic conditions in
the rich countries make it more likely than not – this has radical implications for
the future of the marketing and advertising industries. If we ever reach a stage
where most of the consumers in the industrialized world arc largely ignoring
brand differences when making their buying decisions, what will be the point
of marketing or advertising products by brand name? What then will be the
function of marketers and advertisers?

This is where the direct marketing techniques we discussed in Chapter 14 will
assume even more importance in the future. Closely targeting the likeliest
customers for a given brand looks like becoming far more important to the
marketer and advertiser than the traditional nation-wide campaign (or even
global campaign in the case of brands such as Coke and Pepsi) conducted almost

exclusively in the mass media. Local media (print, radio and television) look set for a boom, with far-reaching repercussions for the economics of the mass media.

■ The Consumer

The own-brand issue highlights anew a theme that has run through this book: while it is true that marketers and advertiser can manipulate consumer choice, it is only true up to a point. When the choice really matters to consumers they will do what is most important to them – whether it looks objectively rational to anyone else or not. In this final section of the final chapter we will take a consumer's eye view of the future and consider the likely patterns of *direct action* and *alternative lifestyles*.

■ Direct Action

Direct action by consumers in defence of their interests is probably as old as the market place. Psychologically it may have become more prominent in the public mind because of the economic recessions of the 1980s and early 1990s. As we have seen, this was a period in which corporate rhetoric about customer service and product quality was at its height. This rhetoric probably increased consumer expectations. We also know that, normally, the average consumer is happy to give producers the benefit of the doubt until a serious failure of service, quality or safety is publicly demonstrated.[10]

Yet the economic hard times of the 1980s and 1990s have conclusively demonstrated how the corporate culture really views the consumer: as necessary profit-making fodder but a very distant second-best to the shareholder – which invariably means the giant financial institutions that hold the largest blocks of company shares. This is but the latest example of the traditional contempt of the producer for the consumer that we first encountered in Chapter 1 and which was enshrined in Henry Ford's famous dictum 'you can have any colour of Model T you like as long as it's black'.

But the producer contempt of modern times is much more pervasive even than Henry's. The effect of his attitude was merely to deny the consumer a trivial choice. However modern producers in hard times will often hit the consumer in two different ways. They will increase prices, reduce service and adulterate quality if they feel this is necessary to maintain profitability, and they will cut costs by firing workers, an individual act whose aggregate effects for the economy as a whole (as Henry Ford warned long ago) is to remove customers and reduce consumer demand.[11] Moreover fewer staff (usually doing more work) in the service sector often means poorer service for the consumer there too. It is this direct action against the consumer that may, I suspect, have helped fuel the direct consumer reaction against the producer. This has taken several forms.

☐   *Boycotts*

The most direct of direct consumer actions is to carry out a *boycott*, named after Captain Boycott, a detested nineteenth-century Irish landlord.   There are boycotts of certain products or companies, or even all products from a particular country as in the case of South Africa during the three decades of apartheid. Individuals often do this for many individual reasons, but what makes a boycott effective is when a sufficient number of individuals are involved and it receives sufficient media attention for the object of the boycott to notice it.

The British journal *Ethical Consumer* keeps track of consumer boycotts and their effects.   In its January 1994 issue it identified more than 50 separate boycotts covering a wide range of goods and services, organizations and issues.[12] Many of these boycotts dealt with well-publicized topics such as environmental degradation and the abuse of animals, particularly in product testing.

It has been calculated that in the United States in 1992 16 per cent of people shopping for groceries were taking part in a boycott, as opposed to only 8 per cent in 1984.[13]   Indeed food products have always been a particularly effective target because they are highly perishable, are purchased frequently by consumers and alternatives are often readily available.

Gauging the effectiveness of a boycott is not always easy.   Sometimes there is a direct link between cause and effect, as when a cosmetics company (for instance L'Oreal) agrees to stop using animals in product testing and has a boycott lifted.   With broader actions (for example that against apartheid) it is more difficult to calculate the effect of a boycott.

It does seem clear, though, that companies that are targeted take the action very seriously indeed.[14]   Obviously the greater the publicity involved the greater the likely effect.   And this is not only because other consumers may join in the boycott – it has been found that a company's stock market performance can be adversely affected fairly quickly.[15]

☐   *Organized Complaints*

We noted in the previous chapter that most companies tend to ignore letters of complaint.   However there are times when they cannot do so.   This can happen, for example when a consumer who feels wronged is willing to go far beyond the letter of complaint stage and devote a considerable part of his or her personal and/or financial resources to the quest for satisfaction.

Such cases are of course rare but their publicity value is great and this is one way in which an individual consumer can inflict incalculable costs on a company. Moreover the consumer is often now treated in the media as a hero ('David versus Goliath') and this may possibly be part of a growing trend to celebrate the *limits* of corporate power whenever possible.

Such a case (and one worth considering in some detail) was that of Jeremy Dorosin, a California consumer who in 1995 took on Starbucks, the largest chain of coffee stores in the United States.[16]   Mr Dorosin's battle with Starbucks concerned an expresso machine he had bought as a wedding present. Mr Dorosin felt he had been insulted by the cashier when he bought the machine – for which the company apologized – but the problem was compounded by the fact that the machine turned out to be defective.

The company, which is proud of its customer care, then offered to refund the customer's money or give him a new machine. But it would not agree to Mr Dorosin's suggestion that amends would properly be made if it sent his friend its 'nicest expresso machine' instead. It would not even agree to its next best machine (at about $150 more than the one purchased).

A very angry Mr Dorosin decided to try direct action. He placed a small advertisement in the *Wall Street Journal* saying 'Had any problems with Starbucks Coffee? You are not alone. Interested? Let's talk'. With the advertisement he provided a freephone number. He received over 1000 calls and the action escalated. Mr Dorosin ran four advertisements in all and received thousands of calls, at a total cost to him of $8200.

After the second advertisement the company responded by sending Mr Dorosin two new expresso machines, two pounds of coffee, a steaming pitcher, condiment shakers, cups and saucers, a $30 refund, a partridge in a pear tree, and letters of apology to him and his friend. He considered this response 'pathetic' and merely a panic reaction to the adverse publicity, which by this time had hit the mass media.

Mr Dorosin's demands escalated to include the provision by Starbucks of a $5 million centre for young runaways in San Francisco. Whatever the objective rights and wrongs of the dispute, business analysts generally believe the company is on a hiding to nothing and feel that Starbucks now has 'to do something very big and very public.' Of course Mr Dorosin is also out of pocket, but then again (this being America) he has a book and a TV movie in the offing.

☐ *Legal Action*

Mr Dorosin shrewdly decided not to sue Starbucks, an action that might have cost him a lot more than $8000. He relied on (mainly free) publicity instead. A consumer complainant would have to be very wealthy indeed to think about taking on a major corporation in court. Or else very poor. Direct legal action is also possible for individual consumers if they qualify for public funds or if they are willing to defend themselves. And that was the situation of two people in London who in 1994 took on one of the biggest corporate giants in the world: McDonald's.

Dave Morris and Helen Steel, known inevitably as the McLibel Two, were members of a small collective (called London Greenpeace but not part of Greenpeace International) who were sued for libel by McDonald's for distributing leaflets attacking the company. The leaflets alleged, amongst other things, that the company's products were lacking in nutrition, fostered the abuse of animals and the degradation of the environment and that the staff were badly paid.

As in the case of Mr Dorosin and Starbucks, the determination of the consumers involved (sometimes known as 'consumer vigilantes') has ensured that, whatever the objective facts of the situation and the eventual legal outcome, there is no way that the company can win. The two-year court battle is costing McDonald's many millions of dollars in legal fees and lost staff time, plus a great deal of negative publicity.

If McDonald's loses it will have to make a public apology to the defendants. If it wins it will gain nothing from the defendants, who are unemployed, have few assets and are defending themselves. If the McLibel Two are ordered not to distribute their leaflets again and persist in doing so they will be jailed, and just imagine what the mass media – and the public – would do with that.[17]

■ Alternative Lifestyles

In the previous chapter when we discussed consumer activism, we did so on the basis of the permanent organizations that groups of consumers have set up over the years to look after their interests. Many of these, such as the co-operative movement, the Consumers Association and Naderism, are still flourishing, though their form may sometimes have changed.

But what seems to have emerged from these organizations, starting in the 1970s, is a movement that is based on the decisions taken by an ever-growing number of individuals to make consumer behaviour an important element of a consciously different, *alternative* form of lifestyle.

Some diverse social, economic and political strands have been identified in this trend, which I think may well be the most important aspect of consumer behaviour for the near future. We will deal very briefly with three leading forms of this alternative lifestyle: *green consumerism, ethical investment* and the *exchange economy.*

□ *Green Consumerism*

The most prominent strand in the alternative lifestyle is probably that of green consumerism, a concern with the effect that products and the way they are produced have on the environment. This is especially true of the action of toxic chemicals on the air, land and water and on the food chain between producer and consumer. Research seems to indicate that half of all American consumers say they are willing to change their buying or consumption patterns to take account of their environmental concerns.[18]

However we have seen throughout this book that there is often a large gap between what people say they will do in a given situation and what they *actually* do. We have already seen in this chapter and the one before that economics can often override good intentions. Moreover there are limits to the average consumer's green behaviour. The more concerned American consumers might choose lead-free fuel for their cars, but how many of them would be willing to give up their cars? Or even use them less?

Yet as we have seen, producers are very concerned about consumers voting with their wallets and will try to accommodate them if the proposed change doesn't threaten profitability. Thus McDonald's has agreed to try out some 42 ideas, suggested by an environmental group, for cutting waste (for example reusing lids) and it has already agreed to use paper wrapping instead of plastic foam cartons.[19]

Of course the entrepreneurial spirit of capitalism will inevitably lead companies to coopt a trend and turn a smart buck whenever they can. Hence the marketing of new (and expensive jeans) that saved their proud owners the bother of ripping them and wearing them out. Thus General Motors, a heroic champion of the God-given right of all Americans to breath polluted air, tried to pass itself off as a champion of the environment on Earth Day 1990. It didn't fool many people though. As one commentator put it, 'Everyone wears green on St Patrick's Day too – but it doesn't make them Irish'.[20]

☐ *Ethical Investment*

This strand of the alternative lifestyle includes green consumerism in its concerns but goes beyond this to embrace both animal and human welfare. Its scope reaches as far as that of the McLibel Two, which we described above. By definition it is largely confined to middle-class consumers who have some spare funds to invest and want to invest them in companies whose activities they approve of. These vary somewhat but generally speaking they avoid companies involved in tobacco, alcohol, weapons, animal abuse, pollution and environmental degradation, and those that have poor industrial relations with their employees.

This is an important and rapidly growing global trend among individual investors that – in the more conservative financial centres such as the City of London – is not yet being reflected in the policies of the 10–15 fund managers who effectively control British investment. Thus while 57 per cent of investors in a recent study considered ethical issues important, only 3 per cent of fund managers and analysts did so.[21] However even the City of London is not totally immune to change, even if it does lead in the direction of greater social responsibility.

☐ *The Exchange Economy*

One consequence of the enormous upheaval in the world of work over the past 20 years is that many people have begun to question the links between full-time job, income and consumption. With millions of people thrown out of full-time employment and widespread insecurity among those still in it, alternative forms of economic exchange have found a receptive and rapidly growing following.

Another important set of orientations towards the world of work lies in what is called the *informal economy*. The formal economy represents the traditional industrial society model of wages paid and taxes collected; of goods and services exchanged for money. The informal economy is much less visible, but no less real for that. It consists of work activities that are not officially recorded in statistics of earnings and taxes. Housework would be included in the informal economy, as would painting one's own house instead of paying to have it done.

Some of the work done in the informal economy is paid for but undeclared to the tax authorities and therefore illegal. This is often known as the *black economy* and is largely confined to people who are also in full-time employment in the formal economy.[21] However there is also a *grey economy*.[23] Unlike the black economy, work in the grey economy is unpaid. It consists of work done in the household or the immediate community in which people live.

As well as all the household tasks that are mostly done by women, the grey economy includes performing the same tasks for other people outside the household – whether from love, friendship, duty or reciprocal agreement – plus anything else that people can do for themselves or others without pay. This latter kind of activity can range from looking after a friend's pet in return for the sorting out of a computer bug, to gardening and cooking for disabled relatives or washing the widows of elderly neighbours.

This kind of work activity is far from marginal. Indeed it has been estimated at 51 per cent of all the work done in both formal and informal economies combined.[24] Moreover work in this sector of the informal economy is probably growing fastest as people generally now spend less time working in the formal economy.

In Canada in 1982 the first attempt was made to organize the trading relationships of the grey economy into something more systematic by means of a Local Exchange Trading System, or LETS. Members of such a system form a network and trade their services and products with each other on the basis of a notional LETS currency, which cannot be converted into cash. So 10 LETS units, say, might get your lawn mowed or 50 might allow you to lease a computer. The LETS idea has since spread successfully to a number of other countries, especially the United States and the United Kingdom. Indeed in some places local traders are now willing to accept LETS units as part payment for their own goods and services.[25]

Gabriel and Lang have succinctly identified six ways in which the LETS idea successfully challenges conventional consumer behaviour:

- 'they focus on unbranded, unadvertised and unmediated goods and services ... they reaffirm the value of hand-made, home-made products...'
- 'they bring together the person as a producer and seller of goods and services with the person as buyer and consumer...'
- '...they enable individuals and groups whose lack of cash would exclude them both from the local economy and involvement in the community...'
- '...they bring together people of different social classes in relations of mutuality, which cross social boundaries and encourage accountability and responsibility...'
- '...they keep capital local...'

- '...they find a legitimate way of generating economic activity which avoids taxation and by-passes the legislative and other apparatuses of the state.'[26]

These new forms of economic exchange may be growing but they have not yet entered the consciousness of our society as a whole. That is, they are not yet seen as a threat to the vested interests that form the framework of our consumer behaviour. But if and when this happens you will be able to recognize it, as governments will start to rubbish these ideas and the corporate world will try to coopt them.

■ Further Reading

Adams, R., J. Carruthers and C. Fisher, *Shopping for a Better World: A Quick and Easy Guide to Socially Responsible Shopping* (London: Kogan Page, 1991). Like it says.

Barnet, R. and J. Cavanagh, *Global Dreams* (New York: Simon & Schuster, 1994). The birth and development of consumer identity and self-image in the light of marketing practices.

Cairncross, F., *Costing the Earth* (London: Business Books/The Economist Books, 1991). An optimistic view of how technological fixes can allow the present consumer society to continue.

Coote, A., *The Welfare of Citizens* (London: Rivers Oram, 1992). An attempt to combine the concepts of citizen and consumer.

Durning, A. T., *How Much is Enough?* (London: Earthscan, 1992). A pessimistic view of the likelihood of maintaining the present consumer society in the face of ecological pressures.

Elkington, J. and J. Hailes, *The Green Consumer Guide* (London: Gollancz, 1988). Comparison of products and companies on environmental criteria.

■ Questions for Discussion

1. Is there any evidence that producers are becoming more aware of the needs of consumers? How convincing do you find it?
2. What is meant by 'business ethics'? Why should businesses be concerned about them? To what extent are they concerned?
3. What is meant by 'deregulation'? What have its effects been on consumer protection?
4. What are 'own-brands'? How have consumers responded to them recently? What is the marketing significance of this?
5. How can the direct action of consumers influence the behaviour of large companies? What significance could this have for future relations between producers, consumers and marketers?

▌References

1 People as Consumers

1. Lutz, R., 'Positivism, rationalism, and pluralism in consumer research: paradigms in paradise', in T. Srull (ed.), *Advances in Consumer Research* 16 (Provo, UT: Association for Consumer Research, 1989).
2. See for example M.B. Holbrook and J. O'Shaughnessy, 'On the scientific status of consumer research and the need for an interpretive approach to studying consumption behavior', *Journal of Consumer Research*, vol. 15 (December 1988), pp. 398–402.
3. Holbrook, M. and E. Hirschman, 'The experiential aspects of consumption: Consumer fantasies, feelings, and fun', *Journal of Consumer Research*, vol. 9 no. 2 (1982), pp. 132–40.
4. Wilkie, W. L., *Consumer Behavior* (New York: John Wiley & Sons, 1994).
5. 'Getting Inside Their Heads', *American Demographics* (August 1989).
6. Smith, A., *On the Wealth of Nations* (Harmondsworth: Penguin, 1982).
7. Drucker, P. F., *Management* (London: Heinemann, 1974), p. 56, emphasis in original.
8. Ibid., p. 57, emphasis added.

2 Market Segmentation

1. Smith, W. R., 'Product differentiation and market segmentation as alternative marketing strategies', *Journal of Marketing*, vol. 21 (1956), pp. 3–8.
2. Serafin, R., 'How GM is shifting gears', *Advertising Age*, vol. 4 (January 1988).
3. Drucker, P. F., *Management* (London: Heinemann, 1974).
4. McKenna, R., Marketing in an age of diversity', *Harvard Business Review* (September-October 1988), pp. 88–95.
5. Larson, J., 'A segment of one', *American Demographics*, December 1991, pp. 16–17.
6. Applebaum, C., *Adweek's Marketing Week*, vol. 9 (March 1992), p. 10.
7. 'Marketing's new look', *Business Week*, 26 January, 1987, p. 64ff.
8. McCarthy, M. J., 'Marketers zero in on their customers', *The Wall Street Journal*, 18 March 1991, p. B1.
9. Barlak, B. and C. G. Schiffman, 'Cognitive age: A nonchronological age variable', in K. B. Monroe (ed.), *Advances in Consumer Research*, vol. 8 (Ann Arbor, MI: Association for Consumer Research, 1981), pp. 602–6.
10. Weiss, M. J., *The Clustering of America* (New York: Harper & Row, 1988).
11. Lohmkuhl, D., 'PRIZM-ACORN-style lifestyle research', *Media World*, April 1982.
12. Plummer, J. T., 'The concept and application of life style segmentation', *Journal of Marketing*, vol. 38 (January 1974), p. 34.
13. Mehrotra, S. and W. D. Wells, 'Psychographics and buyer behavior: Theory and recent empirical findings', in A. G. Woodside, J. N. Sheth and P. D. Bennett (eds), *Consumer and Industrial Buying Behavior* (New York: Elsevier/North-Holland, 1977).
14. Mehrotra and Wells, 'Psychographics and buyer behavior', op. cit., p. 53.

15. Lunn, T., S. Baldwin and J. Dickens, Monitoring consumer lifestyles', *Admap*, November 1982.
16. Mitchell, A., *Nine American Lifestyles: Who We Are And Where We Are Going* (New York: Macmillan, 1983).
17. Barker, S. M. and J. F. Trost, 'Cultivate the high-volume consumer', *Harvard Business Review*, March/April 1973, pp. 118–22.
18. Finkleman, B., 'Ads should reinforce current users, not necessarily convert nonusers of products', *Marketing News*, 15 January 1974, p. 1.
19. Charlton, P., 'A review of brand loyalty', *Journal of The Market Research Society*, vol. 15, (January 1973), p. 1.
20. Norris, E. E., 'Your surefire clue to ad success: Seek out the consumer's problem', *Advertising Age*, 17 March 1975, pp. 43–4.
21. Moffat, S., 'Japan's new personalized production', *Fortune*, 22 October 1990, pp. 132–5.

3 New Products and Innovations

1. Levitt, T., *The Marketing Imagination* (New York: Free Press, 1987).
2. Drucker, P., *Management* (London: Heinemann, 1974), p. 61.
3. Kanter, R. M., *The Change Masters: Innovation and Entrepreneurship in the American Corporation* (New York: Free Press, 1987).
4. Levitt, T., *The Marketing Imagination*, op. cit.
5. Peters, T., *Thriving on Chaos* (London: Pan, 1989).
6. Eklund, C. S., 'Campbell Soup's recipe for growth: offering something for every palate', *Business Week*, vol. 14 (December 1984), pp. 66–7.
7. Harvey-Jones, J., *Getting it Together* (Oxford: Heinemann, 1991).
8. Statt, D. A., *Psychology and the World of Work* (London: Macmillan, 1994), especially Chapters 2 and 6.
9. Schon, D. A., 'Champions for radical new innovations', *Harvard Business Review*, March/April 1963.
10. Peters, *Thriving on Chaos*, op. cit., p. 248.
11. Pascale, R., 'Perspective on strategy: The real story behind Honda's success', in G. Carroll, and D. Vogel (eds), *Strategy and Organization* (Boston: Pitman Publishing 1984).
12. Schon, 'Champions', op. cit.
13. Herr, P. M., F. R. Kardes and J. Kim 'Effects of Word-of-Mouth and Product-Attribute Information on Persuasion: An Accessibility-Diagnosticity perspective', *Journal of Consumer Research*, vol. 17, (1991), pp. 454–62.
14. Chan, K. K. and S. Misra, 'Characteristics of the opinion leader: A new dimension' *Journal of Advertising*, vol. 19, (3 November 1990), pp. 53–60.
15. King, C. W. and J. O. Summers 'Overlap of opinion leadership across consumer product categories', *Journal of Marketing Research*, vol. 7 (February 1970), pp. 43–50.
16. Rogers, E. M. *Diffusion of Innovations*, 3rd edn (New York: Free Press, 1983), p. 5.
17. Robertson, T. S., 'The process of innovation and the diffusion of innovation', *Journal of Marketing*, vol. 31 (January 1967), pp. 14–19.
18. McCarroll, T., 'What New Age?', *Time*, 12 August 1991, pp. 44–5.
19. Rogers, *Diffusion of Innovations*, op. cit.
20. Ohmae, K., 'Managing in a borderless world', *Harvard Business Review*, May–June, 1989, pp. 152–61.
21. Rogers, *Diffusion of Innovations*, op. cit.

4   Perception

1. Abrams, B. and D. Garino, 'Package design gains stature as visual competition grows', *The Wall Street Journal*, 6 August 1981, p. 25.
2. Smith, R. C. and R. Curnow, 'Arousal hypotheses and the effects of music on purchasing behavior', *Journal of Applied Psychology*, vol. 50 (June 1966), pp. 255–6.
3. Milliman, R. E., 'Using background music to affect the behavior of supermarket shoppers', *Journal of Marketing*, vol. 46, no. 3 (Summer 1982), pp. 86–91.
4. Miller, C., 'The right song in the air can boost retail sales', *Marketing News*, vol. 25 (4 February 1991), p. 2.
5. Laird, D. A., 'How the consumer estimates quality by subconscious sensory impressions – with special reference to the role of smell', *Journal of Applied Psychology*, vol. 16 (June 1932), pp. 241–6.
6. *The Wall Street Journal*, 'Hidden costs', 15 February 1977, p. 1.
7. Zajonc, R. B., 'The attitudinal effects of mere exposure', *Journal of Personality and Social Psychology, Monograph Supplement*, vol. 9 (1968), pp. 1–27.
8. Aronson, E., The Social Animal, 6th edn (New York: W. H. Freeman & Co, 1992), p. 68.
9. Allport, G. W. and L. Postman, 'The basic psychology of rumor', in T. Newcomb and E. Hartley (eds), *Readings in Social Psychology* (New York: Holt, Rinehart & Winston, 1947).
10. Allison, R. I. and K. P. Uhl, 'Influence of beer brand identification on taste perception', *Journal of Marketing Research*, vol. 1 (August 1964), pp. 36–9.
11. Weir, W., 'Another look at subliminal facts', *Advertising Age*, 15 October 1984.
12. Zajonc, R. B. and H. Markus, 'Affective and cognitive factors in preferences', *Journal of Consumer Research*, vol. 9 (September 1982), pp. 123–31.
13. Moore, T. E., 'Subliminal advertising: What you see is what you get', *Journal of Marketing*, vol. 46 (Spring 1982), pp. 38–47.
14. Lazer, W. and R. G. Wyckham, 'Perceptual segmentation of department store marketing', *Journal of Retailing*, vol. 45 (Summer 1969), pp. 3–14.
15. Koten, J., 'Car makers use 'image' map as tool to position products', *The Wall Street Jorunal*, 22 March 1984.
16. Cox, D. F. (ed.), *Risk Taking and Information Handling in Consumer Behavior* (Boston: Graduate Business School, Harvard University, 1967).
17. Stone, R. N. and F. W. Winter, 'Risk: Is it still uncertainty times consequences?' in R. W. Belk *et al.* (eds), *1987 AMA Winter Educators' Conference Proceedings* (Chicago: American Marketing Association, 1987).
18. Farley, F., 'The big T in personality', *Psychology Today*, vol. 20 (May 1986), pp. 44ff.
19. Roselius, T., 'Consumer rankings of risk reduction methods', *Journal of Marketing*, vol. 35 (January 1971), pp. 56–61.

5   Personality

1. For a full account of these and other theories see C. S. Hall and G. Lindzey, *Theories of Personality*, 3rd edn (New York: Wiley, 1978) or L. Hjelle and D.Ziegler, *Personality Theories: Basic Assumptions, Research and Applications* (New York: McGraw-Hill, 1987).
2. Statt, D. A., *The Concise Dictionary of Psychology* (London and New York: Routledge, 1990).
3. Kline, P., *Personality: Measurement and Theory* (London: Hutchinson, 1983).
4. Kline, P., *Fact and Fiction in Freudian Theory*, 2nd edn (London: Methuen, 1981).
5. Dichter, E., *Handbook of Consumer Motivation* (New York: McGraw-Hill, 1964).
6. Hathaway, S. R. and J. C. McKinley, 'A multiphasic personality schedule (Minnesota): 1. Construction of the Schedules', *Journal of Psychology*, vol. 10 (1940) pp. 249–54.

7. Murray, H. A., *Explorations in Personality* (New York: Oxford University Press, 1938).
8. Rorschach, H., *Psychodiagnosis: A Diagnostic Test Based on Perception* (New York: Grune & Stratton, 1942).
9. Exner, J. E., *The Rorschach: A Comprehensive System* (New York: Wiley, 1974).
10. Cohen, J. B., 'An interpersonal orientation to the study of consumer behaviour', *Journal of Marketing Research*, vol. 4 (August 1967), pp. 270–8.
11. Slama, M., T. Williams and A. Taschian, 'Compliant, aggressive and detached types differ in generalized purchasing involvement', in M. J. Houston (ed.), *Advances in Consumer Research* vol. 15 (Provo, UT: Association for Consumer Research, 1988), pp. 158–62.
12. Rogers, C. R., 'In retrospect: Forty-six years', *American Psychologist*, vol. 29 (1974), pp. 115–23.
13. See for example W. J. Livesley and D. B. Bromley, *Person Perception in Childhood and Adolescence* (London and New York: Wiley, 1973); J. Suls (ed.), *Psychological Perspectives On The Self* (Hilldsdale, N J: Lawrence Erlbaum Associates, 1982).
14. Guthrie, E. R., *The Psychology of Human Conflict* (New York: Harper & Row, 1938).
15. Grubb, E. L. and G. Hupp, 'Perception of self, generalized stereotypes, and brand selection', *Journal of Marketing Research*, vol. 5 (February 1968), pp. 58–63.
16. Sirgy, M. J., 'Self-concept in consumer behaviour: A critical review', *Journal of Consumer Research*, vol. 9 (December, 1992), pp. 287–300.
17. See for example R. L. Gorsuch, *Factor Analysis*, 2nd edn (Hillsdale, NJ: Lawrence Erlbaum Associates, 1983), or D. Child, *The Essentials of Factor Analysis* (London: Cassell, 1990).
18. Cattell, R. B., H. W. Eber and M. M. Tatsuoka, *Handbook of the Cattell 16 Personality Factor Questionnaire* (Champaign, III: Institute of Personality and Ability Testing, 1970).
19. Rust, J., P. Sinclair and S. Barrow, 'The RPQ: validation of the five-factor model in the workplace', in *Proceedings of the Occupational Psychology Conference* (Leicester: British Psychological Society, 1992).
20. Kassarjian, H. H. and M. J. Sheffet, 'Personality and consumer behavior: An update', in H. H. Kassarjian and T. S. Robertson (eds), *Perspectives in Consumer Behavior*, 4th edn (Englewood Cliffs, NJ: Prentice-Hall, 1991), pp. 281–303.
21. Plummer, J. T., 'How personality makes a difference', *Journal of Advertising Research*, vol. 24 (January 1985), pp. 27–31; K. Sentis and H. Markus, 'brand personality and self', in J. Olson and K. Sentis (eds), *Advertising and Consumer Psychology* (New York: Praeger, 1986), pp. 132–48.
22. Schindler, P. S., 'Color and contrast in magazine advertising', *Psychology and Marketing*, vol. 3 (1986), pp. 69–78.

6 Learning

1. Watson, J. B., 'Psychology as a behaviorist views it', *Psychological Review*, vol. xx (1913), pp. 158–77.
2. Pavlov, I., *Conditioned Reflexes: An Investigation of the Physiological Activity of the Cerebral Cortex* (London: Oxford University Press, 1927).
3. Kreshel, P. J., 'John B. Watson at J. Walter Thompson: The legitimization of "science" in advertising', *Journal of Advertising*, vol. 19, no. 2 (1990), pp. 49–59.
4. Gorn, G. J., 'The effects of music in advertising on choice behavior: A classical conditioning approach', *Journal of Marketing*, vol. 46, no. 1 (Winter 1982), pp. 94–101.
5. Kanner, B., 'Growing pains and gains: Brand names branch out', *New York*, 13 March 1989, pp. 22–4.
6. Skinner, B. F., *The Behavior of Organisms* (New York: Appleton-Century-Croft, 1938).

7. Carey, J. R., S. H. Clicque, B. A. Leighton and F. Milton., 'A test of positive reinforcement of customers', *Journal of Marketing*, vol. 40, no. 4 (October 1976), pp. 98–100.
8. Kassarjian, H. H., 'Presidential address, 1977: Anthropomorphism and parsimony', in H. H. Hunt (ed.), *Advances in Consumer Research*, vol. 5 (Ann Arbor, MI: Association for Consumer Research, 1978).
9. Kohler, W., *The Mentality of Apes* (New York: Harvourt Brace Jovanovich, 1925).
10. Marder, E. and M. David, 'Recognition of ad elements: recall or projection?' *Journal of Advertising Research*, vol. 1 (December 1961), pp. 23–5.
11. Bettman, J. R., *An Information Processing Theory of Consumer Choice* (Reading, Mass.: Addison-Wesley, 1979).
12. Baddeley, A. D., *Working Memory* (Oxford: Oxford University Press, 1986).
13. Meyers-Levy, J. and D. Maheswaran, 'Exploring differences in males' and females' processing strategies', *Journal of Consumer Research* vol. 18 (June 1991), pp. 63–70.
14. Baddeley, *Working Memory*, op. cit.
15. See for example J. R. Anderson (ed.), *Cognitive Skills and Their Acquisition* (Hillsdale, NJ: Lawrence Erlbaum Associates, 1981); G. H. Bower and E. R. Hilgard, *Theories of Learning*, 5th edn. (Englewood Cliffs, NJ: Prentice-Hall, 1981).
16. See for example G. E. Belch, 'The effects of television commercial repetition on cognitive response and message acceptance', *Journal of Consumer Research*, vol. 9 (June 1982), pp. 56–65; R. Batra and M. Ray, 'Situational effects of advertising: The moderating influence of motivation, ability and opportunity to respond', *Journal of Consumer Research*, vol. 12 (March 1986), pp. 432–45.
17. Burke, R. R. and T. K. Srull., 'Competitive interference and consumer memory for advertising', *Journal of Consumer Research*, vol. 15 (June 1988), pp. 55–68.
18. Biron, J. and S. J. McKelvie, 'Effects of interactive and non-interactive imagery on recall of advertisments', *Perceptual and Motor Skills*, vol. 59 (May 1984), pp. 799–805.
19. Brown, P., J. M. Keenan and and G. R. Potts, 'The self-reference effect with imagery encoding', *Journal of Personality and Social Psychology*, vol. 51 (November 1986), pp. 897–906.
20. Burnkrant, R. and H. R. Unnava, 'Self-referencing: A strategy for increasing processing of message content', *Personality and Social Psychology Bulletin*, vol. 15 (December 1989), pp. 628–38.
21. Miller, G. A., 'The magical number seven, plus or minus two: Some limits on our capacity for processing information', *Psychological Review*, vol. 63 (1956), pp. 81–97.
22. Nord, W. R. and J. P. Peter, 'A behavior modification perspective on marketing', *Journal of Marketing*, vol. 44, no. 2 (Spring 1980), pp. 36–47.

7   Motivation

1. Reber, A ., *Dictionary of Psychology* (London: Penguin, 1995).
2. Statt, D. A., *The Concise Dictionary of Psychology* (London and New York: Routledge, 1990).
3. Maslow, A. H., 'A theory of motivation', *Psychological Review*, vol. 50 (1943), pp. 370–96.
4. Maslow, A. H., *Motivation and Personality*, 2nd edn (New York: Harper & Row, 1970).
5. Maslow, *Motivation and Personality*, op. cit.
6. Schrocer, R., 'Maslow's hierachy of needs as a framework for identifying emotional triggers', *Marketing Review*, vol. 46, no. 5 (February 1991), pp. 26–8.
7. Tauber, E. M., 'Why do people shop?', *Journal of Marketing*, vol. 36 (October 1972), pp. 46–59.
8. Lewin, K., *A Dynamic Theory of Personality* (New York: McGraw-Hill, 1935).

9.   'Recalls: Why So Many Are Flops', *Changing Times*, October 1980, p. 29 et seq.
10. Krugman, H., 'The impact of television advertising: Learning without involvement', *Public Opinion Quarterly*, vol. 29 (Fall 1965), pp. 349–56.
11. Richins, M. L. and P. H. Bloch, 'After the new wears off: The temporal context of product involvement', *Journal of Consumer Research*, vol. 13 (September 1986), pp. 280–5.
12. Laurent, G. and J. N. Kapferer, 'Measuring consumer involvement profiles', *Journal of Marketing Research*, vol. 22 (February 1985), pp. 41–53.
13. Ibid.
14. Belk, R. W., 'Effects of gift-giving involvement on gift selection strategies', in A. Mitchell (ed.), *Advances in Consumer Research*, vol. 9 (Ann Arbor, MI: Association for Consumer Research, 1981), pp. 408–11.
15. Zaichkowsky, J. L., 'Measuring the involvement contract', *Journal of Consumer Research*, vol. 12 (December 1985), pp. 341–52.
16. Andrews, J. C., 'Motivation, ability and opportunity in process information: Conceptual and experimental manipulation issues', in M. J. Houston (ed.), *Advances in Consumer Research*, vol. 15 (Provo, Utah: Association of Consumer Research, 1988), pp. 219–25.
17. Wright, P., 'Analyzing media effects on advertising response', *Public Opinion Quarterly*, vol. 38 (Summer 1974), pp. 192–205.
18. Brisoux, J. E. and E. J. Cheron, 'Brand categorization and product involvement', in M. Goldberg, G. Gorn and R. Pollay (eds), *Advances in Consumer Research*, vol. 17 (Ann Arbor, MI: Association for Consumer Research, 1990), pp 101–9.
19. Laurent and Kapferer, 'Measuring consumer involvement', op.cit.
20. Murray, H. A., *Explorations in Personality* (New York: Oxford University Press, 1938).
21. McClelland, D. C., *The Achieving Society* (New York: Van Nostrand, 1961).
22. McClelland, D. C., and R. E. Boyatzis, 'Leadership motive patterns and long-term success in management', *Journal of Applied Psychology*, vol. 67 (1982), pp. 737–43.
23. Dichter, E., *The Strategy of Desire* (New York: Doubleday, 1960).
24. Dichter, E., *Handbook of Consumer Motivation* (New York: McGraw-Hill, 1964).
25. Piirto, E., 'Measuring minds in the 1990s', *American Demographics* (December 1990), pp. 31–5.
26. Alsop, R., 'Advertisers put consumers on the couch', *The Wall Street Journal*, 13 May 1988, pp. 17–21.
27. Packard, V., *The Hidden Persuaders* (New York: Pocket Books, 1957).
28. Dichter, *Handbook*, op. cit.
29. Alsop, R., 'Agencies scrutinize their advertisements for psychological symbolism', *The Wall Street Journal*, 11 June 1987, p. 25.
30. Dichter, *Handbook*, op. cit.

8   Family Influences

1.   Attributed to Margaret Thatcher.
2.   Bennett, A., *Writing Home* (London: Faber and Faber, 1994).
3.   Belk, R., 'A child's Christmas in America: Santa Claus as deity, consumption as religion', *Journal of American Culture*, vol. 10 (Spring 1987), pp. 87–100.
4.   Danziger, K., *Socialization* (Baltimore, MD: Penguin, 1973).
5.   Statt, D. A., 'National identify in United States and Canadian children', in B. Massialas (ed.), *Political Youth, Traditional Schools* (Englewood Cliffs, NJ: Prentice-Hall, 1972).

6.   Grossbart, S., L. Carlson and A. Walsh, 'Consumer socialization and frequency of shopping with children', *Journal of Academy of Marketing Science*, vol. 19 (Summer 1991) pp. 155–63.

7.   Sorce, P., L. Loomis and P. R. Tyler, 'Intergenerational influence on consumer decision making', in T. K. Srull (ed.), *Advances in Consumer Research*, vol. 16 (Provo, UT: Association for Consumer Research, 1989).

8.   Schlossberg, H., 'Kids teach parents how to change their buying habits', *Marketing News* (2 March 1992), p. 8.

9.   Sorce *et al.*, 'Intergenerational influences', op. cit.

10.   Davis, H. L., 'Decision making within the household', *Journal of Consumer Research*, vol. 1 (March 1976), pp. 241–60.

11   Kenkel, W. F., 'Husband-wife interaction in decision making and decision choices', *The Journal of Social Psychology*, vol. 54 (1961), p. 260.

12.   Ferber, R. and L. C. Lee, 'Husband-wife influence in family purchasing behaviour', *Journal of Consumer Research*, vol. 1 (June 1974), pp. 43–50.

13.   Davis, H. L. and B. P. Rigaux, 'Perception of marital roles in decision processes', *Journal of Consumer Research*, vol. 1 (June 1974), pp. 51–62; M. Putnam and W. R. Davidson, *Family Purchasing Behaviour: II Family Roles by Product Category* (Columbus, Ohio: Management Horizons Inc., a Division of Price Waterhouse, 1987).

14.   Putnam and Davidson, ibid.

15.   See for example W. J. Qualls, 'Toward understanding the dynamics of household decision conflict behaviour', in M. Houston (ed.), *Advances in Consumer Research*, vol. 15 (Provo, Utah: Association for Consumer Research, 1988); M. C. Nelson, 'The resolution of conflict in joint purchase decisions by husbands and wives: A review and empirical test', *Advances in Consumer Research*, ibid.

16.   Park, C. W., 'Joint decisions in home purchasing: A muddling-through process', *Journal of Consumer Research*, vol. 9 (September 1982), pp. 151–62.

17.   Kim, C. and J. Lee, 'Sex role attitudes of spouses and task sharing behavior' in T. K. Srull (ed.), *Advances in Consumer Research*, vol. 16, (Provo, Utah: Association for Consumer Research, 1989), pp. 671–9; A. Assar and G. S. Bobinski, 'Financial decision making of baby boomer couples', in H. Holman and M. R. Solomon (eds), *Advances in Consumer Research*, vol. 18 (Provo, Utah: Association for Consumer Research, 1991), pp. 657–65.

18.   Cockburn, C., *Brothers: Male Dominance and Technological Change* (London: Pluto Press, 1991).

19.   Ferri, E. (ed.), *Life at 33: The Fifth Follow-up of the National Child Development Study* (London: National Children's Bureau and the Economic and Social Research Council, 1993).

20.   Ferree, M. M., 'The struggles of superwoman', in C. Bose, K. Feldberg and N. Sokoloff (eds), *Hidden Aspects of Women's Work* (New York: Praeger, 1987).

21.   Wagner, J. and S. Hanna, 'The effectiveness of family life cycle variables in consumer expenditure research', *Journal of Consumer Research*, vol. 6 (June 1983), pp. 12–22.

22.   Wells, W. D. and G. Gubar, 'The life cycle concept', *Journal of Marketing Research*, vol. 2 (November 1966), pp. 355–63.

23.   Dupree, S., 'A snapshot of younger life stage group purchase', *Brandweek* (9 November 1992), p. 28.

24.   Huang, N. S., 'No more toasters please', *Smart Money*, (April 1993), pp. 133–5.

25.   Dupree, 'A snapshot', op. cit.

26.   Fisher, C., 'It's all in the family: Empty nesters, kids moving back home', *Advertising Age*, vol. 3 no. 56 (April 1992), p. 27.

27. Douthitt, R. A. and J. M. Fedyk, 'Family composition, parental time and market goods: Life cycle trade-offs', *The Journal of Consumer Affairs*, vol. 24 (Summer 1990), pp. 110–33.
28. US Bureau of the Census, *Statistical Abstract of the United States*, 112th edn (Washington DC, 1992).
29. Stern, B. B., S. J. Gould and B. Barak, 'Baby boom singles: the social seekers', *Journal of Consumer Marketing*, vol. 4 (Fall 1987), pp. 5–22.

9 Social and Developmental Influences

1. Statt, D. A., *The Concise Dictionary of Psychology* (London and New York: Routledge, 1990).
2. Ibid.
3. Piaget, J., *The Construction of Reality in the Child* (New York: Basic Books, 1954).
4. Danziger, K., 'Children's earliest conceptions of economic relationships', *Journal of Social Psychology*, vol. 47, (1958), pp. 231–40.
5. Lewis, A., P. Webley and A. Furnham, *The New Economic Mind* (Hemel Hempstead: Harvester Wheatsheaf, 1995).
6. Leiser, D., 'Children's conceptions and economics: the constitution of a cognitive domain', *Journal of Economic Psychology*, vol. 4 (1983), pp. 297–317.
7. Lewis *et al*., *New Economic Mind*, op. cit.
8. Ibid.
9. Furnham, A. and P. Thomas, 'Pocket-money: a study of economic education', *British Journal of Development Psychology*, vol. 2 (1984), pp. 205–12.
10. Lewis *et al*., *New Economic Mind*, op. cit.
11. Abramovitch, R., J. L. Freedman and P. Pliner, 'Children and money: getting an allowance, credit versus cash, and knowledge of pricing', *Journal of Economic Psychology*, vol. 12 (1991), pp. 27–46.
12. Newson, J. and E. Newson, *Seven Year Olds in the Home Environment* (London: Allen & Unwin, 1976).
13. Webley, R. A. and S. E. G. Lea, 'Towards a more realistic psychology of economic socialization', *Journal of Economic Psychology*, vol. 14 (1993), pp. 461–72.
14. Kourilsky, M., 'The kinder-economy: a case of kindergarten pupils' acquisition of economic concepts', *The Elementary School Journal*, vol. 77 (1977), pp. 182–91.
15. Jahoda, G., 'European "lag" in the development of an economic concept: A study in Zimbabwe', *British Journal of Developmental Psychology*, vol. 1 (1983), pp. 110–120.
16. Ng, S., 'Children's ideas about the bank and shop profit: developmental stages and the influences of cognitive contracts and conflict', *Journal of Economic Psychology*, vol. 4 (1983), pp. 209–21.
17. Wong, M., 'Children's acquisition of economic knowledge: Understanding banking in Hong Kong and the USA', in J. Valsiner (ed.), *Child Development in Cultural Context* (Norwood NJ: Ablex, 1989).
18. Macklin, M. C., 'Preschoolers' understanding of the informational function of television advertising', *Journal of Consumer Research*, vol. 14 (September 1987), pp. 229–39.
19. Gorn, G. J. and M. E. Goldberg, 'Behavioral evidence of the effects of televised food messages on children', *Journal of Consumer Research*, vol. 9 no. 2 (1982), pp. 200–5.
20. Ward, S., 'Researchers look at the "Kid Vid" rule: Overview of session', *Advances in Consumer Research*, vol. 6 (1979), pp. 7–8.
21. Roedder, D. L., 'Age differences in children's responses to television advertising: An

information-processing approach', *Journal of Consumer Research*, vol.8 (September 1981), pp. 144–53.

22. Belk, R., R. Mayer and A. Driscoll, 'Children's recognition of consumption symbolism in children's products', *Journal of Consumer Research*, vol. 11 (March 1984), pp. 386–97.

23. Gorn, G. J. and R. Florsheim, 'The effects of commercials for adult products on children', *Journal of Consumer Research*, vol. 11 (March 1985), pp. 386–97.

10   The Influence of Small Groups

1. Cockburn, C., 'The gendering of jobs: workplace relations and the reproduction of sex segregation', in S. Walby (ed.), *Gender Segregation At Work* (Milton Keynes and Philadelphia: Open University Press, 1988).

2. Maccoby, E. C. and C. N. Jacklin, 'Sex differences in aggression: A rejoinder and reprise', *Child Development*, vol. 51 (1980), pp. 964–80.

3. Huston, A. C., 'Sex-typing', in P. H. Mussen (ed.), *Handbook of Child Development*, 4th edn. (New York: Wiley, 1983).

4. Bossard, J. H. S., 'Residential propinquity as a factor in mate selection', *American Journal of Sociology*, vol. 38 (1932), pp. 219–24.

5. Festinger, L., S. Schachter and K. Back, *Social Pressures in Informal Groups* (New York: Harper & Bros, 1950).

6. Sundstrom, E., *Work Places* (Cambridge: Cambridge University Press, 1986).

7. Reingen, P. H. and J. B. Kennan, 'Analysis of referral networks in marketing: Methods and illustration', *Journal of Marketing Research*, vol. 23 (November 1986), pp. 370–8; J. J. Brown and P. H. Reingen, 'Social ties and word-of-mouth referral behavior', *Journal of Consumer Research*, vol. 14, (December 1987), pp. 350–62.

8. Voss, P. 'Status shifts to peer influence', *Advertising Age* (17 May 1984) M-10.

9. If you want to follow this up see my book *Psychology and the World of Work*, Chapter 15 (London and New York: Macmillan and New York University Press, 1994).

10. Feick, L. F. and L. L. Price., 'The market maven: A diffuser of marketplace information', *Journal of Marketing*, vol. 51 (January 1987), pp. 85–8.

11. Price, L. L. and L. F. Feick, 'The role of interpersonal sources and external search: An informational perspective', in T C Kinnear (ed.), *Advances in Consumer Research*, vol. 11 (Provo, Utah: Association for Consumer Research, 1984).

12. Asch, S. E., 'Studies of independence and conformity: A minority of one against a unanimous majority', *Psychological Monographs*, vol. 70, no.9 (1956) whole issue, p. 416.

13. Crutchfield, R. S., 'Conformity and character', *American Psychologist*, vol. 10 (1955), pp. 191–8.

14. Milgram, S., 'Behavioral study of obedience', *Journal of Applied Psychology*, vol. 67 (1963), pp. 371–8; S. Milgram, *Obedience to Authority* (New York and London: Harper & Row/Tavistock, 1974).

15. French, J. R. P. and B. H. Raven, 'The bases of social power', in D. Cartwright and A. Zander (eds), *Group Dynamics*, 3rd edn (New York: Harper & Row, 1968).

16. See for example S. B. MacKenzie and J. L. Zaichkowsky, 'An analysis of alcohol advertising using French and Raven's theory of social influence', in K. B. Monroe (ed.), *Advances in Consumer Research*, vol. 8 (Ann Arbor, MI: Association for Consumer Research, 1981), pp. 708–12.

17. Asch, 'Studies', op. cit.

18. Crutchfield, 'Conformity', op. cit.

19. Venkatesan, M., 'Experimental study of consumer behavior, conformity and independence', *Journal of Marketing Research*, vol. 3 (November 1966). pp. 384–7.

20. Midgley, D. F., G. R. Dowling and P. D. Morrison, 'Consumer types, social influence, information search and choice', in T. K. Srull (ed.), *Advances in Consumer Research*, vol. 16, (Provo, Utah: Association for Consumer Research, 1989), pp. 137–43.
21. Milgram, 'Behavioral study', op. cit.
22. Haire. M., 'Projective techniques in marketing research', *Journal of Marketing*, vol. 14 (April 1950), pp. 649–50.
23. Webster, F. E. and F. Von Pechmann, 'A replication of the "Shopping List" study', *Journal of Marketing*, vol. 34 (April 1970), pp. 61–3.
24. Bearden, W. O. and M. J. Etzel, 'Reference group influence on product and brand purchase decisions', *Journal of Consumer Research*, vol. 9 (September 1982), pp. 183–94.
25. Park, C. W. and V. P. Lessig, 'Students and Housewives: Differences in susceptibility to reference group influence', *Journal of Consumer Research*, vol. 4 (September 1977), pp. 102–110.
26. Reingen and Kennan, 'Analysis', op. cit.; Brown and Reingen, 'Social ties', op. cit.

11 The Influence of Social Class

1. Weber, M., 'Class, status, party', in H. Gerth and C. W. Mills (eds), *From Max Weber: Essays in Sociology* (New York: Oxford University Press, 1946)
2. Robinson, R. V., 'Explaining perceptions of class and racial inequality in England and the United States of America', *The British Journal of Sociology*, vol. 34 (1983), pp. 344–63.
3. Veblen, T., *The Theory of the Leisure Class* (New York: Macmillan, 1899).
4. Garfein, R. T., 'Cross-cultural perspectives on the dynamics of prestige', *Journal of Services Marketing*, vol. 3 (Summer 1989), pp. 18–19.
5. Coleman, R. P., 'The continuing significance of social class to marketing', *Journal of Consumer Research*, vol. 10 (December 1983), pp. 265–80.
6. See for example C. Power, K. Fogelman and A. J. Fox, 'Health and social mobility during the early years of life', *Quarterly Journal of Social Affairs*, vol. 2, no. 4 (1986), pp. 397–413.
7. See for example J. Arnold, I. T. Robertson and C. L. Cooper, *Work Psychology*, (London: Pitman, 1991), p. 287.
8. Vanneman, R. and L. W. Cannon, *The American Perception of Class* (Philadelphia: Temple University Press, 1987).
9. See for example *Statistical Abstract of the United States*, 112th edn (Washington, DC: US Bureau of the Census, 1992), p. 446.
10. See for example C. B. Nam and M. G. Powers, *The Socio-economic Approach to Status Measurement* (Houston: Cap and Gown Press, 1983); *The Gallup Poll*, July 1993.
11. *Methodology and Scores of Socio-economic Status* Working Paper no. 15 (Washington DC: US Bureau of the Census, 1963).
12. Coleman, 'The continuing significance', op. cit.
13. Warner, W. L., M. Meeker and K. Eels, *Social Class in America* (New York: Harper & Row, 1960).
14. Stern, B. B., 'Literary criticism and consumer research: Overview and illustrative analysis', *Journal of Consumer Research*, vol. 16 (December 1989), pp. 322–34.
15. Sonfield, M. C., 'Marketing to the carriage trade', *Harvard Business Review*, vol. 3 (May-June 1990), pp. 112–17.
16. Hirschman, E. C., 'Consumption styles of the rich and famous: The semiology of Saul Steinberg and Malcolm Forbes', in M. Goldberg, G. Gorn and R. Pollay (eds), *Advances in Consumer Research*, vol. 17 (1990), pp. 850–55.

17. Rotzoll, K. B., 'The effect of social stratification on market behavior', *Journal of Advertising Research*, vol. 7 (1967), pp. 22–7.
18. Andreasen, A. R., 'Consumer behavior research and social policy', in T. Robertson and H. Kassarjian (eds), *Handbook of Consumer Behavior*, (Englewood Cliffs, NJ: Prentice-Hall, 1991), pp. 459–506.
19. See for example D. Monk, 'Social grading on the National Readership Survey', Research Services Ltd (London: Joint Industry Committee for National Readership Surveys, 1970).
20. 'NRS deficit changes: housewives or shoppers?', *Market Research Society Newsletter*, July 1992.
21. Gilbert, D. and J. A. Kahl, *The American Class Structure: A New Synthesis* 3rd edn (Homewood, Ill: The Dorsey Press, 1987).
22. Duncan, G. J. (ed.), *Years of Poverty, Years of Plenty* (Ann Arbor, MI: Institute for Social Research, 1984).
23. Larson, J., 'Reaching downscale markets', *American Demographics*, November 1991, pp. 38–41.
24. Dickson, J. P. and D. L. MacLachlan, 'Social distance and shopping behavior', *Journal of the Academy of Marketing Science*, vol 18 (Spring 1990), pp. 153–61.
25. Thomas, E. G., S. R. Rao and R. G. Javalgi, 'Affluent and nonaffluent consumers' needs: Attitudes and information-seeking behavior in the financial services market place', *Journal of Services Marketing*, vol. 4 (Fall 1990), pp. 41–54.

12 Cultral Influences

1. Statt, D. A., *The Concise Dictionary of Management* (London and New York: Routledge, 1991).
2. Linton, R., *The Cultural Background of Personality* (Englewood Cliffs, NJ: Prentice-Hall, 1945).
3. Shouby, E., 'The influence of the Arabic language on the psychology of the Arabs', *Middle East Journal*, vol. 5 (1951), pp. 284–302.
4. Ricks, D. A., *Big Business Blunders: Mistakes in Multinational Marketing* (Homewood, Ill: Dow Jones-Irwin, 1983).
5. Lynch, M., 'When slogans go wrong', *American Demographics*, vol. 14 (February 1992), p. 14.
6. See for example E. T. Hall and M. R. Hall *Hidden Differences: Doing Business with the Japanese* (Garden City, NY: Anchor Press/Doubleday, 1985).
7. Blackwell, R. D., W. W. Talarzyk and J. F. Engel, 'Miele', in *Contemporary Cases in Consumer Behavior* (Hillsdale, Ill: Dryden, 1990), pp. 473–80.
8. Belk, R. W. and R. W. Pollay, 'Images of ourselves: The good life in twentieth century advertising', *Journal of Consumer Research*, vol. 11 (March 1985), pp. 887–97.
9. Belk, R. W., 'Materialism: Trait aspects of living in the material world', *Journal of Consumer Research*, vol. 12 (December 1985), pp. 265–80.
10. Statt, D. A., *Psychology and the World of Work* (London: Macmillan; New York: New York University Press, 1994), p. 69.
11. Ibid.
12. McClelland, D. C., *The Achieving Society* (New York: Van Nostrand, 1961).
13. Ward, A., 'Americans step into a new fitness market', *Advertising Age*, vol. 3 December 1990, p. 33.
14. Statt, D. A., 'National identity in United States and Canadian children', in B. Massialas (ed.), *Political Youth, Traditional Schools* (Englewood Cliffs, NJ: Prentice-Hall, 1972).

15. Lipset, S. M., *Continental Divide: The Values and Institutions of the United States and Canada* (New York: Routledge, 1990).
16. Wallendorf, M. and M. D. Reilly, 'Ethnic migration, assimilation and consumption', *Journal of Consumer Research*, vol. 10 (1983).
17. Alvarez, M., 'Sabor Hispano - the flavor of the Hispanic market', *Marketing Review*, January 1990, pp. 25–6.
18. Updegrave, W. L., 'Race and Money', *Money*, December 1989, p. 154.
19. Elizabeth Hirschman's work seems to be about it: E. C. Hirschman, 'Ethnic variation in leisure activities and motives', in B J. Walker *et al.* (eds), *An Assessment of Marketing Thought and Practice* (Chicago: American Marketing Association, 1982); and E. C. Hirschman, 'American Jewish ethnicity: its relationship to some selected aspects of consumer behavior', *Journal of Marketing*, vol. 45 (Summer 1981), pp. 102–10.
20. See especially H. H. Kassarjian, 'Content analysis in consumer research'', *Journal of Consumer Research*, June 1977, pp. 8–18; J. Naisbitt, *Megatrends* (New York: Warner Books, 1982).
21. Price, B. A., 'What the baby boom believes', *American Demographics*, May 1984, pp. 30–3.
22. *The Public Pulse* (New York: The Roper Organization, 1991).
23. Ibid.
24. Ibid.

13 Attitudes

1. See for example B. Ryan, *It Works! How Investment Spending in Advertising Pays Off* (New York: American Association for Advertising Agencies, 1991).
2. Mackenzie, S. B., R. J. Lutz and G. E. Belch, 'The role of attitude toward the ad as a mediator of advertising effectiveness: A test of competing explanations', *Journal of Marketing Research*, vol. 23 (May 1986), pp. 130–43.
3. Statt, D. A., *The Concise Dictionary of Psychology* (London and New York: Routledge, 1990).
4. Cited in G. H. Bower, R. R. Bootzin and R. B. Zajonc, *Principles of Psychology Today* (New York: Random House, 1987), p. 479.
5. Bagozzi, R. P., H. Baumgartner and Y. Yi, 'Coupon usage and the theory of reasoned action', in R H. Holman and M. R. Solomon (eds), *Advances in Consumer Research*, vol. 18 (Provo, UT: Association for Consumer Research, 1991), pp. 24–7.
6. Marks, L. J. and M. A. Kamins, 'The use of product sampling and advertising: Effects of sequence of exposure and degree of advertising claim exaggeration on consumers' belief strength, belief, confidence and attitudes', *Journal of Marketing Research*, vol. 25 (August 1988), pp. 266–81.
7. Fishbein, M. and I. Ajzen, *Belief, Attitude, Intention and Behavior*, (Reading, MA: Addison-Wesley, 1975); I. Ajzen and M. Fishbein, *Understanding Attitudes and Predicting Social Behavior* (Englewood Cliffs, NJ: Prentice-Hall, 1980).
8. Ajzen and Fishbein, *Understanding Attitudes*, op. cit.
9. See for example B. Sheppard, J. Hartwick and P. Warshaw, 'The theory of reasoned action: A meta-analysis of past research with recommendations for modifications and future research', *Journal of Consumer Research*, vol. 15 (December 1988), pp. 325–43.
10. See for example Fazio, R., R. M. Powell and C. Williams, 'The role of attitude accessibility in the attitude-to-behavior process', *Journal of Consumer Research*, vol. 16 (December 1989), pp. 280–8.
11. Aronson, E., *The Social Animal*, 6th edn (New York: W. H. Freeman, 1992), p. 68.

12. Mitchell, A. A. and J. C. Olson, 'Are product attribute beliefs the only mediator of advertising effects on brand attitudes?', *Journal of Marketing Research*, vol. 18 (August 1981), pp. 318–32.
13. Gorn, G. J., 'The effects of music in advertising on choice behavior: A classical conditioning approach', *Journal of Marketing*, vol. 46 (Winter 1982), pp. 94–101.
14. Lutz, R. J. and J. R. Bettman, 'Multi-attribute models in marketing: A bicentennial review', in A. G. Woodside, J. N. Sheth and P. D. Bennett (eds), *Consumer and Industrial Buying Behavior* (New York: North Holland, 1977), pp. 137–49.
15. See for example A. Achenbaum, 'Advertising doesn't manipulate consumers', *Journal of Advertising Research*, vol. 12, no. 2 (April/May 1972), pp. 3–13.
16. Festinger, L., *A Theory of Cognitive Dissonance* (Stanford: Stanford University Press, 1957).
17. Festinger, L. and J. M. Carlsmith, 'Cognitive consequences of forced compliance', *Journal of Abnormal and Social Psychology*, vol. 58 (1959), pp. 203–10.
18. Ehrlich, D., I. Guttman, P. Schonbach and J. Mills, 'Postdecision exposure to relevant information', *Journal of Abnormal and Social Psychology*, vol. 57 (1957), pp. 98–102.
19. Brehm, J., 'Postdecision changes in the desirability of alternatives', *Journal of Abnormal and Social Psychology*, vol. 52 (1956), pp. 384–9.
20. Zanna, M. P., 'Attitude-behavior consistency: Fulfilling the need for cognitive structure', *Advances in Consumer Research*, vol. 16 (1989), pp. 318–20; C. T. Allen, K. A. Machleit and S. S. Kleine, 'A comparison of attitudes and emotions as predictors of behavior at diverse levels of behavioral experience', *Journal of Consumer Research*, vol. 18, no. 4 (March 1992), pp. 493–504.

14 Communication and Persuasion

1. McGuire, W. J., 'Attitudes and social change', in G. Lindzey and E. Aronson (eds), *Handbook of Social Psychology*, 3rd edn, vol. 2 (New York: Random House, 1985), pp. 233–346.
2. Walster, E., E. Aronson and D. Abrahams, 'On increasing the effectiveness of a low prestige communicator', *Journal of Experimental Social Psychology*, vol. 2 (1966), pp. 325–42.
3. Aronson, E., *The Social Animal*, 6th edn (New York: Freeman, 1992), Chapter 3.
4. Miller, N., G. Maruyama, R. J. Beaber and K. Valone, 'Speed of speech and persuasion', *Journal of Personality and Social Psychology*, vol. 34 (1976), pp. 615–24.
5. Cook, T. D., C. L. Gruder, K. M. Hennigan and B. R. Flay, 'History of the sleeper effect: Some logical pitfalls in accepting the null hypothesis', *Psychological Bulletin*, vol. 86 (1979), pp. 662–79.
6. Eagly, A. and S. Chaiken, 'An attribution analysis of the effect of communicator characteristics on opinion change: The case of communicator attractiveness', *Journal of Personality and Social Psychology*, vol. 32 (1975), pp. 136–44. See also K. Dion, E. Berscheid and E. Walster, 'What is beautiful is good', *Journal of Personality and Social Psychology*, vol. 24 (1972), pp. 285–90.
7. See for example Aronson, *Social Animal*, op. cit.
8. This section is very well summarized in Aronson, *Social Animal*, op. cit.
9. Leventhal, H., 'Findings and theory in the study of fear communications', in L. Berkowitz (ed.), *Advances in Experimental Social Psychology*, vol. 5 (New York: Academic Press, 1970); H. Leventhal, D. Meyer and D. Nerenz, 'The common sense representation of illness danger', in S. Rachman (ed.), *Contributions to Medical Psychology*, vol. 2 (New York: Pergamon Press, 1980).

10. Leishman, K., 'Heterosexuals and AIDS', *The Atlantic Monthly* (February 1987), pp 39–58.
11. Nisbet, E. R. and L. Ross, *Human Inference: Strategies and Shortcomings of Social Judgment* (Englewood Cliffs, NJ: Prentice-Hall, 1980).
12. Gonzales, M., E. Aronson and M. Costanzo, 'Increasing the effectiveness of energy auditors: A field experiment', *Journal of Applied Social Psychology*, vol. 18 (1988), pp. 1049–66.
13. Hovland, C., A. Lumsdaine and F. Sheffield, *Experiments on Mass Communication* (Princeton, NJ: Princeton University Press, 1949).
14. Tesser, A. and D. Shaffer, 'Attitudes and attitude change', in M. Rosenzweig and L. Porter (eds), *Annual Review of Psychology*, vol. 41 (Palo Alto, CA: Annual Reviews Inc., 1990).
15. Miller, N. and D. Campbell, 'Recency and primacy in persuasion as a function of the timing of speeches and measurements', *Journal of Abnormal and Social Psychology*, vol. 59 (1959), pp. 1–9.
16. Aronson, E., J. Turner and J. M. Carlsmith, 'Communication credibility and communication discrepancy as determinants of opinion', *Journal of Abnormal and Social Psychology*, vol. 67 (1963), pp. 31–6; W. J. McGuire, 'Attitudes and attitude change', in G. Lindzey and E. Aronson, *Handbook of Social Psychology*, 3rd edn, vol. 2 (New York: Random House, 1985), pp. 233–346.
17. Zellner, M., 'Self-esteem, reception and influenceability', *Journal of Personality and Social Psychology*, vol. 15 (1970), pp. 87–93.
18. Marlowe, D. and K. Gergen, 'Personality and social interaction', in G. Lindzey and E. Aronson (eds), *Handbook of Social Psychology*, 2nd edn, vol. 3 (Reading, MA: Addison-Wesley, 1969).
19. McGuire, W. J. and D. Papageorgis, 'The relative efficacy of various types of prior belief-defence in producing immunity against persuasion', *Journal of Abnormal and Social Psychology*, vol. 62 (1961), pp. 327–37.
20. Freedman, J. and D. Sears, 'Warning, distraction and resistance to influence', *Journal of Personality and Social Psychology*, vol. 1 (1965), pp. 262–6.
21. Kiesler, C., *The Psychology of Commitment* (London: Academic Press, 1971).
22. Lewin, K., 'Group decision and social change', in E. E. Maccoby, T. Newcomb and E. L. Hartley (eds), *Readings in Social Psychology*, 3rd edn (New York: Holt, Rinehart & Winston, 1958).
23. Kiesler, *Psychology*, op. cit.
24. Gardner, M. P., 'Mood states and consumer behavior: A critical review', *Journal of Consumer Research*, vol. 12 (December 1985), pp. 281–300.
25. See for example R. Batra and D. M. Stayman, 'The role of mood in advertising effectiveness', *Journal of Consumer Research*, vol. 17 (September 1990), pp. 203–14.
26. Goldberg, M. E. and G. J. Gorn, 'Happy and sad TV programs: How they affect reaction to commercials', *Journal of Consumer Research*, vol. 14 (December 1987), pp. 387–403.
27. Kamins, M. A., L. J. Marks and D. Skinner, 'Television commercial evaluation in the context of program induced mood', *Journal of Advertising*, vol. 20 (June 1991), pp. 1–14.
28. Petty, R. E. and J. T. Cacioppo, *Communication and Persuasion: Central and Peripheral Routes to Attitude Change* (New York: Springer Verlag, 1986). See also R. E. Petty, R. Unnava and A. J. Strathman, 'Theories of attitude change', in T. Robertson and H. Kassarjian (eds), *Handbook of Consumer Behavior* (Englewood Cliffs, NJ: Prentice-Hall, 1991), pp. 317–38 for a broader discussion.

29. Mitchell, A. A. and J. C. Olson, 'Are product attribute beliefs the only mediators of advertising effects on brand attitudes?', *Journal of Marketing Research*, vol. 18 (August 1981), pp. 318–32; T. Shimp, 'Attitudes towards the ad as a mediator of consumer brand choice', *Journal of Advertising*, vol. 10, no. 2 (1981), pp. 9–15.

30. Mitchell and Olson, 'product attribute beliefs' op. cit.; Shimp, 'Attitudes', op. cit.; see also for example, P. H. Homer, 'The mediating role of attitude towards the ad: Some additional evidence', *Journal of Marketing Research*, vol. 27 (February 1990), pp. 78–86; R. I. Haley and A. L. Baldinger, 'The ARF copy research validation project', *Journal of Advertising Research*, vol. 31, no. 2 (1991), pp. 11–32 (ARF = Advertising Research Foundation).

31. Rossiter, J. R. and L. Percy, *Advertising and Promotion Management* (New York: McGraw-Hill, 1987). For a general discussion of this issue see D. A. Aaker and D. E. Bruzzone, 'Causes of irritation in advertising', *Journal of Marketing*, vol. 49 (Spring 1985), pp. 47–57.

32. See for example R. W. Olshavsky, 'Customer-salesman interaction in appliance retailing', *Journal of Marketing Research*, vol. 10 (May 1973), pp. 208–12; L. A. Crosby, K. R. Evans and D. Cowles, 'Relationship quality in services selling: An interpersonal influence perspective', *Journal of Marketing*, vol. 54, no. 3 (July 1990), pp. 68–81.

33. Gold, L. N., 'The evolution of television advertising sales measurement: Past, present and future', *Journal of Advertising Research*, (June/July 1988), pp. 19–24.

34. Zimbardo, P., E. Ebbesen and C. Maslach, *Influencing Attitudes and Changing Behavior*, 2nd edn (Reading, MA: Addison-Wesley, 1977).

35. Weinberger, M. G. and C. S. Gulas, 'The impact of humor in advertising', *Journal of Advertising*, vol. 21, no. 4 (December 1992), pp. 35–59.

36. Soley, L. and G. Kurzbard, 'Sex in advertising: A comparison of 1964 and 1984 magazine advertisements', *Journal of Advertising*, vol. 15, no. 3 (1986), pp. 46–54.

37. Yovovich, B. G., 'Sex in advertising – the power and the perils', *Advertising Age*, 2 May 1983, pp. 4–5.

38. Sciglimpaglia, D., M. A. Belch and R. F. Cain, 'Demographic and cognitive factors influencing viewers' evaluations of "sexy" advertisements', in W. Wilkie (ed.), *Advances in Consumer Research*, vol. 6 (Ann Arbor, MI: Association for Consumer Research, 1979), pp. 62–5.

15 Approaching a Decision

1. Fiske, S. T. and S. E. Taylor, *Social Cognition* (New York: McGraw-Hill, 1991).

2. Tversky, A. and D. Kahneman, 'Judgment under uncertainty: Heuristics and biases', *Science*, vol. 185 (1974), pp. 1124–31.

3. Pratkanis, A. R., 'The attitude heuristic and selective fact identification', *British Journal of Social Psychology*, vol. 27 (1988), pp. 257–63.

4. Tversky and Kahneman, 'Judgment', op. cit.

5. Urbany, J. E., P. R. Dickson and W. C. Wilkie, 'Buyer uncertainty and information search', *Journal of Consumer Research*, vol. 16 (September 1989), pp. 208–15.

6. There are several relevant articles in R. H. Holman and M. R. Solomon (eds), *Advances in Consumer Research*, vol. 18 (Provo UT: Association for Consumer Research, 1991): see J. R. Stoltman, J. W. Gentry and K. A. Anglin (pp. 430–40); J. Meoli, R. A. Feinberg and L. Westgate (pp. 441–4); P. H. Bloch, N. M. Ridgway and J. E. Nelson (pp. 445–52); and P. A. Doherty and J. E. P. Kulikowski (pp. 453–61).

7. Hirschman, E. C. and M. K. Mills, 'Sources shoppers use to pick stores', *Journal of Advertising Research*, vol. 20 (February 1980), pp. 47–51.

8. Biehal, G. J., 'Consumers' prior experiences and perceptions in auto repair choice', *Journal of Marketing*, vol. 47 (Summer 1983), pp. 87–91.

9. See for example J. W. Newman, 'Consumer external search: Amount and determinants', in A. G. Woodside, J. N. Sheth and P. D. Bennett (eds), *Consumer and Industrial Buying Behavior*, (New York: North-Holland, 1977), pp. 79–94, and W. L. Wilkie and P. R. Dickson, 'Consumer information search and shopping behavior', in H. Kassarjian and T. Robertson (eds), *Perspectives in Consumer Behavior*, 4th edn (Englewood Cliffs, NJ: Prentice-Hall, 1991).

10. Dickson, P. R. and A. G. Sawyer, 'The price knowledge and search of supermarket shoppers', *Journal of Marketing*, vol. 54 (July 1990), pp. 42–53.

11. Ibid.

12. Duncan, C. P., 'Consumer market beliefs: A review of the literature and an agenda for future research', in M. E. Goldberg, G. Gorn and R. W. Pollay (eds), *Advances in Consumer Research*, vol. 17 (Provo, UT: Association for Consumer Research, 1990), pp. 729–36.

13. Dickson and Sawyer 'The price knowledge', op. cit.

14. Engel, J. F., D. A. Knapp and D. E. Knapp, 'Sources of influence in the acceptance of new products for self-medication: Preliminary findings', in R. M. Haas (ed.), *Science, Technology and Marketing* (Chicago: American Marketing Association, 1966).

15. Hauser, J. R. and B. Wernerfelt, 'An evaluation cost model of consideration sets', *Journal of Consumer Research*, vol. 16 (March 1990), pp. 393–468.

16. Ursic, M. L. and J. G. Helgeson, 'The impact of choice phase and task complexity on consumer decision making', *Journal of Business Research*, vol. 21 (1990), pp. 69–90.

17. Petroshius, S. M. and K. B. Monroe, 'Effects of product line pricing characteristics on product evaluations', *Journal of Consumer Research*, vol. 13 (March 1987), pp. 511–19.

18. Hoyer, W. D., 'An examination of consumer decision making for a common repeat purchase product', *Journal of Consumer Research*, vol. 11 (December 1984), pp. 822–9.

19. Crane, F. G. and T. K. Clarke, 'The identification of evaluative criteria and cues used in selecting services', *Journal of Services Marketing*, vol. 2, no. 2 (Spring 1986), pp. 54–8.

20. See for example J. Jacoby, 'Perspectives on information overload', *Journal of Consumer Research*, vol. 10 (March 1984), pp. 432–5; J. G. Helgeson and M. L. Ursic, 'Information load, cost/benefit assessment and decision strategy variability', *Journal of the Academy of Marketing Science*, vol. 21, no. 1 (Winter 1993), pp. 13–20.

16 The Decision and its Consequences

1. Bloch, P. H., N. M. Ridgway and J. E. Nelson, 'Leisure and the shopping mall', in R. H. Holman and M. R. Solomon (eds), *Advances in Consumer Research*, vol. 18 (Provo, UT: Association for Consumer Research, 1991), pp. 445–52.

2. Tauber E. M., 'Why do people shop?' *Journal of Marketing*, vol. 36 (October 1992), pp. 47–8.

3. Langrehr, F. W., 'Retail shopping mall semiotics and hedonic consumption', in R. H. Holman and M. R. Solomon (eds), *Advances in Consumer Research*, vol. 18 (Provo, UT: Association for Consumer Research, 1991), p. 428.

4. McNeal, J. U. and D. McKee, 'The case of antishoppers' in R. F. Lusch *et al.* (eds), *AMA Educators' Proceedings* (Chicago: American Marketing Association, 1985), pp. 65–8.

5. Fram, E. H. and J. Axelrod, 'The distressed shopper', *American Demographics*, October 1990, pp. 44–5.

6. Monroe, K. B. and J. B. Guiltinan, 'A path-analytic exploration of retail patronage influences', *Journal of Consumer Research*, vol. 2 (June 1975), pp. 19–28.

7. Putnam, S. A., W. R. Davidson and K. Martell, *The Management Horizons: Six Shopper Typologies* (Columbus, OH: Management Horizons Division of Price Waterhouse, 1987).
8. Craig, C. S., A. Ghosh and S. McLafferty, 'Models of the retail location process: A review', *Journal of Retailing*, vol. 60 (Spring 1984), pp. 5–36.
9. Reynolds, F. R. and W. R. Darden, 'Intermarket patronage: A psychographic study of consumer outshoppers', *Journal of Marketing*, vol. 36 (October 1972), pp. 50–4.
10. Lumpkin, J. R., J. M. Hawes and W. R. Darden, 'Shopping patterns of the rural consumer: Exploring the relationship between shopping orientations and outshopping', *Journal of Business Research*, vol. 14 (1986), pp. 63–81.
11. Waldrop, J., 'Mall shoppers want the basics', *American Demographics*, October 1991, p. 16.
12. Gardner, M. P., 'Mood states and consumer behavior: A critical review', *Journal of Consumer Research*, vol. 12 (December 1985), pp. 292–3.
13. Kotler, P., 'Atmospherics as a marketing tool', *Journal of Retailing*, vol. 49 (Winter 1973–4), pp. 48–65.
14. Berry, L. L. and L. G. Gresham, 'Relationship retailing: Transforming customers into clients', *Business Horizons*, (November–December 1986), pp. 43–7.
15. Kendall, K. W. and I. Fenwick, 'What do you learn standing in a supermarket aisle?', in W. L. Wilkie (ed.), *Advances in Consumer Research*, vol. 6 (Ann Arbor, MI: Association for Consumer Research, 1979), pp. 153–60.
16. See for example Park, C. W., E. S. Iyer and D. C. Smith, 'The effects of situational factors on in-store grocery shopping behaviour: The role of store environment and time available for shopping', *Journal of Consumer Research*, vol. 15 (March 1989), pp. 422–33.
17. Rook, D. W., 'The buying impulse', *Journal of Consumer Research*, vol. 14 (September 1987), pp. 189–99.
18. Curhan, R. C., 'Shelf space allocation and profit maximization in mass retailing', *Journal of Marketing*, vol. 37 (July 1973), pp. 56, 54–60.
19. Gagnon, J. P. and J. T. Osterhaus, 'Effectiveness of floor displays on the sales of retail products', *Journal of Retailing*, vol. 61 (Spring 1985), pp. 104–16.
20. See for example Scott, C. A., 'The effects of trial and incentives on repeat purchase behavior', *Journal of Marketing Research*, vol. 13 (August 1976), pp. 263–9; and A. N. Doob, J. M. Carlsmith, J. L. Freedman, T. K. Landayer and T. Soleng, 'Effects of initial selling price on subsequent sales', *Journal of Personality and Social Psychology*, vol. 11, no. 4 (1979), pp. 345–50.
21. Dickson, P. R. and A. G. Sawyer, 'The price knowledge and search of supermarket shoppers', *Journal of Marketing*, vol. 54 (July 1990), pp. 42–53.
22. Rosenberg, L. J. and E. C. Hirschman, 'Retailing without stores', *Harvard Business Review*, vol. 58 (July/August 1980), p. 105.
23. Garland, S., 'Stores brush up Fuller's image', *Advertising Age*, 14 September 1987, p. 107.
24. See especially H. K. Hunt, 'CS/D: Overview and future research directions', in H. K. Hunt (ed.), *Conceptualization and Measurement of Consumer Satisfaction and Dissatisfaction* (Cambridge, MA: Marketing Science Institute, 1977), and R. L. Oliver, 'A cognitive model of the antecedents and consequences of satisfaction decisions', *Journal of Marketing Research*, vol. 17 (November 1980), pp. 460–9.
25. Hunt, 'CS/D', op. cit.
26. Westbrook, R. A. and J. W.. Newman, 'An analysis of shopper dissatisfaction for major household appliances', *Journal of Marketing Research*, vol. 15 (August 1978), pp. 456–66.
27. La Tour, S. A. and N. C. Peat, 'The role of situationally produced expectations, others' experiences and prior experience in determining consumer satisfaction', in J. C. Olson (ed.), *Advances in Consumer Research*, vol. 7 (Ann Arbor, MI: Association for Consumer Research, 1980), pp. 588–92.

28. Halstead, D. and C. Droge, 'Consumer attitudes towards complaining and the prediction of multiple complaint responses', in R. H. Holman and M. R. Solomon (eds), *Advances in Consumer Research*, vol. 18 (Provo, UT: Association for Consumer Research, 1980), pp. 210–16.

29. Ehrlich, D., I. Guttman, P. Schonbach and J. Mills, 'Postdecision exposure to relevant information', *Journal of Abnormal and Social Psychology*, vol. 57 (1957), pp. 98–102.

30. Brehm, J., 'Postdecision changes in the desirability of alternatives', *Journal of Abnormal and Social Psychology*, vol. 52 (1956), pp. 384–9.

31. See for example D. Finkelman and T. Goland, 'The case of the complaining customer', *Harvard Business Review*, vol. 3 (May–June 1990), pp. 9–25.

32. Singh, J., 'Consumer complaint intentions and behavior: Definition and taxonomical issues', *Journal of Marketing*, vol. 52 (January 1988), pp. 93–107.

33. Morganowsky M. N. and H. M. Buckley, 'Complaint behavior: Analysis by demographics, lifestyle, consumer values', in M. Wallendorf and P. Anderson (eds), *Advances in Consumer Research*, vol. 14 (1987), pp. 223–6.

34. See for example K. J. Cobb, G. C. Walgren and M. Hollowed, 'Differences in organizational responses to consumer letters of satisfaction and dissatisfaction', in M. Wallendorf and P. Anderson (eds), *Advances in Consumer Research*, op. cit., pp. 227–31.

35. See for example M. J. Bitner, B. M. Booms and M. S. Tetreault, 'The service encounter: Diagnosing favourable and unfavourable incidents', *Journal of Marketing*, vol. 54 (January 1990), pp. 71–84; and C. A. Kelley and J. S. Conant, 'Extended warranties: consumer and manufacturer perceptions', *Journal of Consumer Affairs*, vol. 25 (Summer 1991), pp. 68–83.

36. Richins, M. L., 'Negative word-of-mouth by dissatisfied customers: A pilot study', *Journal of Marketing*, vol. 47, (Winter 1983), pp. 68–78; N. Nanna and J. S. Wagle, 'Who is your satisfied customer?', *Journal of Consumer Marketing*, vol. 6 (Winter 1989), pp. 53–62; and C. Goodwin and I. Ross, 'Consumer evaluations of responses to complaints: What's fair and why', *Journal of Consumer Marketing*, vol. 7 (Spring 1990), pp. 29–48.

17 The Organization as Purchaser

1. Buchanan, D. and A. Huczynski, *Organizational Behavior* (London: Prentice-Hall International, 1985), p. 3.

2. Schein, E., *Organizational Psychology*, 3rd edn (Englewood Cliffs, NJ: Prentice-Hall, 1988), p. 12

3. Buchanan and Huczynski *Organizational Behavior*, op. cit., p.5.

4. Schein, *Organizational Psychology*, op. cit., p. 15.

5. Kempner, T. (ed.), *The Penguin Management Handbook*, 4th edn (London: Penguin, 1987), p. 361.

6. Weber, M., *The Theory of Social and Economic Organization* (Oxford: Oxford University Press, 1922).

7. Pugh, D. S. (ed.), *Organization Theory: Selected Readings* (Harmondsworth: Penguin, 1971).

8. Allport, G. W., *Pattern and Growth in Personality* (London: Holt, Rinehart & Winston, 1963).

9. Hosking, D. and I. Morley., *A Social Psychology of Organizing* (London: Harvester Wheatsheaf, 1991).

10. Statt, D. A., *Psychology: Making Sense* (New York and London: Harper & Row, 1977).

11. Dahl, R. A., 'The concept of power', *Behavioral Science*, vol. 2 (1957), pp. 201–18.

12. French, J. R. P. and B. H. Raven., 'The bases of social power', in D. Cartwright and A. Zander (eds), *Group Dynamics*, 3rd edn (New York: Harper & Row, 1968).
13. Pettigrew, A., *The Politics of Organizational Decision-Making* (London: Tavistock, 1973).
14. Bachrach, P. and M. S. Baratz, 'Two faces of power', *American Political Science Review*, vol. 56 (1962), pp. 947–52.
15. Hickson, D. J., 'Politics permeate', in D. C. Wilson and R. H. Rosenfeld (eds), *Managing Organizations* (Maidenhead: McGraw-Hill, 1990), pp. 175–81.
16. Dror, Y. and T. Romm., 'Politics in organizations and its perception within the organization', *Organization Studies*, vol. 9, no. 2 (1988), pp. 165–80.
17. Hickson, 'Political permeate', op. cit., p. 175.
18. Kotter, J. *The General Manager* (New York: Free Press, 1982).
19. For a fuller discussion of this topic see S. B. Bacharach and E. J. Lawler, *Power and Politics in Organizations* (London: Jossey-Bass, 1980).
20. Nichols, R. G., 'Listening is good business', *Management of Personnel Quarterly*, vol. 4 (1962). p. 4.
21. Katz, D. and R. L. Kahn, *The Social Psychology of Organizations*, 2nd edn (New York, Wiley, 1978).
22. Schein, E. H., *Organizational Culture and Leadership*, 2nd edn (San Francisco: Jossey Bass, 1992).
23. Hofstede. G., *Culture's Consequences: International Differences in Work-Related Values* (Beverly Hills: Sage, 1980).
24. Barsoux, J. and P. Lawrence, *The Challenge of British Management* (London: Macmillan, 1990).
25. Crittendon, V., C. A. Scott and R. T. Moriarity, 'The role of prior product experience in organizational buying behavior', *Advances in Consumer Research*, vol. 14 (1980), pp. 387–91.
26. Williams, K. and R. Spiro, 'Communication style in the salesperson-customer dyad', *Journal of Marketing Research*, vol. 22 (November 1985), pp. 434–42.
27. Webster, F. E. and Y. Wind, 'A general model for understanding organizational buying behavior', *Journal of Marketing*, vol. 36, no. 2 (1973), pp. 12–19.
28. Janis, I. L., *Groupthink* (Boston: Houghton Mifflin, 1982).
29. Reason, R., 'The Chernobyl errors', *Bulletin of the Psychological Society*, vol. 40 (1987), pp. 201–6.
30. Feldman, D. C. and H. J. Arnold, *Managing Individual and Group Behavior in Organizations* (New York: McGraw-Hill, 1983).

18   Consumer Awareness

1. Gabriel, Y. and T. Lang, *The Unmanageable Consumer* (London: Sage, 1995), p. 187. I have drawn extensively on this work throughout the present chapter.
2. Ibid.
3. Bell, D., *The Cultural Contradictions of Capitalism* (London: Heinemann, 1976). For a more recent extension of this issue see Z. Bauman, *Freedom* (Milton Keynes: Open University Press, 1988).
4. Herrmann, R. O., 'Consumerism: Its goals, organizations, and future', *Journal of Marketing*, vol. 35 (October 1970), pp. 55–60.
5. Gabriel and Lang, *The Unmanageable Consumer*, op. cit.
6. Marglin, S. A., 'What do bosses do? The origins and functions of hierarchy in capitalist production', *Review of Radical Political Economics*, vol. 6 (1974), pp. 33–60.
7. Thompson, E. P., 'Time, work, discipline and industrial capitalism', *Past and Present*, vol. 29 (1967), pp. 50–66.

8. Smith, M., *An Introduction to Industrial Psychology* (London: Cassell, 1952).

9. Gabriel and Lang *The Unmanageable Consumer*, op. cit., p. 156.

10. Barnet, R. and J. Cavanagh, *Global Dreams* (New York: Simon & Schuster, 1994).

11. For a discussion on this topic see R. J. Lampman, 'JFK's four consumer rights: A retrospective view', in E. S. Maynes (ed.), *The Frontier of Research in the Consumer Interest* (Columbia, MO: American Council on Consumer Interests, 1988).

12. See 'Coming: A rush of new consumer-safety rules', *US News and World Report*, 18 July 1977, p. 61.

13. Nader, R., *Unsafe At Any Speed: The Designed-in Dangers of the American Automobile*, 2nd edn (New York: Knightsbridge Publishing, 1991).

14. Brimelow, P. and L. Spencer, 'Ralph Nader Inc.', *Forbes*, vol. 146, no. 6 (17 September 1990), pp. 117–29.

15. Aronson, E., *The Social Animal*, 6th edn (New York: W. H. Freeman, 1992), p. 67.

16. Kamins, M. A. and L. J. Marks, 'Advertising puffery: The impact of using two-sided claims on product attitude and purchase intention', *Journal of Advertising*, vol. 16, no. 4 (1987), pp. 6–15.

17. 'Procter and Gamble: On a short lease', *Business Week*, 22 July 1991, p. 76.

18. Nader, R., in J. S. Turner (ed.), *The Chemical Feast: The Ralph Nader Study Group Report on Food Protection and the Food and Drug Administration* (New York: Grossman, 1970), p. v.

19. See for example R. Dardis, 'International trade: The consumer's stake', in E. S. Maynes (ed.), *The Frontier of Research in the Consumer Interest* (Columbia, MO: American Council on Consumer Interests, 1988), and D. Morris (ed.), *The Economic System in the UK*, 3rd edn (Oxford: Oxford University Press, 1985).

20. Burnett, J., *Plenty and Want: A Social History of Diet in England from 1815 to the Present Day*, 2nd edn (London: Scolar Press, 1979); and S. Lebergott, *Pursuing Happiness: American Consumers in the Twentieth Century* (Princeton: Princeton University Press, 1993).

21. Pantzar, M., 'The growth of product variety – a myth?', *Journal of Consumer Studies and Home Economics*, vol. 16 (1992), pp. 345–62; J. Benson, *The Rise of Consumer Society in Britain 1880–1980* (London: Longman, 1994).

22. Paxton, A., *Food Miles* (London: Sustainable Agriculture, Food and Environment Alliance SAFE, 1994).

23. Gabriel and Lang *The Unmanageable Consumer*, op. cit., p. 124.

24. Cohen, D., 'Remedies for consumer protection: Prevention, restitution or punishment', *Journal of Marketing*, vol. 39 (October 1975), pp. 24–31.

25. Schwartz, J., 'Earth day today', *American Demographics* (April 1990), pp. 40-1.

26. Schlossberg, H., 'Americans passionate about the environment? Critic says that's "nonsense"', *Advertising Age*, 16 September 1991, p. 8.

27. Hume, S., 'Consumer doubletalk makes companies wary', *Advertising Age*, 28 October 1991, GR-4.

28. See for example, Hume, S., 'Consumers target ire at databases', *Advertising Age*, 6 May 1991, p. 3 and D. Fost, 'Privacy concerns threaten database marketing', *American Demographics*, (May 1990), pp. 18–21.

29. Davies, S., *Big Brother: Britain's Web of Surveillance and the New Technological Order* (London: Pan, 1995).

19 The Future Consumer

1. See for example Peters, T., *Thriving on Chaos* (New York: Alfred Knopf, 1987).

2. Freeman, L., 'Japan Rises to P & G's No 3 Market', *Advertising Age*, 10 December 1990, p. 42.

3. Womack, J. P., D. T. Jones and D. Roos, *The Machine That Changed the World* (New York: Rawson Associates, 1990), p. 13.
4. Hoger, B., 'What's behind business' sudden fervor for ethics?', *Business Week*, 23 September 1991, p. 65.
5. Lacniak, G. R. and P. E. Murphy, *Marketing Ethics* (Lexington, MA: Lexington Books, 1985).
6. Pride, W. M. and O. C. Ferrell, *Marketing: Basic Concepts and Decisions*, 4th edn (Boston: Houghton Miffin, 1985).
7. See for example 'Need for government oversight', *Adweek*, 12 October 1987, p. 78; A. R. Andreasen, 'Consumer behavior research aand social policy', in T. Robertson and H. Kassarijian (eds), *Handbook of Consumer Behavior* (Englewood Cliffs, NJ: Prentice-Hall, 1991), pp. 450–506; and J. R. Burton, C. D. Zick and R. N. Mayer, 'Consumer views of the need for government intervention in the airline market', *Journal of Consumer Affairs*, vol. 27, no. 1 (Summer 1993), pp. 1–22.
8. See for example J. Deighton, C. M. Henderson and S. A. Neslin, 'The effects of advertising on brand switching and repeat purchasing', *Journal of Marketing Research*, vol. 31, no. 1 (February 1994), pp. 28–44.
9. McCarthy, M. J., 'Soft-drink giants sit UP and take notice as sales of store brands show more fizz', *Wall Street Journal*, 6 March 1992, p. B1 ff.
10. See for example S. A. Greyser and S. L. Diamond, 'US consumers view the marketplace', *Journal of Consumer Policy*, vol. 6 (1983), pp. 3–18.
11 Gabriel, Y., 'The unmanaged organisation', *Organisation Studies*, vol. 16, no. 3 (1995), pp. 481–506.
12. 'Special anti-consumerism issue', *Ethical Consumer*, vol. 27 (Manchester: Ethical Consumer Research Association, 1994).
13. Herrmann, R. O., 'The tactics of consumer resistance: group action and marketplace exit', *Advances in Consumer Research*, vol. 20 (1993), pp. 130–4.
14. Smith, N. C., *Morality and the Market: Consumer Pressure for Corporate Accountability* (London: Routledge, 1990).
15. White, R. E. and D. D. Kare, 'The impact of consumer boycotts on the stock prices of target firms', *Journal of Applied Business Research*. vol. 6, no. 2 (1990), pp. 6–71.
16. Heft, R. K., 'Full head of steam', *The Scotsman*. 28 July 1995, p. 17.
17. Boseley, S., 'Bun fight', *Guardian*, 11 July 1995, p. 5.
18. Schwartz, J. and T. Miller, 'The Earth's best friends', *American Demographic*, February 1991, pp. 26–35.
19. Fierman, J., 'The big muddle in green marketing', *Fortune*, 3 June 1991, pp. 91–102.
20. Vidal, J., 'Clean money talks', *The Guardian*, 18 May 1995, p. 4.
21. Garfield, B., 'Beware: Green overkill', *Advertising Age*, 29 January 1991, p. 26.
22. Pahl, R. E., *Divisions of Labour* (Oxford: Blackwell, 1984).
23. Handy, C. B., *The Future of Work: A Guide to a Changing Society* (Oxford: Blackwell, 1984).
24. Rose, R., *Getting by in Three Economies* (Glasgow: Centre for the Study of Public Policy, University of Strathclyde, 1983).
25. Kellaway, L., 'Twelve acorns for a haircut', *Financial Times*, 30 November 1993, p. 13.
26. Gabriel Y. and T. Lang, *The Unmanageable Consumer* (London: Sage, 1995), p. 148.

Name Index

Subject Index